Franz Kafka
The Jewish Patient

PRAHA FRANZE KAFKY

FRANZ KAFKA
The Jewish Patient

by

Sander L. Gilman

ROUTLEDGE
New York and London

Published in 1995 by

Routledge
29 West 35TH Street
New York, NY 10001

Published in Great Britain in 1995 by

Routledge
11 New Fetter Lane
London EC4P 4EE

Printed in the United States of America
Design: Jack Donner

Library of Congress Cataloging-in-Publications Data

Gilman, Sander L.
Franz Kafka, the Jewish patient
p. cm.
Includes bibliographical references and index.
ISBN 0–415–91177—X
1. Kafka, Franz, 1883–1924—Health. 2. Tuberculosis—Patients—Austria—Biography. 3. Authors, Austrian—20th century—Biography. 4. Kafka, Franz, 1883–1924—Religion. 5. Jews in Literature. 6. Tuberculosis in Literature. I. Title
PT2621.A26Z7336 1995
833'.912—dc20 94–29322
CIP

For my friend and colleague

U.H. Peters

Contents

Acknowledgments

The present book was delivered as the Danz Lectures for 1994 at the University of Washington, Seattle, as well as the Gale Lecture for 1993 at the University of Texas, Austin, and as lectures at Harvard and Jerusalem. I am grateful to Hillel J. Kieval for his comments on this material and for his hospitality during my stay in Seattle. The substance of the book was worked through as a graduate as well as an undergraduate seminar at Cornell University and as a German Academic Exchange Service Seminar for College Teachers. I want to thank the participants in that seminar: John Bormanis, David Brenner, Iris Bruce, Gabi Cooper, Karin Doerr, Linda Feldman, Mark Gelber, Sabine Gölz, Sonja Hedgepath, Diana Hinze, Chris Kenway, Scott Spector, Denis Sweet, Steven Taubeneck, Istvan Varkonyi. Misha Kavka helped find a number of manuscripts reflecting Kafka's illness in Prague, and has been helpful throughout this project. The manuscript was read in whole or in part by Mark Anderson, Robert von Hallberg, Edward S. Brinkley, and A. A. Nassar. The Appendix was transcribed and translated from the German and the Czech by Misha Kavka and Frank Kavka.

The textual history of Kafka's works is complex. In general, I have made use of the edition of Max Brod: Franz Kafka, *Gesammelte Werke*, 8 vols. (Frankfurt a. M.: Fischer, 1989). All of the available volumes of the critical edition (*Kritische Ausgabe*) by Jürgen Born, Gerhard Neumann, Malcolm Pasley, and Jost Schillemeit (Frankfurt a. M.: Fischer, 1982) have been consulted. In addition, I have cited, as AS, from the

Ämtliche Schriften, edited by, Klaus Hermsdorf, Windfried Possner, and Jaromir Louzil (Berlin: Akademie-Verlag, 1984) in my own translation.

The English translations of the texts and letters do not always reflect the latest German textual scholarship. I have checked each passage against the original and have made changes and additions where necessary.

The original translations cited are:

The Trial, trans. Willa and Edwin Muir (New York: Schocken, 1984), cited as T;

The Complete Stories, ed. Nahum N. Glatzer (New York: Schocken, 1971), cited as S;

The Castle, trans. Willa and Edwin Muir (New York: Alfred E. Knopf, 1992), cited as C;

Parables and Paradoxes (New York: Schocken, 1963), cited as P;

"Letter to the Father," trans. Ernst Kaiser and Eithne Wilkens, revised by Arthur S. Wensinger, in Franz Kafka, *The Sons*, intro. Mark Anderson (New York: Schocken, 1989), cited as L;

The Diaries, 1910–1913, ed. Max Brod, trans. Joseph Kresh (New York: Schocken, 1948), cited as D1;

The Diaries, 1914–1923, ed. Max Brod, trans. Martin Greenberg and Hannah Arendt (New York: Schocken, 1949), cited as D2;

Letters to Friends, Family, and Editors, ed. Max Brod, trans. Richard and Clara Winston (New York: Schocken, 1977), cited as LF;

Letters to Felice, ed. Erich Heller and Jürgen Born, trans. James Stern and Elisabeth Duckworth (New York: Schocken, 1973), cited as LFe;

Letters to Milena, trans. Philip Boehm (New York: Schocken, 1990), cited as LM;

Letters to Ottla and the Family, trans. Richard and Clara Winston, ed. N. N. Glatzer (New York: Schocken, 1982), cited as LO.

Kafka's experience is too Jewish:

The writer Franz Kafka is not an Übermensch in Nietzsche's sense of the word, for as a Jew he has not yet transcended Christianity.

—from a recent study of Kafka published in Germany, Dagmar Fischer's *Der Rätselcharakter der Dichtung Kafkas* (1985): 404.

Kafka's experience is not Jewish enough:

Kafka emerged from an inner world and tried to get some grip on reality, and I came from a world of detailed, empirical reality, the camps and the forests.... At first I tried to run away from myself and from my memoirs, to live a life that was not my own and to write about a life that was not my own. But a hidden feeling told me that I was not allowed to flee from myself and that if I denied the experience of my childhood in the Holocaust I would be spiritually doomed.

—The Israeli survivor/novelist Ahron Appelfeld in the words attributed to him in Phillip Roth's novel, *Operation Shylock: A Confession* (1993): 56.

Kafka's experience is Christian:

Kafka, however unmistakable the ethnic source of his "liveliness" and alienation, avoided Jewish parochialism, and his allegories of pained awareness take upon themselves the entire European—that is to say predominantly Christian—malaise.

—The great American WASP novelist, John Updike, in the Introduction to *The Complete Stories of Franz Kafka* (1983): xx.

And then comes me.

one

On Difference, Language, and Mice

THE LONG TURN OF THE CENTURY

With this book, I want to return to the long *fin de siècle*, that age that begins self-consciously in the final decades of the nineteenth century and ends in the trenches of World War I. Rather than return to Vienna, I want to turn to Prague, and to the one writer who has come in the course of the later twentieth century to be seen as an archetype of a precise set of "universals" that shape human beings in our age—Franz Kafka.[1] I want to read in the light of the language of Kafka's time a series of texts written by Kafka that constructed specific differences among human beings, differences that may seem to us universal but that in his time had specific forms and directions (Plate 1). These stereotypes of the differences among human beings shaped Kafka's sense of himself so intensely that he too may well have been unaware of their historical specificity. Our temporal distance from Kafka provides us some ability to examine the rhetoric that shaped these stereotypes.

Yet it is very clear from his texts that Kafka does not merely appropriate and/or resist the stereotypes of his world to provide a vocabulary of images for his literary texts. (The exceptions to this rule, such as his tale "The Bucket Rider" [1916–17], show that he was quite capable of

"Vy d'you vear all dem ringth, Ithaacth?"

"Vell, you thee, I travelth a good deal, and ven I gets into converthation with a gentleman, ten to vun I thells him a ring, don'd yer know."

"But all the sthoneth ith turned inthide."

"You thilly fool! I don'd talk like that!——

PLATE 1: The language of the Jew as the salient marker of difference.
From *The Butterfly* (May – October, 1893) (Source: Private Collection, Ithaca).

doing so.) His texts self-consciously generate a sense of their own "transhistorical" nature. It is of little surprise that the adjective "kafkaesque" now exists in all of the languages of Europe and the Americas. Kafka consciously moved from a language marked by the discourses of his time to one that he and his contemporaries saw as "modern" and therefore, they hoped, universal, transnational, and infinitely interpretable in

I talks like thith ! ! ! ”

the ideological strife of their own age. However, all of these qualities—in their negative formulations, we might add—are components of the stereotype of the Jew at the turn of the century. The Jew is nomadic, uncentered, and infinitely mutable—immutably so. We must reconstruct the contemporary discourses that Kafka consciously or unconsciously repressed by reinscribing them into a new literary tradition, the high modern. According to Karl Menninger, writing in the 1930s, "For the present, our social heritage is such that the average Jew thinks of himself as a biological entity and he is so regarded by the average Gentile."[2] To separate himself from this biological categorization, Kafka selects from the grab bag of discourses available to him. Like a *bricoleur*, Claude Lévi-Strauss's image of the creator of myths and legends, he shops about, taking bits and pieces from various discourses that have deep meaning for him. By sublimating them he can try to control them or believe that he can.

For organizational reasons, I will be addressing three discursive complexes from which Kafka borrows—the discourses of his time about race, illness, and gender—and these will form the three divisions of this book. This division is not intended to create discrete categories of analysis; the discourses that I am analyzing were not discrete and are not so in Kafka's text. The very messiness of these three categories is at the heart of my project: we could add an extended index of further messy constructions. These categories are not ahistorical principles of psychic organization, but rather the historical articulation of deeper psychic categories. They reflect the inherently interlinked representation of reality at the *fin de siècle*. It was impossible to think about race at the *fin de siècle* without also thinking about gender and illness—it is impossible to invoke one such categorization without implying them all. It is not desirable for us analytically to separate what is interlinked in the object of our analysis. This is quite different from the most recent "postmodern" evocation of the ever-expanding body as communicative system in the work of Jean Baudrillard. Baudrillard's failure to understand the subtlety of the constructed body—the profusion of meanings that the same sign can have for differently situated individuals—leads to his claims for a universal body.[3] For me, all of the categories that together construct the body are aspects of the *fin de siècle* definition of "difference." It is a difference understood in the aesthetic terms of the equation of beauty with health and ugliness with illness. What I shall be undertaking in these five intertwined, overlapping, and inexorably intersecting chapters is to show, first, how contemporary discourses of gender, illness, and race inform the language of Kafka's world; and second, how Kafka's struggle with the claims of these discourses forms and is in turn formed in his texts. As Kafka wrote in a letter to the tubercular Jewish physician Robert Klopstock in April 1922, "A Jew, and a German besides, and sick besides, and in difficult personal circumstances besides—those are the chemical forces with which I propose to straightway transmute gold into gravel or your letter into mine, and while doing so remain in the right" (LF, 324). Here the discourses on race ("Jew"), nationality/language ("German"), health ("sick"), and class ("difficult personal circumstances") imply the missing category of gender. In much of my recent work, I have shown that the idea of the Jew as gendered male at the turn of the century was a commonplace.[4] The very phrase "the Jew" meant a male Jew. This image of the "Jew" as male in turn evokes further images. The male Jew is associated with ideas of illness, of not being part of a nation, because of his imagined inability to serve in the armed forces, and of being the "breadwinner," itself a gendered concept in Kafka's time. From all of these images, both those consciously present and those implied, Kafka indeed makes his world of words. Whether or not we share Kafka's aesthetic judgment that he transmuted gold into gravel, his creative world has grasped our fantasies for at least fifty years now.

The theme of this volume evokes Kafka's illness, his role as a "Jewish patient." Kafka's illness(es) came to define his sense of self. His final illness was pulmonary and laryngeal tuberculosis, of which Kafka wrote, "the larynx patient, for instance (blood brother of a consumptive but far sadder), who sits across from you so friendly and harmless, looking at you with the transfigured eyes of the consumptive and at the same time coughing into your face through his spread fingers drops of purulent phlegm from his tubercular ulcer" (LF, 264). But Kafka's illness was also the axis on which he and his world turned. Like Vladimir Nabokov's butterflies, Kafka felt himself physically impaled. To his fiancée Felice Bauer, in 1917, he described tuberculosis as "a knife that stabs not only forward but one that wheels around and stabs back as well" (LFe, 544). It is not only his real, palpable illness that is the secret of Kafka's sense of self, but the fact that the illness comes as no surprise. Kafka sees his imagined body as pierced with hidden arrows. In 1912, he wrote that "I am supposed to pose in the nude for the artist [Ernst] Ascher, as a model for St. Sebastian" (D1, 222). St. Sebastian, of course, was almost martyred by being shot full of arrows. These arrows, as we shall see, represent Kafka's anxiety about his own masculinity, an anxiety as closely tied to his sense of self as his anxiety about his illness. Each category transforms into the other; each is linked to the other in Kafka's expressions of his sense of who he is in his time and his place. For they all contribute to the complex notion of "difference" at the heart of Kafka's self-conception, a complex that defined the Jew, the man, and the patient at the *fin de siècle*.

Imagine a time and a place where fathers have lost their power; where they represent not authority but the abdication of authority; where the space occupied by fathers is replaced by another powerful belief system—such as science. Such was the situation in Prague, at least among younger Prague Jews, at the close of the nineteenth century. Their fathers had moved far from the organized religious belief system of their grandfathers. Religion had lost its centrality in their life, and their own children came to see the power of all patriarchy as weak. Their model was the weakened patriarchal religion that their fathers had westernized, modernized, and reformed, weak in terms of the religious authority to which they now demanded they defer. Not quite of the "old world" and yet not quite integrated into the new, these fathers were marked by their accents, their table manners, their physical difference. Smaller than their children, these children literally had to look up to them as they grew. And their children, among them Franz Kafka, saw in their own bodies the potential repetition of the failures marked on the bodies of their fathers. As Elaine Scarry has remarked:

> at particular moments when there is within a society a crisis of belief—that is, when some central idea or ideology of cultural construct has ceased to elicit a population's belief either because it is manifestly fictitious or because it has for some reason been divested of ordinary forms of transubstantiation—the sheer material factualness of the human body will be borrowed to lend that cultural construct the aura of "realness" and "certainty."[5]

It is this realness and certainty ascribed to an imagined Jewish body at the turn of the century that haunted Franz Kafka and his contemporaries.

Yet for all the failure of the fathers, they remained fathers. They were the representatives of imagined power in the lives of their children (male and female). And yet this power was questioned at every moment. How big and powerful can a father really be when he is frightened by the anti-Semitic bullies on the street, uncertain of his role and place in society because of his marginal economic position, unsteady in his religious beliefs and practices? This ambiguity, too, is mirrored in the fathers' bodies—bodies that are imagined to safeguard the child yet betray because of their weakness, imagined to be powerful and revealed constantly to be weak, imagined to be the ideal model for the son and yet represent the fearful potential of what the son will inevitably become.

Kafka effaced the world he experienced in his writing. Hannah Arendt employed an apt yet evocative image for this effacement. For her, Kafka "... spit on everything sacred so that against the background of this gloomy scene the foulness and depravity of bourgeois conditions do not stand out so clearly."[6] It is indeed Kafka's spit that is of interest to me—the skewer that pinned Kafka to his time and his place in society, but also the bloody tubercular sputum that both fascinated and repelled him (and us). The infected and infecting "spit" of the tubercular Kafka obscures the discourses of his own day, even the discourses of illness and race. To reconstitute these discourses in our world, the world after the *Shoah*, runs the risk of reestablishing these boundaries between the Jew and the Aryan, healthy and the sick, the beautiful and the ugly. Thus what this study offers is not a comprehensive interpretation of Kafka's works, but tiny, intimate glimpses into the fragments left partially obscured by Kafka's desire to mask and thus to control his world through his act of writing. This present study does not claim to provide a "reading" of Kafka's creative work, but rather a small attempt to see what is unobscured or only partially masked in his *oeuvre*. It is a reading of the historical imaginary in Kafka's world seen through all of Kafka's texts, from his fiction to his letters. And my reading of Kafka's imaginary world must be in light of my own fantasy of my world, a world after the *Shoah*.

Eric Santner has commented that after the *Shoah* there has been a "radical rethinking and reformulation of the very notion of boundaries and borderlines, of that 'protective shield' regulating exchange between the inside and the outside of individuals and groups."[7] These protective boundaries existed at the turn of the century, and we must take them seriously as the means by which Jews were able to cope with and even resist the meaning inscribed on their bodies by the imagination of those who needed to generate images of Jewish difference. These images of Jewish physical difference grew in proportion to the actual cultural and social integration of Jews into the world of the European Diaspora. The theological difference of the Jew from the Christian came to be translated in the course of the nineteenth century into biological difference of the Jew from the Aryan. Jewish biological difference came to be understood as immutable and inscribed on the Jew's imagined body. In the world of Diaspora Jewry it mattered little how the Jew defined him or herself. No matter what the self-definition of the Jew—whether religious, ethnic, cultural, or political—this construction of the Jew's body came to be reflected in the Jew's self-perception and self-actualization. This could and did take a range of forms, from the social formation of sports organizations to the construction of the idea of the Jewish patient. But all of these forms of response or resistance were rooted in the internalization of ideas of Jewish physical and mental difference.

Kafka's anxiety is about the inevitability of becoming that which he fears he must become. Whether that means becoming the Eastern Jew, whom he imagines as poor, ill, unable to command the language of high culture, and by definition male; whether it is becoming his own or any father, the very model of masculinity and disease for the turn of the century; whether it is becoming the patient, revealing the illness to which he is predisposed. This is the fear that takes the form of the knife "that stabs not only forward but one that wheels around and stabs back as well." It is the anxiety of becoming what one is condemned to become. It is a fear engendered by the images associated with the Jewish male in Kafka's world. It provides for him a vocabulary with which to clothe his innermost unspoken anxieties about himself, a vocabulary that distorts or represses this central anxiety, the anxiety of transformation and change, the anxiety leading unto death.

The articulated structures of Kafka's psychic world—like ours—are constructed. Or, rather, they are constantly under construction. Unlike the psychotic, whose detailed, complex, rigid world becomes his substitute for the ever-shifting world of mental activity, Kafka's world is ambiguous because of his own awareness of the need to constantly construct this world of fantasy. His is the world of the "normal neurotic." The vocabulary that enables him to articulate this world is taken from that world of words that most closely articulates his own anxieties—and also precipitates them. This world of words is as powerful as the real world. His sense of disease is thus as intense as its reality. As Elias Canetti notes, in his reading of Kafka's letters to Felice Bauer, the most "authentic" line in the correspondence is Kafka's claim: "I am a mendacious creature; for me it is the only way to maintain an even keel; my boat is fragile."[8] Kafka's mendacity represents the sense of slippage in all our psychic constructs, in all our struggles with the sense of not being quite complete, not being quite in control. Kafka's sense of incompleteness is presented within his overriding fear of change as articulated within the model of transformation—the fear of becoming what one fears one is fated to become, the sense of predestination or predisposition inherent in the discourse of "difference" at the *fin de siècle*, especially in regard to the Jews.

MICE

My basic thesis is not at all unusual in the writing about Kafka. Ernst Pawel, in perhaps the best biography of Kafka, states quite baldly, "Kafka grew up hating his body."[9] Stanley Corngold, in one of the most incisive studies of the writer, adds the notion of a double renunciation. Kafka first renounces the body in order to write and then, when the writing goes beyond the human limits, even the very act of writing is depleted.[10] My task in this study is analogous to that of Corngold, to "disclose, in Nietzsche's words, 'the secret alphabet-script' of Kafka's bodily self in his work, especially in its literal aspect—its play with the body of the letter"(7). My argument is that this "bodily self" that Kafka constructs when he looks into the mirror reflects certain basic *fin de siècle* discourses about the meaning of the body, discourses that, on the one hand, are not limited to Franz Kafka and yet, on the other hand, are not universal. Tracing the way that these discourses shaped and are shaped by Kafka's sense of his own identity is at the center of this book, and in this I believe I can add to the sum of the extraordinary literature on this extraordinary individual.

My own "new psychohistorical" approach to the world of Kafka's text is indebted to much of the most recent work done on Kafka.[11] My debt to the literally hundreds of books and articles on Kafka I examined in the preparation of this volume will become apparent in the course of the book; yet my own material is original enough in terms of my earlier work on literary identity formation that I believe I can claim that my contributions are unique and substantial additions to the literature on Kafka's world, if not on his work.[12] But I make no claims at providing a total reading of Kafka's work. Rather, my readings attempt to uncover the relationship between either the masked or the effaced discourse of high modernism that dominates Kafka's writing and the contemporary discourses in which he found himself enmeshed.

There are a few recent studies of Kafka that deserve special mention as they have elaborated my own approach to this writer and built upon it in interesting and exciting ways. Mark Anderson proposed—following my work on the "hidden language of the Jew"—that Kafka's internalization and deterritorialization of the discourse on the nature of the imagined Jew's body be understood as serious moments in the construction of Kafka's project.[13] (I use the term "deterritorialization" to mean the creation of a seemingly universal discourse by liminal writers. This discourse replaces and represses those discourses that demean or denigrate one's ability to command the language of the high culture with which one identifies .) Anderson's brilliant book stresses Kafka's preoccupation with physical externals, his clothes and outward appearance. It is well known that clothes make the *man* (the masculine being rather than the person), but Anderson is the first to show us a Kafka hyperconcerned about his appearance, his body, his manners, and the manners of others, especially his parents. Kafka's dandyism affects not only how he understands himself as a man, but equally his literary production. Kafka's imagined body becomes the place where his art is contested and where the images in his art are forged.

Anderson's readings of Kafka's major literary works are compelling in their clarity and directness, but especially notable is his reading of the Jewish voice in Kafka's final tale, "Josephine the Singer, or the Mouse Folk." He provides a highly sophisticated reading of Kafka's internalization, in this story, of the discourse on the Jewish voice at the *fin de siècle*. His persuasive reading is rooted in the culture of the time, and fully reflects the complex give and take about language in Kafka's culture (Plate 2). His method underlines the movement from Kafka's larger discursive world, to his construction of his own body, to his construction of literary texts. In other words, Anderson shows the structural centrality in Kafka's texts of fantasies about the body; the real "body in pain" becomes accessible in Anderson's reading of Kafka's narrative of pain.

My present approach will parallel Anderson's approach to Kafka as a dandy. I shall examine Kafka's self-construction in fiction, letters, and diaries to show how some of his most important identities—a man, a sufferer from illness, a Jew—relate to his fear of becoming exactly what the world says he must become. For Anderson, Kafka compensated for this lack in his dress; I see his anxiety present deep in his imagined body and his understanding of its dangers and limitations. More importantly for the reader of Kafka's texts, I will relate these constructions to his construction of a literary body. It is his ill, Jewish body that Kafka attempts

PLATE 2. The corrupt image of Jewish culture. From Eduard Schwechten's parody of Schiller's "Song of the Bell," *Das Lied vom Levi* (1895), drawings by Siegfried Horn (reprint: Düsseldorf: J. Knippenberg, 1933) (Source: Private Collection, Ithaca).

to cover with the clothes of the dandy; it is his irreducibly Jewish voice that he tried to transmute into high modernism.

In practice, this meant that Kafka hoped to accomplish what no Jewish writers had yet accomplished: to be acknowledged by the mainstream of German writing on their own terms. For example, Berthold Auerbach's *Tales from the Black Forest* became the most acclaimed example of the German Late Romantic style of the latter half of the nineteenth century. But Auerbach finally had to recognize that anti-Semitism could misread or distort even the most perfect embodiment of German literary style. For anti-Semitism understood the Jew as only capable of mimicking style, thus totally incapable of fulfilling it with the "truths" that it should represent. But the success of Kafka's undertaking has made the historically determined fantasies that underlay it again seem universal. The universality of Kafka's text is based on a heightened self-awareness of the dangers of his project. This danger is confronted by a strange but successful mix of compulsive precision and distanced irony, a mix that shapes Kafka's literary world. A Jewish *fin de siècle* writer's modernity is inseparable from his allegedly diseased nature. Modernity is either the cause of or the result of Jewish illness, depending on whom one reads at the turn of the century. Kafka struggles in his fantasy to find a language that is unmarked by difference, by disease, by heteronomy, yet he is aware that such a discourse can never exist. If we are to understand how he thought of his physical and literary body, we must understand the patterns of self-understanding that dominate his age, such as the relationship between mind and body, and we must place that too in a half-ironic, half-serious discourse.

Kafka's membership in the Jewish minority in Prague, the third city of the Austro-Hungarian Empire; a father who had originally spoken Yiddish, then Czech, and only then German; and his employment in the new Czech Republic as the only ethnic "German" in a workmen's compensation company—all these reinforced his sense of marginality. The center to which he was marginal was the German language, and this remained true even within the discourse of high modernism to which he contributed so much. The world of words could not protect him from charges that Jews could never fully command language, any more than they could become true citizens merely by means of civil emancipation. Furthermore, during the course of the late nineteenth and early twentieth centuries these charges had become part of the discourse on the biological difference of the Jew. Social position and ideology all became reflexes of the innate biology of the Jew. Kafka's fantasies indeed reflect the biological discourses of the time, even while he translates them into literature in order to limit their power over his imagined body. Kafka's own life spanned that period—bounded by the Dreyfus case in France and the accession to power of the Nazis in Germany—during which the claims about the biological difference of the Jew were passionately contested.[14] Hidden behind all of Kafka's attempts to undermine the notion of the biological difference of the Jew, the worm burrowed into flesh—maybe "they" are right after all, maybe we are biologically different from "them."

The transformation of the Jewish body was desirable but inherently impossible. The model for Kafka was that of religious conversion. By the end of the nineteenth century the very notion of conversion from Judaism to Christianity was considered as impossible as converting from one race to another. Throughout Kafka's writing such transformation is always an impossible wish: the rider who merges with his horse in "Desire to Become an Indian" (1913); Gregor Samsa's horrid transformation into a giant vermin in "The Metamorphosis" (1915); the incomplete and pathetic metamorphosis of ape into man in Kafka's "Report to an Academy" first published in Martin Buber's journal *The Jew* in November 1919. Once transformed, Samsa sinks into a decline that is marked by his loss of human epistemology. He becomes different in the way that he sees the world, losing even an internal language. He comes to represent the world with the perceptual limitations of the bug.[15] The ape becomes "human," that is, he acquires a human manner of seeing the world with his acquisition of language. But he remains marked by sexual passion for his "kind." All these transformations reflect both Jewish and anti-Semitic accusations against Jewish assimilation: Jews will never become true Germans; their Germanness is a mere sham. The more they try to change, the more they reveal themselves as fundamentally defective. Jews see and represent the world differently from Germans; their sexuality, their bodies remain as different as the bug's or the ape's.

No healthy assimilation is possible, not even in the fantasy world of Kafka's texts. Even the French historian Anatole Leroy-Beaulieu (1842–1912), a member of the French Academy and a staunch defender of the Jews at the time of the Dreyfus Affair, noted that irony is the weapon by which "the baptized Jew takes vengeance upon the God of the

Christians and upon their social system, for the disgrace of compulsory baptism."[16] Kafka is aware not only that conversion is impossible, but that marrying outside the "race" can lead to ghastly results. This can be seen in his understanding of the particular nature of the *Mischling*, the offspring of race-mixing between Jew and non-Jew.[17] The *Mischling* had a special status in the culture of the period, for the *Mischling* magnified the most egregious aspects of both "races." These children of Jews and non-Jews, these *Mischlinge*, are Jews, but in heightened form, bearing all the stigmata of degeneration that exist in incestuous or inbred families. Like the sign of congenital circumcision, the myth that male Jews are born circumcized, the mark of the decay of the Jew is present even (or especially) in the *Mischling*: "The children of such marriages [between Jews and non-Jews] . . . even though they are so very beautiful and so very talented, seem to lack a psychological balance that is provided by pure racial stock. We find all too often intellectually or morally unbalanced individuals, who decay ethically or end in suicide or madness."[18] There is no place one can hide; there is no means of becoming invisible. The *Mischling* is the end product of the process of Jewish degeneration that produces children that reveal the hidden racial difference of the Jews, their "blackness."[19]

Certainly a major literary representation of this trope is to be found in William Thackeray's *Vanity Fair*, which was as much a part of the German as of the Anglophone canon in the nineteenth century.[20] In the very first chapter, we are introduced to a Miss Schwartz, "the rich woolly-haired mulatto from St. Kitts," who goes into "downright hysterics" when Amelia Sedley and Becky Sharp leave school (8). She is depicted as neither very bright nor very talented. She retains her "primitive" love of ornament: "her favorite amber-coloured satin with turquoise bracelets, countless rings, flowers, feathers, and all sorts of tags and gimcracks, about as elegantly decorated as a she chimney-sweep on May-day" (200). This hysterical type is a *Mischling* in the German sense of the word, as her German name, "black," suggests. But her patrimony is not German, but Jewish: "Her father was a German Jew—a slave-owner they say—connected with the Cannibal Islands in some way or another," who has died and left his children a large inheritance (194). In the novel she is anomalous, an exotic whose sexuality is written on her body. Even her wealth does not cancel this out. Thus George Osborne rejects a potentially lucrative match with her, exclaiming: "Marry that mulatto woman? . . . I don't like the colour, sir. Ask the black that sweeps opposite Fleet Market, sir. *I'm* not going to marry a Hottentot Venus" (204). The reference to the Hottentot Venus evokes the body of the African woman and her "primitive sexuality." But this figure represents a literary reworking of the *Mischling*'s atavism. It also evokes the German Jew's supposed willingness, even eagerness, because of his or her innate sexual difference, to cross racial lines.

The model of the *Mischling*, however, comes to represent the "essential" nature of the Jew in racist culture of the twentieth century. In Josefa Berens-Totenohl's best-selling novel of the Third Reich, she describes the Jew as "a *Mischling* in blood and home, in language and promise, in thinking and acting. No one really knew him."[21] His physiognomy likewise gives him away; his eyes and his hair color reveal that he does not belong. Even the dogs of the farm know that, barking at his approach. The *fin-de-siècle* literary Jew is no longer "pure" in anything, not even racially. The Jew now provokes the anxiety associated with the boundary-crossing *Mischling*. This *Mischling* is manifestly, ineradicably different.

Nowhere is this anxiety more powerful at the turn of the century than in Kafka's Prague. In 1909 Max Warwar published a biting feuilleton on the front page of the Zionist periodical, *Self-Defense* (*Selbstwehr*), a periodical of which Kafka was a fervent reader and sometime correspondent. Warwar bemoans the "flight from the type," the anxiety of Jews about their own bodies as signs of their inherent difference.[22] "There are reportedly Jews," writes Warwar, "who stand for hours before the mirror and like vain women observe their exterior with jealousy and distaste, complaining against nature that had so irrationally formed them in the light of the laws of their development. These Jews feel their profile as a band of shame, and suffer for they have not learned to experience what is there as beautiful." These male Jews are like women, but women who are constantly unhappy with what nature has provided them in the way of beauty. They are ashamed of their own "type." This "type," of course, according to the Zionist Warwar, is a pure type, but these Jews act as if their bodies represented a mixed type. Some try to escape their bodies through conversion, by "crawling to the cross," but the conversion fails, and they do not acquire any respect for their "external being" from the "other" through conversion. Conversion is no escape from race, as it is only the desire to appear like the "other," in Warwar's term, that motivates their false conversions. What they wish to escape is the "Jewish type," being a "true, black-haired Jew." It is blackness that marks the Jews as different in Prague. Blackness, for Warwar, is a sign of the pure type; a sign of inherent difference. These "black Jews," seen by Warwar in the singer's self-representation in the *Song of Songs*, can be beautiful: "For the soul even of the blackest of Jews can be as pure as gold." And it is indeed the blackness of the Jew that should be the erotic center of their attraction: "Perhaps it is this very fire that burns in the eyes of Jewish men and women, that extends an inescapable attraction to all that come close to it. And the blacker such a type is, the more demonic and darker the fires burn in the eyes, and the more intimate the magic that such a Jew can exude." Warwar sees, however, that this is precisely not the case in contemporary Prague. There the sexual attraction to such a "type" is felt only by "Christians, Teutons, and Romans," not by Jews. And this attraction leads then to crossing racial boundaries, and the creation of mixed racial types. In this argument, Jews must remain true to their own "type," to their own body, and to their cultural difference as "Orientals."[23]

In this ideological construct, the Jews as "Oriental" are as marked by the color of their skins, by their yellowness or their blackness, as Africans. In addition to their moral, psychological, and physiological failings, all inscribed so that they can be read by the physician, the *Mischling* is proverbially creative. This is a negative quality of the Jew that has its roots in the nineteenth-century discussion about the relationship between genius and madness. Creativity was understood by physicians as early as mid-century as a symptom pointing to some form of underlying degenerative pathology. This labeled the creativity of writers (such as Heinrich Heine) as a sign of their pathology and this pathological nature was embodied in the writer's use of language. The Jews' creativity is in the Jewish use of the German language.[24] But they cannot become too like Aryan Christians, for then they are inauthentic: "If the Jew differs from us, so much the better; he is the more likely to bring a little variety into the flat monotony of modern civilization. I am rather inclined to find fault with these sons of Shem—as I find fault with the Orientals who adopt our customs—for resembling and copying us too closely."[25] The inauthenticity of the Western Jew, copying "us" too closely, is the inauthenticity of the convert, whether a religious or a cultural convert. Jews have the "remarkable faculty of taking on a new skin, without at bottom ceasing to be a Jew."[26] For Leroy-Beaulieu knows where the "real" Jew lies—it is in the East where the essence of the Jew is revealed and cannot be masked by conversion: "There seems to be something of the reptile in him [the Eastern Jew], something sinuous and crawling, something slimy and clammy, of which not even the educated Israelite has always been able to rid himself. . . . This is a quality that transforms him again . . . into an Oriental; it is a racial feature, an inherent vice, not always to be washed away by the water and salt of baptism."[27] And it is the voice that reveals the Jew even after his seeming transformation into a "Frenchman": "The metamorphosis was often too sudden to be complete. . . . A glance, a word, a gesture, all of a sudden lays bare the old Jew at the bottom."[28] It is the face and the voice that reveal the hidden Jew.

One might add that, at the close of another century, the old *Mischling* seems the antithesis of the "cosmic race" imagined by contemporary thinkers such as Gloria Anzaldúa, where "this mixture of races, rather than resulting in an inferior being, provides hybrid progeny, a mutable, more malleable species with a rich gene pool."[29] For her, this is the true genius of the *mestiza*, the New World *Mischling*. This rescuing of the concept of hybridity generates an image of a culture that embodies difference for Anzaldúa, on the analogy of the gay man and lesbian, "the supreme crossers of cultures," who are the focus of cultural exchange. Contemporary theory, in attempting to rescue the *mestiza*, provides a further rehabilitation of notions of continually crossing ideas of race and gender. The Canadian film maker Christine Welsh effects a similar, necessary rehabilitation of the anxiety about being *Métis*, of mixed race: the *Métis* becomes a type of one.[30] By positing the "cosmic race" as "healing the split at the foundation of our lives," she removes the stigmata of "illness" from those at the borderlands.

In Kafka's world, such a solution is not available, neither for Kafka as a writer nor as a person. Earlier options of cultural and biological integration are also seemingly closed to him. Visiting Meran in April of 1920, his visibility as a Jew becomes even more evident to him. His very language reveals him as a Jew to the "Germans" there (LF, 232), in a way that is most telling for a writer. In this same account, he rails against the *Taufjude* and the *Mischling*: "What horrid Jewish energies live on close to bursting inside a baptized Jew, only to be modulated in the Christian children of a Christian mother!" (LF, 232). Here, the promise of eventual integration into an ideal society, as the Christian child of a Christian mother, is the result of the process of the physical transformation of the Jew. The intermediate stage of this transformation is the baptized Jew. This baptized Jew represents, in Kafka's vocabulary of images, the status of the westernized, acculturated, perhaps even assimilated Jews, whose only hope is in the eventual total physical acceptance of their offspring who have become physically identical with the Germans (but not the Czechs). As Ernst Lissauer observed in 1912:

> The Jews are in an intermediary stage. The emancipation of the Jews is but a hundred years hence; it began only a hundred years ago and is not yet completed. These hundred years are but a very short span of time. Our poorly educated sense of history often allows Jews and Non-Jews to forget that the Jews were in the Diaspora for 1700 years, under extraordinary pressure and need, and that the effects of such an extended time cannot be eradicated in a century. When we tabulate these figures, the "Jewish Question" acquires quite a different image. One can thus see that the Jews still possess many of the characteristics that come from the Ghetto and that awake the hate of the Non-Jew, but also that on the other hand many of these characteristics have been lost, as assimilation has been relatively successful.[31]

Among the markers of difference that seem not to have been lost but only repressed, in the fantasies of Western Jews, is the inability of the Jew to command the language of high culture. And Jews who speak differently look different. Kafka meets a Jewish goldsmith from Cracow who had been long in America, and whose "German was disturbed by an English pronunciation and English expressions; his English was so strong that his Yiddish was given a rest." And this traveler looked different: "He had long, curly hair, only occasionally ran his fingers through it, very bright eyes, a gently curving nose, hollows in his cheeks, a suit of American cut, a frayed shirt, falling socks" (D2, 263). Here is what the Eastern Jew becomes when he attempts to transform himself—an individual without language, without culture, marked by the physiognomy of the Jew.

Here we have the other side of the "double helix," to use Stanley Corngold's felicitous image, of Kafka's struggle with his body as an assimilated Jew. No transformation will change his future, not even marriage "outside of the race." No Christian children by a Christian wife will redeem him. In an earlier letter of June 3, 1919 to Josef Körner, on Körner's work on the Romantics, Kafka wrote: "Bettina [von Arnim] gives the impression of having been a distraught half-Jewish young man dressed in woman's clothes, and I don't understand how she could have had that happy marriage and those seven children. Should the children have led halfway normal lives, it would have been a miracle" (LF, 215). It is the child who suffers from the sins of the parents, the "half-Jews" who inherit the worst of both parents. These parents are cultural cross-dressers of the most aberrant kind, and their children, by definition, must be even more abnormal than their parents. For the biological rule of the time was that in such marriages, there was a renewed appearance in the children of the signs of difference that the parents had repressed. Thus Thackeray's Miss Schwartz possesses magnified defects of both her parents, especially their innate tendency toward hysteria.

Kafka's tale, "A Crossbreed" (1917), the tale of an animal, "half kitten, half lamb" (426), demonstrates his awareness of this debate.[32] The animal bears the qualities of both: the head and claws of the cat, the size and shape of the lamb. But more importantly, it incorporates the inherently contradictory mind-sets of both animals: it lies in the sun and purrs, or it scampers on the meadow. But it "cannot mew and it loathes rats." It is unique, for when it confronts other cats and lambs, there is no "scene of recognition": "The animals gazed calmly at each other with their animal eyes, and obviously accepted their reciprocal existence as a divine fact." The narrator's response is to see the animal as a true extension of himself:

> Once when, as may happen to anyone, I could see no way out of my business problems and all that they involved, and was ready to let everything go, and in this mood was lying in my rocking chair in my room, the beast on my knee, I happened to glance down and saw tears dropping from its huge whiskers. Were they mine, or were they the animal's? Had this cat, along with the soul of a lamb, the ambitions of being a human being? I did not inherit much from my father, but this legacy is quite remarkable.

The only humane solution for this hybrid is "ritual" slaughter: "Perhaps the knife of the butcher would be a release for this animal; but as it is a legacy I must deny it that. So it must wait until the breath voluntarily leaves its body, even though it sometimes gazes at me with a look of human understanding, challenging me to do the thing of which both of us are thinking" (427). This knife certainly evokes again that "knife that stabs not only forward but one that wheels around and stabs back as well." It is also a knife that is both ritually clean (one is ritually permitted to butcher lambs) and simultaneously unclean (one is forbidden to butcher cats). Thus the "knife of the butcher," as we shall see in Chapter Three, with all of its evocations of slaughter and disease, encompasses all the contradictions of a masculinity defined by ritual circumcision and ritual murder trials.

Kafka's butcher knife is also Kafka's legacy: that which he fears and acknowledges he has inherited and must fulfill. For his father's father, Jakob Kafka, had been a kosher butcher in the tiny Czech village of Wossek. Kafka's very rejection of meat and his becoming a vegetarian in 1909 is read by him, in a letter to Milena Jesenská in June, 1920, as a type of magical gesture to ward off the inevitable. He writes that it is part of the inheritance that simply shapes him, like his lack of musical ability: "Unmusicality is not as clearly a misfortune as you say—in the first place it isn't for me: I inherited it from my predecessors (my paternal grandfather was a butcher in a village near Strakonitz; I have to not eat as much meat as he butchered) and it gives me something to hold on to; being related means a lot to me" (LM, 59).[33] Kafka's legacy is not only his lack of musical ability, it is those qualities of mind and character inherited from his totally differing ancestors. The problem of mixed inheritance was a means of describing his own background as complex and antithetical, unlike the racialist label that saw all Jews as essentially the same. The problem of a mixed inheritance is also its advantage. Kafka's anxiety is that he will become what he must become. He will inherit the qualities of his ancestors—as well as their guilt. He will be unmusical, but he must also atone for the ritual slaughter of animals. But this diversity is also an answer to the label that he is simply a "Jew." His construction of his Jewish ancestry points to its diversity while continuing to evoke a level of anxiety because of its Jewishness. For Kafka as the writer, an answer to mixed breeds is ritual murder/butchery, but in his own inverted manner of representing this dilemma, this demands that the victim be seen as "human." Is the mixed breed truly human? And why is the narrator suddenly in the position of ritual butcher?

Kafka understands his own imagined body and psyche as that of a *Mischling* who can never become "normal," as in this story. The *Mischling* has a German Romantic pedigree, nonetheless, beginning with the divided soul of Goethe's Faust, that is then racialized in Thomas Mann's "Tonio Kröger" (1903), about the son of German father and an

Italian mother. Kafka certainly sees himself in this lineage. In the "Letter to the Father," part fiction, part autobiography, all construction, written in 1919, he describes himself as "a Löwy [his mother's family] with a certain Kafka [his father's family] component" (L, 115), a mix that results in a distorted body and a hysterically nervous psyche. All of the qualities, however, that Kafka ascribes to the "mix" between the Löwys and the Kafkas are the qualities ascribed to the Jew by *fin-de-siècle* culture. What seems in this text to be an intense introspection on his Oedipal struggle with his father uses the language and images of psychoanalysis (a language and imagery that Kafka knew well and found inadequate) to mask the anxiety about his biological and psychic stability, about his fear of becoming his parents, just as his culture claimed that he inevitably would.

But it is not just the social construction of the Jew that forced Kafka to deal with contradictions in his construction of himself. As I noted earlier, it is impossible to invoke the concept "Jew" without immediately invoking concepts of masculinity and pathology. For *the* Jew at the *fin de siècle* is the male Jew. The act of circumcision marks the male Jew as different, and as different precisely for reasons of "hygiene," the rationale for infant male circumcision among European and American Jews of the time. The Jew is seen in Europe as "the circumcised pariah," according to Leroy-Beaulieu.[34] Circumcision thus marked the Jewish male's character as well as his body. Indeed, in 1891 one could read toilet graffiti to the effect that: "You without a foreskin / shouldn't be too pushy." (*"Ihr ohne Vorhaut / Seid nicht vorlaut."*)[35] Of course, masculinity in general came to be highly contested in the 1890s. With the rise of the homosexual emancipation movement and the German Youth Movement, the monolithic definition of the male was drawn into question. Nonetheless, the position of the male Jew, his body clearly marked, remained radically defined. The shifts in the meaning of disease with Pasteur, Koch, Wassermann, the discovery of germ theory, asepsis, and anesthesia by the end of the century were also impacted by complex theories of predisposition and inheritance that looked at "race" and "gender" as two potent variables. All of these qualities are reflected in Kafka's self-image and his works.

How Kafka restructures his self-image as a patient, a Jew, and a man is complex but understandable. Here the concept of the "masochist text" can be helpful. It is masochism not as self-abnegation or self-flagellation, but as a demand on the part of the author that the literary representation of the sense of powerlessness be understood as a tool to shape those who claim to have power over oneself. The projection of power may be onto the culture in its entirety or onto an individual in that culture. That sense of power and powerlessness is mirrored in the relationship that the individual has with the parent—the power of the parent having been internalized by the child, and the child needing that sense of power beyond him/herself, especially when the parent ages and weakens. Masochism comes to be an acting out of the conflict felt between the claims lodged against the individual and the inability of that individual to counter these claims completely because of the underlying incompleteness, the transitoriness of all constructions of the self. This is heightened when the model for this conflict is the model of child/parent interaction. In such a model the parent must remain powerful for the child to have any sense of his/her relationship to the source of power. The illusion of control that the child has becomes part of a real sense of loss as the child sees the parent's "power" waning. The inevitability of decay and death of the self becomes the repressed moment in this masochistic scene. Thus each person is incomplete within him/herself. *But in a culture in which the inevitability of decay is projected onto specific categories of difference, those who understand themselves as belonging to a stigmatized category can only partially repress this anxiety*. This sense of the incomplete self is parallel to the claims of the culture about the nature of the male, of the Jew, of the patient—when all three are taken simultaneously as markers for the difference of any given individual from the arbitrary norms of the culture that define control, health, and positive sexuality.

Gilles Deleuze and Félix Guattari espoused a similar view in their analysis of Kafka's term, "minor" (or "little") literature.[36] This concept is especially useful for any analysis of a literature that self-consciously positions itself outside a cultural mainstream to which it certainly belongs. The term "minor literature" is taken from Kafka's diary entry for December 25, 1911. It is clear that Kafka would not necessarily have included what he wrote in German while living in Prague under the rubric of a "minor" literature.[37] His examples are Yiddish literature in Poland and Czech literature in Prague. But for Kafka (if not for Deleuze and Guattari) a "minor literature" is written in a discourse that must simultaneously be employed and transcended. It is a language and style that the "minority" is accused of not being able to command that is captured in a special way by the writers in that minority. This is a highly psychologized political literature, for the creation of a "minor literature" requires a struggle with the image of the self that is both private, psychological—and here the model of the masochist is appropriate—as well as public, political, since resistance to one's internalization of others' labeling of oneself is inherently political. And central to the existence of a minor literature is a clear association with the discourse about the body of the writer—bodies and biographies are never peripheral to the construction of a "minor literature." The writer's body, in Deleuze's later formulation, comes to be an extension of the imagined body of the father. For Deleuze, and as we shall see, for Kafka, it is not that the father is the (positive) Oedipal aggressor dominating the son; rather, the father is "not so much the beater as the beaten. . . . Is it not precisely the father-image in him that is miniaturized, beaten, ridiculed and humiliated? What the subject atones for is his resemblance to the father and the father's likeness in him: the formula of masochism is the humiliated father."[38] Or at least the anxiety that the son must eventually become like the father, and the father's status is marked by the decay of power, by the father's increasingly marked role as the old, ill male. In terms of one of the central anxieties in Kafka's life and work—one is fated to become the father. On one level this takes place in the world of the imaginary, yet it also has specific symbolic significance in the structuring of the masochist's world out of historical rhetoric. For Kafka, the model of son and father, of youth and age, of progress and regression, of health and illness replicates the rhetoric of the relationship of the Jews to Western and/or Christian culture. The Jew is old, is regressive, is ill, while the Christian or secularized Western culture in which he dwells is the opposite. When Kafka imagines the decay of his aging father from the powerful, "modern" citizen of the Empire into the status of the aged Jew, he also understands that his body remains inevitably Jewish.

Identity, the seemingly fixed summary of the internalization of a series of external norms about oneself, is rooted in both the physical sense of oneself as well as one's ability to write autobiography. It is a minor literature formed within the ethnopsychology of the group: "A small nation's memory is not smaller than the memory of a large one and so can digest the existing material more thoroughly,"[39] Kafka writes, using the ethnopsychological argument of Jewish thinkers of the late nineteenth century such as Heymann Steinthal, Moritz Lazarus and Sigmund Freud. For Kafka, all of this plays itself out within a psyche that retains historical experience across generations, and that shapes even the writer who has not experienced the realities of history firsthand. And the image of the collective into which the writer is forced by the hegemonic discourse of the society and its literature in which the writer dwells, or which determines the writer's cultural orientation, is always encapsulated in that society's image of the body. It is a body that remembers things that it has not experienced personally, but that the group has experienced.

The writer's tongue is but an extension of that fantasy body. As Deleuze and Guattari note: "Rich or poor, each language always implies a deterritorialization of the mouth, the tongue, and the teeth" (19). This is a tongue intimately connected, as Alexander Kluge and Oskar Negt have argued, with self-presentation in the public sphere.[40] It is a tongue with at least the potential for resistance. It is this body, inscribed in and inscribing language, which both dominates and resists. This is the masochist's body, with the weakness and incompleteness of a child's body. It is a construct of the author (as much as the writer constructs the entire fiction), for a writer's use of social constructions inevitably becomes masochistic, since his self-construction involves his domination by others (the readers) and his supposed dominance of them. The fiction of control is at the heart of the concept of a "minor literature." For in the fictive scene the writer creates the image of the dominated and the dominating using a language over which the writer is denied control. It is the writer's reenactment of this scene of domination which puts the writer in imaginary control over the fictive bodies in the text. This position is analogous to the position that the "minor" writer has to the dominant culture. The writer is part of that culture, part of the masochistic contract between the dominated and the dominating, and yet separated from it by the same conceptual space that separates the dominated from the dominating.

Kafka's concept of a minor literature is framed by this complex discourse on the body of the male Jew, his language, and their relationship. It is not an anxiety about Yiddish, German, Czech, or Hebrew that creates Kafka's sense of the slipperiness of language, as Deleuze and Guattari claim (25). Rather it is the sense that none of the "real" languages—not even Yiddish—is an authentic language for the Western Jewish writer. Kafka's language is the language ascribed to the *Mischling*; it is the language that slips out even when you think that you are in command of an "authentic" language. It is *Mauscheln*, the language the Jew tries to hide.

A German proverb of the time says that "One can inherit *Mauscheln* but one can not unlearn it."[41] *Mauscheln* is the term for the language ascribed to the Jews. It is not merely bad German, but a specific form of German that reveals the Jew hidden in its texts. Its overt model in *fin-de-siècle* German culture may lie in the way that Yiddish speakers articulate German, but the concept is older and more all-encompassing. In 1924, Arthur Schnitzler's Fräulein Else, the young girl about to be sacrificed to an older man for the sake of her bankrupt father, comments in an interior monologue on the art dealer to whom she is about to sell her virtue:

> You might as well be an old-clothes man as an art dealer—But, Else Else, what makes you say a thing like that?—O, I can permit myself a remark of this sort. Nobody notices it in me. I'm even blonde, a strawberry blonde, and Rudi [her brother] looks absolutely like an aristocrat. Of course, one can notice it easily in Mother, especially in her speech, but not at all in Father. Really they ought to notice it in me. More than that—let them notice it.

The "it," of course is the hidden taint, the visible invisibility of the Jewishness of her parents, a visibility inscribed in her mother's language, that she believes (hopes) is unnoticeable in hers. *Mauscheln* is a reflex of her Jewishness, her inherent difference. It is also the language of Kafka's parents: unlike Schnitzler's middle-class Jews, they never quite lost their Yiddish accents and their use of Yiddishisms in their writing.[42]

Even if the body appears to be "Aryan," it will, it must reveal itself as Jewish. The anti-Semitic proverb is precisely the antithesis of the claim Kafka makes in Paris in 1911, that German has the "faculty of sounding beautiful in the mouths of foreigners who haven't mastered it, and for the most part don't intend to, either" (D2 275). For Jews in "German" culture, his culture, this is precisely not the case. It was understood that the farther East one went, the more Eastern Jews, speaking German as a second language, came to embody the impossibility of German-speaking Jews having command over their own discourse and tongues. On April 10, 1920, Kafka writes to Max Brod and Felix Weltsch from Meran about how the guests at the hotel in which he was staying attempted to identify his accent (LF, 232–233). One of them, an Austrian general with "true German military eyes," demanded that he tell him where he was from. Kafka admitted to being from Prague, but that was not sufficient for his interlocutors. For after dinner, they began again: "He once more began to wonder about the sound of my German, perhaps more bothered by what he saw than by what he heard." Kafka came to realize in his recording of this exchange that it was not only his accent, the sound of his German, but his appearance that drew his status in this middle-class hotel into question. He notes that people doubted their eyes as well as their ears. As soon as he announced he was Jewish, the dining room cleared, leaving Kafka to wonder, "Why must I be a thorn in their flesh?" The language of the Jew was understood even by Jews as but a reflex of the body of the Jew.

Jewish savants, such as ethnopsychology's cofounder Heymann Steinthal, claimed in 1893 that *Mauscheln* was a reflex of the "organ of speech" of those born in the East, but would not appear among those born in Germany. Steinthal's prediction of the acculturated Western Jew's psychical and physical transformation is reflected in the debates about the nature of the Jew's language and body.[43] Kafka's close friend and literary executor, Max Brod, as late as the early 1930s, upheld the notion that each "type" (*Art*) of human being possesses its own stylistic form, and when it attempts to speak another language it falls into a rigidity and superficiality that it did not have in its own language. It is style (*Stilart*) that is affected.[44] This reflects the views of writers such as Martin Buber, who accepted a racialist model of the Jew tied to the authenticity of a Jewish discourse.

Kafka's text deterritorializes all of these anxieties and permits them to be performed and displayed within the modernist, written text. In his early work he permits himself to contextualize these charges by enacting them in his own text. There he exposes his own vulnerability, the ambiguities in his sense of self. His invention of his modernism and its discourse to displace the language about the Jews and the language of the Jews is quite different from that of the Viennese Jew Theodor Herzl, for example. While Wilhelm II can dismiss Herzl as *Mauschel* and Herzl in turn can savage the Jewish opponents of Zionism as *Mauschel*, Kafka must take a different tack. He enacts such charges in a number of his texts, ranging from "The Report to the Academy" to "Josephine, the Singer," but removes any specifically "Jewish" overtones. Wilhelm II's and Herzl's attacks on Jews as possessing a different and evil discourse evoke the rhetoric of anti-Semitism; Kafka sublimates his anxiety about language and its control as a means of combating the rhetoric of his own difference. But as his own literary tools are drawn into question, a further ambiguity arises.

Kafka is clearly looking for an "authentic" language in which to write. Kafka's romanticization of Yiddish as found in the popular

Yiddish theater in Prague has been taken as his response to the European (and Western Jewish) condemnation of "Yiddish," a language of "raggedy and makeshift character."[45] But Kafka's discovery of "Yiddish" as the language of itinerant players such as his friend Yitshak Löwy comes at precisely the point in the literary history of Yiddish when its greatest authors—Shalom Aleichem, Peretz, and the young Sholem Asch—were writing, and being read in Prague, if only in German translation, as serious works of world literature. Indeed, Löwy read from many of these works in his public presentations in Prague.[46] A few years before, Nathan Birnbaum, a leading cultural Zionist, had called the first conference in Czernowitz to regularize the Yiddish language and make it a "real" language with "real" grammatical rules. More importantly Kafka, not to mention his contemporaries, could have had access to much of this literature through numerous translations and reviews, some of them in Martin Buber's journal, *The Jew*, to which Kafka contributed. Kafka's discovery of Yiddish writing in Warsaw as a "minor" literature is the projection of his own desire for authenticity. Yiddish literature in all of its diverse forms serves for Kafka as the location of Jewish linguistic authenticity.

Yiddish thus comes to represent not only the authentic language but the authentic Jew. In his "Speech on the Yiddish Language," which he gave on February 18, 1912 to introduce a reading by Yiddish actor Yitshak Löwy, at the Jewish Town Hall, Kafka imagines the nature of Yiddish and sees in it the idealized but tormented place of the Western European Jew confronting his own language.[47] His audience was composed of German-speaking Prague Jews, whose rejection of Yiddish was profound. Yiddish marked the world from which they had come, and was, for Western culture, a sign of the linguistic degeneracy of the Jews. Kafka demands that his audience acknowledge that they can understand Yiddish (306). This theme is so powerful that Kafka can claim by the middle of his talk, "luckily everyone who comprehends the German language is also able to understand Yiddish" (308). There is an authentic language of the Jew, no matter whether the Jew acknowledges his understanding of Yiddish or of German. Hidden within the Jew is this language that is "everything, words, Hassidic melodies, and the essence of the Eastern Jewish actors themselves." Once the Western Jew acknowledges this potential inscribed on the Jewish psyche, then this "language will have captured him." "Then you will come to feel the unity of Yiddish so strongly that you will come to fear not the language but yourselves" (309). The language is the actor in Kafka's world, for it is identical with the Jew. "Our" language, according to Franz Rosenzweig in 1921, does not have a "spirit" (*Geist*), but rather a "life" (*Leben*). "One *lives* in a language."[48] For Kafka, too, language is not the ephemeral spirit but the very body, the very life of the Jew.

Such a language would be untranslatable. And thus Kafka stresses that Yiddish cannot be translated into German because the "relationship between the two languages is too delicate and meaningful," because they are indeed two halves of a whole. Here Rosenzweig would have objected, for he believed that the translator needs to create a new language when a truly great work like the Bible is brought into another language: "Translations into a Jewish German wouldn't hurt." For Kafka, seeing the interchangeability of Yiddish and German, German is already a Jewish German that is so transparent that its speakers can understand Yiddish intuitively. This is a desire, a desire that the two languages live together like the two halves of the Platonic body, each yearning for the other to complete its wholeness. But it is a fantasy, a masochistic wish-projection of control over German that designates it merely Yiddish in another form.

The masochistic wish for domination by language, by the Jew within, is an acknowledgment in reverse of the discourse on the hidden language of the Jews, whose discovery the acculturated Jewish audience must fear, a "fear that you would like to forget." But the purpose of the evening is not to punish this audience, but to let them enjoy at a distance what they must fear becoming—Yitshak Löwy, the Eastern Jew. The language, the body of the Eastern Jew are but one generation or a few hundred kilometers removed from the audience, hence their anxiety that they must again become authentic Jews. Löwy was an actor, who by theatricalizing his audience's fear of his language and body enabled them to experience catharsis. But Löwy's ever-shifting body also enacted an anti-Semitic canard of the time, that Jews make the best actors because of their intrinsic mutability. Actor and audience thus have control only in the masochistic context of the performance; on the street, they again become simply "Jews," according to anti-Semites no more able than Eastern European Jews to command their discourse.

The image of a "primitive" language that needs rescuing was Kafka's own, and it spoke to his need to redeem his Jewish linguistic identity. His writings, those of Karl Kraus, and somewhat later those of the "Jewish" Ludwig Wittgenstein deal quite concretely with internalized allegations that German Jewish literature is illegitimate. Wittgenstein observed, "even the greatest of Jewish thinkers is no more than talented. (Myself, for instance.) I think there is some truth to my idea that I really only think reproductively. . . ."[49] Kafka turned this anxiety about control into a theory of linguistic praxis that was, however, self-consciously not to be read as Jewish but as "modern" (at a point when these two traditions were not yet labeled as interchangeable). Unlike his friend Max Brod, who attempted to craft a new German Jewish discourse in some of his novels, Kafka restrained his enthusiasm for the new language of the Jew—the discourse of the East—and mirrored it only within the most complex of high literary conventions, such as the animal fable, which in the nineteenth century had taken its place within the literary fairy tale as part of German "high culture."[50]

Kafka's language use is closely linked to the contemporaneous charge of the "illegitimacy of German-Jewish literature." What haunts Kafka's text is the voice attributed to the other marginal category to which Kafka self-consciously belonged: that is, the discourse of the tubercular patient. (Ironically, Kafka adopted this convention *even before* he was diagnosed as having tuberculosis.) The language of the patient with tuberculosis was clearly described in the medical literature of the period, but was also equally in the popular literature of the time. Not merely Thomas Mann and the expressionist Klabund but an entire raft of tales, ranging from the naturalistic to the highly expressionistic, represented the voice of the tubercular patient following the *fin de siècle*. Overheated, highly charged, highly sexual, this language was the other major model for a linguistic tradition that Franz Kafka saw as potentially contaminating his own text. The highly controlled world of dream images is the language both ascribed to and experienced by the patient with tuberculosis (in the light of this ascription). Kafka detoxifies this discourse and makes it his own.

The discourse of the Jew, whether tubercular or not, is male, as it is defined by circumcision, while the language of the tubercular patient is clearly ungendered. It is this latter fact, the self-consciously ungendered nature of Kafka's language, especially in those scenes where male sexuality is represented, as in *The Castle* or "A Country Doctor," that are a response to these associations. Kafka's language represents the "feminine" within the language of the tuberculosis patient of whatever gender, whose social role in the asylum was analogous to a middle-class woman's. This is the view of the tubercular in the work of Herbert Böhme, for example, whose 1932 dissertation (first published in 1939) stresses the predisposition of tubercular writers not only to the disease but to the language that is an inevitable reflex of it. Böhme stresses the feminization of the writer's discourse, its intense sexuality, its overblown and pathetic tone.[51] But equally important, as we shall see, he relates this to the asthenic body form that marks the tubercular (11). This widely accepted version of the relationship between the mind and the body of the tubercular is, of course, analogous to the prejudice against *Mauscheln*. It is of little surprise that Böhme also sees the discourse of the tubercular as "reminiscent of that of the Jew" (51). I would argue that the discourses about the body that swirled around and impacted on the Jewish, tubercular, male, German-language writer, Franz Kafka, in the Prague of his time are reflected in the high modernism of his text, with good reason. But, as we shall see, his modernist claim to a position above such problems is constantly in doubt.

A Jewish accent marks the soul of the Jew just as it marks his body. Kafka's tale "Josephine the Singer, or the Mouse Folk" (1924), in which singing may not be singing at all but merely the usual piping of the mice, presents a series of associations, all of which relate to the representation of the body. Mark Anderson stresses the connection between this image and the claim, by writers of *fin-de-siècle* Viennese culture such as Otto Weininger, that Jews are congenitally unable to sing; as Kafka's mouse narrator states, "we are quite unmusical" (S, 360). The most obvious biographical association is not with Kafka's Jewishness, however, but with his illness. Kafka wrote the tale after he developed laryngeal tuberculosis, which forced him to communicate, like the deaf Beethoven, through notes. His silence was heard, a silence that signified only his wish to communicate. This was a physical analogy to the speechless state that his Jewishness placed upon his command of the language of modernism. Kafka's consciousness of language is found in his visceral sublimation of the anxiety about his voice, his literary as well as physical voice, into the discourse of the female, who is also the primitive. For Josephine is both.

But the image of the mouse had long haunted his sense of his own sanity. He writes in December, 1917, about the mice that haunt his apartment:

> My reaction toward the mice is one of sheer terror. To analyze its source would be the task of the psychoanalyst, which I am not. Certainly, this fear, like an insect phobia, is connected with the unexpected, uninvited, inescapable, more or less silent, persistent, secret aims of these creatures, with the sense that they have riddled the surrounding walls through and through with their tunnels and are lurking within, that the night is theirs, that because of the nocturnal existence and their tininess they are so remote from us and thus outside our power (LF, 174).

Kafka sees these mice as figments of the madness that he fears, as he writes to Milena Jesenská in September 1920: "something dark and squeaky with a long tail fell out and immediately disappeared under the bed. That could have very easily been the mouse, couldn't it? Even if the squeak and the long tail were just in my imagination? In any case I couldn't find anything underneath the bed (as far as I dared look)" (LM, 186). Anthony Storr sees these mice as a sign of Kafka's calling as an author: "indeed, for people of Kafka's temperament, the gift of being able to write is an ideal way of expressing oneself, since it does not involve direct contact with others."[52] But Storr does not address the form of the fantasy. This hallucination may well be but the fear of an hallucination—the fear that, like his mother's family, he may be predisposed to melancholy and suicide or conversion, another form of madness for the *fin-de-siècle* Jew.[53] But why mice as a source of anxiety? They may generally be images of contamination, but at the turn of the century they have a very particular meaning. If one examines these passages closely, the rhetoric of anti-Semitism appears. For all of the attributes that Kafka sees in his mice are attributed to the Jews. Again the proverbial literature of the time states it boldly: "Jews have as much value in the world as mice in corn," or "Jews are as usual in a country as mice in the granary or moths in clothing."[54] In the rhetoric of political anti-Semitism, the Jews turn out to be "golden rats and red mice," as the arch-anti-Semite Wilhelm Marr put it.[55]

Mice are also associated with Jews through the popular etymology of *Mauscheln* as meaning "mouselike."[56] Kafka was well aware of this association. In an extensive letter to Max Brod in June of 1921, Kafka wrote about Karl Kraus, the Viennese satirist, thus:

> The wit principally consists of Yiddish-German, *Mauscheln*: no one can *Mauscheln* like Kraus, although in this German-Jewish world hardly anyone can do anything else. This *Mauscheln*—taken in a wider sense,

> and that is the only way it should be taken—consists in a bumptious, tacit, or self-pitying appropriation of someone else's property, something not earned, but stolen by means of a relatively casual gesture. Yet it remains someone else's property, even though there is no evidence of a single solecism. That does not matter, for in this realm, the whispering voice of conscience confesses the whole crime in a penitent hour. . . . But why should Jews be so irresistibly drawn to this language? German literature existed before the emancipation of the Jews and attained great glory. After all, that literature was, as far as I can see, in no way less varied than today—in fact, today there may be less variety. And there is a relationship between all this and Jewishness, or more precisely between young Jews and their Jewishness, with the fearful inner predicament of these generations. Psychoanalysis lays stress on the father-complex, and many find the concept intellectually fruitful. In this case I prefer another version, where the issue revolves not around the innocent father but around the father's Jewishness. Mostly young Jews who began to write German wanted to leave their Jewishness behind them, and their fathers approved of this, but vaguely (this vagueness was what was outrageous to them). But with their posterior legs [*Hinterbeinchen*] they were glued to their father's Jewishness and with their waving anterior legs [*Vorderbeinchen*] they found no new ground. The ensuing despair became their inspiration. (LF, 286–289)

The depth-psychological explanation (Kafka has read his Freud) is linked to the Jewishness of the father. Kafka reads the depth in terms of the surface but sees his position as an intermediate figure, as a *Mischling*, whose language must be *Mauscheln*. These writers are becoming what they were fated to become, not their fathers but also not separate from their fathers. The result of this conflict, Kafka goes on to write, is a "literature impossible in all respects." Jewish writing in German becomes "a Gypsy literature which had stolen the German child out of its cradle and in great haste put it through some kind of training, for someone has to dance on the tightrope" (LF, 286–289, here 289). It is not a "minor literature." Rather it is the "family romance" that results in an offspring as crossbred as is the cat/lamb of Kafka's tale—a language-using, trained mouse, its four legs straining between the Jewishness of the father and the ungroundedness of "modern" culture. It is of little surprise that Kafka evokes the glue mousetrap in this context. The transformation of the Jewish writer's body into the mouse of his hallucination, which becomes the unheard singing mouse of his tale displaces the anxiety about the difference of the Jewish language as a reflex of the Jew's body.

Here, too, the notion of the act of writing becomes a quality ascribed to the body. The model is one of the most evident commonplaces of *fin-de-siècle* culture—the notion of the essential linkage of the mind and the body. This model, stated here in aesthetic terms, also has a medical corollary in the notion of psychosomatic illness, one that we shall explore in this analysis.[57] But Kafka links his comments on *Mauscheln* with the special status of the Jew's writing, of the minor literature. The passage from Kafka's diaries which I quoted above seems to have as its point of departure Kafka's "understand[ing] of contemporary Jewish [read: Yiddish] literature in Warsaw through [Yitshak] Löwy and of contemporary Czech literature partly through my own insight. . . ." (D1, 190–196). The passage was written at Christmas—not the most productive time to think about one's Jewishness separate from the Christian culture in which one lives, and yet only a week away from the Feast of the Circumcision, when the infant Christ ritually became part of the covenant. Jews as Christians; Christians as Jews, seemingly interchangeable yet inherently different. Kafka comes to understand his own writing not as part of the "minor literature" but in terms of his own Jewish body suspended between the rituals of Eastern Jewry and those of Westernizing Christianity.

Framing his long and complex Christmas Eve discourse on the aesthetics and society of a "minor" literature are two entries about the authentic character of Jewish identity. The first recounts his nephew's circumcision as a sign of the "historical character" of the present-day Jews of Prague; the second discusses circumcision in Russia, a quite different subject. But both frame the notion that minor literature is a product of the ethnopsychology of a group, and is in some way as much inscribed on their unconscious by their social circumstances and historical experiences. In Prague, at the circumcision of his nephew, Kafka stresses the distance that Westernized Jews have from the intrinsic meaning of the ritual. Indeed, what Kafka describes is the contrast between the safe, clean, but forgetful world in Prague, and the dirty, yet vibrant and wholesome world of Eastern Judaism.

For Kafka the Jewishness of the male is inscribed upon his body through the act of circumcision, an act in the East that ends with the *mohel*, the ritual circumciser, with his "red nose and reeking breath," performing *metsitsah*: "It is therefore not very pleasant when, after the operation has been performed, they suck the bloody member with this mouth, in the prescribed manner" (D1, 196). (An herbed wine in the *mohel*'s mouth stanches the blood.) The long association of the *metsitsah* with the transmission of disease and its elimination in virtually all "Western" Jewish communities points to the further association of the Jew's body and his diseased nature. The arguments against the practice of *metsitsah* in the nineteenth century were supposed to be "hygienic" rather than theological, and were separated from the ritual meaning of circumcision. By the close of the nineteenth century, the practice of *metsitsah* had been either abandoned or, in those Western orthodox communities that insisted on its retention, modified by the introduction of a glass tube over the penis through which the *mohel* could draw blood that was filtered before it reached his mouth. The initial purpose of the procedure, to stanch the blood, was abandoned, but the form of the ritual remained. But it is tuberculosis as well as syphilis that is spread by the *mohel*, according to the medical literature of the time[58] (Plate 3). If the child survives the initial infection, the medical literature observed, the child develops pulmonary tuberculosis rather than any other form of the infection.[59] Indeed, tuberculosis comes to be understood in the first decades of the twentieth century as a "disease caused by immoral or intemperate habits," like syphilis.[60] Kafka sees this act in the East, however, as a part of a ritual of redemption and healing. It does not transmit disease. Following *metsitsah*, "the member is then sprinkled with sawdust and heals in about three days." In the East this becomes a narrative of healing, and moreover a healing in three days, the model for which is the story of the Resurrection. Kafka uses the term "heals" (*"heil"*), a term that evokes, especially about the time of the Festival of the Circumcision, the Christian myth of redemption, the "Heilsgeschichte." And, indeed, redemption for Kafka at that moment could only be found in this fabled East, where it is healing rather than illness that follows in three days, where the disease of being a Jew, in Heine's phrase, is transformed into the source of health and healing.

In Kafka's world, the link between syphilis and tuberculosis as "social diseases," as Jules Héricourt labels them at the turn of the century, shows the problem in all its confusion.[61] For if Jews are putatively supposed to suffer from syphilis and tuberculosis, they are also supposed to be immune from syphilis and tuberculosis. This is the contradiction that Kafka senses in the East—Jews there are dirty, superstitious, and marked by their physiognomy and ritual, but they are authentic and therefore healthy. These Jews, too, cannot avoid what they are fated to become,

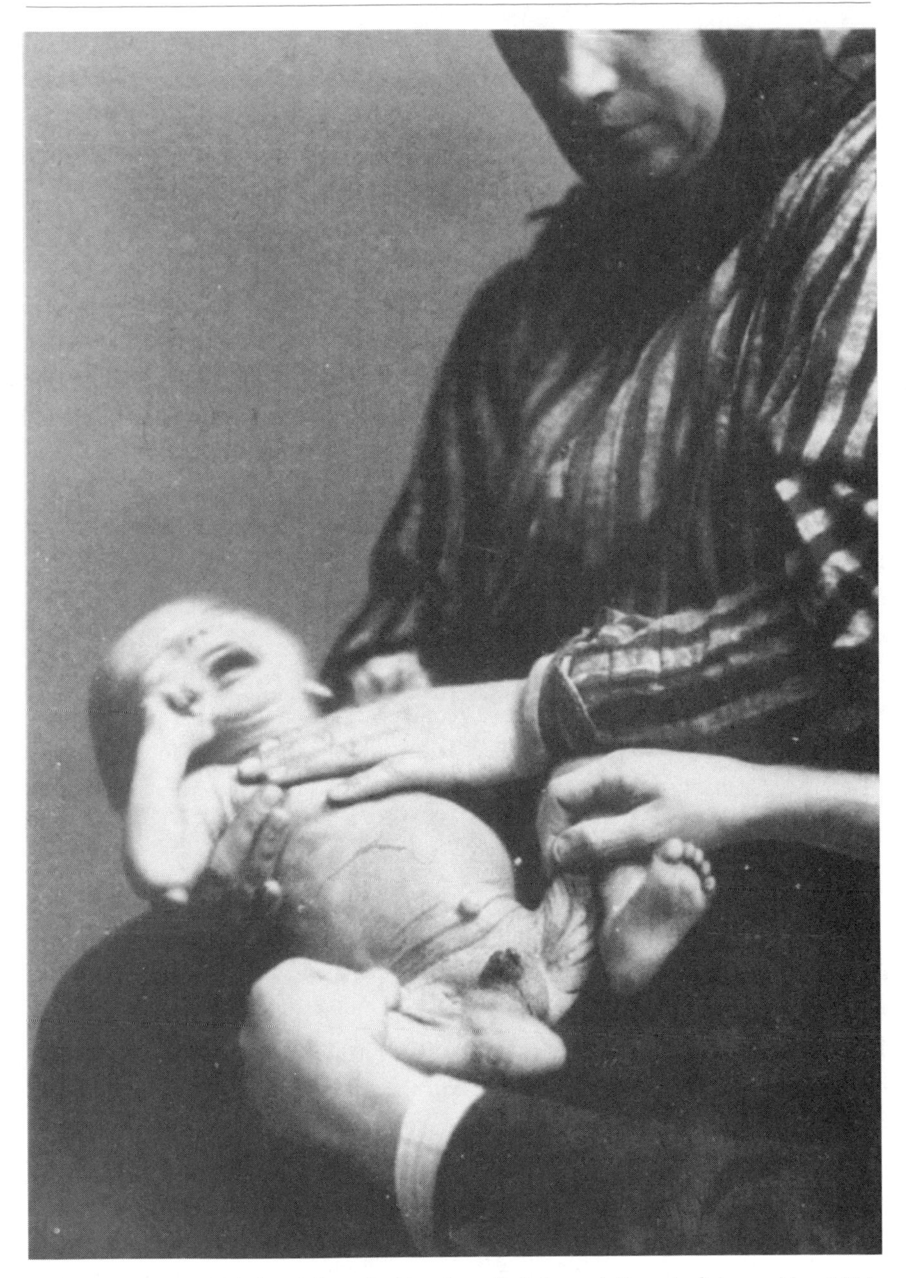

PLATE 3: "The Jewish infant infected with tuberculosis through the act of circumcision," I.M. Arluck and I.J. Winocouroff, "Zur Frage über die Ansteckung an Tuberkulose jüdischer Kinder während der Beschneidung," *Beitrage zur Klinik der Tuberkulose* 22 (1912): Supplementband 3: 341–349 (From the pediatric clinic of the Jewish Hospital at Odessa) (National Library of Medicine, Bethesda).

but this is a "pure" identity rather than a "mixed" identity. In this complex of associations, masculinity, Jewishness, and disease are inexorably linked to these definitions of a positive and a negative identity.

The traditional image of the diseased Jewish child dying of the tuberculosis transmitted to him through the act of circumcision contrasts markedly with Western Christianity's idealized images of circumcision (Plate 4). Here Kafka makes a contrast between the rational, safe, yet boring image of the circumcision in Prague and the dirty, risky, yet authentic image in the East. Using "an ordinary knife, a sort of a fish knife," the *mohel* in Prague performs the circumcision (Plate 5). In Prague the *mohel* "drinks some wine and with his fingers, not yet entirely unbloody, carries some wine to the child's lips." The act of *metsitsah,* with its evocation of fellatio, is missing from the ritual. Circumcision as it is performed in Prague is a sign of the death of Western Judaism: "these forms . . . have reached their final end [and] have merely historical character, even as they are practiced today. . . ." Such practices are of interest only because they are "something out of history." The Jews at the ceremony are awakened from their indifference by the ritual: "only a short time was needed this very morning to interest the people present in the obsolete custom of circumcision and its half-sung prayers by describing it to them as something out of history." But it is also inscribed on their psyches because they are Jews. They may no longer experience the essential nature of the ceremony, as do the Eastern Jews, but they intuitively respond to it.

The experience of acculturated Western Jewry seems to be essentially embedded in their memory, a memory that reaches across the ages to mark them, no matter how unwillingly, as Jews. This construction of Jewish memory is tied to the circumcision that defines Jewish masculinity as effeminate, castrated, potentially ill. In Kafka's account of the animal in the Thamühler Synagogue, written in 1922 in the final stage of his tuberculosis, the "authentic" Jewish discourse of memory is to be found in the dying *shtetl.* This unpublished text contains the only overtly Jewish reference in Kafka's "literary" work. The reader finds him/herself in a "congregation in this little town of ours in the mountains that is becoming smaller every year and that is already having trouble in raising the money for the upkeep of the synagogue" (P, 51). Jonathan Boyarin, in his brilliant book on the politics of Jewish memory, points out that this text "reminds us that we are not the first generation to find that loss is

PLATE 4: The image of circumcision as Christian ritual, in an engraving by François le Parmesan (Girolamo Francesco Maria Mazzola) of the circumcision of Christ. Note the form of the knife (National Library of Methesda, Bethesda).

PLATE 5: The knife used in the act of circumcision, from volume one of Georg Herlitz and Bruno Kirschner, eds., (Berlin: Jüdischer Verlag, 1927). This image reproduces an older image from 1756 (National Library of Medicine, Bethesda).

the heart of our connection." It is the loss, the turning of active memory into the memory of a "mere" history, the "frozen, defensive posture" of his father's religious identity, that Kafka bemoans in Western Jewry.[62]

There is an "animal about the size of a marten" of "pale blue-green color" that haunts the old synagogue (P, 49). Kafka translates his anxieties about loss into an animal metaphor that parallels the mice of his dreams. Unlike those dirty, disease-bringing vermin, this unnamed animal is an "uncommonly quiet animal of settled habits." In spite of this, in the synagogue, the women, who sit separate from the men in the balcony of this orthodox synagogue, "are afraid of the animal" (P, 49). This fear is generated by the distance of the "woman" from the meaning of the ritual. These women have seemingly lost the authenticity of the

Jewish religious experience, for they are not at all religious, and use the animal as an excuse not to pray. Here the women in the balcony become like the Western Jews, such as Kafka's father, whose rare attendance at synagogue came to devalue any religious significance for his son. But the reason for their fear seems to be the animal's physical appearance, its physiognomy: "it looks frightening, particularly the long neck, the triangular face, the upper teeth, which jut out almost horizontally, and on the upper lip a row of long, obviously hard, pale bristles" (P, 49). The relationship between these women and this animal is at the very heart of the tale. It is the animal, whose color and body mark it as different that is seen as frightening, but only for the women. "The men have long ceased to bother about it, one generation has pointed it out to the next" (P, 51). It has become part of their ritual experience; for the women, it remains ever new and frightening. And the animal itself is closely associated by the narrator with the women, for "it seemed, at least until recently, to be not much more intelligent than our women" (55).

Jewish intelligence and superiority, as the discourses of the late nineteenth century would have it, are but parodies of the "real" thing.[63] They are the equivalent of the seeming incomparability of the "superior degenerate" whose life is completely maladaptive. They can produce what seem to be works of aesthetic value, but which reveal themselves in the course of time to be simply shallow imitations. This is the theme of much of Thomas Mann's work, from "Little Mr. Friedmann" to *Death in Venice.* And in all cases, the "superior degenerate," like the male Jew, is feminized. Here, too, the little animal that haunts the synagogue is no smarter than the women in the balcony. Kafka is quite aware of the power of the argument about the feminization of the male Jew and the unnatural superficiality of his discourse. Indeed, these women are the essential aspects of the acculturated Jew that Kafka has displaced to the West. The geography of the synagogue, with its balcony and floor level, are a fantasy geography of Western and Eastern Jewry, opposed in mind-set as well as space. For Kafka's Eastern "male" Jews have simply acculturated to the secular Western world, and function separate from that beast that haunt the synagogue, a cousin to the mice that haunts Kafka's dreams. The acculturated Jew is fated to become ill, effeminate, and sterile, separated from the wellspring of Jewish experience and authenticity. Kafka, dying of tuberculosis, had come to see his study of Hebrew as giving him three possible languages for the Jew—German, Yiddish, and Hebrew. And German was the most damaged, the most infected, and yet simultaneously the only one in which he could express the complexity of his literary desire to control the randomness of the world. Does he then have the ability to control the language of his texts, or does he function in the awareness of the illusion of masochistic control that is necessary to write? Or both simultaneously?

The question of a self-perceived authenticity is the dilemma posed by Kafka's discourse about "minor literature," where there is an "acceptance of what is foreign only in reflection." In Kafka's world of letters, he is the "foreign," the exotic, whose control over the dominant language can be proven only through his control over the new discourse of the high modern. That this discourse itself is highly suspect in its claims and its representation of Jewish difference makes this even more problematic. But Kafka must sign a masochist contract written in German that places him in the position of perpetual victim but that also gives him control over how he is treated—at least in his fantasy world of the literature he writes. Inscribing the victimization of the liminal in his texts, he is constrained to suppress or repress the language and discourse taken from the streets about himself. Here Kafka tries to resolve the ambiguity of his Czech- and German-speaking father in terms of placing himself with the framework of "high" German culture. Yet Kafka remains bilingual in everything but his writing. Indeed, reading his office correspondence (see the appendix) shows that Kafka's written (bureaucratic) Czech improved remarkably between 1919 and 1922. The German anti-Semites on the streets and in the coffee houses of Prague and Berlin did not recognize Jewish self-abasement (or Jewish self-hatred) as control over the Jews themselves. Kafka therefore needs to efface any reference to an external world that questions his control over his language and his body. And the high modern permits, indeed, encourages this effacement in its striving for seeming universals and its reduction of its characters to types. But it is this world in which this reflection of Kafka's internalization of the stereotypes of the Jew is not "something out of history," but rather, immediate and authentic. One is born into these worlds—one will become what one is predetermined to become. And the act of circumcision, with all of its contrary risks and meanings, comes to circumscribe the very idea of writing.

two

Kafka's Body in the Mirror of His Culture

Reading Bodies and Character

What did Franz Kafka see when he looked in the mirror? Or what did he imagine he saw? Let us begin with Kafka's body, at least with a baseline for his body. On October 1, 1907, Dr. Wilhelm Pollack, a physician working for Kafka's new employer, the Trieste-based Assicurazioni Generali Insurance Company, found their new employee weighed 61 kilograms (133 pounds) and was 1.82 meters tall (under six feet). He was almost six feet tall, while the average Czech man was five foot five to six, and the average Slavic Jew was much shorter—five foot to five foot one.[1] Pollack's findings, written on the standard form used to examine those applying for insurance, were as follows:

> The unmarried Dr. Franz Kafka, born on July 3, 1883, is in good health and has neither suffered from recent illness nor had any surgical operations. He has not been in any bath-cures or at any sanatoria. His parents are 57 (father) and 48 (mother) years old. His sisters are 18, 17, and 15, and the oldest and youngest both suffered from meningitis. The older at l and 1/2 years old; the younger at six months. His body is thin and delicate (*gracil*). He is relatively weak. His stride is secure, relaxed. The circumference of his neck is 37 cm. He shows no

> signs of goiter. His voice is pure and strong. He looks younger than his age. The form and structure of his chest—his breast is raised, his clavicle is drumstick-shaped and indented at its ends. He has weak chest muscles. With a deep breath his chest circumference at level of his nipples is 82 cm and on expiration it is 78 cm. Both halves of his chest are equally developed but weak. He takes 16 breaths a minute when resting; and 19 per minute with exercise. The percussion of right upper lobe of his lung is dull as a result of an earlier rachitic deviation. No anomalies by auscultation; no anomalous sounds. His pulse is 78 beats per minute resting, with exercise, 84 beats per minute. There are no abnormal heart sounds. No anomalies in the lower body. The circumference of the waist at the level of the navel is 72 cm. There are no anomalies of the urinary track. His urine showed no anomalies; neither protein nor sugar. There are no anomalies of mental sensibility or motility. Both of his pupils are equally open and each reacts to the light equally. The plantar reflex is present. All past illnesses are truly healed (especially syphilis). The only residue present is the sign of childhood rickets. His general health is good. He shows neither alcoholism nor other excesses. He is a delicate (*zart*) but healthy man.[2] (Plates 6–8)

This is the sort of information which any citizen of Europe would have been asked to provide, not only for employment, but even for a simple life insurance policy. But I would like to read this information from the standpoint of Franz Kafka, a Prague Jewish male, born in 1883, twenty-four years old, to see how he understood his own body, and I would like to search for the discourses which formed his understanding. One could claim, quite correctly, that Kafka's sense of self was unique, but he articulated it very much within the bounds of his culture.

The requirement of such physical examinations is transmuted into a literary trope in Kafka's diaries for July 1914, where "Bauz, the director of the Progress Insurance Company" informs the unnamed job applicant:

> "You're tall enough. . . . I can see that; but what can you do? Our attendants must be able to do more than lick stamps. . . . Your head is shaped peculiarly. Your forehead recedes so. Remarkable. . . . Naturally, we can employ only people in good health. Before you are taken on you will have to be examined by a doctor. You are quite well now? Really? Of course, that could be. Speak up a little! Your whispering makes me nervous. . . . As long as you're already here, have the doctor examine you now; the attendant will show you the way. But that doesn't mean you will be hired, even if the doctor's opinion is favorable. . . . Go along and don't take up any more of my time." (D2, 73–74)

External appearance signals the applicant's health or illness. In particular, the shape of the head provides insight not only into character but also into morbidity. Nervousness and the somatic are closely linked in this body.

Kafka's body is long and thin, a statement in a world where corpulence was a sign of success, of substance:

> It is certain that a major obstacle to my progress is my physical condition. Nothing can be accomplished with such a body. . . . My body is too long for its weakness, it hasn't the least bit of fat to engender a blessed warmth, to preserve an inner fire, no fat on which the spirit could occasionally nourish itself beyond its daily need without damage to the whole. How shall the weak heart that lately has troubled me so often be able to pound the blood through the length of these legs. It would be labor enough to the knees, and from there it can only spill with a senile strength into the cold lower parts of my legs. But now it is already needed up above again, it is being waited for, while it is wasting itself below. Everything is pulled apart throughout the length of my body. What could it accomplish then, when it perhaps wouldn't have enough strength for what I want to achieve even if it were shorter and more compact. (D1, 160)

But Kafka's equation of thinness with a lack of "inner fire," of spirit, his reading of his outer body as a sign of his soul, are part of the common wisdom of the nineteenth century. This conception of the relationship between the mind and the body informs many different discourses—medical, historical, and cultural. The medical view was set at the turn of the century with the rise of the concept of psychosomatic illness—illness that arises in the mind but has somatic as well as psychological symptoms. Building on the work of the German Romantic psychiatrists, such as Johann Heinroth, physicians such as F. Krauss in Berlin evolved complex ideas of the relationship between illnesses of the mind and those of the body. Your body is therefore what your mind deems it to be. The complex interaction between mind and body can also have an historic dimension, as we have seen in Kafka's acceptance of the basic argument of ethnopsychology in his diary entry on "minor literature." You are what your ancestors were. This is the Jewish masochist's internalization of the stereotypical representation of the Jew in *fin-de-siècle* culture.

How does the Jew's physiognomy signify in the late nineteenth century? The pseudonymous French anti-Semite "Docteur Celticus" provides a handbook on the vocabulary of Jewish physical difference[3] (Plates 9–11). Of course, the Jew is male, as we shall see again and again. His hand, his

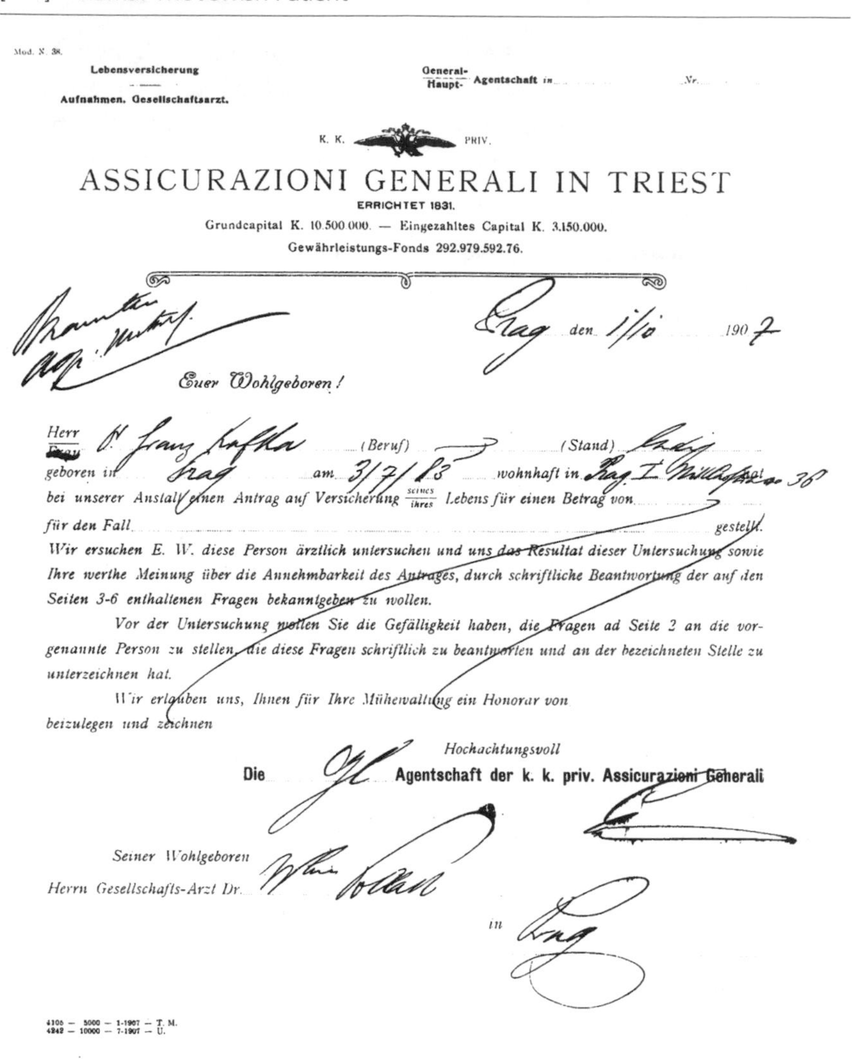

Mod. N. 38.

Lebensversicherung
Aufnahmen. Gesellschaftsarzt.

General-/Haupt- Agentschaft in ... Nr. ...

K. K. PRIV.

ASSICURAZIONI GENERALI IN TRIEST

ERRICHTET 1831.

Grundcapital K. 10.500.000. — Eingezahltes Capital K. 3.150.000.

Gewährleistungs-Fonds 292.979.592.76.

Prag den 1/10 1907

Euer Wohlgeboren!

Herr Dr. Franz Kafka (Beruf) (Stand) ...
geboren in Prag am 3/7/83 wohnhaft in Prag I ... 36
bei unserer Anstalt einen Antrag auf Versicherung seines/ihres Lebens für einen Betrag von ...
für den Fall ... gestellt.
Wir ersuchen E. W. diese Person ärztlich untersuchen und uns das Resultat dieser Untersuchung sowie Ihre werthe Meinung über die Annehmbarkeit des Antrages, durch schriftliche Beantwortung der auf den Seiten 3-6 enthaltenen Fragen bekanntgeben zu wollen.

Vor der Untersuchung wollen Sie die Gefälligkeit haben, die Fragen ad Seite 2 an die vorgenannte Person zu stellen, die diese Fragen schriftlich zu beantworten und an der bezeichneten Stelle zu unterzeichnen hat.

Wir erlauben uns, Ihnen für Ihre Mühewaltung ein Honorar von ... beizulegen und zeichnen

Hochachtungsvoll

Die ... Agentschaft der k. k. priv. Assicurazioni Generali

Seiner Wohlgeboren
Herrn Gesellschafts-Arzt Dr. Wilhelm Pollack
in Prag

4106 — 5000 — 1-1907 — T. M.
4242 — 10000 — 7-1907 — U.

PLATES 6–8. Kafka's first medical record from his October 1, 1907, examination by Dr. Wilhelm Pollack, a physician working for the Trieste-based Assicurazioni Generali Insurance Company (Assicurazioni Generali, Trieste).

---

foot, his nose all mark him as different, not theologically but racially. As the Viennese anti-Semite Ritter von Schönerer wrote at the turn of the century: "The Jew's belief is nothing / it's race that makes him swinish!"[4] Every aspect of the Jew points towards his difference. The German-language proverbial literature of the time is full of such references: "He walks like a Jew. He has flat feet like a Jew. God protect us from trichinosis and Jew's noses." But it also points to the diseased nature of the

2

Fragen, die die Gesellschaft durch ihren Vertrauensarzt an die zu untersuchende Person stellt:	Antworten der zu untersuchenden Person:
1. Wie ist Ihr gegenwärtiger Gesundheitszustand?	1. Ein guter
2. Welche Krankheiten oder Leiden haben Sie in den letzten zehn Jahren überstanden? Haben Sie sich chirurgischen Operationen unterzogen? Welchen Operationen?	2. Keine Nein
3. Haben Sie je an einer der nachstehend genannten *Krankheiten* oder *Gebrechen* gelitten? Wann? An welchen leiden Sie etwa noch? ***Hals- oder Brustkrankheiten — Bluthusten — Herzklopfen — Ohnmacht oder Schwindelanfälle — Kurzer Athem — Epileptische Krämpfe — Lähmungen — Ohrenfluss — Gicht — Wechselfieber — Hämorrhoidalblutungen — Harnverhaltung — Harnröhrenverengerung — Venerische oder syphilitische Krankheiten — Gallen- oder Nierenkolik — Harnsand — Traumatische Verletzungen — Bruch — Krampfadern — Geschwülste u. dlg. mehr?***	3. Nein
4. Welchen Arzt ziehen Sie gewöhnlich für sich selbst oder für Ihre Familie zu Rathe?	4. Dr Kohn Melantrichg
5. Welche Aerzte haben Sie sonst konsultiert: von welchen Aerzten haben Sie sich behandeln oder operiren lassen? Aus welchem Anlasse? Wann?	5. " " "
6. *a)* Haben Sie Mineralwässer als Trink- oder Badekur gebraucht oder Kaltwasserkuren unternommen? Welche? Wo? Wie oft? Wann? *b)* Haben Sie sich krankheitshalber in klimatischen Curorten oder in Heilanstalten aufgehalten? In welchen? Wie oft? Wann?	6. *a)* Nein *b)* Nein
7. Wie ist? *a)* der Appetit? *b)* die Verdauung? *c)* der Stuhl? *d)* die Harnentleerung?	7. *a)* … *c)* … Normal
8. Wie alt sind Ihre Eltern?	8. *Vater* 54 *Jahre* *Mutter* 48 *Jahre*
9. Wenn diese nicht mehr am Leben sind, wie alt und an welcher Krankheit sind sie gestorben?	9. *Vater* … *Jahre* *Krankheit:* *Mutter* …
10. In welchem Alter stehen Ihre Geschwister und Ihre Kinder, die noch am Leben sind? — In welchem Alter und an welcher Krankheit sind die anderen gestorben?	10. (see table below)
11. Sind Sie von anderen Anstalten abgewiesen worden? Von welchen Anstalten? Wann? Welcher Arzt hat Sie untersucht?	11. Nein
Bei Frauen:	
12. *a)* Sind die Menstruationen regelmässig oder unregelmässig, reichlich oder spärlich? Wie sind sie gefärbt? *b)* Wie oft haben Sie entbunden? *c)* Haben Sie bei den Entbindungen ärztliche Hilfe benöthigt? Wie verliefen die Wochenbette? *d)* Haben Sie Fehlgeburten gehabt? Wie oft und mit welchen Folgen? *e)* Sind Sie gegenwärtig Schwanger, in welchem Monate? *f)* Leiden oder litten Sie an Gebärmutterfluss oder Blutung?	12. *a)* *b)* *c)* *d)* *e)* *f)*

Lebende Geschwister: Alter Jahre	Verstorbene Geschwister: Alter Jahre	Krankheit	Lebende Kinder: Alter Jahre	Verstorbene Kinder: Alter Jahre	Krankheit
18	1 1/2	Meningitis	/	/	/
17	1/2	Meningitis			
15					

Obige Angaben, die ich als wahrheitsgetreu erkläre, sollen zur Beurtheilung meines Versicherungsantrages vom über dienen, und ich bin dessen vollkommen bewusst, dass jede Unwahrheit in diesen Angaben die Ungiltigkeit der Police laut § 13 der allgemeinen Versicherungsbedingungen nach sich zieht.

Datum Prag *den* 1. X 1907

(Eigenhändige Unterschrift der zu untersuchenden Person) Dr Franz Kafka

PLATE 6b (reverse side).

Jew: "There are no Jews without the mange. He is as proud of his work as the Jew of his skin disease. He is as scabby as a Jew."[5] The significance of such images for Kafka provides some insight into the meaning of the Jew's body at the *fin de siècle*.

There is no better source for the meaning of the Jew's body during the late nineteenth century than the monograph *Israel among the Nations: A Study of the Jews and Anti-Semitism* by the non-Jewish

Die Herren Aerzte sind gebeten die nachstehenden Fragen eingehend und vollständig, in bestimmten Ausdrücken zu beantworten; Striche oder sonstige Zeichen an Stelle der Worte sind unzulässig.

Befund der ärztlichen Untersuchung

des Herrn / der Frau Dr Franz Kafka

1. a) Kennen Sie bereits die zu versichernde Person? — Nein
   b) Seit wie lange?
   c) Wenn nicht, wodurch ist ihre Identität festgestellt?
   d) Sind die Angaben ad Seite 2 in Ihrer Gegenwart datirt und unterschieben worden? — Ja
   e) Wo haben Sie die Untersuchung vorgenommen? In Ihrer eigenen, oder in der Wohnung der zu untersuchenden Person, oder wo?
   f) An welchem Tage? Zu welcher Stunde? — 1. X 07, 5 Uhr Nachm.
   g) Sind Sie Hausarzt der Person? — Nein
   h) Haben Sie sie an körperlichen oder geistigen Krankheiten behandelt oder sind Sie von ihr wegen solcher Krankheiten consultirt worden? — Nein
   i) Wenn dies der Fall ist, an welchen Krankheiten und wann?
   k) Haben Sie je über diese Person für unsere oder für eine andere Gesellschaft ein Zeugniss ausgestellt? Für welche Gesellschaft? Wann? — Nein

2. a) Körperlänge und Körpergewicht der Person? — 2. a) *Körperlänge Centimeter* 181 *Gewicht Kilo:* 61
   b) Wie ist der Körperbau? — schlank
   c) Sind Anomalien in der Richtung der Wirbelsäule vorhanden (Scoliosis, Kyphosis)? — Keine
   d) Wie ist der allgemeine Ernährungszustand? — mässig
   e) Wie sind die Muskeln entwickelt? — schwach
   f) Wie ist der Gang, insbesondere bei geschlossenen Augen, und die Haltung? — sicher, legère
   g) Wie ist die Farbe und der Ausdruck des Gesichtes? — Blass, frisch
   h) Wie ist die Beschaffenheit der Haut, namentlich am Gesichte? Ist sie gedunsen? — Normal
   i) Sieht man Narben, Geschwüre, Exantheme, skrophulose Drüsen, Neugebilde? — Nein
   k) Ist das Aussehen dem angegebenen Alter von 24 Jahren, oder welchem Alter entsprechend? — Erscheint juveniler

NB. Es ist wünschenswerth, dass die Person abgewogen werde. Ist dies nicht thunlich, so wolle man das Körpergewicht nach Schätzung oder nach Angabe der Person mittheilen, und die Bemerkung: ***laut Schätzung*** oder ***laut Angabe*** hinzufügen.

3. a) Sind Anomalien am Kopfe bemerkbar? Welche? — Keine
   b) Wie ist das Kopf- und Barthaar in Beziehung auf Dichtigkeit und Farbe? — Dicht braun
   c) In welchem Zustande befinden sich die Zähne? Wie viele Zähne fehlen? — sehr gut, keiner fehlt
   d) Sind am Munde, an der Zunge, in der Rachenhöhle krankhafte Erscheinungen nachweisbar? — Nein
   e) Sind insbesondere an der Zunge Narben sichtbar, namentlich von Bisswunden? — Nein
   f) Ist Strabismus vorhanden, welcher Art und seit wann? Besteht Schwerhörigkeit oder Ohrenfluss, und wenn dies der Fall ist, wird beim Drucke auf die Warzenfortsätze Schmerz hervorgerufen, und ist überhaupt Verdacht auf Caries vorhanden? — Nein
   g) Sind überhaupt Anomalien an den Sinnesorganen vorhanden und welche? — Keine

PLATE 7a.

historian Anatole Leroy-Beaulieu, where the liberal discourse about Jewish physical difference attains full flower.[6] Leroy-Beaulieu defends the Jews against the arguments of inherent racial difference, but not of innate biological inferiority. Jews are biologically and psychologically different, he states, but this difference is not to be explained by the immutable category of race. The Jew's difference lies in "the Jew's historic education, by the antiquity of his culture, by the protracted training to which he has been subjected for centuries, in one word, by hereditary selection—the cruel selection of two thousand years of suffering and struggle" (232).

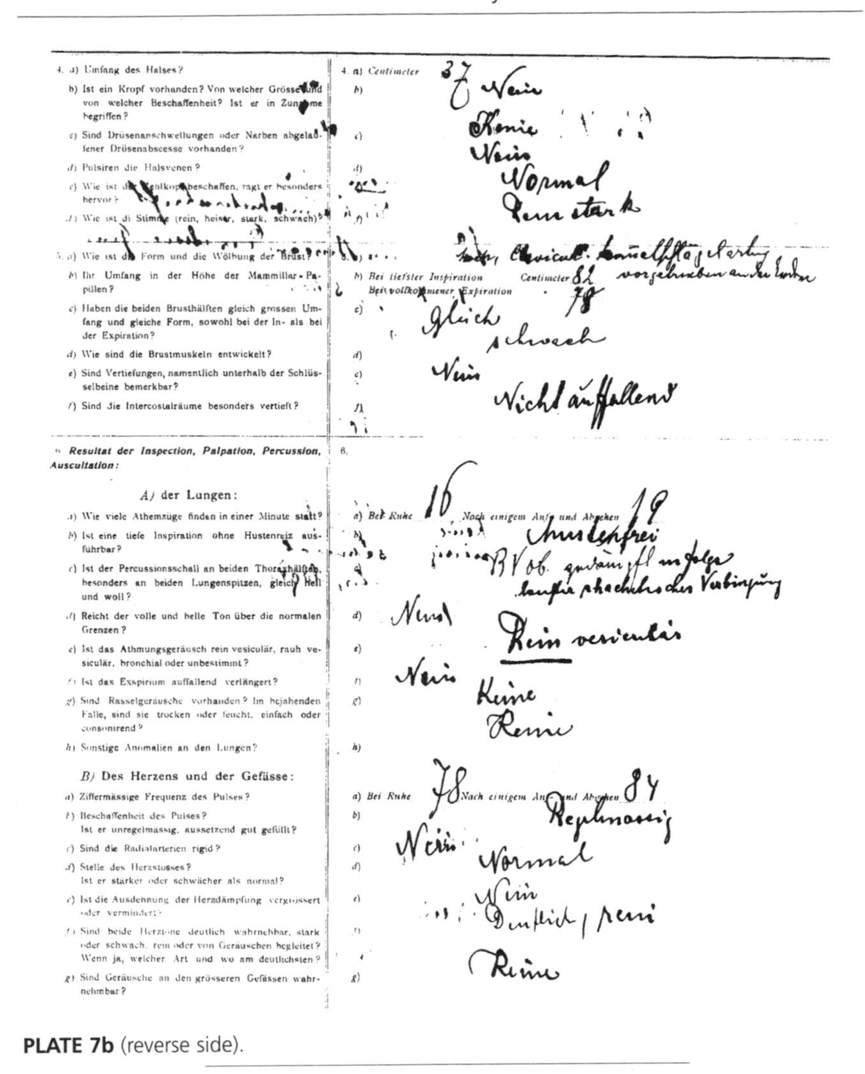

4. a) Umfang des Halses?	4. a) Centimeter 37
b) Ist ein Kropf vorhanden? Von welcher Grösse und von welcher Beschaffenheit? Ist er in Zunahme begriffen?	b) Nein
c) Sind Drüsenanschwellungen oder Narben abgelaufener Drüsenabscesse vorhanden?	c) Keine
d) Pulsiren die Halsvenen?	d) Nein
e) Wie ist der Kehlkopf beschaffen, ragt er besonders hervor?	e) Normal
f) Wie ist di Stimme (rein, heiser, stark, schwach)?	f) Rein stark
5. a) Wie ist die Form und die Wölbung der Brust?	5. a) [illegible]
b) Ihr Umfang in der Höhe der Mammillar-Papillen?	b) Bei tiefster Inspiration Centimeter 82 Bei vollkommener Expiration 78
c) Haben die beiden Brusthälften gleich grossen Umfang und gleiche Form, sowohl bei der In- als bei der Expiration?	c) Gleich
d) Wie sind die Brustmuskeln entwickelt?	d) schwach
e) Sind Vertiefungen, namentlich unterhalb der Schlüsselbeine bemerkbar?	e) Nein
f) Sind die Intercostalräume besonders vertieft?	f) Nicht auffallend
6. ***Resultat der Inspection, Palpation, Percussion, Auscultation:***	6.
A) der Lungen:	
a) Wie viele Athemzüge finden in einer Minute statt?	a) Bei Ruhe 16 Nach einigem Auf- und Abgehen 19
b) Ist eine tiefe Inspiration ohne Hustenreiz ausführbar?	b) Hustenfrei
c) Ist der Percussionsschall an beiden Thoraxhälften, besonders an beiden Lungenspitzen, gleich hell und voll?	c) [illegible]
d) Reicht der volle und helle Ton über die normalen Grenzen?	d) Nein
e) Ist das Athmungsgeräusch rein vesiculär, rauh vesiculär, bronchial oder unbestimmt?	e) Rein vesiculär
f) Ist das Exspirium auffallend verlängert?	f) Nein
g) Sind Rasselgeräusche vorhanden? Im bejahenden Falle, sind sie trocken oder feucht, einfach oder consonirend?	g) Keine
h) Sonstige Anomalien an den Lungen?	h) Keine
B) Des Herzens und der Gefässe:	
a) Ziffermässige Frequenz des Pulses?	a) Bei Ruhe 78 Nach einigem Auf- und Abgehen 84
b) Beschaffenheit des Pulses? Ist er unregelmässig, aussetzend gut gefüllt?	b) Regelmässig
c) Sind die Radialarterien rigid?	c) Nein
d) Stelle des Herzstosses? Ist er stärker oder schwächer als normal?	d) Normal
e) Ist die Ausdehnung der Herzdämpfung vergrössert oder vermindert?	e) Nein
f) Sind beide Herztöne deutlich wahrnehbar, stark oder schwach, rein oder von Geräuschen begleitet? Wenn ja, welcher Art und wo am deutlichsten?	f) Deutlich / rein
g) Sind Geräusche an den grösseren Gefässen wahrnehmbar?	g) Keine

PLATE 7b (reverse side).

The Jewish body is the result of "confinement in the Ghetto," and the "Jewish race" so produced was the "artificial product of the rabbinical code and of medieval laws." The Jew is the sum of all of the "cruelties" lodged against him by others and himself (148). Jews are inferior because of their poor treatment in the past and their inheritance of those characteristics that mark them as ill. But Jewish character is not so marked. It remains virtually inalterable even though it is not "racial." Leroy-Beaulieu also argues that Jews are marked by "their Oriental self-restraint, which distinguishes them so conspicuously from

h) Ist der zweite Ton der Pulmonalarterie accentuirt?
i) Sind die Temporalarterien besonders geschlängelt?
k) Sonstige Anomalien an den Circulations-organen?

C) des Unterleibes:

a) Wird bei der Inspection, Palpation und Percussion des Unterleibes irgendetwas Abnormes wahrgenommen?
Ist namentlich die Magengegend bei Druck empfindlich?
b) Wie weit reicht die Leberdämpfung nach unten?
c) Ist die Milz vergrössert?
d) Ist ein Bruch (Leisten-Schenkel-Nabelbruch) oder eine Erweiterung der Bruchpforten vorhanden, und wenn dies der Fall ist, wird ein gehörig schliessendes Bruchband getragen?
e) Umfang des Bauches in der Nabelhöhe?
f) Sonstige Anomalien am Unterleibe?

NB. Bei Vorhandensein nichtbandagirter Brüche hat der Herr Untersuchungsarzt dem Versicherungswerber das Anlegen und beständige Tragen eines Bruchbandes wärmstens zu empfehlen und sich dann, einige Tage später durch einen unerwarteten Besuch zu überzeugen, ob das Bruchband angelegt worden ist und seinem Zwecke gut entspricht.

7. a) Wie geht die Harnemission von Statten?
b) Wurde der Harn in Ihrer Gegenwart abgelassen?
c) *bei Männern:*
Können Harnröhrenstricturen und Prostatahypertrophie ausgeschlossen werden?
c) *bei Frauen:*
α) Ist Vorfall, Senkung oder eine sonstige Lageveränderung des Uterus vorhanden?
β) Erregen Narben oder Knoten and den Brüsten den Verdacht einer operirten oder sich entwickelnden bösartigen Neubildung?
d) Sonstige Anomalien and den Harn- und Geschlechtsorganen?

e) Resultat der Harnuntersuchung:

α) Aussehen, Farbe, Reaction, spec. Gewicht?
β) Enthält der Harn Eiweiss?
γ) " " " Zucker?
δ) Sind andere abnorme Bestandtheile, als Schleim, Eiter, Blut, Concretionen u. dgl. m. nachweisbar?

NB. Die Harnuntersuchung soll ohne jede Ausnahme vorgenommen werden, wenn die Versicherungssumme den Betrag von Achttausend Kronen ö.-u. W. (Zehntausend Francs) erreicht oder übersteigt. Die Harnuntersuchung soll aber auch bei geringeren Versicherungsummen vorgenommen werden, wenn der leiseste Verdacht auf krankhafte Zustände besteht, die durch die Harnuntersuchung constatirt werden können.

8. Wie ist die Beschaffenheit der Extremitäten rücksichtlich der Haut, Muskeln, Knochen und Gelenke?

9. Sind Varices vorhanden?

10. a) Sind Störungen in der Sensibilität oder Motilität oder in den geistigen Funktionen nachweisbar? Wenn ja, in welchem Grade, in welcher Ausdehnung? Ist die Sprache stotternd?
b) Sind beide Pupillen von gleicher Weite? Reagiren sie auf Licht gleichmässig oder ungleichmässig?
c) Ist der Patellar-Sehnenreflex (Kniephänomen) vorhanden? Deutlich oder undeutlich, gesteigert oder vermindert?
d) Wird die Zunge gerade oder mit seitlicher Abweichung oder zitternd ausgestreckt?

PLATE 8a.

the Northern peoples, Slav or Semitic, into the mists of which the eddies of history have whirled them" (160). Here is the conception of innate racial predestination important to such racial anti-Semites as Houston Stewart Chamberlain, and another, biological conception of Jewish difference as the result of Christian persecution and Jewish religious practice.

In any case, the ethnopsychological dimension of Jewish experience is unaltered. The Jewish psyche remains "Oriental." The biological argument hinges on the notion of the inheritance of acquired characteristics, so that the changes in the Jew's body that occurred over thousands of years

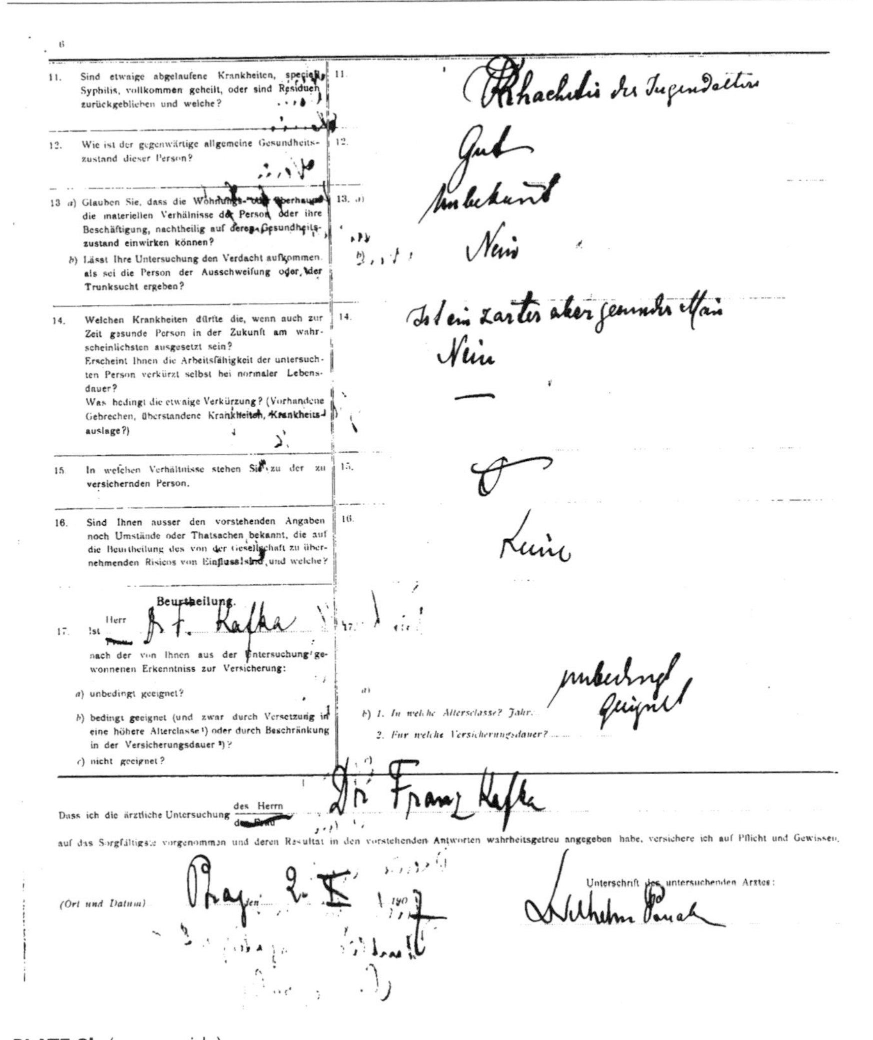

6

11. Sind etwaige abgelaufene Krankheiten, speciell Syphilis, vollkommen geheilt, oder sind Residuen zurückgeblieben und welche?
— 11. Rhachitis der Jugendzeit

12. Wie ist der gegenwärtige allgemeine Gesundheitszustand dieser Person?
— 12. Gut

13 a) Glauben Sie, dass die Wohnungs- oder überhaupt die materiellen Verhälnisse der Person oder ihre Beschäftigung, nachtheilig auf deren Gesundheitszustand einwirken können?
— 13. a) Unbekannt

b) Lässt Ihre Untersuchung den Verdacht aufkommen, als sei die Person der Ausschweifung oder der Trunksucht ergeben?
— b) Nein

14. Welchen Krankheiten dürfte die, wenn auch zur Zeit gesunde Person in der Zukunft am wahrscheinlichsten ausgesetzt sein?
— 14. Ist ein zarter aber gesunder Mann

Erscheint Ihnen die Arbeitsfähigkeit der untersuchten Person verkürzt selbst bei normaler Lebensdauer?
— Nein

Was bedingt die etwaige Verkürzung? (Vorhandene Gebrechen, überstandene Krankheiten, Krankheitsauslage?)
— —

15. In welchen Verhältnisse stehen Sie zu der zu versichernden Person.
— 15. 0

16. Sind Ihnen ausser den vorstehenden Angaben noch Umstände oder Thatsachen bekannt, die auf die Beurtheilung des von der Gesellschaft zu übernehmenden Risicos von Einfluss sind, und welche?
— 16. Keine

Beurtheilung.

17. Ist Herr Dr F. Kafka nach der von Ihnen aus der Untersuchung gewonnenen Erkenntniss zur Versicherung:

a) unbedingt geeignet?
b) bedingt geeignet (und zwar durch Versetzung in eine höhere Alterclasse [1]) oder durch Beschränkung in der Versicherungsdauer [2])?
c) nicht geeignet?

— 17. a) unbedingt geeignet
b) 1. In welche Altersclasse? Jahr.
2. Fur welche Versicherungsdauer?
c)

Dass ich die ärztliche Untersuchung des Herrn Dr Franz Kafka auf das Sorgfältigste vorgenommen und deren Resultat in den vorstehenden Antworten wahrheitsgetreu angegeben habe, versichere ich auf Pflicht und Gewissen.

(Ort und Datum) Prag den 2. X 1907

Unterschrift des untersuchenden Arztes: Wilhelm Pollak

PLATE 8b (reverse side).

will take an equally or at least very long period to return to the Christian norm. Thus even emancipated Jews, with no experience of the ghetto, nonetheless perpetuate their fathers' history and all its biological pathologies. Their psyches remain inherently Jewish, though their bodies may seem to change. William Osler, one of the preeminent physicians of the early twentieth century, in his "Israel and Medicine" (1914), wrote:

> In estimating the position of Israel in the human values we must remember that the quest for righteousness is oriental, the quest for knowledge occidental. With the great prophets of the East—Moses,

PLATE 9.

PLATE 10.

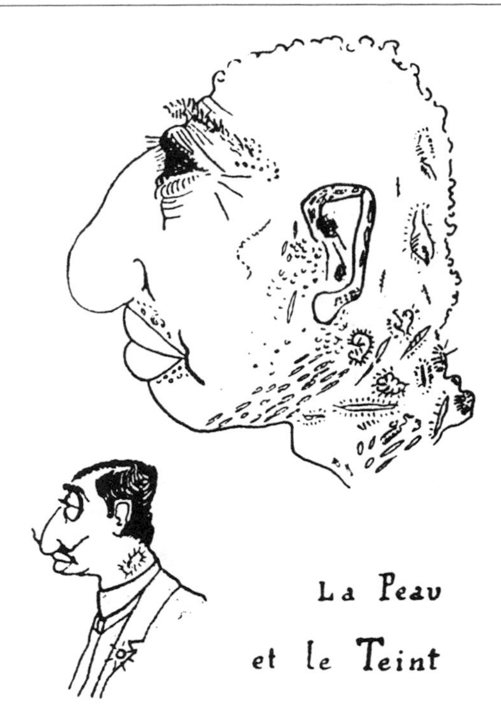

PLATES 9-11. The image of Jewish hands and feet, eyes, and skin from the anti-Semitic physiological study of the Jew's imagined body by "Docteur Celticus," *Les 19 Tares corporelles visibles pour reconnaître un Juif* (Paris: Librairie antisémite, 1903) (National Library of Medicine, Bethesda).

> Isaiah, Mahomet—the word was "Thus saith the Lord"; with the great seers of the West, from Thales and Aristotle to Archimedes and Lucretius, it was "What says Nature?" They illustrate two opposite views of man and his destiny—in the one he is an "angelus sepultus" in a muddy vesture of decay; in the other, he is the "young light-hearted master" of the world, in it to know it, and by knowing to conquer.[7]

The imagined Jewish body still bears within it an ancestral irrationalism.

In no other realm is Jewish biological predestination clearer than in the relationship to illness. The common view was that Jews were more diseased than other groups. Their spiritual difference would ultimately manifest itself physically, no matter how long it had been repressed. The Jews have a special relationship to disease. Yet Leroy-Beaulieu argues that Jews also inherit a special resistance to certain illnesses. Living in the ghetto, "they had become inured to its infectious streets" (149). "It has been remarked that in several countries the Jews seem to possess immunity from certain infectious diseases" (157). For the liberal Leroy-Beaulieu, the Jews are the handmaidens of the new cult of hygiene, his defense against arguments that they are inherently diseased: "Judaism has made religion the handmaiden of hygiene; it has utilized piety for the preservation of health" (157). Of course, this contradicts the notion that it is the Jewish law, and not just persecution by Christians, that has caused the present state of the Jew's body. Jewish longevity becomes a proof of the prophylactic power of biblical law: "The first thing to surprise us is the fact that the Jew lives longer than the Christian. In spite of his frail body and look of privation, he seems often to unite within himself two qualities apparently contradictory: precocity and longevity" (151). "His longevity, his resistance to disease, his immunity from certain disorders, are a legacy from his ancestors, and are due to his laws, his customs, and his sobriety. On the other hand, his feebleness and the defects of his physical constitution are due to our laws, our Ghettos, and our system of confinement" (165). Anti-Semitism as the cause of the illnesses of Jews presupposes a historical memory inscribed on their bodies. This idea of "real" Jewish illnesses (or their antithesis, the immunity to illness) as the product of social experience became somewhat of a commonplace among Jews in the early twentieth century. As Diana Trilling wrote: "Indeed, Jewish men were at that time [1920s] said to be free not only of alcoholism but also of schizophrenia; Jewish women were thought to be immune to cancer of the cervix."[8] This assumption (whatever the presumed etiology) set the Jew apart.

The Jew is also supposed to be more fecund than the Christian, which, given the anxiety in France and Germany about the low birthrate at the close of the nineteenth century, is an important issue for Leroy-Beaulieu to raise. Here it becomes an argument in favor of the healthy physiology of the Jew, in spite of his evident pathology. "The Jew multiplies, as a rule, more quickly than his Christian neighbors" (152). "Almost everywhere, at present, the Jews have proportionally fewer children than the non-Jews" (154). Yet these few children have a lower infant mortality. "We should not be justified, however, in regarding their superiority as a racial phenomenon of a purely physiological nature; it is doubtless due entirely to the difference in customs, to the family spirit of the Jews, to their devotion as parents, to the care of the mother for her children, and also to the chastity of the marriage relation, to the prescriptions of the Law, and to the consideration and respect shown by the husband for the health of his wife" (155). The Law, the *Torah*, is at the bottom of all dissimilarities that exist between the Jews and their neighbors (156–157). And it is one specific aspect of the law, the practice of infant male circumcision, which is the most evident indicator of the healthiness of the Jew. It is circumcision which marks the health of the Jew foremost: "Despite the risk which the new-born infant may incur under the knife of the peritomist, circumcision seems to have a twofold value: it may—although this has not been conclusively proven—decrease the chances of contagion from the most repulsive diseases; it may also—and this would be of no lesser benefit—blunt the desires and weaken the stimulus to carnal passion. At any rate, I know Jews who are convinced that such results are secured, and who, while caring little for the *Thora* [sic], persist in having their sons circumcised, and in eating *kosher* meat, as a matter of hygiene" (161). This link between hygiene and Jewish practice is one of the central secular reinterpretations of Judaism, not as a religion, but as a series of worldly practices, that was undertaken in the course of the latter half of the nineteenth century by Jews and non-Jews alike. We shall see how important the link between the ritual slaughter of animals and circumcision, the creation of the physical difference of the Jewish male, comes to be.

The link between ritual slaughter and circumcision is not as evident to us as it was in Leroy-Beaulieu's time, when the two dread diseases were syphilis and tuberculosis. For acculturated Jews who see Jewish ritual practice as having hygienic importance, the prophylaxis for the former is circumcision; for the latter, the eating of kosher meat. These become commonplaces in discussions of Jewish health, as in William Z. Ripley's 1899 study of racial topology: "The Jews have abnormally small proportions of deaths from consumption and pneumonia. . . . This immunity can best be ascribed to the excellent system of meat inspection prescribed by the Mosaic Laws."[9] Jews, whose bodies are already marked as different, also eat different foods and thus remain healthy, unlike the rest of the population that is at extraordinary risk from tuberculosis.

But if the Jew is "healthy" because of his social practices, what accounts for a physiognomy that is marked by disease and reveals the disease hidden within the individual? For Leroy-Beaulieu, the ghetto breeds not only illness (and its antithesis, resistance to disease) but also ugliness: "Such warrens could not breed a comely race. . . . The race is not handsome." But the Jew—always male for Leroy-Beaulieu and his contemporaries, inasmuch as the Jew is defined by circumcision—is not only ugly, he is feminized. "There is a singular contrast between the Jew's persistent vitality and his bodily infirmity. His feebleness often gives him a somewhat unmanly appearance." (163). Leroy-Beaulieu repeats the liberal explanation for such emasculation—it is not the essence of the Jew we see before us, but only the product of Judaic practice and Christian intolerance: "The Jew is, moreover, often misshapen. . . . The reason for this lies not only in their early marriages and their marriages between near relations, but also, and above all, in their age-long confinement, their lack of exercise, of pure air and wholesome nourishment" (164). The association of beauty with health and ugliness with illness is important to Kafka's era. Here it marks the qualities of the Jew associated with hygiene or its lack. Here, of course, "health" (and "beauty") implied by social practices, such as circumcision and ritual slaughter, comes into conflict with the "illness" (and "ugliness") of social practices such as early marriage and confinement in the ghetto.

The male Jew is thus visualized in terms of this image of illness, specifically the image of the tubercular female, simultaneously "beautiful" but "diseased." The Jew's "bodily infirmity" is marked by his "unmanly appearance." He is like but not identical to the tubercular woman, specifically the tubercular Jewish woman. The Jew's visage is like "to those lean actresses, the *Rachels* and *Sarahs*, who spit blood, and seem to have but the spark of life left, and yet who, when they have stepped upon the stage, put forth indomitable strength and energy. Life, with them, has hidden springs" (150). It is the tubercular Jewish woman whom the healthy male Jew resembles. It is Sarah Bernhardt (1844–1923) and Rachel Félix (1820–1858), the two best known Jewish actresses of the nineteenth-century Parisian stage, both tubercular, who define the normal physiognomy of the *male* Jew.

The popular image of Sarah Bernhardt is an extraordinarily good example. Not only was she a Jewish actress closely identified with traditionally male roles, such as Hamlet (Plate 12), she was decried as a masculine woman because of her outspokenness.[10] She also echoed her own illness, not as a Jewish actress but as a figure of the French demimonde, when she starred as the tubercular heroine of Dumas's *Lady of the Camellias* (Plate 13). Tuberculosis becomes as powerful an indicator of the Jewish nature as syphilis. Leroy-Beaulieu uses tuberculosis as a means of distinguishing between two classes of Jews—the "healthy" and the "sick." And being a tubercular Jewish male is being doubly feminized—

PLATE 12. The masculinized body of the tubercular Sarah Bernhardt playing Hamlet at the Adelphi Theater in London (June 12, 1889) (Victoria and Albert Museum).

PLATE 13. The tubercular body of Sarah Bernhardt as the tubercular "Dame aux Camélias" (Victoria and Albert Museum).

for if circumcision is the first act that "unmans" the Jewish male, acquiring tuberculosis is the second:

> Let us take tuberculosis, the disease that creates most havoc in Europe. Although in London, even in the most squalid dens of Whitechapel, consumption is, according to medical testimony, less frequent among the Jews than the Christians, it has been proved that in Poland and Russia the Jews are often subject to consumption as well as

PLATE 14. The armed forces and the imagined Jewish body: the Jew as shirker, from *L'Assiette au Beurre* (July 30, 1904) (Source: Private Collection, Ithaca).

to scrofulous diseases. Indeed, they seem predisposed to these evils. The Jews of Lithuania, Poland, and Little-Russia are frequently characterized by narrow chests. This alone would suffice to render them liable to consumption. The Russian councils of revision are well aware of this. They are obliged yearly to reject as invalids, or to put off for future examination, a number of Jewish conscripts whose chests are not sufficiently developed. The narrowness of chest must not be ascribed to the origin of the race or to its Semitic blood. . . . (162)

The "healthy" are those males who can serve in the military; the "sick" cannot, and thus are feminized (Plate 14).

Now there is a basic contradiction in Leroy-Beaulieu's argument typical of the discourse about the Jewish body in the late nineteenth and early twentieth centuries. On the one hand, Jews have an immunity to certain diseases, such as tuberculosis, though an affinity for others, such as neurasthenia and hysteria. On the other hand, the male Jew's body is depicted in terms of the *habitus phthisicus*, the tubercular patient,

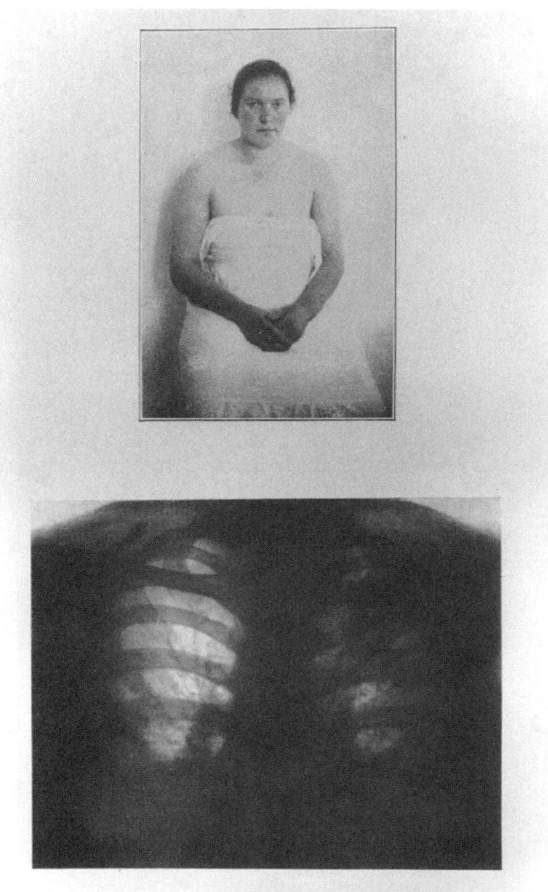

Abb. 1.
Blühendes, gesundes Aussehen, kräftiger Brustkorb.
Schwere offene kavernös-zirrhotische Phthise.

PLATES 15–16. By the early twentieth century the easy equation of body type and predisposition for tuberculosis was being drawn into question. Two images, the first showing a "blooming, healthy appearing, powerful chest cavity" with a severe case of pulmonary tuberculosis and

especially the female tubercular patient (Plates 15–16). How can the Jew be both immune to and defined by tuberculosis? Here the stereotype's peculiar power to accommodate antitheses comes into play. At the turn of the century, Jews are both the arch-bankers and the arch-revolutionaries, both the false nobility of Paris and the Wandering Eastern Jews of Warsaw, all things to all groups who need to define outsiders. Thus their supposed immunity, whether racial or acquired, is a sign of their "nature," as is the assumption that the Jew, because of his body form, is

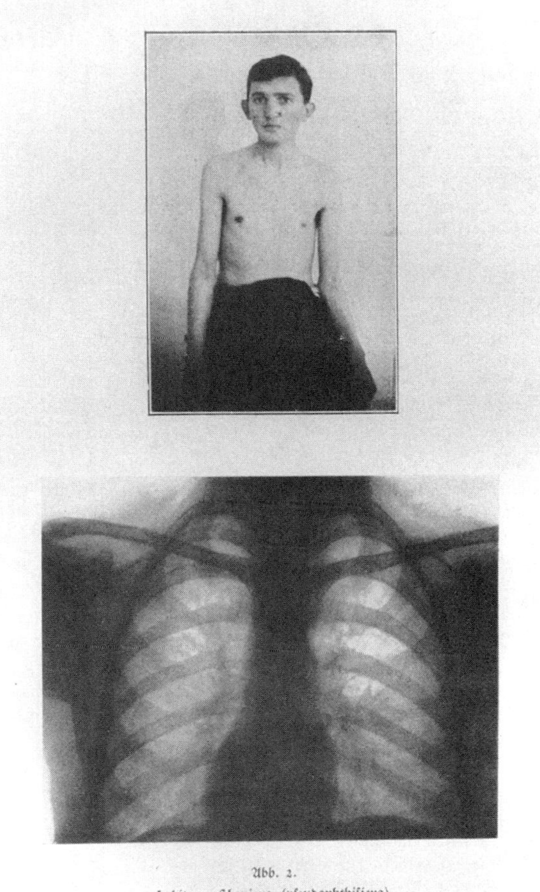

Abb. 2.
Habitus aſthenicus (pſeudophthiſicus).
Geſunde Lunge.

the second, the *habitus asthenicus* with healthy lungs. Taken from K. Nicol and G. Schröder, *Die Lungentuberkulose: Lehrbuch der diagnostischen Irrtümer* (Munich: Otto Gmelin, 1932), 52–53 (National Library of Medicine, Bethesda).

predisposed to tuberculosis. Both point to a close association between the body of the Jew and the Jew's character. This difference from an established norm of "beauty/health" comes to be inscribed on every part of the Jew's anatomy, especially the chest.

The narrowness of the Jew's chest, a sign of his predisposition to tuberculosis, as I shall discuss in Chapter Four, becomes the focus of Jewish concern about masculinity. In 1902, the Jewish physician Moses Julius Gutmann observed that, from 1886 to 1897, the average chest circumference of Polish Jews was less (811 mm) than that of the general population in Poland (863 mm). In examining some two hundred Jews in Warsaw, he found that they had an average chest circumference of 839 mm to a body length of 1611 mm, while Galician Jews showed only an average chest circumference of 794 mm. Yet Gutmann, following the liberal Jewish line, argues that in Austria and Russia their ability to serve in the military was not affected. During 1901 in Russia, he notes, 5.73 percent of Jews were in the army but Jews made up 4.1percent of the general population.[11] Jews, according to Gutmann (and Leroy-Beaulieu) are "decadent but not degenerate." This is exactly the reverse of the argument used by anti-Semites, who see Jewish "decadence" as a sign of the inherent "degeneration" of the type.[12]

Westernized Jews were constrained by the power of science to accept the argument for Jewish physical insufficiency. Martin Engländer commented in 1902, "the inheritance and the quality of life [in the ghetto] evidenced two grotesque parallel facts: the skull size of the Jews is on average greater than that of the non-Jewish population; on the other hand, their chest circumference absolutely and relatively in relationship to body length is less than for non-Jews."[13] Engländer did not need to interpret these "facts" for his Jewish readership, as they could easily do it for themselves: thin-chested Jews may have "insufficient muscles and badly developed breathing apparatus," may "live with poor nutrition and conditions which harbor infection," and may therefore "have an enormous rate of tuberculosis," but they are smarter than non-Jews. Intelligence is the compensation for the physical weakness signified by small chest circumference and tuberculosis. This is a quality ascribed not only to male Jews in German society, but of course to women, in such texts of high culture as Kant's *Anthropology*, Schopenhauer's essay "On Women," and Nietzsche's aphorisms on the nature of the feminine in *The Gay Science*.

Heinrich Singer, another Jewish physician of the *fin de siècle* fascinated by the charges of Jewish pathology, argued, "In general one can see in the body form the closeness of the Jew to the female type." One quality which marks this feminized body is that the "chest is constructed smaller, its circumference is relatively small, a natural result of the long standing curvature and poor economic circumstances." He provides the following table. Of one thousand military draftees, a greater percentage of Jews have a chest circumference less than half of their body height:[14]

	smaller	*at the half*	*greater*
Christians	128	36	836
Jews	491	57	452

Leroy-Beaulieu sees the decay for the modern Jew as increasing over time: "Their wretched physique is the result of their wretched living. Their physical strength, their muscular power, has diminished in each generation" (163). Only the escape offered by the physical assimilation of the Jews into the West will provide for the recuperation of the Jew's body, otherwise, not even the consumption of "healthy" meat presumably free from tuberculosis will lessen the risk for illness and effeminization.

Such are the contradictions of late nineteenth-century popular and medical culture. For a victim of pulmonary tuberculosis, such as Franz Kafka in 1917, this contradiction takes on special significance. For does his tuberculosis not prove the validity of those anxieties about his masculinity that had haunted him for decades? Kafka distances this anxiety by framing it in terms of military service. The Jew unable to serve in the military because of his weakened constitution is incorporated into "The Conscription of Troops" (1920). Here the regular conscription of troops, "often necessary on account of the never-ending frontier wars," is represented as inevitable but also manly. Whenever the soldiers come to recruit new soldiers, someone is always missing. This person is not really trying "to evade military service, it's only fear that has prevented him from turning up." When he finally appears from his hiding place, he is punished by the weak nobleman who heads the regiment, and then is permitted to join the ranks. Everyone must serve.

And yet in each town there is some woman who compulsively follows the conscripting soldiers: "This is something women have to go through, a debt which they pay their sex" (440). She is dressed in conspicuous finery, but is a stranger coming from a foreign place to take part in a conscription that is not her own.

> She feels shame to a degree which our women possibly feel at no other time; only now is she fully aware of having forced her way into a foreign conscription, and when the soldier has read out the list and her name is not on it and there comes a moment of silence, she fled, stooped and trembling out of the door, receiving in addition a blow in the back from a soldier's fist. Should the person not on the list be a man, his only desire is to be conscripted with the others, although he does not belong to this house. But this is too utterly out of the question, an outsider of this kind has never been conscripted and nothing of the sort will ever happen. (441)

The false conscript is inherently feminine. She cannot serve in the military because of the form of her body; here "anatomy is destiny."

Here the movement that Kafka's modernist discourse permits is clear. Kafka takes the debate about the feminized body of the Jewish conscript, deterritorializes it by placing it in a never-never land without cultural and social signposts, and transmutes the feminized Jewish male into a woman, a stranger in a foreign culture who is driven to undergo recruitment. What remains is the relationship of the masculine military service, and the disqualification and mockery of bodies inappropriate for such service. It is a cultural imperative that drives the women, the call of the group, "something women have to go through, a debt that they pay their sex." It is inscribed on their psyches because it is ascribed to their bodies. The sign of their irrational mental state is their misapprehension that they too can become soldiers.

The Jewish Patient

For all of his sense that the Jew was made stronger ("tougher") by his experience of persecution (as viewed shared by his contemporary, Friedrich Nietzsche), Leroy-Beaulieu comments that "the Jew is particularly liable to the disease of our age, neurosis" (168). And this "nervousness" is a sign of the Jew's modernity, for modernity and nervousness are interchangeable at the *fin de siècle*: "The Jew is the most nervous and, in so far, the most modern of men. He is, by the very nature of his diseases, the forerunner, as it were, of his contemporaries, preceding them on that perilous path upon which society is urged by the excesses of its intellectual and emotional life, and by the increasing spur of competition" (169). Kafka's own illnesses prior to the outbreak of his tuberculosis in 1917 are understood by his physicians as "nervousness." On August 18, 1909, Dr. Siegmund Kohn attested to Kafka's employer that his patient showed signs of "nervousness," and was in need of an extended holiday. On June 11, 1912, Kohn repeated his contention, stating that Kafka's "nervous problems make it absolutely necessary" that his patient have an extended stay in a sanatorium at Riva for his problems.[15] Kafka's "nervousness" was a sign of the times.

In 1913, again Kafka spent time at the Hartmann Sanatorium at Riva. The guests that year included the writers Hermann Sudermann and Thomas and Heinrich Mann.[16] But for a Jew, such a sojourn had to provoke fear of racial predestination. Even a Jew understood the "Jewish patient" as different. Drawing on much of my earlier work on this topic, Edward Shorter has recently shown how the discourse about the imagined Jew's body led to the incorporation of hypochondriasis into *fin-de-siècle* Jewish self-representation.[17] Anti-Semitic jokes circulated about Eastern European Jews who seek out a second opinion when bathing is required as a treatment, or who are so poor that they cannot read the numbers on an eye chart, or who take money for a cure from a physician and then use it to pay for a second opinion. Jewish hypochondria is central to such jokes:

> Frau Schminkeles, a woman who had emigrated to Berlin from Galicia, is always excessively upset by illnesses in her family. The doctor can never come fast enough, for there is always someone, in her view, "about to die." One day, when the doctor opened his waiting room door, Mrs. Schminkeles pushed her way in front of a couple who were about to enter. The doctor said: "Dear Mrs. Schminkeles, here everything goes according to order." Mrs. Schminkeles screams angrily: "Schminkeles is dying! and Schminkeles does not die in order!"[18]

Even in Jewish sources, such images of the demanding patient, whose illnesses are usually trivial, are at center stage. In a Jewish joke book of the turn of the century, the following story is told about two converts to Christianity: "'Have you retained anything in your memory from your former religion, Rosalie?' the baptized Mrs. Rosenthal asked her longtime friend. 'You can't forget everything?' 'Not everything,' admits Mrs. Rosenthal, 'I still know two Jewish words.' 'And what are those?' '*Chuzpa* (pride) and hypochondriac'."[19]

In 1914, the Prague Zionist journal *Self-Defense (Selbstwehr)* presented an ironic yet intensely focused account of this "Jewish patient":

> The Jewish patient does not suffer from the illness itself but rather from the fear of the illness and its consideration. Almost every Jewish patient presents the same question: "Is there no danger?" even when the illness is trivial. Even the friends, relatives, acquaintances ask: "You can tell me. . . . Is there really no danger?" And the report of the doctor is not sufficient; the patient continues to ruminate about himself and collects all of the comments of other "experts" and repeats them in the greatest detail. He describes every symptom exactly. One example: Once a Jewish woman came to the author with a pain in her side. She began to explain how a cow had butted her in the side, described the cow exactly, talked with ever greater fervor, explained about the owners of the cow, of a trial, that she had with them, etc. She talked about twenty minutes until she finally came to her pain, just like Shalom Aleichem.
>
> To interrogate a Jewish patient is not easy. The Christian patient answers the doctor simply and directly; the Jewish patient answers the questions often with counter questions, starts to debate with the doctor, presents his own diagnosis and confuses the doctor with every new complaint, out of the fear that he did not present his complaint clearly enough. Well-known is the classic statement of the Jewish patient: "And generally I am not very well." Here are other examples of typical answers of Jewish patients:
>
> "How old are you?" "Well, just because I'm old, does that mean I have to die?"
>
> "How is your stomach?" "It's not my stomach," the patient answered with an discontented tone.
>
> "How often did you vomit?" "What, is twice too seldom? How often should I have vomited?"
>
> "How long have you been sick?" "My friend, I came into this world with my illness."
>
> "Do you eat well?" "Food is carefully measured."
>
> "How is your stomach?" "Since I eat, how should my stomach be?"
>
> "Do you have palpitations?" "That's because I'm a weak person."
>
> And if the doctor prescribed a course of treatment, the Jewish patient has all sorts of objections. If one suggests that she go to the sea, she says: "The Jewess from Globok has exactly the same illness as do I, and baths have helped her—perhaps baths will also help me."
>
> While the Christian patient comes to terms with it when he learns that his illness can not be healed and that there is no hope, the Jew does not accept the inevitable end and says over and over again:
>
> "Give me some advice, what I should do?" Or: "One *must* be able to find a cure. . . ."

> Often the interest in the cure of the illness is so great, that it separates itself from the illness itself. His cure becomes a goal in itself, on which he spends all of his strength. He knows only that passionate desire, it becomes for him almost a cult, like a pious deed, and shapes the entire content of his life.[20]

The Jewish patient in the sanatorium is thus understood as different, even if he or she manifests the same illness as his or her non-Jewish counterpart. The Jewish patient is obsessive, the search for the disease comes to reflect the same nervousness as do all other factors in the Jew's life. What is described here, and in all of the discussions of the Jewish patient at the turn of the century, is the presumed gain from illness. Thus Gregor Samsa, in Kafka's "The Metamorphosis" (1915), initially struggles against assuming the passive and dependent patient role, even though his mother insists that he is ill, rather than transformed. This gain is to be found in the ability of the patient to call upon the defined role of the patient with all of its clearly delineated borders. Anti-Semites see this as a reflection of the essential nature of the Jew, his grasping at every advantage he can accrue; Jews understand this as a reflex of the displacement of Jewish anxiety in a world no longer fixed in its Enlightenment promise of Jewish equality. This model projects these qualities onto the body and illness (sham or real) results.

Kafka's role as a Jewish patient was understood as reflected in his body. In one of the first letters to Felice Bauer in the winter of 1912 (he still addresses her as "Fräulein Felice"), Kafka writes: "Just as I am thin, and I am the thinnest person I know (and that's saying something, for I am no stranger to sanatoria), there is also nothing to me which, in relation to writing, one could call superfluous, superfluous in the sense of overflowing. . . ." No one knows sanatoria quite like the Jewish patient. Kafka's following account of his day places emphasis on his illness, his "unbearable weakness," "the slight pain in my heart and twitching stomach muscles," his insomnia (LFe, 21–22). In other words, Kafka as a Jewish patient is a nervous patient.

This nervousness shows on his face: "I have often noticed the pensiveness of the Jewish face; it is one of the characteristics of the race" (172). Here Leroy-Beaulieu cites one of the major authorities on the Jewish face, the British eugenist Francis Galton. When the turn-of-the-century Jew looked in the mirror, he saw not only a sick Jew looking back at him, but also a corrupt and degenerate Jew. Francis Galton had tried to capture this "Jewish physiognomy" in his composite photographs of "boys in the Jews' Free School, Bell Lane"[21] (Plate 17). Galton believed that he had captured the "typical features of the modern Jewish face." Galton's trip to the Bell Lane school confronted him with the "children of poor parents, dirty little fellows individually, but wonderfully beautiful, as I think, in these composites." There, and in the adjacent "Jewish Quarter," he saw the "cold, scanning gaze of man, woman, and child," the gaze of the Jew as the sign of their difference, of their potential pathology, of their inherent nature: "There was no sign of diffidence in any of their looks, nor of surprise at the unwonted intrusion. I felt, rightly or wrongly, that every one of them was coolly appraising me at market value, without the slightest interest of any other kind."[22] In the Jews' gaze, the pathology of their soul, which reveals their materialism, their avarice, their greed can be found. At the turn of the century, Carl Heinrich Stratz noted this "vivacity of the eye" as a sign of the "remarkable persistence" of the Jew's physiognomy.[23] This view is at least as old as the seventeenth century: Robert Burton writes in the *Anatomy of Melancholy* of the "goggle eyes" of the Jews, as well as "their voice, pace, gesture, [and] looks" as a sign of "their conditions and infirmities."[24]

Using Galton's photographs, the German racialist anthropologist Hans F. K. Günther in the 1920s, attempted to describe the "sensual," "threatening" and "crafty" gaze of the Jew as reflecting the essence of the Jewish soul.[25] Günther's importance to acculturated German Jews of the period cannot be underestimated. The Eastern European Jewish novelist Joseph Roth wrote to the German Jewish novelist Stefan Zweig on April 6, 1933, that it was the Nazis who looked different and inferior: "The SA Storm troopers destroy the shop windows. You can find *their* images in the work of the racial theorist [Hans] Günther as that of the typical Semite."[26] Even the anti-Semites look Jewish! It is not merely that Jews "look Jewish" but that this look marks them as inferior: "Who has not heard people characterize such and such a man or woman they see in the streets as Jewish without in the least knowing anything about them? The street arab who calls out 'Jew' as some child hurries on to school is unconsciously giving the best and most disinterested proof that there is a reality in the Jewish expression."[27] When the non-Jew sees the Jew's physiognomy, the face is immediately translated into bad character. And this character is fixed in the Jew's eyes. The Jewish "race," as we have seen, could never be truly beautiful.[28] Most writers fix on the Jewish gaze

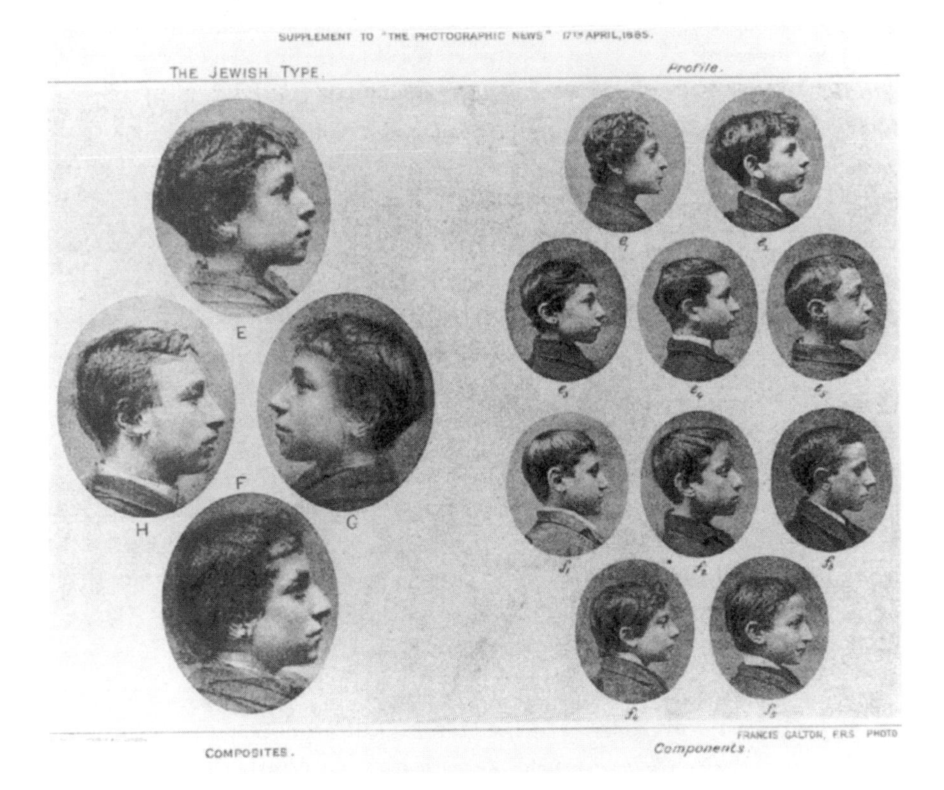

PLATE 17. Francis Galton's original photographs of Jewish students at a London school. Galton then superimposed the original photographs to produce a form of multiple exposure, and created an image of the "essence" of the Jew. From *The Photographic News* 29 [April 17, 1885 and April 24, 1885] (Source: Private Collection, Ithaca).

in particular. Arthur de Gobineau noted, "French, German and Polish Jews—they all look alike. I have had the opportunity of examining closely one of the last kind. His features and profile clearly betrayed his origin. His eyes especially were unforgettable."[29]

This meaning of the "crafty" gaze of the Jew is reversed when the liberal Leroy-Beaulieu observes, about the comparative intelligence of the Germans (but not the French) and the Jews, "I have heard Germans urge this intellectual precocity of the Jews as a reason for debarring their children from the schools and colleges attended by other children. 'The struggle,' they said, 'between the sons of the North, the pale Germans with their blond hair and sluggish intellects, and these sons of the Orient with their black eyes and alert minds, is an unequal one'" (171–172). Not only are these displaced "Orientals" different in terms of their bodies and their psyches, but as in their resistance to illness, they are cleverer (not smarter) than other groups (at least the Germans). The Jew's gaze reflects his way of seeing and recording the world; it marks his body as different and as potentially more advantageous. However, that advantage was not in terms of the idealized male body of the age, the body of the soldier. For the Jew's chest condemned him to be a poor soldier, a male who is not fully a male. He is a feminized intellectual whose nervousness can be read on his body like Sarah Bernhardt's tuberculosis. His tuberculosis is of the soul, a sign of the hypochondria of the Jewish patient. His body marks a loss of status as a "real" man or a status yet to be gained. This is the marked body of the exemplary Jewish soldier of Kafka's age.

The Soldier's Body

It is with the Jew's gaze as the point where his mind and body meet that we can leave Leroy-Beaulieu's construction of the Jew, and turn to the formative political event for Jews of Kafka's generation, the Dreyfus Affair. Hannah Arendt was quite right when she wrote in the late 1940s, "Not the Dreyfus case with its trials but the Dreyfus affair in its entirety offers a foregleam of the twentieth century."[30] But it was not only the trial's place in debates about national identity which affected acculturated European Jews; Alfred Dreyfus's body and its literary representation haunt Jewish self-representation at the beginning of this century.

At the close of the nineteenth century, the Dreyfus trial is the event which more than any other focuses the anxiety of assimilated Jews about their physical integration into the world where they find themselves. There had been a complex discourse about the physical assimilation of the Jews during the nineteenth century, which mirrored the rather quick social integration of the Jews into European society during the century from Joseph II's edict of toleration to the Dreyfus "affair" of the 1890s.[31] From the Jewish perspective, they were physically becoming "Europeans" as their bodies and minds left the ghetto; in other words, as even "philo-Semitic" thinkers such as Leroy-Beaulieu observed, they were simply becoming less authentically Jewish.

All of the fantasies about the difference of the Jewish body returned in the image of Captain Alfred Dreyfus. Franz Kafka, like every Jew of his age, understood his Jewishness in terms of Dreyfus's experience. Such thoughts permeated even into Kafka's subconscious. As late as 1922, in a letter to Max Brod about Brod's support for a controversial Czech sculptor, František Bílek, Kafka wrote, "It's a great delight to me that you really mean to try something that I dared mention only as a purely fantastic wish; I don't have the strength for more. In my opinion it would be a fight of a par with the fight for [Leoš] Janáček, if I understand the matter rightly (I almost wrote: with the fight for Dreyfus)" (LF, 348). This self-conscious "almost" slip of the pen is one of the very few "slips" which Kafka, as meticulous in his letters as in his fiction, acknowledges. The very word "fight" (*Kampf*) evokes Dreyfus even when he wishes to think about the cultural struggle about the Czech composer Leoš Janáček. Dreyfus remains at the back of Kafka's unconscious as a model—but as a model for the body of the Jew that is also Franz Kafka.

The Dreyfus Affair haunted Kafka all his adult life. In 1894 Alfred Dreyfus was charged with spying for the Germans, and was convicted as much for being the first Jew to have been assigned (even temporarily) to the French General Staff as for treason. Kafka was eleven at the time of the thirty-five-year-old Dreyfus's degradation in 1895; at the time of Dreyfus's second trial in 1899, he was sixteen; he was twenty-three when Dreyfus was finally acquitted and twenty-five when a final attempt was made to assassinate Dreyfus. All of these events haunted the front pages of the newspapers in Prague as elsewhere in the world. Kafka's life paralleled the public events of Dreyfus's life. Franz Kafka died in 1924; Alfred Dreyfus died in 1935.

For the opening decade of the twentieth century, the seminal texts in the Dreyfus Affair (not the trial, to follow Hannah Arendt's view) were the various versions of Dreyfus's letters and autobiography. Published in 1901 in French and then translated immediately into most European languages, these were the texts that gave educated, bourgeois Jews access to Dreyfus's inner life. They captured Dreyfus's self-representation for the Jewish reader safe in an armchair in London or Berlin or Prague. In Dreyfus's letters and diaries, the reality of his body became textualized. Dreyfus became a part of the literary world of educated Jews. His letters (unsent from Devil's Island), his diary entries, and his immediate autobiographical comments provided a textual corpus through which the decay of the body of the acculturated Jew, one of the new muscle Jews, could be measured.

Dreyfus's texts appeared as documents attempting both to establish his innocence through an examination of his mind-set, and to prove the universal experience of having been snatched from an established, unexceptional, middle-class life: "A brilliant and easy career was open to me; the future appeared under the most promising auspices. After my day's work I found rest and delight at home."[32] But on "Saturday, the 13th of October, 1894, I received a service-note directing me to go the following Monday, at nine o'clock in the morning, to the Ministry of War for the general inspection. It was expressly stated that I should be in *tenue bourgeoise* (civilian dress). The hour seemed to be very early for the general inspection, which is usually passed late in the day; the mention of civilian dress surprised me as well" (5–6). Dreyfus is confronted with the accusation of being a traitor, and his body responds: "Commander du Paty arose and, placing his hand on my shoulder, cried out in a loud voice: 'in the name of the law, I arrest you; you are accused of the crime of high treason.' A thunderbolt falling at my feet would not have produced in me a more violent emotion; I blurted out disconnected sentences, protesting against so infamous an accusation, which nothing in my life could have given rise to" (9). This moment of surprise as represented by a physical response, the collapse of speech, is echoed in a number of the trial and judgment themes in Kafka's literary work. It is the *globus hystericus*, the inability to speak, the central, determining symptom of hysteria, a feminizing illness, that marks these Jewish males as ill.

The trial of Alfred Dreyfus is "the archetypal court case in the background of *The Trial*," according to Frederick Karl, but it is even more than that.[33] It provides a model for the decline of the healthy body of the acculturated, westernized, male Jew into the sick, decaying body of the essential Jew he is concealing, the *exemplum* of racial predestination. Certainly Dreyfus was considered an example of the Jewish type by his enemies; "his sly and vain character betray[s] all the pride and all the ignominy of his race," wrote one.[34] But even his supporters judged him by his appearance. Forzinetti, the Commandant at the Cherche-Midi Prison, where Dreyfus was taken after his initial trial, became his advocate because of his deportment: "He was in a state of extraordinary excitement. He looked like a madman; his eyes were bloodshot, and the things in his room had been upset. I had great difficulty in calming him. I had then the intuition that this officer was innocent" (42). Guilt or innocence was written on Dreyfus's body.

Alfred Dreyfus was seen as different in a specific, visible way, as different as the Cracow Jew whom Kafka met on the train. On the day of

Dreyfus's public degradation, Saturday, January 5, 1895, the French writer and journalist Léon Daudet wrote this eyewitness account: "His was the color of treason. His face was ashen, without relief, base, without appearance of remorse, foreign, to be sure, debris of the ghetto. . . . This wretch is not French. We have all understood as much from his act, his demeanor, his physiognomy."[35] The anti-Dreyfusard journalist Maurice Barrès was likewise present at the ceremony: "His foreign physiognomy, his impassive stiffness, the very atmosphere he exuded revolted even the most self-controlled of spectators."[36] A contemporary historian summarized the conventional image of Dreyfus: "Even his physique, his myopia and, of course, his physiognomy, ended up bearing witness against him: Dreyfus seemed flat, commonplace, livid, cunning, colorless, awkward, and prodigiously antipathetic."[37] When he is degraded, military police "tear off the braid from his cap and sleeves, the buttons from his jacket, his shoulder-straps, all the marks of his rank. . . . [His] uniform [is] reduced to tatters. . . ."[38] In rags, he now approximates the contemporaneous image of the Wandering Jew. His Jewish appearance was proof after the fact of his heinous crime, for no Frenchman could have betrayed France as Dreyfus was accused of having done. That he looked and sounded Jewish was the same as looking and sounding guilty.

This leads back to the claim that Jews cannot really lay claim to the language of the nation in which they dwell. By November 1894 the newspapers such as *La Libre Parole* and *La Croix* used the accusations against Dreyfus to campaign for the exclusion of Jews from the military. "The frightful Jews, vomited up into France by the ghettos of Germany, can barely jabber our language."[39] When Rabbi J. H. Dreyfuss, the Grand Rabbi of Paris, served as a character witness for Alfred Dreyfus, Jean Sandherr, the head of the Section for Statistics of the Army at the time of the accusation, mocked his Yiddish accent when recounting his testimony.[40] Dreyfus was multilingual: he spoke German "thoroughly," which made him "the perfect choice for the miserable and shameful mission."[41] The quality of his voice betrays him: "Face unpleasant, eyes short-sighted and deceitful, voice dry, toneless, metallic, 'a voice of zinc'."[42] His is the Jew's voice, a voice betraying his essential difference from all Frenchmen.

If one returns to Dreyfus's texts today, the *fin-de-siècle* discourse about his exemplary Jewish body is easy to reconstruct. These texts, published in 1901 after his return from Devil's Island, had been written as letters and notes during his imprisonment and immediately after the second trial.[43] They were an immediate best-seller, and were his contemporaries' first real look into Dreyfus's understanding of his own situation. They provided a grid for the self-understanding of his Jewish contemporaries about their own situation. In particular, his portrayal of his body under torture implies the contemporary discourse on madness. We can begin with Dreyfus' removal from France following the first trial:

> I was taken to the Orleans railway station in a prison van, and thence brought in a roundabout way to the freight entrance, where the cars built specially for the transportation of convicts . . . were waiting. These cars are divided into narrow cells, each barely accommodating a man in sitting posture, and when the door is closed it is impossible for the occupant to stretch his legs. I was locked up in one of these cells, with my wrists handcuffed and irons on my ankles. The night was horribly long; all my limbs were benumbed. (74)

Dreyfus stresses again and again how far removed his body was from the bourgeois body which he had inhabited till then: "My body was benumbed, my head on fire, and my hands and ankles bruised by the handcuffs" (76). His is a body in pain, but not pain that the soldier could bear with honor; rather, it is the pain of degradation and torture.

For the anti-Dreyfusards, Dreyfus's conviction reveals the deformed Jewish body, its deformed chest hiding beneath the dress uniform of the soldier Dreyfus could never be (Plates 18–19). The imagined diseased body of the Jew was the imagined circumcised body of Alfred Dreyfus. No uniform, no code of conduct, no national identity could obscure the physical difference of the male Jew. Such bodies could never truly become soldiers, argued the anti-Dreyfusards. The unmasking of Dreyfus's body revealed the Jew within the uniform. And it was the Jew as the disease within the body politic.

When Dreyfus arrives at the prison on Devil's Island, he records in his diary his solitary confinement in a seventeen-foot-square hut under constant surveillance by hostile guards: "Until now I have worshipped reason, I have believed there was a logic in things and events, I have believed in human justice! Anything irrational and extravagant found difficult entrance into my brain" (103–104). Madness haunts his sense of self, and links more and more his awareness of his body's decay:

> APRIL 15, 1895*:* At ten o'clock they bring me my day's food—a bit of canned pork, some rice, some coffee berries in filthy condition, and a little moist sugar. I have no means of roasting the

PLATE 18. The image of Dreyfus on board the cruiser *Sfax* in 1899. From Alfred and Pierre Dreyfus, *The Dreyfus Case*, trans. Donald MacKay (New Haven: Yale University Press, 1937), opposite p. 106 (Olin Library, Cornell University).

coffee, which in derision is given to me raw. I throw it all into the sea. . . . What an agony of my being! What a sacrifice I have made in giving my pledge to live! Nothing will be spared me, neither mental torture nor physical suffering. (112) Again I had only a bit of bread for my dinner, and I was fainting. (113)

APRIL 16, 1895: As to my bill of fare for dinner, it is very simple—bread and water.

APRIL 22, 1895: I have such a mingling of physical weakness and extreme nervousness that, the moment I am in bed, the nerves get the upper hand, and I am tortured with anxiety about my dear ones. (121)

MAY 9, 1895: This morning . . . I had a fit of weakness followed by a copious perspiration. I had to lie down on my bed. I must struggle to support my body; it must not yield until my honor is restored. (133)

MAY 9: A frightful day. Violent nervous chills.

MAY 10: High fever last night.

MAY 11, 12, 13: Bad Days. Fever, stomach trouble, disgust for everything.

MAY 16: Continual fever. A stronger attack yesterday evening, followed by congestion of the brain. (134)

DECEMBER 30, 1895: My nerves trouble me so that I am afraid to lie down. (140)

Dreyfus fears that he will be unable to cope with increasing psychic debility. His nervousness seems to be caused equally (in his estimation) by the quality of the food he is given and by the violation of his innocence. On June 19, 1895, he writes: "I am all covered with pimples from the bite of mosquitoes and all sorts of insects. But that is nothing! What are physical sufferings as compared to the horrible tortures of the soul?" (145). Here the tortures he experiences begin to come solely from without himself. They are in part projections of his sense of having been violated. Even mosquitoes, which violate the private body, represent his false imprisonment, and they inscribe his sentence on his body.

It is not food or bad living conditions, but the sense of innocence violated that begins to destroy his body: "December 11, 1895: My heart feels as though pierced by a dagger . . . I wish to tear my flesh so as to forget in physical pain this mental torture" (183). The soldier's bearing is beginning to collapse. Dreyfus's comment on his "mental torture" comes at a point where he is being physically tortured. By December 1896, the measures taken against him are increased, and he begins to be tortured not only by his physical decline and sense of innocence but by being strapped into a diabolical apparatus:

> On the 4th of September my jailers received from M. [André] Lebon, Minister of Colonies, the order to keep me, until further notice, confined to my hut through the twenty-four hours, with the "double boucle" at night. . . . From the 6th of September, I was put in the "double boucle" at night; and this torment, which last nearly two months, was of the following description: two irons in the form of a "U"—AA—were fixed by their lower parts to the sides of the bed. In these irons an iron bar—B—was inserted, and to this were fastened two boucles—CC.

PLATE 19. Alfred Dreyfus's imagined body from the anti-Semitic Viennese turn-of-the-century journal *Kikeriki* presenting Dreyfus's deformed skeleton. From Eduard Fuchs, *Die Juden in der Karikatur* (Munich: Langen, 1921) (Private Collection, Ithaca).

> At the extremity of the bar, on one side, there was a head "D" and at the other a padlock, "E," so that the bar was fastened into the irons "AA," and consequently to the bed. Therefore, when my feet were inserted into the two rings, it was no longer possible for me to move about. I was fastened in an unchangeable position to my bed. The torture was hardly bearable during those tropical nights. Soon also the rings, which were very tight, lacerated my ankles. (221) (Plate 20)

What is striking about this passage is its cool, dispassionate, yes, even distant tone. This tone, that of the engineer, was necessary for Dreyfus to deal with his torture in his retrospective account.

PLATE 20. The torture machine from the German edition of Dreyfus's memoirs and letters. Alfred Dreyfus, *Fünf Jahre meines Lebens* (1901; reprint Berlin: Globus, 1930), 153 (Olin Library, Cornell University).

In a letter of December 9, 1896, Dreyfus comments on the arrival of the "new commandant of the islands," who "came yesterday evening. He told me the last measure which had been taken against me was not a punishment, but a 'measure of precaution.' . . . Putting in irons a measure of precaution!" (214). Dreyfus had again been falsely accused.

> In the early part of September 1896 a rumor that Dreyfus had escaped was current in Paris. It was promptly denied—Dreyfus had done nothing whatever to justify a supposition of this kind. But André Lebon, the Colonial Minister, took his role as jailer in the tragic vein, and telegraphed an order to confine Dreyfus to his cell and to put him in irons. . . . Fearing that his orders might not be executed with sufficient rigor, Lebon summoned one Deniel, who had a reputation for brutality and who was at that time in France. The Minister gave Deniel a lecture and dispatched him to the Salvation Islands as new head of the penitentiary. . . . Riveted to his bed by chains stained in blood, tortured by vermin and torrid heat, racked by spiritual torment, Dreyfus felt that his suffering had passed the limits of human endurance and that he should die.[44]

On Devil's Island (once used, as Dreyfus notes, to isolate lepers) Dreyfus's body undergoes a metamorphosis. He begins with the body of a French army officer, relatively well proportioned, handsome, though revealing in his physiognomy his Jewish ancestry. His chest measurements are sufficient to pass muster. He is a soldier. Then his body is tortured until it is virtually no longer recognizable.

The torture of Dreyfus is recognized by his contemporaries as such. Maurice Paléologue comments on the beginning of the second court-martial, on August 16, 1899, at Rennes: "The first hour in court today was taken up with consideration of the measures of constraint and confinement to which Dreyfus was subjected during his five years on Devil's Island. In comparison with his atrocious treatment, the system in the Russian convict prisons as described by Dostoevski in *The House of the Dead* or Kropotkin in his *Memoirs of a Prison of State* seem the gentlest, the most charitable, the most civilized form that the vindication of society could take. It made the most painful impression on the public; heads were lowered even among the witnesses for the prosecution. During this long reminder of his tortures, the prisoner did not once speak. At the end, when Colonel Jouaust asked him if he had anything to say he replied coldly: 'I am not here to talk about the abominable tortures to which I have been subjected; I shall speak only to defend my honor.'"[45] Dreyfus acts like a healthy soldier but his emaciated and aged body now reveals him to be a diseased victim.

What Dreyfus's second trial meant differed from his supporters to his opponents. What strikes everyone is his "extraordinary emaciation."[46] "His trousers flapped about his legs, which had neither muscle nor flesh, as though they were sticks. He had his uniform padded to give himself a semblance of stature."[47] Maurice Barrès, who had seen in his physiognomy the reason for his degradation, now sees "his thin and contracted face. His sharp stare from behind the pince-nez!"[48] Maurice Paléologue looks and him and wonders: "But how worn and emaciated he was, what a wreck of a human being he was reduced to! His arms were withered, his knees so thin that they seemed to pierce the cloth of his trousers. There were just a few white hairs on his bald pate. Only the staring eyes behind his pince-nez gave some slight animation to his cadaverous face. Ecce homo!"[49] (Plate 21) Even original anti-Dreyfusards such as Barrès see Dreyfus as a Christ figure, the ultimate Jewish victim (of Jews?). The crucifix becomes their means of defining Dreyfus's tortured body — it becomes the torture machine. And Dreyfus becomes the archetypal victim of injustice. But even that seemed not to be sufficient for many of his opponents. During this second trial, with its inevitable negative outcome, it was vital for Dreyfus to again present himself as a military man. This was read as a sign of his Jewish duplicity and guilt.

Dreyfus's trial and imprisonment transform his body into the body of the Jew. He moves through the shock of being revealed as different, to acknowledging that he is seen as different, to seeing his body made different through starvation and torture. Readers of his diary who had participated in the "struggle for Dreyfus" (*"Kampf für Dreyfus"*), in Kafka's phrase, are supposed to empathize with his spiritual and physical decline, with his emasculation. In a letter from September 24, 1899, Dreyfus's supporter Mark Twain recommends a certain London physician for "the restoration of Captain Dreyfus's health. . . . [He] can cure any disease that any physician can cure, and that in many cases he can restore health where no physician can do it, and where no physician will claim to be able to do it."[50] He recommends him as the physician to Nathaniel Rothschild of Vienna and the daughter of a Mr. Cohen of London, among others. This doctor had helped other Jews, so perhaps he could help Dreyfus.

PLATE 21. Alfred Dreyfus as Christ from the pro-Dreyfus *Le Sifflet* (1898) (Olin Library, Cornell University).

However, it is important to note that Dreyfus nowhere refers to himself as a Jew, even though it is clear to him from the beginning that this is the reason for his betrayal. Not just Judaism as a religious practice or ethical system, but the contemporary biological definitions of the Jew are missing from Dreyfus's account. The very word "Jew" does not appear in his texts. As Hannah Arendt puts it, "Jewishness was for the individual Jew at once a physical stain and a mysterious personal privilege, both inherent in a 'racial predestination.'"[51] This view dominated the discussion about the Jews in Zionist circles such as Martin Buber's, with which Kafka was acquainted, even though he did not especially like Buber.[52] The concept of racial predestination is at the center of the question of Dreyfus's body.

In the course of his autobiographical account, Dreyfus's body metamorphoses from the body of the French soldier to that of the imaginary diseased Jew. Franz Kafka's tale "The Metamorphosis" (1915) evokes a similar pattern of imagined decay. In that tale Gregor Samsa awakes "transformed into a gigantic insect [*Ungeziefer*]" (89). According to the standard Nazi collection of "popular wisdom," Jews were traditionally labeled as the "insects of humanity" [*Ungeziefer der Menschheit*]. It is because "the Jew is corrupt in his very soul and therefore feels himself only well in the swamp."[53] Jews are "insects [*Ungeziefer*] like lice and cockroaches, that generate general disgust among all humanity." Thus Jews are traditionally compared with insects and through this association with illness, specifically illness of the skin, carried by (or believed to be carried by) bugs. Dreyfus's skin and Gregor Samsa's carapace are marred by the scars and the infections that represent their pariah state.

In Kafka's tale, Gregor is labeled as "sick." At least his mother calls a doctor to come and "cure" him when she becomes aware of his transformation into a "gigantic insect." But is it a real or an imagined illness, or is it an illness at all? Could it be a natural metamorphosis? At least Gregor Samsa is afraid that the "sick-insurance doctor" would be called, "who of course regarded all mankind as perfectly healthy malingerers" (S, 91). Is Gregor Samsa sick, or is he merely "transformed" into his real (read: inner) state, as the imagined Dreyfus came to be? Is illness merely the return of the fancied Jewish body to its "natural" state?

This "illness" or transformation is marked by the "gigantic insect" being unable to find his correct food. Indeed, the fresh milk and bread supplied to the newly transformed Gregor Samsa by his sister fills him with repulsion (S, 105). Gregor is "hungry enough" and yet is "dying of starvation" (S, 129). As Gregor's body decays, as he collapses and becomes more and more bug-like, his father abandons his own hypochondria and inaction and puts on a "smart blue uniform with gold buttons, such as bank messengers wear" (S, 121). Here is the reverse of Dreyfus's degradation. For the father goes from being a raggedy figure to a uniformed one, one who has again assumed power within the family structure. But Kafka's tale only evokes the Dreyfus Affair in the most marginal manner.

Kafka works through the overt question of the Dreyfus case in "In the Penal Colony" (1914). Its setting, as virtually every commentator has observed, is more than similar to Devil's Island. Indeed, even the map of Devil's Island which Dreyfus provides in his memoirs looks like the island of the fictive penal colony (Plate 22). Even the primary literary source for the novel, Octave Mirabeau's *The Garden of Torturers* (1898–1899; 1902 in German) was written under the influence of the images of the Dreyfus Affair. Mirabeau himself was a Dreyfusard. Other texts, such as those by Charles Dickens on prisons and workhouse which have

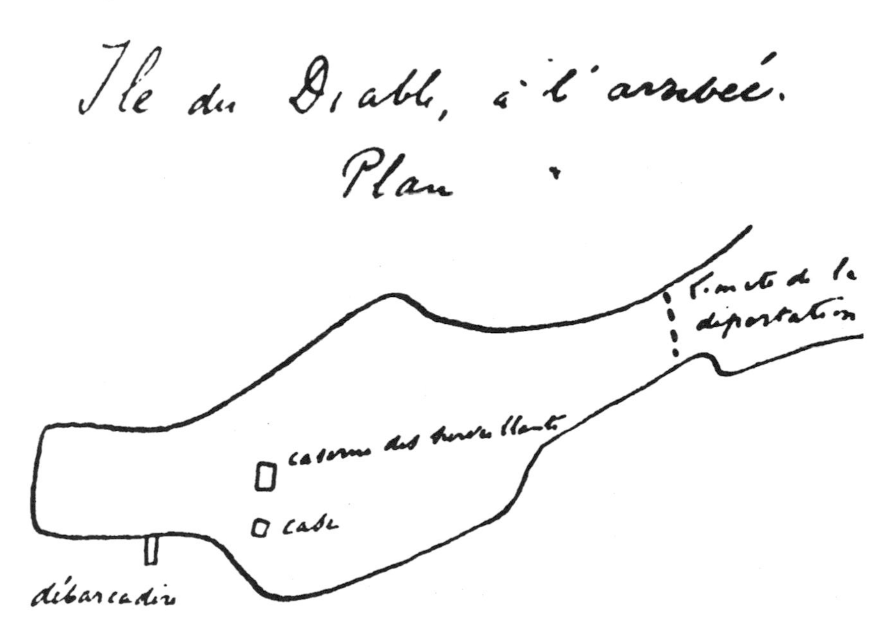

PLATE 22. Dreyfus's island from the German edition of Dreyfus's memoirs and letters. Alfred Dreyfus, *Fünf Jahre meines Lebens* (1901; reprint Berlin: Globus, 1930), 66 (Olin Library, Cornell University).

plausibly been proposed as sources, were read by Central European Jews at the turn of the century in the light of the Dreyfus trial and punishment. It is the overriding paradigm of military life for the Jews of the age.

Yet Kafka, like Dreyfus, avoids any mention of the Jewishness of the prisoner. Neither the word "Jew" nor any easily decoded reference appears in either of these texts. Kafka's prisoner, "a stupid-looking, wide-mouthed creature with bewildered hair and face" (S, 140), like Dreyfus, appears in chains, in stark contrast to the officer in his hot and stuffy, but proper, uniform. Each is Dreyfus. The latter is Dreyfus as uniformed French soldier; the former, Dreyfus in rotting rags in his cell. They turn out to be interchangeable. Indeed, the self-degradation of the officer in Kafka's tale parallels Dreyfus's degradation. He strips himself of rank and uniform and finally: "He drew [the sword] out of the scabbard, broke it, then gathered all together, the bits of sword, the scabbard, and the belt, and flung them so violently down that they clattered in the pit" (S, 163). His dereliction of duty might have been to fall asleep while on guard duty, a meaningless duty, as he is to salute his officer's door every hour on the hour. He is awakened by the captain's whip and threatened: "'Throw that whip away or I'll eat you alive'" (S, 146). He is accused by the captain, which is sufficient for his condemnation ("that's the evidence" [S, 146]). Like Dreyfus, he is accused of a military crime, here, insubordination. What is central to his crime, however, is that his guilt is proven by the accusation.

The officer's colonial language (and that of the narrator/observer) is represented by Kafka's German. The officer represents the regime of the old commandant who built the machine that dominates the penal colony, rather than the new commandant who wishes to discredit it. The officer's vocabulary when describing the torture machine evokes Dreyfus's account of his shackling. But Kafka also places the machine into a very different context. The officer, describing the operation of the machine, provides this analogy for the visitor: "You will have seen similar apparatus in hospitals. . . ." (S, 143). In hospitals, too, such machines exist, but their object is to heal, not to torture, unless one understands hospitals as places for the inflicting of pain. Hospitals are where bodies are cut up on tables, and the blood that results must go somewhere, for, as we shall see, blood pollutes. The hospital is also the abattoir. The machine is constructed to provide for the runoff of blood that results from the slow inscription of the "crime" onto the body of the condemned man. The needles cut ever so slowly into the skin, spray water onto the wound to make the inscription legible, and "blood and water together then [are] conducted here through small runnels into this main runnel and down a waste pipe into the pit" (S, 147). Pain and machines are closely linked to images of the ill body. Indeed, the inscription of pain to teach a lesson evokes Dreyfus's account of his torture. The body understands the crime: "You have seen how difficult it is to decipher the script with one's eyes, but our man deciphers it with his wounds" (S, 150). Here it is no longer the gaze of the Jew that reveals him as different, but his very body. By use of the machine the crime and the individual become one.

The prisoner's body, his ragged clothes, the gruel that keeps him alive to be tortured, all evoke the image of Dreyfus's self-representation. They also pervade Kafka's description of "A Hunger Artist" with "his ribs sticking out so prominently" (S, 268) who dies in his cage lined with dirty straw. However, there is another detail in "In the Penal Colony" which requires comment: the torture machine is constructed so that as the stylus inscribes the "lesson" into the body, the body is turned over onto a bed of cotton-wool which enables the lesson to be inscribed yet again. "The Harrow is beginning to write; when it finishes the first draft of the inscription on the man's back, the layer of cotton wool begins to roll and slowly turns the man's body over, to give the Harrow fresh space for writing. Meanwhile the raw part that has been written on lies on the cotton wool, which is specially prepared to stanch the bleeding and so makes all ready for a new deepening of the script" (S, 149). This detail ties the prisoner, and later the officer who is impaled on the malfunctioning machine, to the Jew.

Dreyfus's body is already inscribed when he arrives on Devil's Island. He was the circumcised Jew for, in the mythmaking of the anti-Semites, all male Jews were marked by their physical difference. For the image of the male Jew included his circumcision, and implied the entire debate about the hygiene of this practice, especially *metsitsah*, the sucking of the infant's penis after the removal of the prepuce. Remember that Kafka comments on this practice in his account of circumcision in Russia, where it is "not very pleasant when, after the operation has been performed, they suck the bloody member with this mouth, in the prescribed manner." During the late nineteenth century, the anxiety about the spread of disease through infant male circumcision led to the gradual abolition or modification of this practice among Western Jews. But the mythical association of syphilis with circumcision persisted. In the standard medical handbook on syphilis, written by Jonathan Hutchinson in 1887 and quickly translated into German, he moves away from the *mohel*'s direct transmission of syphilis through *metsitsah*, though still acknowledging it as a potential problem.[54] He describes other practices which transmit syphilis from one Jewish male to another without the intervention of a female. Thus newly circumcised infants are exposed to the blood of infected infants when the *mohel* stores the amputated prepuce in the same container as the lint used to staunch the bleeding.[55] It is the lint which absorbs the infected blood which is thus the source of the illness.

The discourse on circumcision and feminization has a long history among acculturated Western Jews. Spinoza commented on the centrality of circumcision for the definition of the feminized Jewish male. Spinoza's text, often cited and commented on in the late nineteenth century, names circumcision as the primary reason for the survival of the Jews, as "they have incurred universal hatred by cutting themselves off completely from all other peoples." It also made them "effeminate," and thus unlikely to assume a political role in the future.[56] This sense that the marked Jewish male body can never function in "real" society is reflected in the discussion of Jewish chest circumference and in the role that Jewish males are permitted to take in this imagined society. For Kafka, the marking the body, with all of its associations with masculinity and disease, becomes a leitmotif in his representation of the impossibility of social roles. This marking of the body reoccurs in Kafka's "A Country Doctor" in the ill child whose plight calls the eponymous protagonist out "in a thick blizzard of snow" (S, 220). The child patient he finds suffers from an open wound, an ulcer: "in his right side, near the hip, was an open wound as big as the palm of my hand. Rose-red, in many variations of shade, dark in the hollows, lighter at the edges, with irregular clots of blood, open as a surface mine to the daylight" (S, 223). Is this not the tubercular/syphilitic lesion created by the attentions of the diseased *mohel*? It is the transmutation of the biblical leper into the "modern" syphilitic/tubercular. In another sketch, Kafka describes a woman covered with leprous "ulcers" (D1, 286). The cotton lint is also here, for the patient's "sister [comes] fluttering a blood-soaked towel" (S, 223). Clearly there has been a displacement, but the basic pattern of bloodletting and disease is repeated. Circumcision becomes for Kafka the "mark of Cain" that sets the ill Jew apart. Here the doctor and his patient share this role, much like the officer and victim in the penal colony. For the doctor is as much victim as is the patient. At the close of the story he is pictured wandering through the snow, unsure of his direction, of his calling, of his identity.

Throughout Kafka's "In the Penal Colony" there are encrypted references to Dreyfus, torture machines, cotton lint, and sexually transmitted diseases that mark the Jewish male as unable to serve as a soldier. For it is the body with sexually transmitted diseases that cannot be a true soldier (Plate 23). One might note that this association of sexually transmitted diseases and the Jews reappears in Kafka's account in the form of vile rumors concerning Jewish draft dodging during World War I, of Jews avoiding service as "real" men because of illness: "War stories provide many opportunities for . . . [anti-Semitism]; for instance that a sick East European Jew, the evening before his unit was marching to the front, sprayed germs of the clap into the eyes of twelve other Jews; is that possible?" (LF, 237). Here, a Jewish collective avoids service, providing the antithesis to Dreyfus's military dedication, or, seen another way, the embodiment of his imprisonment.

For Kafka, the lesson of the Dreyfus case was that Dreyfus was never truly freed from Devil's Island. He remained the condemned Jew, even with the honors and awards heaped upon him after his innocence was proven. The visitor, like the mythic Wandering Jew, can barely escape the Penal Colony at the close of the tale, but the vision of the eternal repetition of Dreyfus' fate haunts this and other tales by Kafka. The seemingly inevitable transformation of soldier into victim is marked on the prisoners' bodies.

Kafka's own fantasy is full of evocations of Dreyfus. He recounts a dream on August 3, 1917:

> Once more I screamed at the top of my voice into the world. Then they shoved a gag into my mouth, tied my hands and feet and blindfolded me. I was rolled back and forth a number of times, I was set upright and knocked down again, this too several times; they jerked at my legs so I jumped with pain; they let me lie quietly for a moment, but then, taking me by surprise, stabbed deep into me with something sharp, here and there, at random. (D2, 173–174)

This passage evokes both Dreyfus's torture on the island, as well as the cultural fantasy of ritual murder and ritual slaughter that we shall discuss

PLATE 23. A French poster by Théophile-Alexandre Steinen from World War I that warns about the dangers of sexually transmitted diseases undermining the ability of the soldier to fight (Ithaca: Private Collection).

below. But it is the association of pain with elaborate machinery that Kafka takes from the Dreyfus case. In a letter to Milena Jesenská, he provides a description as well as a drawing of his torture machine:

PLATE 24. Kafka's torture machine from a letter to Milena Jesenská in March, 1920. From *Letters to Milena*, trans. Philip Boehm (New York: Schocken, 1990) (Olin Library, Cornell University).

> So you can see how I'm keeping myself "occupied," I'm enclosing a drawing. There are 4 posts, with poles running through the two middles ones to which the "delinquent's" hands are fastened; poles for the feet are run through the two posts on the outside. Once the man is thus secured, the poles are slowly pushed outward until the man is torn apart in the middle. The inventor is leaning against the column with his arms and legs crossed, putting on airs as if the whole thing were his original invention, whereas all he really did was watch the butcher in front of his shop, drawing out a disemboweled pig. (Plate 24) (LM, 201)

Kafka's masochism machine is part rack, part abattoir. It is written in the same cool, distanced style as that of Dreyfus's representation of the rack into which he was fastened nightly. Here both torturer and victim are viewed. Kafka is, of course, both. He is the creator of the machine and the machine's essential victim. But Kafka's reference here to Dreyfus is through his evocation of the unclean, filthy food that drives Dreyfus to the edge of madness as surely as his torture. For Kafka's machine is that of the pork butcher, with all the overtones of ritual uncleanness, not only for Kafka the Jew but for Kafka the food faddist and quasivegetarian. The pig butcher reappears as the image of Kafka's torment. On May 4, 1913, he writes: "Always the image of a pork butcher's broad knife that quickly and with mechanical regularly chops into me from the side and cuts off very thin slices which fly off almost like shavings because of the speed of the action" (D1, 286–287). This is certainly not the kosher butcher selling ritually prepared meat. It is not Jakob Kafka, Hermann Kafka's father, in his butcher shop in the village of Wossek, selling meat prepared according to Halakha. And yet that meat, too, evoked disgust and uncleanness in the adult Kafka's mind: "my paternal grandfather was a butcher in a village near Strakonitz; I have to not eat as much meat as he butchered" (LM, 59).[57] The victim, the torturer, the butcher, and the butcher's knife, which will come to be so important in Kafka's response to ritual murder, are elided. All of these images refer back to the discourse about the uncleanness of pork, of illness, of the imagined torture of Kafka's body, of the nature of the Jew's body, as well as to the idea of inheritance. And yet by evoking the uncleanness of the pork butcher, Kafka is again displacing the discourse of Jewish ritual practice into another world, that of the Christian West and the world of the seemingly acculturated Western Jew.

MENS NON SANA IN CORPORE INSANO

The literary body in "The Penal Colony" is neither Dreyfus's nor Kafka's, but it bears the mark of both insofar as it raises the question of biological predestination. Kafka's sense of such predestination as an inscription on his own body can be judged in yet another text, his "Letter to the Father" (1919), since its publication one of the touchstones of Kafka interpretation, since it so clearly echoes themes from Kafka's fiction. However, despite its confessional form, it is also an elaborate fiction about Kafka's anxiety about his own body's predestination to become his father's. This is not the strong, paternal body, but the ill body of a father who manipulates his illness for his own ends, at his son's expense.

In 1911 Kafka wrote a short autobiography in his diary[58] (D1, 197–198). In it he traces his lineage through the Löwys, his maternal family, which begins with his namesake, his mother's maternal grandfather, Adam (Amschel) Porias (1794–1862), "a very pious and learned man" who "bathed in the river every day, even in winter." (Kafka's Hebrew name is Amschel.) These begats, in the matrilineal Jewish tradition, return to his mother's mother who "died before her time of typhus." Her death at the age of twenty-nine so affected her mother (Franz Kafka's great-grandmother) "that she became melancholy" and committed suicide in 1860. Then comes his mother's grandfather, a miracle rabbi, whose four sons "all died young," except for his namesake Amschel, who was known as "Crazy Uncle Nathan," and one daughter, his mother's mother. One of the brothers converted and became a physician. What Kafka does not mention is that his mother, who had "weeping spells and melancholy," was orphaned at three, and was raised with her two brothers and three half brothers, one of whom, Kafka's Uncle Rudolph, was also a convert. Kafka's father, according to the letter Franz never sent him, agreed that his wife's family was tainted by madness, demonstrated by their apparent hereditary predisposition to a whole range of illnesses for which madness was the master category. For Jews of the time, madness was definitively proven by symptoms such as melancholy or conversion, for only a mad person would try to convert out of a race. Kafka sees himself half-ironically as in that maternal tradition. In a letter to Hedwig Weiler from April 1909 he writes: "If there is anything you want to know about me . . . my mother is due for an operation next week; my father is more and more on the downgrade; my grandfather collapsed unconscious today; and I'm not so well myself" (LF, 53).

Kafka's notion of inheritance is perhaps best documented in his story, "Eleven Sons" (1917), in which the inheritance of illness is central. The sons inherit not only the positive qualities of the parent but also their physical anomalies. The smaller left eye of the second son is equated with a "small irregularity of the spirit . . . a kind of stray poison in the blood. . ." (S, 420). The sixth son is not ill; "his health on the contrary is very good—he sometimes staggers, especially at twilight, but he needs no help, he never falls. Perhaps his physical growth is the cause of this phenomenon, he is much too tall for his age. That makes him look ugly in general, although he has remarkable beauty in detail, in hands and feet, for instance. His forehead, too, is ugly; both its skin and its bone formation are somehow arrested in their development" (S, 421–422). The eleventh son is the frailest, a frailty that masks an inner strength. It is not incidental that there are eleven *sons*. It is the masculinity of the father, which is the equivalent of his Jewishness, which is present in the sons. And along with all of the positive qualities ascribed to this inheritance, Kafka also stresses the pathological—the very form of the body reflects the inheritance from the father.

Yet it is not the illnesses ascribed to his mother's family that form the centerpiece of his concern, but rather his anxiety that he must become his father. He writes on October 16, 1911, "the whole staff gave Father notice. By soft words, cordiality, effective use of his illness, his size and strength, his experience, his cleverness, he wins almost all of them back. . . ." (D1, 97). His father's heart pains haunt his own sense of himself. In the famed passage about the writing of his first great story, "The Judgment," Kafka wrote, on September 23, 1912: "As the maid walked through the anteroom for the first time I wrote the last sentence. Turning out the light and the light of day. The slight pains around my heart" (D1, 276). He feigns "nervousness and cardiac excitability" to quit the job he disliked at the Assicurazioni in July, 1908.[59]

There is a detailed literature that claimed that Jews had a much higher incidence of heart illness, which was nonetheless a vague category in the nineteenth century. The forensic psychiatrist Cesare Lombroso, in his 1894 study of Jews and anti-Semitism, argued that Jews in Verona between 1855 and 1864 showed a nine percent morbidity rate due to heart disease, as against four percent for the general population.[60] Lombroso's explanation was the environment in which they were forced to live, their "passionate temperament, the anxiety of wagering and profit, the force that results from poor living conditions." This mix of predisposition and context was typical of debates about Jews and heart disease, but ultimately the Jewish character, Jewish nervousness, is the deciding factor. According to Martin Engländer, it is the "struggle of modern life, the haste and drive, the hunt for happiness," coupled with the weakness of the Jewish nervous system caused by centuries of oppression, which are at the core of their "nervousness and neurasthenia."[61] According to the German psychiatrist Otto Binswanger, "among the European nations the Jews supply, relatively, the largest contingent of neurasthenics."[62] Even James Jackson Putnam, the leading American specialist in nervous diseases, could claim that without exception "the psychoneuroses in general are particularly common to the Latin and Hebrew races."[63]

This nervousness is represented in Kafka's own struggle with the trope of the inherent instability of the Jew. In February 1911, Kafka writes, "as I was getting out of bed this morning, I simply collapsed, and for a very simple reason, I am badly overworked. Not in the office but because of my other work. . . . To me this means leading a horrible double life, from which madness probably offers the only way out" (D1, 44). In July, 1912,

Kafka spent three weeks at Jungborn Sanitarium because of "a pathological nervous condition manifesting itself in nearly continuous digestive disturbances and sleep problems."[64] (Kafka, like many Central Europeans at the *fin de siècle*, often spent his "holidays" at health spas.) At least, this was his claim when asking for extended leave. He observes his mental state as a sign of his own decline: "Am I in decline? Almost all signs speak for it (coldness, apathy, state of my nerves, distractedness, incompetence on the job, headaches, insomnia); almost nothing but hope speaks against it" (D2, 140). In 1913, he records in his *Diaries* a list of his symptoms: "1. Digestion 2. Neurasthenia 3. Rash 4. Inner insecurity" (D1, 287). The neurasthenia of the Jew, like the Jew's hysteria, is a product of the Jew's inbreeding and the confining spaces of the city in which the Jew has been housed. Indeed, Kafka believes that he has found the cure for his neurasthenia in gardening, until he learns in May of 1913 that the local gardener had committed suicide. On October 6, 1915, he again notes: "Various types of nervousness" (D2, 138).

But in a letter to his fiancée Felice Bauer on November 5, 1912, he attempts to persuade her that his health is fine, that his "nervousness and cardiac excitability" are but the signs of a sensitive soul destined to be a writer: "My heart may be comparatively sound, but for any human heart to stand up to the sorrows of bad writing and the joys of good writing is not easy. I was in sanatoria only on account of my stomach and my general weakness, not forgetting my self-enamored hypochondria. One day I shall have to write at length about all this" (LF, 27). Later, on August 4, 1913, he provides further documentation of the state of his heart: "Lately, however, I have had palpitations, followed by stabs and pains in the region of the heart, which are no doubt caused largely, if not altogether by the unbearable separation from you. But they are also partly due to the fact that I have recently been swimming too much." (LFe, 296). His biographers record how Kafka attempted to alter his body through sports of all types, including swimming.[65] But he could not avert his destiny, which was to become—his father and all that his father represented—the ill Dreyfus, the diseased Jew.

The analogy is not at all forced. For his father had in fact been a soldier. Hermann spent three years in the Austrian army, evidently a high point in his life, quitting the service with the rank of sergeant.[66] Indeed, the image of his father as a healthy soldier haunts even Kafka's dreams. In 1916, he dreams of a regiment of soldiers marching by, whereupon the figure of his father comments in the dream, "One has to see this, as long as one is able. . . ."[67] For Kafka this attribute of the father is literally inscribed on the father's body. In "The Judgment" (1912), in Kafka's account his first "real" piece of writing, the ill father mocks his son in a very specific way. The father may be ill, but in the eyes of the son he is still "a giant of a man" (S, 81). This sickly figure suddenly metamorphoses into his former self when he mocks his son because of his engagement: "'Because she lifted up her skirts,' his father began to flute, 'because she lifted her skirts like this, the nasty creature,' and mimicking her he lifted his skirt so high that one could see the scar on his thigh from his war wound. . . ." (S 85) This "war wound" marks the father's body as the soldier's body, and mocks the son as a male in thrall to a woman and unable to serve. Kafka has the ill father enact the seductive woman's role! The scarred warrior and the feminized male Jew with a high voice merge in the figure of the father. Thus the "son" who later writes to his father in 1919, "You encouraged me, for instance, when I saluted and marched smartly, but I was no future soldier . . ." (L, 120) uses his father's desire to have a soldier as a son in order to draw his own masculinity into question.

The father's unnamed illness in "The Judgment" seems to make him into an invalid. In *The Trial* (1914), the lawyer to whom Joseph K.'s uncle brings him in the dead of the night clearly suffers from a heart condition. K.'s uncle asks immediately upon being told that his friend is ill: "Is it his heart?" (T, 100). When they finally see the lawyer, the uncle attempts to dismiss his illness: "Are you really in a bad way? . . . I can't believe it. It's one of your heart attacks and it'll pass over like all the others." But the lawyer's diagnosis is more pessimistic: "Maybe . . . but it's worse than it's ever been before, I find it difficult to breathe, can't sleep at all, and am losing strength daily." This exchange encapsulates the mythmaking that Kafka is able to spin about heart disease. On the one hand, from the external point of view, it is not truly serious; it happens over and over again, but there is always a recuperation. Indeed, it might really only be a form of hypochondria. Thus it is analogous to the miraculous recuperation of the father in "The Judgment." On the other hand, as seen from within, it is a sign of morbidity, of the decay that will eventually lead to death. The lawyer's description of his symptoms, moreover, ring true as an image of Kafka's own "illness" as well as those symptoms ascribed to his father.

By April, 1916, Kafka was diagnosed as having a "cardiac neurosis," for which the prescribed treatment (which he did not do) was electrotherapy, used for traumatic neurosis at the time.[68] His own reading of his ill body, perhaps already in the first stages of pulmonary tuberculosis, was in terms of mental illness. He writes on September 1,1916: "Since yesterday, after three days remarkably free of headaches, I have been feverish—from the tips of my toes to those of my hair. . . . (My fits of despair send me not through a window, but to a doctor's office.)" (LF, 495). Somatic illness (fever) clarifies the mind (a point that Kafka will make after the first appearance of his pulmonary tuberculosis, as discussed in Chapter Four.) His "neurosis" does not drive him to suicide (as it had a number of his ancestors), but rather manifests itself in somatic form, as hysterical symptoms, for which he seeks treatment (as a Jewish patient) from a physician. He knows, however, that such a course of action cannot change the inevitability of the outcome of his illness unto death.

In the "Letter to the Father" it is inheritance, becoming like his ancestors, but especially like his father, that is at the center of his litany of woes: "(In this, by the way, I have inherited a great deal from you and taken much too good care of my inheritance, without, admittedly, having the necessary counterweights in my own nature, as you have.)" (L, 117–118). Kafka is like his ancestors, but less than they. There has been a decay in his generation. And the sign of this decay is the sickly relationship between mind and body, the sick mind in the sick body, or the sick body caused by the sick mind—*mens non sana in corpore insano*. This is the dominant model of inheritance for Kafka. Inheritance is the curse that his father recognizes. His father condemns his grandson, Felix (Kafka's nephew), when ". . . he does anything that is in your opinion unclean, you are not content to say to him, as you used to say to me: 'You are a pig,' but add: 'a real Hermann' or 'just like your father'" (L 125). Kafka's fear is that he will become "just like his father," the parvenu with "unclean" table manners (L, 124). The image of the pig, tortured in Kafka's place in his nightmares, is the Jew. Here is a further intrusion of Devil's Island and the penal colony into the domestic sphere. Kafka is the "pig" and his father, the "pig butcher." This is the powerful father, a proud soldier like Dreyfus, who haunts Kafka's nightmares.

Kafka sees himself as a poor combination of the worst qualities of both sides of his family:

> I . . . a Löwy with a certain Kafka component which, however, is not set in motion by the Kafka will to life, business, and conquest, but by a Löwyish spur that impels more secretly, more diffidently, and in another direction, and which often fails to work entirely. You, on the other hand, a true Kafka in strength, health, appetite, loudness of voice, eloquence, presence of mind, knowledge of human nature, a certain way of doing things on a grand scale. . . . (L, 117)

His younger sister Ottla, who rebels against her parents with Franz's support, on the other hand, is "a kind of Löwy, equipped with the best Kafka weapons" (L, 141), namely Hermann Kafka's "strength, health, appetite, loudness of voice, eloquence, presence of mind, knowledge of human nature, a certain way of doing things on a grand scale." This is the ideal which Kafka projects onto his father in order to imagine himself to have this potential, but his own body seems to have decayed next to his father's imagined health. When bathing, Kafka feels himself to be "a little skeleton, unsteady, barefoot on the boards." The image of a skeleton with bare feet encapsulates all the contradictions in the discourse about the male Jewish body, acutely aware that it is being read for signs of difference: "I felt best when you sometimes undressed first and I was able to stay behind in the hut and put off the disgrace of showing myself in public . . . I was grateful to you for not seeming to notice my anguish, and besides, I was proud of my father's body" (L, 121). Kafka himself is a sickly survivor, whose ". . . brothers died when they were small" (L, 117).

But there is a counterweight to this image, and that is the image of Kafka's father as the sick Jew. Like Dreyfus, the father's strength is revealed to have crumbled. Kafka documents his image of the father as an ill Jew. He records his father's complaints to him: "I have never come to you when you were in the synagogue, never visited you in Franzenbad," where his heart condition was being treated (L, 115). Even among the ill, he appears healthy: "In fact, in the group photographs taken at Franzenbad, for instance, you always looked big and jolly, among those sulky little people, as a king on his travels" (L, 144). Kafka has him accounting for his "imperious temperament": "In recent years you have been explaining this as due to your nervous heart condition. I don't know that you were ever essentially different. Rather, the nervous heart condition is a means by which you exert your domination more strongly" (L, 126). Here there is no question of the "reality" of the father's heart condition—he is truly ill in Kafka's representation—but he still appears more healthy than the "really" ill. The ambivalent representation of his father's heart condition represents his desire for a powerful father (whom he fears) and a sickly father (whom he fears to become). In addition, the heart condition comes to be an explanation for the erratic mental state of the father.

Kafka presents his own "heart condition," or at least the feigned "nervousness and cardiac excitability" by means of which he quit his job at the Assicurazioni in July 1908, as the result of his identification of his former employer with his ill but still abusive father: ". . . you gradually began to terrify me on all sides . . . the way you treated the staff. . . . I don't know, perhaps it was the same in most businesses (in the Assicurazioni Generali, for instance, in my time it was really similar, and the explanation I gave the director for my resignation was, though not strictly in accordance with the truth, still not entirely a lie: my not being able to bear the cursing and swearing, which incidentally had not actually been directed at me; it was something to which I had become too painfully sensitive from home)" (L, 136). But the father's abuse is not random—it falls on those hirelings whom he feels are not carrying their weight in the business: "your constant complaint about a clerk with TB: 'The sooner that sick dog croaks the better.' You called the employees 'paid enemies'" (L, 136). Here the weak heart from which Kafka did not suffer is replaced with tuberculosis. This tactic is unmistakable in the fall of 1917. On August 29, 1917, Kafka writes to his sister Ottla about his first bout with tuberculosis. In this letter, as we shall discuss in more detail in Chapter Four, Kafka begins to structure his tuberculosis as part of an inherited predisposition to mental illness rather than to somatic disease. Madness is the illness he inherited from his mother's family. Yet on September 2, 1917, he writes to Ottla that he has closed his "cold, stale, ill-smelling" apartment, an act that he compares to dying, and had moved back with his parents. His coughing has become the prime symptom of his tuberculosis, and he lies awake in his parent's apartment where "the door to the bedroom [was] left open so that I could hear Father coughing. Poor Father, poor Mother, poor Franz" (LO, 20). The father's heart condition has suddenly become marked by his coughing: Kafka has reshaped his father's illness to match his own symptoms.

Kafka maintained that all his illness was the result of his nervousness, an inherited hypochondria culminating in real illness, as real as the heart disease of his father:

> . . . the worry about my health; it began imperceptibly enough, with now and then a little anxiety about digestion, hair falling out, a spinal curvature, and so on; intensifying in innumerable gradations, it finally ended with a real illness. But since there was nothing at all I was certain of, since I needed to be provided at every instant with a new confirmation of my existence, since nothing was in my very own, undoubted sole possession, determined unequivocally only by me—in sober truth a disinherited son—naturally I became unsure even to the thing nearest to me, my own body. I shot up, tall and lanky, without knowing what to do with my lankiness, the burden was too heavy, the back became bent; I scarcely dared to move, certainly not to exercise, I remained weakly; I was amazed by everything I could still command as if by a miracle, for instance, my good digestion; that sufficed to lose it, and now the way was open to every sort of hypochondria; until finally under the strain of the superhuman effort of wanting to marry (of this I shall speak later), blood came from the lung, something in which the apartment in the Schönborn Palais—which, however, I needed only because I believed I needed it for my writing, so that even this belongs here under the same heading—may have had a fair share. So all this did not come from excessive work, as you always imagine. There were years in which, in perfectly good health, I lazed away more time on the sofa than you in all your life, including all your illnesses. (L, 152)

The son's response to his illnesses, including his tuberculosis, cannot match the father's in his forbearance. What should be a narrative of illness is actually a narrative of acting ill out of psychic necessity. It is a narrative of hypochondriasis, notwithstanding Kafka's very "real" tuberculosis. This is the story of the Jewish patient, whose anxiety is located in the body, but whose real source is the social displacement felt by Jew's in *fin-de-siècle* European society.

The "illnesses" of Kafka's childhood, from the dyspepsia to spinal curvature, mark his body as a diseased Jewish body. Now the theme of Kafka's letter is his anxiety about becoming his father, that is, becoming Jewish: "Jewish schoolboys in our country tend to be odd" (L, 151). Indeed, Kafka attributes his special perceptual gifts to this nervousness: as a child, he had been "acutely observant from sheer nervousness" (L, 148). He describes even his religious observances in terms of the congenital weakness attributed to the nervous *fin-de-siècle* Jew. Religious feeling at home was "confined to the first Seder, which more and more developed into a farce, with fits of hysterical laughter, admittedly under the influence of the growing children . . ." (L, 147). Hysteria characterized the response of the children to the idea of ritual, especially a child, like Franz, already understood as nervous. This is the nervousness, inherited along with his faith from his mother, capable only of a "few flimsy gestures . . . little souvenirs of earlier times" (L, 148). Furthermore: "As a child I reproached myself, in accord with you for not going to the synagogue often enough, for not fasting and so on" (L, 146). The refusal to attend synagogue is a sign of the changing manners of the westernized Jew. His father's atrocious table manners distinguish him as a partially acculturated westernized Jew. All of this is again little more than the "historical character" of contemporary Prague Jewry. But the idea of Judaism as a "gastronomic cult," so Ludwig Feuerbach's claim that the Jews see the world through their stomachs, is part and parcel of the idea of the Jew in the cultural realm of Prague.

The role of the father as a young *author's* ancestor is also important. Conventional wisdom at the turn of the century held that Jewish families were ill. Theodor Gomperz, a leading philologist of the late nineteenth century, could write in 1886 to his sister, "looking around our family circle, there are not too many bright points. Nearly everywhere, at the least, irritable and excited nerves—the inheritance of a very old civilized race and of the urban life."[69] The literary antidote to this inheritance was to be high culture. So it is in books that Kafka seeks a "healthy" father and a "healthy" son. Hermann Kafka reads Benjamin Franklin's memoirs, which his son gave him, "because of the relationship between the author and his father, as it is there described" (L, 149). In the German edition available at the time, Franklin's father is introduced wisely talking the younger Franklin out of a wasted life as a poet and writer, and persuading him to become a printer instead.[70] The healthy father persuades his young son to do precisely what Kafka has no desire for—to take part in mundane reality as a replacement for the world of words.

The key for Kafka seems to be marriage, the ability to have children of his own, yet this is impossible: "I would have a family. . . . I would be your equal" (L, 162). To marry a Jewish woman would be to perpetuate the curse of the Jewish body; to marry outside of the group would be a sure sign of madness and degeneracy. For to be less than his father means to inherit all of his flaws and inexorably build upon them: "It is as if a person were a prisoner, and he had not only the intention to escape, which would perhaps be attainable, but also, and indeed simultaneously, the intention to rebuild the prison as a pleasure dome for himself. But if he escapes, he cannot rebuild and if he rebuilds he cannot escape" (L, 162). Here the world of Dreyfus, of the prisoner, reappears as the model of the narcissistic Jew.

Kafka's discourse of decay, even in the light of apparent gains by acculturated Jewish children against the older, Eastern European adults, is riddled with contradictions. The children are weaker, more nervous, less masculine than their sick parents. All of the apparent physical acculturation cannot mask the predisposition of the children to becoming Jews. This is a common theme in the culture of the time. It is the theme of Thomas Mann's novel of the degeneracy of the Lübeck patricians, *Buddenbrooks* (1901), which for European Jews reversed a powerful myth. For if the patricians of Lübeck were sliding down the slippery slope of modernity toward degeneration and eventual disappearance, European Jews had only very recently begun to believe that they were climbing that very slope.

By the latter half of the nineteenth century, Western European Jews believed themselves to have become indistinguishable from other Western Europeans in matters of language, dress, occupation, location of their dwellings, and the cut of their hair. Indeed, if Rudolf Virchow's extensive study of over ten thousand German school children published in 1886 was accurate, they were also indistinguishable in terms of skin, hair, and eye color from the greater masses of those who lived in Germany.[71] Virchow's statistics sought to show that wherever a greater percentage of the overall population had lighter skin or bluer eyes or blonder hair there a greater percentage of Jews also had lighter skin or bluer eyes or blonder hair. But although Virchow attempted to provide a rationale for the sense of Jewish acculturation, he still assumed that Jews were a separate and distinct racial category. George Mosse has commented: "The separateness of Jewish schoolchildren, approved by Virchow, says something about the course of Jewish emancipation in Germany. However rationalized, the survey must have made Jewish schoolchildren conscious of their minority status and their supposedly different origins."[72] Nonetheless, even though they were labeled as different, Jews came to parallel the scale of types found elsewhere in European society.

A similar shift in the perception of the Jewish body can be found in the twentieth century in the United States. In 1910 the famed German

Jewish anthropologist (and the founder of modern American anthropology) Franz Boas authored a detailed report for Congress on the "Changes in Bodily Form of Descendants of Immigrants."[73] This report documented the change in body size, cephalic index, even hair color of the offspring of Jews, Sicilian, and Neapolitan immigrants born in the United States. Unlike their siblings born abroad, first-generation immigrants were bigger, had greater brain capacity, and lighter hair color. Boas attempted to argue that racial qualities, even to the color of hair, change when the environment shifted and that racial markers were at least to some degree mutable. Needless to say, this view was contested in the science of his time—arguments against this view ranged from the impact being merely the shift from rural to urban life to the reversal of the "degenerate" types which developed in Europe and the reemergence of the "pure" and therefore healthier original European types. The image that there could be a "new human race" evolving under American conditions startled European scientists. But it was not only that these Eastern European Jewish immigrants were physically becoming more and more like other Americans, they were also growing into American culture.[74] As the body type altered, their culture also changed.

In Europe, however, being physically bigger than one's parents did not necessarily meaning being better. One powerful reading of the meaning of this shift in the body—becoming taller and smarter than one's parents—was that this was a sign of degeneration. It is the "early mature, super-intelligent, physically mostly extraordinarily developed children" who will quickly wilt and enter into the decline of the degenerate.[75] Premature maturity and seemingly "healthy" growth is a sign of the gradual decline of a people, whose decline of population will soon become evident. Kafka's body is thus both a sign of potential positive but also of potential negative development. The signs that it sends its possessor are contradictory. The state's "cure" for such seemingly healthy individuals, whose presence places the entire society at risk, is to isolate them on islands, where they will be forced to work and will be restrained from reproducing. These islands, according to a contemporary commentator, must be humane, unlike the French penal colonies such as Devil's Island.[76] Only such moves will lead to the eventual regeneration of the race and the elimination of such maladaptive individuals from society.

By the beginning of the twentieth century, at least for a number of westernized Jews, the very opposite seemed to be happening. Jews were reverting to the illnesses of their ancestors, their birthrate was declining, and because of their biological predisposition they were increasingly unable to deal with the pressures of modern life, thus becoming neurasthenic or hysteric. Kafka's "heart" trouble was a sign of his internalization of the image of the Jew's physical decay. His body was also his father's body. But unlike his father, whose aging first reveals his weakness, Kafka's body was marked from before his birth as ill.

three

Males On Trial

Trials and Tribulations

Was Franz Kafka a real man? George Mosse has described "the idealization of masculinity as the foundation of the nation and society."[1] A failure to be "masculine" is seen in the national arena as pathological. I would add that the pathologization of the male Jew's body is also his feminization. Of course, "masculinity" is a complex and even contradictory construction, as will become clear in my analysis of the Dreyfus Affair. What is striking are its similarities to the blood libel cases that loomed so large in Kafka's world. On precisely this analogy, contemporaries such as Richard Lichtheim considered the Dreyfus case a sign of "how deep the old Jew hatred is rooted in the 'people' [*Volk*]."[2] We will see how Kafka's anxiety about such accusations is at the same time an anxiety about "masculinity."

Acculturated Jews in Central Europe relied on stable political and social structures for their identity, indeed their physical safety. When the stability of these boundaries was drawn into question, to whom could a Jew turn? Denounced suddenly, arrested, and tortured, would he be like Alfred Dreyfus, steadfastly protesting his innocence, or would he recant, like Shabbethai Tzevi (1626–1676)? Tzevi declared himself the Messiah, was eventually arrested by Turkish authorities, and converted rather than face execution. His followers believed the conversion to be part of his Messianic trial. It is of little surprise that there was an increased fascination with these aspects of Jewish history among acculturated Central European Jews at the beginning of the twentieth century. Gershom Gerhard Scholem's work, begun in the late 1920s, argued that the integration of Jewry into Western culture began with Tzevi rather than with the Enlightenment. For Scholem, it was Tzevi's action that marked the beginning of the deleterious movement toward assimilation and conversion of European Jewry.[3] Conversion merges into acculturation for Scholem. These were two fantasy solutions to the Jewish anxiety about the collapse of "good enough authority."[4] Both masochistically combine self-assertion and self-denial. On the one hand, the brave Dreyfus never acknowledges his Jewishness; on the other hand, the apparent coward Shabbethai Tzevi came to be seen by some of his followers as the hidden Messiah, the essential Jew. Betrayal becomes affirmation, and *vice versa*. In the face of such paradoxes, how can one show that one is a "real man"?

The Dreyfus Affair reached its peak with the Dreyfus trial, and the trial violated the promise of stability that had grown out of the elementary principles of the Enlightenment. No group had internalized these principles more than the acculturated European Jews, for their entire sense of place in European society depended on them. Hannah Arendt noted that:

> The Dreyfus case, the various trials of the Jewish Captain Alfred Dreyfus, are quite typical of the nineteenth century, when men followed legal proceedings so keenly because each instance afforded a test of the century's greatest achievement, the complete impartiality of the law. It is characteristic of the period that a miscarriage of justice could arouse such political passions and inspire such an endless succession of trials and retrials, not to speak of duels and fisticuffs. The doctrine of equality before the law was still so firmly implanted in the conscience of the civilized world that a single miscarriage of justice could provoke public indignation from Moscow to New York.[5]

Dreyfus's conviction thus defined a rupture in the Enlightenment itself for some Jews, such as the *Viennese Free Press*'s crack reporter at the trial, Theodor Herzl. This is the same violation that Kafka's Josef K. experiences at the very beginning of *The Trial*: "K. lived in a country with a legal constitution, there was universal peace, all the laws were in force; who dared seize him in his own dwelling?" (T, 4). Despite this rupture, most acculturated Jews expected Dreyfus, clearly innocent, to be exonerated at his second trial, a show trial held at Rennes in 1899. Nonetheless, he was again convicted and sentenced to ten years. The President of France finally had to overturn this parody of justice by unconditionally pardoning Dreyfus in 1906.

The conception of the trial of law as an affirmation of order was destroyed. The best-known Yiddish writer of the day, Shalom Aleichem, depicted the dislocation felt by Jews reading newspaper accounts of the Dreyfus trial in his prototypical *shtetl*, Kasrilevka.[6] There the sole means of learning about the progress of the case is the newspaper to which the local secular intellectual, Zeidel, subscribes. The Jews are amazed by such an ugly thing happening " . . . in Paris: It didn't do any credit to the French" (272). Toward the end of Dreyfus's retrial, the Jews of Kasrilevka awaited the expected innocent verdict at Zeidel's doorstep. The guilty verdict caused an outcry against Zeidel:

> "It cannot be!" Kasrilevka shouted with one voice. "Such a verdict is impossible! Heaven and earth swore that the truth must prevail. What kind of lies are you telling us?"
>
> "Fools!" shouted Zeidel, and thrust the paper into their faces. "Look! see what the paper says!"
>
> "Paper! paper!" shouted Kasrilevka. "And if you stood with one foot in heaven and the other on earth, would we believe you?"
>
> "Such a thing must not be. It must never be! Never! Never! Never!"
>
> And—who was right? (273)

Problems of textual representation thus became the focus for Jewish readers. Who is to be believed, the witness to the truth, whose testimony clearly defies belief, or the world as it must be? There had been a link between the text as the locus of Enlightenment reason and the trial as a testing ground of its principles. That link is the witness, and he happens to be always male, like Zeidel with his newspaper. This is the essential problem of *The Trial* (1914–15): "someone must have been telling lies (*verleumdet*) about Josef. K., for without having done anything wrong he was arrested one fine morning" (T, 1). The controversy of his trial and the authorities who eventually condemn him to being slaughtered "like a dog" all revolve about the opening problem—who betrayed him before the very opening of the novel? What false witness denounced this petty bureaucrat living his peaceful, repetitive life? At the end of the novel,

Josef K.'s guilt or innocence is unresolved, but the question of false testimony also remains unresolved.

Dreyfus had suffered not only in body, but in spirit. His conviction had broken the promise of Jewish integration into Western culture. However, this integration impinged again on the representation of the male Jewish body. Nowhere was his integration more problematic than in that essentially masculine component of the nation where the antithesis between national and Jewish identity was most clearly defined, namely the military. In Arthur Schnitzler's psychogram of the Austrian officer, *Leutnant Gustl*, which appeared in 1901, the same year as Thomas Mann's *Buddenbrooks*, the simple-minded protagonist considers Jews incapable of the soldierly bearing that defines the real man. Yet they are everywhere in his society, capable of corrupting it with their presence alone: "Oh, what a nose!—Jewess . . . .Another one. It's amazing, half of them are Jews. One can't even hear an oratorio unmolested these days."[7] Debates about the Jewish presence in the military in France, Germany, and Austro-Hungary turned on the distinction between the healthy, male body, fit to be a citizen-soldier, and the sickly, effeminate body which was not. At the same time, an ever-growing number of Jews wanted to become members of the officer corps. The debate about chest circumference, outlined in the second chapter, certainly overlaps with this other debate. This is the context of the real anxieties which we find in displaced form in the texts of Jewish writers.

Kafka frequently represented his body as that of a soldier, but this body is always attenuated. According to his application for employment at the Assicurazioni Generali on October 2, 1906, Kafka claimed an exemption from military service "due to weakness."[8] Yet his exclusion, even desire for exclusion, did not preclude him from fantasizing about his body as that of a soldier. On October 3, 1910, he comments thus about his chronic insomnia: "While falling asleep a vertically moving pain in my head over the bridge of the nose, as though from a wrinkle too sharply pressed into my forehead. To make myself as heavy as possible, which I consider good for falling asleep, I had crossed my arms and laid my hands on my shoulders, so that I lay there like a soldier with his pack" (D1, 75–76). The healthy, sleeping soldier's body stands in for the sickly Kafka who cannot sleep.

Once World War I actually begins, Kafka is carried on the reserve rolls of the 28th Royal and Imperial Infantry Regiment. In June, 1915, and again June, 1916, he was found fit for active duty, but was not released from his position at the Workmen's Accident Insurance Institute for the Kingdom of Bohemia in Prague because he was considered "indispensable" in this war work (AS, 402–405). On May 11, 1916, he discussed a long leave with the director of his Institute:

> Asked for a long leave later on, without pay of course, in the event that the war should end by fall; or, if the war goes on, for my exemption to be canceled. It was a complete lie. . . . He said nothing at all about the army, as though there had been nothing in my letter about it. . . . [He] made incidental remarks in the role of a lay psychiatrist, as does everyone. . . . I was weak, though I knew that it was almost a life-and-death matter for me. But insisted that I wanted to join the army and that three weeks were not enough. Whereupon he put off the rest of the discussion. If he were only not so friendly and concerned!" (D2, 153).

Kafka's conflicted desire to serve and not to serve is complex.

Even when his tuberculosis becomes manifest in 1917, this imagery does not cease. On October 12, 1917, he writes to Max Brod: "Where would I crawl off to, when all the big guns start booming, with my toy pistol of a lung?" (LF, 156). He now understands his tuberculosis as part of a war, a war that cannot be won with the present tactics. He writes to Max Brod from the sanitarium at Matliary in April, 1921: "I am willing to believe that tuberculosis will be controlled; every disease will ultimately be controlled. It is the same with wars—each one will come to its end but none ever stops. Tuberculosis no more has its origin in the lungs than, for example, the World War had its cause in the ultimatum. There is only a single disease, no more, and medicine blindly chases down this one disease as though hunting a beast in endless forests" (LF, 275). By 1920, this sense of his body as a soldier's body continues, but now in service to his illness. He writes to Milena Jesenská on August 26, 1920: "For a few days now I have been performing my 'military service'—or more correctly 'maneuvers,' which is sometimes the best thing for me, as I discovered years ago. In the afternoon I sleep in bed as long as I can, then walk around for two hours, then stay awake as long as I can" (LM, 169). It is not surprising that Kafka, writing in the context of the "War to End All Wars" would revert to military metaphors and allusions, but this language should be understood in the light of a discourse that incorporates qualities of his sense of his male, Jewish, and afflicted body.

The soldier's body is certainly not the nervous, diseased body of the

Jewish male. Yet Kafka's body becomes a battlefield on which a different war takes place. Max Nordau's often-cited call for the Jews to become "muscle Jews," published in 1900, responded to the commonplaces about Jewish effeminacy.[9] For Nordau, the reform of the Jew's body would reform his mind, and finally his discourse. Nordau's title recalls the "Muscular Christianity" of the late nineteenth century, with its advocacy of regular exercise to improve the body and to control "lascivious thinking." Nordau's Zionism also shares with German nationalism the code of *mens sana in corpore sano*. The legacy of Friedrich "*Turnvater*" Jahn, a father of German nationalism, had been heavily mixed with anti-Semitism since the founding of the Second *Reich*. Nordau's demand from within Zionism that the Jews reform their bodies is yet another adaptation of an element of anti-Semitic rhetoric for Jewish ends. His call for a "new muscle Jew" is intended as the antidote to centuries of Jewish degeneration, physical and mental, "in the narrow confines of the ghetto." The "new Jews" must purge their bodies of the diseases of the past. Implicit in Nordau's call is the condemnation of the "old" Jew's attitude toward life. Zionism demands that the new muscle Jew have a healthy body and a healthy mind. Thus Nordau condemns his critics as not only having weak bodies but weak minds! In the inner circles of the Zionist movement, opponents were typically accused of possessing the qualities, including madness, that anti-Semites ascribed to them. Nordau's call echoed loudly in Prague, where Kafka had been training his body. His friend Felix Weltsch writes in *Self-Defense* (*Selbstwehr*) that the Jews must "shed our heavy stress on intellectual preeminence . . . and our excessive nervousness, a heritage of the ghetto. . . . We spend all too much of our time debating, and not enough time in play and gymnastics. . . . What makes a man a man is not his mouth, nor his mind, nor yet his morals, but discipline. . . . What we need is manliness."[10] Of course, manliness is healthiness.

One sign of the Jew's inability to be a soldier is his foot, as much as his small chest.[11] At the turn of the century, when more and more Jews were actually becoming soldiers and officers, the charge that the flat feet of the Jews made it impossible for them to fulfill their masculine role in the new nation-state became important.

If Kafka's internalization of his father's heart ailment is finally his internalization of certain standard tropes about the Jew's body, his image of the foot is part of his more generalized image of the Jewish male, along with his small chest as a sign of his difference, his effeminacy. He links these particular signs in a letter of July, 1916, to Max Brod, about a visit to a Hasidic miracle rabbi: "Outside the rabbi walks with difficulty; one of his legs, the right one, gives him trouble. He also must have a good cough, while his followers stand respectfully around him" (LF 122).

Kafka's feet increasingly prevent him from undertaking the strenuous physical activity that he needs to reform and transform his body, a hopeless task given the persistence of the Jew's body. In early October, 1910, he dislocates his big toe (LF, 67). He writes, "The foot in particular is enormously swollen—but it is not very painful. It is well bandaged and will improve" (LF, 67). The physical foot may improve, but Kafka's symbolic foot never will: it will inexorably become the limping foot of the miracle rabbi. It represents an inability to be a real man. It is a sign of the Jew, the devil, and the cripple: "I frightened Gerti [Kafka's young niece] by limping; the horror of the club foot"[12] (D2 140). The limping Jew is the evil Jew.

The limping foot is conspicuous in anti-Semitic discourse of the time. In Oskar Panizza's *fin-de-siècle* drama, *The Council of Love*, the Devil appears as a Jewish male, his corruption written on every aspect of his body, including his foot: "The Devil stands before them, leaning on one foot and supporting the other with his hands. He wears a black, close-fitting costume, is very slender, close-shaven with a fine-cut face, but his features wear an expression that is decadent, worn, embittered. He has a yellowish complexion. His manners recall those of a Jew of high breeding. He leans on one foot, the other is drawn up."[13] The "yellowish" skin color, the limping leg, the degeneracy of the Jew form Panizza's image of the seducer of humankind. His limping signifies his Jewish illness and effeminacy.

His yellow, "Oriental" skin is also part of the standard image of the diseased Jew. Johann Jakob Schudt, Günther's seventeenth-century authority, cited the male Jews' physical form as diseased and repellent: ". . . among several hundred of their kind he had not encountered a single person without a blemish or other repulsive feature: for they are either pale and yellow or swarthy." [14] Schudt saw the diseases of the Jews as a reflex of their "Jewishness," their stubborn refusal to acknowledge the truth of Christianity. But the yellow skin reappears two centuries later as a marker of the ill Jewish male. Otto Weininger, the quintessential Jewish self-hater of the turn of the century, stressed that Jews "possess a certain anthropological relationship with both Negroes and Mongolians."[15] From the former, they get their "readily curling hair," from the latter, their "yellowish complexion." This yellow skin color later marks the bearded "friend in Russia" in Kafka's tale "The Judgment" (1913), whose "skin was growing so yellow as to indicate some latent disease" (77). He bears the symptoms associated with the diseased Jew, including his skin color. "Even three years ago he was yellow enough to be thrown away" (S, 87). This "yellowness" suggests the jaundice that signals a number of "Oriental" illnesses, such as malaria and thalassemia.

This parallels the more standard trope of the "swarthiness" or "blackness" of the Jew's skin. In 1923, Joseph Roth, perhaps the most important Jewish novelist writing in German whose origin was in the Yiddish-speaking areas of Eastern Europe, described the Jewish protagonist of his piece in the Viennese *Workers' News* as "black."[16] Likewise, writing to Milena Jesenská in 1920, Kafka can comment quite casually, "naturally for your father there's no difference between your husband and myself; there's no doubt about it, to the European we both have the same Negro face" (LM, 136). When the non-Jewish writer Jesenská herself turns, in 1938, to write about the persecution of the Jews and other minority peoples of Central Europe by the Germans, she writes about them as "the Negroes of Europe."[17] In what was more than an analogy, Jews understood themselves as "black," another marker of their predisposition to disease. (Plate 25) In his use of this trope, Kafka selects the image of the Jew as "Oriental," as the individual bearing the stigmata of illness, rather than as the image of the politically liminal figure (the Jew as black). Kafka's displacement is an important one, as it places the marginal nature of the ill and the Jew as qualities essentially in the body, rather than qualities superimposed on the body by its political and social context. For Kafka the Jew is truly ill, rather than having been forced to see him or herself as ill.

All aspects of the Jewish body are represented as pathological, from the skin to the feet. The limping Jew is a sign of the exclusion of the Jewish male from qualities associated with the masculine at the *fin de siècle*.[18] Panizza's Devil as Jew as Devil clearly limps:

> The Devil turns on his right heel, smiles sardonically, and shrugs his shoulders. He feigns regret. Very much the Jewish merchant. A painful moment. . . .

PLATE 25. The male Jew and the male African are seen as equivalent dangers to the "white" races in the anti-Semitic literature of the late nineteenth century. From Eduard Schwechten's parody of Schiller's "Song of the Bell," *Das Lied vom Levi* (1895), drawings by Siegfried Horn (reprint: Düsseldorf: J. Knippenberg, 1933) (Source: Private Collection, Ithaca).

> MARY: By the way how is your foot?
>
> THE DEVIL: Oh, so-so! No better! But no worse, actually! Oh, god! (Hitting his shorter leg a blow.). There's no change any more! Blasted thing!
>
> MARY (in a lower voice): Your fall did that?
>
> (The Devil, not reacting, is silent for a while; then he nods gravely.) (91–92)

The limping Devil and the limping Jew are interchangeable at the turn of the century: both are understood within a secularized (for Panizza, anti-Christian) model of the Jewish disavowal of Christ's divinity. At the *fin de siècle*, it is the syphilitic who limps, as the Parisian neurologist Joseph Babinski showed in 1896, when he proved that a diminished plantar reflex was a sign of neurosyphilis. But the symbolic association of Jewish or Satanic limping with syphilitic limping was already well established in the culture of the late nineteenth century, by means of the intermediate image of the "yellow" skin of the Jew.

Panizza's Devil's limping reveals him to be a syphilitic Jew. He thus prefigures the central theme of the play—the introduction of syphilis into the Europe of the Renaissance. He is already infected with his "disease," his Jewishness, and he will presumably spread it by using the Jews as intermediaries. Syphilis was actually considered a Jewish disease as early as its first modern outbreak in the fifteenth century, and Panizza as well presents it as such, personified in a Jewish, male Devil.[19]

The disease that pervades the Jew is found in his blood. "Blood is a very special fluid," as Mephisto observes in Goethe's *Faust I*, especially for the Central European Jew at the *fin de siècle.* (It is in blood that illness as well as the potential for cure seem to be located at the turn of the century. Thus it is no accident that Emil von Behring closes his basic essay on diphtheria with this quote from Goethe.[20]) And it is blood that presents the next trial of the Jew and his sense of control over his body. Syphilis is the means—according to the anti-Semitic literature of the early twentieth century—through which the Jew corrupts the Aryan. This view is to be found in Adolf Hitler's discussion of syphilis in *fin-de-siècle* Vienna in *My Struggle* (1925). Like his Viennese compatriot, Bertha Pappenheim, the original of Josef Breuer's patient, Anna O.,[21] but with a very different intent, he links it to the Jew, the prostitute, and the power of money:

> Particularly with regard to syphilis, the attitude of the nation and the state can only be designated as total capitulation. . . . The invention of a remedy of questionable character and its commercial exploitation can no longer help much against this plague. . . . The cause lies, primarily, in our prostitution of love. . . . This Jewification of our spiritual life and mammonization of our mating instinct will sooner or later destroy our entire offspring.[22]

Hitler's views also linked Jews with prostitutes and the spread of infection. Jews were the archpimps; Jews ran the brothels; but Jews also infected their prostitutes and caused the weakening of the German national fiber.[23] But Hitler also associates Jews with the false promise of a "medical" cure separate from the social "cures" that he wishes to impose—isolation and separation of the syphilitic from the body politic. Hitler believes that the fields of dermatology and syphilology were especially dominated by Jews, who used their medical status to sell quack cures.

The notion that the Jews' disease is written on their skin is echoed again in Kafka's image of his own body. His image is at bottom the Viennese Jew's image of the Eastern Jew and his Eastern diseases, such as the fabled *Judenkrätze*, the skin and hair disease also attributed to the Poles as *plica polonica*.[24] When one sees such Eastern Jews, there can be no question that they suffer from Jewishness. In the eighteenth century, Joseph Rohrer, stresses the "disgusting skin diseases" of the Jew as a sign of the group's general infirmity.[25] The essential Jew for the Bavarian traveler to Vienna, Johannes Pezzl, even worse than the Polish Jew, is the Galician Jew from the Eastern reaches of the Hapsburg Empire.[26] This theme reappears in Arthur Schopenhauer's mid-nineteenth century evocation of the Jews as "a sneaking dirty race afflicted with filthy diseases (scabies) that threaten to prove infectious."[27]

The eruption of such a skin disease feminizes Kafka. In the fall of 1910, he goes to Paris, a city always associated with sexuality, but for German-speaking Jews of Kafka's time, with the image of the syphilitic Heinrich Heine. On October 8, on the way to Paris, he develops an attack of *furunculosis*, which forces him to abort his trip. This intense, painful, and for the time dangerous skin disease focuses his anxieties about his own body. On October 20, 1910, in Prague again, he writes to Max and Otto Brod, who are still in Paris:

> A brief fainting spell deprived me of the pleasure of shouting at the doctor. I had to lie down on his sofa, and during that time—it was very odd—I felt so much like a girl that I tried with my fingers to tug down my skirt. For the rest, the doctor declared himself horrified by the appearance of my backside; the five new abscesses are no longer important since a skin eruption has appeared that is worse than all the abscesses, will take a long time to heal, and is and will be the real cause of the pain. (LF, 67)

The backside scarred by ulcers signifies the leprous wife for Kafka: "The leper and his wife: The way her behind—she is lying in bed on her belly—keeps rising up with all its ulcers again and again although a guest is present. The way her husband keeps shouting at her to keep covered" (D1, 286). Here the question of being infected rather than infecting, of being the female as infected patient rather than the male as agent of infection, is tied to the notion of a "skin disease." This anxiety about the body diseased reverses the "normal" perspective of the male. But this should not surprise. The hyper-conscious Jewish male, aware that he is "infected" already, that his masculinity is in doubt because of the very nature of the body, seeks out the role of the woman. This sense of the body at risk for those diseases hidden within reappears when Kafka is confronted with diseases that have a powerful association for him. He senses that "you are what you are fated to become"—the diseased, syphilitic female who endangers male society.

Over and over again Kafka experiences his body as the showplace of a trial. It is a place where the betrayal of the body reveals it to be the antithesis of the soldier's body. But even the Jewish soldier is at risk. Kafka's sense of his body as a battlefield reflects the trope of the illness of the Jewish body as the reflection of millennia of persecution and the attendant ills. It is a body marked by repeated losses of "good enough" authority, the illusion of a stable world and a "healthy" (unchanging) body. Not only the state, with Dreyfus's body, but even Hermann Kafka's body seems to be in decay. Kafka's father, once strong and glorying in his military service, becomes an old, sick man with a chronic (perhaps hypochondriacal) heart condition. Kafka's body, like his father's, is diseased in ways that externalize his felt loss of masculinity as his society defined it. His body does not know whether it is condemned to have Dreyfus's fate, or simply to collapse into a myriad of diseases, all of which reveal his essential effeminacy. The trials of this body are rooted in the Jew's blood. In this way, Kafka's body represented his inheritance of a Jewish identity, whether that identity was essentially Jewish or formed by millennia of persecution.

Blood Libels

The Jew infects the Aryan's blood, in the anatomical and racial senses, by means of both syphilis and intermarriage. However, the Jew has a special relationship to blood not only in metaphors of infection, but in images of outright murder. The Dreyfus trial may have been the most famous case of Kafka's time, but it was not unique in Jewish experience. For the late nineteenth century saw the resurgence of the medieval blood libel. The traditional charge had been that Jews killed Christian boys and girls for their blood, which they required for the production of unleavened Passover bread in a parody of the communion wafer. This blood, furthermore, was supposed to cure Jews of their diseases, especially those associated with bleeding, such as male menstruation, and by extension phthisis (the nineteenth century term for pulmonary tuberculosis). By the close of the nineteenth century, the accusation had changed: male Jews were now reputed to kill post-pubescent Aryan women, for reasons having to do with the mysteries of blood.[28] (The one exception is the Beilis case in Russia where the victim is a young boy.). In any case, the Jews are still supposed to eat the blood baked in flat, unleavened bread.

The charge that the Jews, either historically or presently, sacrificed to the god Moloch has an uninterrupted tradition at least back to the Enlightenment.[29] Thus Voltaire argued, "Jewish Law expressly ordered the immolation of men dedicated to the Lord. . . . Human blood sacrifices were thus clearly established. No historical detail is better attested. A Nation can only be judged by its own archives."[30] The "archives," of course, are the Hebrew scriptures. In the early nineteenth century, Voltaire was revised by Georg Friedrich Daumer, who placed Jewish blood rituals in the present rather than in the distant, biblical past. Daumer brought the charge up to date with the example of the 1840 accusation against the Jewish community in Damascus, that they had murdered a friar to obtain blood for their rituals. Such accusations persist throughout the nineteenth century, but are transformed into the accusation of *Lustmord*—the sexually motivated murder of an attractive young woman by a cabal of Jews. The *Lustmord* pervades the literature and art of the period, as exemplified by the image of Jack the Ripper as a Jew.[31] In this tradition, Jewish males are fated to become ritual murderers.

But how does one become a ritual murderer, a Jewish Jack the Ripper? The central question of *fin-de-siècle* "human science" is stated in the subtitle of Friedrich Nietzsche's *Ecce Homo*: "How one becomes what one is?" Jews lived in terror, even greater than Nietzsche's, that they were fated to become what they were said to be.[32] Nietzsche proposed, ". . . I am merely my father once more" (44). Just as important, however, was what one ate: "how to nourish yourself so as to attain your maximum of strength." His view is that what one eats, makes one what one is: "German cookery in general—what does it not have on its conscience. . . . The German spirit is an indigestion, it can have done with nothing" (52). "Selectivity in nutriment" (56). If Jews are believed to eat the blood of Christians in their ritual foods, this is an index of who they are, what their essence is, what they desire to be.

Kafka lived when the charge of ritual murder still appeared regularly in the newspapers of Prague.[33] In 1882 the charge appeared in Hungary; in

1899 in Czechoslovakia; 1891 on Corfu; in 1911 in Kiev.[34] In Corfu, the charge lead to riots that decimated the Jewish community; in the Austro-Hungarian Empire to sensationalistic trials that were the talk of everyone in Prague.[35] Indeed, it was difficult to pick up an issue of the Viennese *New Free Press* without reading about the blood accusation being raised somewhere in Europe. At least fifteen cases appear between 1881 and 1900.[36] For example, on November 26, 1899, in the *New Free Press*, there is a long article on the attempt to hide the body of a dead infant in a Jewish bar in Podgorze near Cracow. Karl Kraus, the Viennese Jewish satirist intensely read by Kafka, commented on the poor taste of respectable Christian citizens of Vienna who assured their Jewish neighbors that they were sure that they were incapable of committing ritual murder![37]

That Kafka knew about the major trials for ritual murder is clear; he comments on them explicitly.[38] Indeed, it is quite possible that while at law school he had read the proposal of one of his law professors, Hans Gross, that ritual murder be defined as a crime under the new category of "psychopathological superstition."[39] Gross attacks a Jewish colleague, A. Nussbaum, who believes that accepting ritual murder as a legal concept would support the reality of the charge, which would then cause "a persecution of the Jews." For Gross, "ritual murder" is a sign of the madness of the accuser and of the accuser's culture, and does not reflect on the Jews as the accused at all. Kafka's fascination with these charges continues until the final year of his life, when he planned a story on a ritual murder trial in Odessa.

The trials that often resulted from these charges were widely covered and intensively debated throughout the German-speaking world, and especially in Prague. Indeed, it was T. G. Masaryk, the founder of the Czech Republic, who published one of the most widely cited attacks on the very idea of blood libel during the trial of Leopold Hilsner in 1899, which resulted from the murder of Agnes Hrunz in Polna (Bohemia).[40] The charges against Hilsner had great currency; they were even debated in the Viennese parliament[41] and the Prussian Chamber of Deputies.[42] Masaryk's legal analysis of the faulty nature of the Polna trial, in contrast to Émile Zola's impassioned "I accuse" attacking the persecutors of Dreyfus, placed Czech nationalism (quite against its will) on the side of the Jews. This was not unimportant to the understanding of this case at the time as the "Austrian Dreyfus Affair."[43] Masaryk himself was quite cool to any self-consciously Jewish participation in the new nationalist movement, but saw the advantage to the rule of law in the claims of the Czechs. Kafka, himself a lawyer, must have been struck by Masaryk's rational response to these irrational claims.[44]

Kafka responded deeply to the implications of the blood libel trials, seeing them in terms of the charges of the exploitation of Aryan women by Jewish men. On June 20, 1920, Kafka writes to his non-Jewish woman friend, Milena Jesenská, expressing his anxiety about a scandal concerning his Jewish friend Willy Haas and Jesenská's Czech friend Jarmila Ambrozová, whose husband committed suicide when he found out about their affair. The pair were forced to flee provincial Prague for Berlin:

> First of all what most terrifies me about the story is the conviction that the Jews are necessarily bound to fall upon you Christians, just as predatory animals are bound to murder, although the Jews will be horrified since they are not animals, but rather all too aware. It is impossible for you to imagine this in all its fullness and power, even if you understand everything else in the story better that I do. I don't understand how whole nations of people could ever have thought of ritual murder before these recent events (at the most they may have felt general fear and jealousy, but here there is no question, we see "Hilsner" committing the crime step by step; what difference does it make that the virgin embraces him at the same time?). But on the other hand, I also don't understand how nations could believe that the Jew might murder without stabbing himself in the process, for that is what he does—but of course the nations don't need to worry about that.
>
> Once again, I am exaggerating, these are all exaggerations. They are exaggerations, because people seeking salvation always throw themselves at women, and these women can be either Christian or Jewish. And what is meant by the girls' innocence is not the usual chastity, but the innocence of sacrifice, an innocence that has just as much to do with the body. (LM 51)

Kafka's image is that of the inexorable relationship between Jewish men, robbed by the society in which they live of their masculinity, who turn to the woman, whether Jewish or Aryan, for salvation. This is the key to his understanding of the blood libel trial. And yet this level of revelation also masks the hidden agenda of the attractiveness and anxiety of these trials.

The blood libel trials have all the elements of the Dreyfus trial: an innocent man suddenly accused of a heinous crime, a trial, and, more often than not, a conviction and false imprisonment. The Jew accused of ritual murder comes to represent not merely himself but his entire "race," and

PLATES 26-28.. The nude Marianne, the female symbol of France, as the true victim of the Dreyfus Affair, from the pro-Dreyfus *Le Sifflet* (1898) (Olin Library, Cornell University).

that he is a Jew serves as the rationale for his crime. His victim is a young and beautiful woman. (In the case of Dreyfus, Marianne, the pubescent female who symbolizes France, is the victim, Plates 26–28). There is a

Nº 10. — 2e Année. — 7 Avril 1899. PARAIT LE VENDREDI Le numéro : 10 centim

LE SIFFLET

ABONNEMENTS
Un An : France, 6 francs; Étranger, 8 francs.

DIRECTEUR
ACHILLE STEENS

BUREAUX
10, Galerie du Théâtre-Français
(Palais-Royal, Paris.)

Ressaisissement

PLATE 27.

spectacular trial, the representatives of the state frame the accused, and he is finally imprisoned under cruel conditions. They also share the problem of the credibility of witnesses. This was an issue in the Polna trial, to

A VERSAILLES

— La tombera! la tombera pas!

PLATE 28.

which Kafka refers above, the most important Czech trial during Kafka's lifetime. But it becomes clearest in the earlier trial of József Scharf and its literary transmutation. Scharf was accused of having murdered Esther Solymosi at Tisza-Eszlar in Hungary during 1882.

The problem of credibility haunts the literature on the blood libel trials written by Jews at the turn of the century. It is the central problem in the case of Tisza-Eszlar, which received an extraordinary account in the French Jewish physician Hippolyte Bernheim's study of suggestion.[45] Bernheim described the background of the Tisza-Eszlar case in great detail. He recounted how a fourteen-year-old Christian girl in the village vanished, and how thirteen "unlucky" local Jews were arrested and accused by the public prosecutor, who "was a great enemy of Israel," and had a "blind hatred" of the Jews. The public prosecutor seized the thirteen-year-old son of the caretaker at the synagogue and held him for three months isolated from his family. The child then proceeded to give detailed testimony as to how he observed the murder of the girl through a keyhole in the synagogue door by three Jews, and he maintained this account even under cross-examination: "I saw it!" Eventually the accused were freed, "justice prevailed and all friends of Hungary and the civilized world could breathe freely."

Bernheim wanted to understand how a child could have given such monstrous testimony. He dismissed the idea that he was simply blackmailed into lying by threats to himself and his family. Rather, he assumed that the child came to believe that he had actually seen the events described to him by the public prosecutor. Bernheim sets the scene: The "small, weak child, raised in the direst poverty, is brought before this august person, who incorporates all justice and power." This "poor, isolated being is overwhelmed by him" and listens as he describes the Jews as "a damned race, who see it as their pious undertaking to spill Christian blood, in order to dampen the dough for the unleavened Easter bread." The power of such rhetoric has an "impact on the weak character" of the child, and this "extreme suggestion permeates his hypnotized brain." He comes to believe that he actually saw the events described to him by the public prosecutor.

Bernheim proposed that the child's testimony was a "retrospective hallucination such as one can generate in a deep trance." This model carries within it all of the aspects of Freud's later, major debt to Bernheim—the replacement of the world of trauma with the world of fantasy. The testimony of the child, like that of Freud's neurotics, was manifestly false, so how could he maintain it under oath? Not because he was consciously lying, but because he had come to believe the reality of the experience that he had imagined rather than experienced. The reason for this was the suggestibility of the child (the product of his environment) and the presence of this over-life-sized figure of power and authority (the father-surrogate). The child, who comes to believe that he has seen a murder committed by his coreligionists, is the ultimate victim. The only thing that he can do is to forget what he has actually seen. The child becomes what the world wants him to become.

Bernheim's answer to why Jews betray other Jews is part of a long debate about the Jewish role in maintaining the blood libel myth. Felix Goldmann offered an explanation in his study, *Baptized Jews and Anti-Semitism* (1914).[46] Goldmann's view—well-established by the time he published his study—is that the very act of conversion to Christianity is a form of mental illness, a psychosis that turns one against one's own people. He begins by tracing the textual representation of the blood libel myth from the convert Paolo Sebastiano Medici in the early seventeenth century through to contemporary figures such as Paulus Meyer, who was baptized in 1882 (42). These figures called upon their own "authentic" knowledge of the Jews to lodge the charge that Jews murder Christians for their blood. Goldmann's call is "Struggle against Baptized Jews!" for it is the baptized Jew who is "our enemy, and is the enemy of Christendom, of any religion, any world view, that stands on a moral foundation" (95). For baptized Jews, to Goldmann, are "egocentric." They embody all the qualities ascribed to the Jew by the discourse of the anti-Semites, but most of all earn the central charge against the Jews, that they violate all of the norms of society by eating human blood. This cannibalism places them morally beyond the pale.

It is the consumption of such "food" that makes the Jew different. This difference does not vanish when the Jew is converted to Christianity. For the baptized Jew eats the body and the blood of Christ at the Mass out of "egoistic" self-interest, rather than true belief in the transubstantiation of the host and the wine. Thus the baptized Jew, unlike the believing Christian, is thus merely a Jew acting like a Jew. He is a cannibal—eating the body and blood of Christ rather than consuming the host in the true Christian spirit.

In this version of the ritual murder trials, there is a further notion of racial predestination. Kafka was presented with a copy of Abraham Grünberg's autobiographical 1916 pamphlet on the 1906 pogrom in Siedlice, which also discussed the ritual murder allegations. The following epigram from the chapter "On Reading and Writing" from Nietzsche's *Thus Spoke Zarathustra* (another well-read text in Kafka's library) appears on its title page:

> Of all that is written I love only what a man has written with his blood. Write with blood, and you will experience that blood is spirit. It is not easily possible to understand the blood of another . . . [47]

Here the quote ends abruptly . . . but in the original, Nietzsche continues: "I hate reading idlers"[48] (40). It is not the Jew who is the implied Other as the quote's revision by Grünberg seems to imply, but rather "the idler." But blood, whether the blood of the Jews which flows in the pogroms or the blood that the Jews are accused of having shed through the charges of ritual murder, blood is that "most special liquid." And later in *Zarathustra*, Nietzsche warns, "blood is the worst witness of truth; blood poisons even the purest doctrine and turns it into delusion and hatred of the heart" (93). It is in the "law of the blood," according to Houston Stewart Chamberlain, that the Jew must finally become what he truly is.[49] Or at least in a world once removed from its reality, in the world of representations that are at least nominally under the control of those who create them.

Kafka Weeps

Kafka's experience of the blood libel trials, like his experience of the Dreyfus affair, is mediated through texts. In the case of the blood libel trials, the text is from high culture, a play by Arnold Zweig. It is a text from a culture which Kafka desires to enter. Mediated experience is foremost for Kafka—the transformation of experience into the world of words over which he is supposed to have no control. Reading about these experiences of trial and torture in such a text reinforces Kafka's sense of the pathological nature of his own ill body. The victim of "In the Penal Colony" "deciphers" his sentence with his wounds (S, 150), reflecting Kafka's own internalization of the image of the corrupted and corrupting Jew. The opposition of beauty and health with ugliness and illness in definitions of masculinity recur in Kafka's response to the ritual murder trial.

The anxiety that he is fated to become a Jewish murderer brings him to tears. On October 28, 1916, he writes to Felice Bauer:

> The other day I read "Ritual Murder in Hungary" by [Arnold] Zweig; its supernatural scenes are as feeble as I would have expected from what I know of Zweig's work. The terrestrial scenes on the other hand are intensely alive, taken no doubt from the excellent records of the case. Nevertheless, one cannot quite distinguish between the two worlds; he has identified himself with the case and is now under its spell. I no longer see him [it] the way I used to. At one point I had to stop reading, sit down on the sofa and weep aloud. It's been years since I wept.[50] (LFe, 530)

What about this tale moved him to tears that he had not shed for years? Is it Zweig's extensive quotations from the "reality" of the ritual murder trial, or is it his literary restructuring? And do "real" men—military men—weep?

Dreyfus does not weep. Indeed, he reads the welling up of emotions as a sign of an incipient mental collapse. "Real" soldiers, especially Jewish soldiers, don't cry. On the other hand, Dreyfus's stoic and soldierly bearing was taken by his opponents as a sign of his guilt, for a truly innocent man would be violently emotional in his protestations of innocence. Kafka's innocent, if unmasculine, tears may well be part of *his* Jewish reading of the Dreyfus case—how would he have reacted to these circumstances? The case of Tisza-Eszlar presented an equally compelling anxiety inherent in debates about Jewish identity: Under what circumstances would I capitulate and turn on my fellow Jews? Could I thus "convert" and come to believe everything "they" say about the Jews? Am I really totally without morals, can I become anything if it serves my own purpose? Is there really the "Wandering Jew" within me, who will appear when I am confronted by the accusations of the *goyim*, or am I the steadfast Dreyfus? Am I Shabbethai Tzevi?

When one reads Arnold Zweig's play of 1914, *Ritual Murder in Hungary*, these questions are inscribed in an account of the trial at Tisza-Eszlar. In his reading, Kafka immediately discounts the "supernatural scenes" derivative of *Faust*. (Zweig evidently felt the same. He recast the play substantially in 1920 and reworked much of this material.[51]) The struggle between the "black," limping Satan, Semeal, "resting on his staff," and the pure voice of God opens the drama (9). Here, as in the work of Oskar Panizza, the limping Devil represents evil on the stage. God's desire, as in Panizza's drama, is to test his people, here the Jews, and force them to pray for their deliverance by the Messiah. God's device is the "lie of the blood" that the Devil spreads (12).

In its nonsymbolic scenes, Zweig's drama kept very close to newspaper accounts of the trial.[52] As Kafka knew, Zweig quotes from actual trial transcripts from major newspapers and journals of the day. Zweig's dramatization of the case, however, reframes it in terms of the Jewish anxiety about trials. The opening, reminiscent of *Faust*, leads into the murder itself, a real *Lustmord*, the rape and murder of the (in Zweig's version) almost eighteen-year-old Esther Solymosi. The audience sees the crime committed by the landlord, the Baron Géza von Onody, who is described as "a big man with a red, instinctual, now angry face, a strong mustache" (14). (In actuality, Onody was an Independence Party deputy in the Hungarian Diet, a supporter of the most outspoken Hungarian anti-Semite of the time, Gyözö Istóczy, and his "advisor" on rural affairs.) His innately criminal sexuality, in Zweig's version, is written on his face, along with his anti-Semitism. The audience witnesses the actual murder. Onody's rape of the girl ends in her death from suffocation, and he disposes of her body in the river. Her death scream is overheard by two passing Jewish peddlers, who choose not to get involved for fear of being themselves accused of the crime.

These Jews, who are first introduced in the same scene as the murderer, are wandering peddlers, and Zweig makes sure that we understand the central problem for them: anxiety at a world where social stability seems to be collapsing. They initially speak about the very low birthrate among Jews in the town, an important commonplace at the turn of the century. Low birthrate is a trope for the collapsing of boundaries and the general sense of instability in this world. The anxiety about low rates of reproduction seems to be ubiquitous among most cultures in Western Europe at the turn of the century as a corollary of a greater sense of social and cultural change. This anxiety marked a loss of control over the future.

The best example of the fear that (Western) Jews were in danger of vanishing is Felix Theilhaber's 1911 work.[53] Theilhaber's work on the "decline of the Jews" presented the demographic case for the disappearance of the Western Jew in greatest detail. He accepted most of the negative evidence, including the greater incidence of disease and insanity, as signs of the degeneration of the Jew. Indeed, he relied heavily on medical authorities for the evaluation of the clinical status of the Jews as the object of special study, without ever drawing their findings into question.

Medicine has a much greater authority for him than, say, social statistics. Central to his argument is the decline in the Jewish birthrate, because of late marriages, the emancipation of Jewish women, and mixed marriages. According to Theilhaber, mixed marriages have an especially low rate of reproduction. Indeed, he notes, if it were not for the "primitive sexuality of the *Ostjuden*," the birthrate of the Jews in Germany would be even lower.[54] Theilhaber's prediction of the eventual disappearance of Western European Jewry had been anticipated in 1904 by the founder of German Jewish demography, Arthur Ruppin.[55] Ruppin warned that Western European Jews might become extinct while the birthrate of Eastern European Jews continued to rise.[56] Franz Kafka attended Theilhaber's public lecture in Prague on the "decline of Germany Jewry" in January, 1912.[57] There, Theilhaber recapitulated the thesis of his controversial book: that urbanization, the struggle for profit, as well as mixed marriages and baptism, were causing German Jewry to vanish. (The latter argument was a social variant on the older biological argument that "mixed marriages between Jews and Aryans had a noticeably lower fecundity."[58]) Kafka took notes:

> A week ago a lecture in the banquet room of the Jewish Town Hall by Dr. Theilhaber on the decline of the German Jews. It is unavoidable, for (1) if the Jews collect in the cities, the Jewish communities in the country disappear. The pursuit of profit devours them. Marriages are made only with regard to the bride's settlement. Two-child system.(2) Mixed marriages (3) Conversion. (D1, 229)

The urban Jew Franz Kafka's anxiety about the decline of the Jews centers on the theme of betrayal, whether through mixed marriages or through conversion.

Zweig introduces this motif as a sign among the Jews of their own instability, but an instability, as Kafka would have read the scene, tied to the decay of the body and the reproductive potential of the Jew. Another theme of Theilhaber's reappears in Zweig's opening scene, in the mouth of the young woman who will be the murder victim: anxiety about the economic power of the Jews, whom, she claims, are owed money by everyone in the town. Indeed, she is at the river fishing in order to have something on her family's table (14). Here the accusation of Jewish economic dominance, for Theilhaber an element in the decay of Western Jewry, is lodged against the Jews as a rationale for the charges of ritual murder.

The Jewish danger to the body politic is articulated by Zweig's Hungarian nobleman, Györö Istóczy. Istóczy's address in the play invokes the entire network of images about Jews and disease: the Jews are leeches (*Blutegel*) who suck the best blood from the Hungarians; they are "damned Vampires" who cover Hungary like a "skin infection" (*Krätze*), like a "rash" (*Ausschlag*); they should be killed like "rats" who attack a lamb, regardless of which rat actually did the deed; they serve Satan, and the proof is that "from 1869 to 1870 36,000 people died of cholera and other plagues in Hungary and Rumania: but almost no Jews. Does the plague come from God or the Devil?" The Jews, says Istóczy, who attack our lands, should not be permitted to drink the blood of our children (63–65). His speech contained quotes from the most infamous (and widely read) tractate on the blood libel, *Der Talmudjude* (1871), by the most notorious proponent of this myth, the Prague theologian August Rohling. All of these charges reflect Kafka's discourse about the difference of his own body and the language used to represent the various "literary" bodies in his world of fiction.

The frame of the drama has now been set: Jewish anxiety and the anxiety about the Jews have both been articulated. The next scene introduces the male protagonist, the thirteen-year-old Moritz (actually Móric) Scharf, the son of the *schammes* (synagogue official) in the local synagogue. His youthful desire is to become a soldier and serve the "Kaiser in Vienna" (17). Here the "childish" desires of the thirteen-year-old center about establishing his identity through undertaking a patriotic and masculine role, that of the soldier. This role seems completely fanciful for a Jewish child in this tiny Hungarian city, with its tight-knit Orthodox Jewish community.

The plot moves along as Esther Solymosi's disappearance is registered by her mother, who is persuaded by a gypsy fortune teller that the Jews are at fault, as they need Christian blood for their matzos (25). Now the townspeople become obsessed with the notion that this event has indeed happened, and that they have even seen it. One of the peasant shouts: "I saw it. Yesterday evening I saw it: a couple of Jews dragged a girl into the synagogue. Scharf opened the door. My wife was there." His wife supports him, noting "I also saw it, Scharf was there. We wanted to bring him interest. I think it was the girl" (26). The role of Josef (actually, József) Scharf, Moritz Scharf's father, as one of the communal leaders and the *schammes*, the official in charge of the synagogue, exemplifies the dramatic theme of generation conflict; Josef's conflict with Moritz exemplifies the collapse of order and the rise of anti-Semitism in the play, as Zweig implies that it is Jewish acculturation that also plays a role in the rise of anti-Semitism. For the father, who has allowed his family to live in a town inhabited by Jews and non-Jews, blames himself for his son's apostasy.

Once the accusation of ritual murder is made, the mob attacks the male Jews leaving the synagogue. The real murderer, Onody, appears on the scene, and orders all the Jews arrested for the murder. He then suborns the magistrate to prosecute the case, stressing, however, that it is only the twenty-seven Jewish men of the town who are guilty, not the women. This sexualized crime by men against a woman mirrors his own rape and murder of the victim. Indeed, it is striking that the defendants in ritual murder trials of the nineteenth century are exclusively male Jews. This is a reflex of the centrality of the male in Jewish ritual, but is also consistent with the anti-Semitic image of the hypersexual Jewish male. Ritual murder in the nineteenth century is a gendered category.

However, the state must still be able to make a case against the Jews. The magistrate points out to Onody the unreliability of peasants. They decide that the best witness would be a Jew, perhaps a woman or a boy who could have seen the crime through the keyhole (33). Thereupon the judge and two policemen go to Josef Scharf's home, expecting to find children there, because (as Theilhaber would have it) the Eastern Jews bred so quickly (35). Unexpectedly and seemingly randomly, they arrest the thirteen-year old Moritz, who because of his age is legally an adult and can be sworn in to give testimony (35).

To this point all the characters except the Jews are speaking High German, which represents the Hungarian spoken by the real participants. The Jews, who in reality also spoke Hungarian, in the play speak a theatrical (that is highly mediated) *Mauscheln* that contains no Hebrew or Yiddish words but only grammatical inversions and minor lexical changes. The language of the Jews is represented as inherently different from that of the other participants. Thus when Moritz Scharf is taken off in chains to the prison in the regional capital of Nyiregyhaza, he is examined by the magistrate, who interrogates him. He is aided by a secretary who understands the boy's *Mauscheln*, and serves as a cultural as well as linguistic interpreter for the magistrate. When asked how he knows this "Gemauschel," he answers "Here you have to after a while" (38). This interrogation of the naive and helpless boy extends over three pages. The child tells the magistrate exactly what happened, how his father returned from the synagogue, and prepared the Sabbath at home. He narrates this in an ironic tone, quite aware that the "ignorant" *goyim* do not really understand the intricacies of the ritual, even though the secretary (for an "am horaz," an ignoramus) seems to grasp some of this. This truthful narrative is presented in the child's *Mauscheln*.

The truthful narrative is precisely not what the magistrate wishes to hear, and he orders the child taken out and beaten by one of the policeman until he stops "lying" (40). He is brought back into the room, frightened and in tears from pain. He still states that he has told the truth, that he knows nothing about the murder, and the magistrate orders him locked into a cell without food or drink for three days. Every time he begins to fall asleep, he is to be wakened by blows. Here the evocation of Dreyfus is evident. The physical torment of the child is used to break his spirit and to make him testify against his father and the other male Jews of the town.

The third act opens with what is now clearly going to be the central question of the play, as it was Bernheim's central question in his reading of the case—how do the conspirators get Moritz Scharf to testify to the guilt of his father and the other Jews? We find ourselves in the prison cell with Moritz, his face "pale and sunken," disfigured by whiplashes. He begs the guard not to beat him any more; to give him food and water. The magistrate appears and Moritz asks him why he has "tortured" him so and the magistrate replies, "because you have lied" (50). Moritz refuses to admit to knowing anything about the murder and faints.

The magistrate is about to have him beaten again, but he reconsiders, has him moved into a bigger, cleaner cell, and orders that he be given food and drink and be permitted to walk two hours a day in the prison garden. At the end of the week, the magistrate calls Moritz to him and promises him continued good treatment, good food, good clothes. He promises him: "Anything you want. We'll take care of you, you will be sent to a good school. We will get you a good job; you can even go to university, and become a judge like me" (52). Moritz's response is immediate: "Even a soldier?" Here Zweig's earlier representation of the child's fantasy of what it means to become a man in the "Royal and Imperial" (KuK) society of the Hapsburg monarchy reappears. Real men serve their emperor as soldiers. The promise of this society, which is Zweig's and Kafka's as well, is that if you follow the rules and become a "good" citizen, the "good enough authority" will protect you and reward you with the bounty of true citizenship. The Jew's body will stop being the tortured body, and instead become the soldier's body in a reversal of Dreyfus's fate.

Once the trap is baited, now with the promises of acculturation rather than beatings, Moritz capitulates. The magistrate sets a series of questions: Who opened the door? Who held the girl? Who butchered her? Who collected the blood? Where was the body disposed? He states that he will return the next day to hear the answers. What the magistrate wishes to have substantiated is how the "Jews butchered" the victim (52) (to use the set phrase employed by him as well as subsequently by the victim's mother [67]). The image of the "butchering" of the victim is taken from the rhetoric of the persecutors. For the analogy in this scene (as in the actual trial) is to the Christian fantasy of the Jewish ritual slaughter of animals, a crucial index of Jewish difference at the turn of the century. This analogy appears on the pages of *Self-Defense* (*Selbstwehr*) in 1912, with a full-page reproduction of one of the Czech accusations of ritual murder.[59] The image of the victim is reproduced, and the full text is translated into German. It details the butchering of the living child, the child's bleeding, and the collecting of its blood for consumption.

Young Moritz considers the magistrate's request, and decides to tell him what he wants to know, but not out of conviction, as Bernheim suggests; rather, Zweig shows us the mind of the Jew attempting to cope with the pressure of the now suborned institution of the trial. This is a trial that is not seeking after truth, but merely someone to blame. Moritz reflects that the magistrate wants him to lie, so it cannot be a sin. All the Jews will know that he lied. His testimony will have little effect on the court, as they will clearly prefer the word of the adults accused of the crime to his childish statement. He then proceeds question by question to answer the magistrate and to repeat his questions as statements.

At the trial Moritz substantiates each stage of the ritual murder. The Jews, including his father, place the naked victim on a table covered in red cloth. The ritual slaughter of the victim is undertaken by "the butcher (*Schächter*) [who] cut her throat with the big calf knife and the others caught her blood in large, silver bowls" (76–77). The body is then dismembered and cut into twelve pieces, one for each of the tribes of Israel, and each piece is wrapped in linen and buried in a different child's grave in the cemetery. This story is repeated by Moritz in an ever clearer and more articulate German.

When Moritz is finally brought into the courtroom to testify, he is dressed "like a Hungarian peasant boy, with high boots, white shirt, and blue linen pants. His hair is cut short, so that his sidelocks (*payess*) are missing" (74). In perfect High German, without a trace of his earlier *Mauscheln*, he recounts in detail the confession that had been presented to him by the magistrate. He no longer appeals to his Jewish audience's understanding that his testimony is false. The details he recounts are precisely those narrated by the magistrate, down to the ritual dismemberment of the body. And he has come to believe them. Following his testimony, he is confronted by his father before the court:

> SCHARF: Mr. President, is this my son Moritz? Come here, let me look at you. Are you my son Moritz?
> MORITZ: I don't want to.
> SCHARF: Are you my son?
> MORITZ: Sure, I'm your (*Ihr*) son.
> SCHARF: You say "*Sie*" to me, to your father?!
> MORITZ: Should I say "noble lord" to a Jew?
> SCHARF: God save my thoughts.
> MORITZ: You helped butcher Esther, I saw it. . . .
> SCHARF: Then I am lying?
> MORITZ: That's right, You (*Sie*) are lying. (79–80)

Moritz's father mourns his son as if he were dead or a convert (87). But he sees in his son's apostasy his own failure to be a good Jew and father. He has led his child into the temptations of a big city without enough Jewishness to protect him, and had neglected his Jewish education. Here is the crux of Zweig's rationale for Moritz's apostasy—he was not Jewish enough, as revealed to the reader through his childish dreams of becoming a soldier of the emperor.

After Moritz's testimony, the trial continues, with the prosecutor revealing that the exhumation of the body showed no signs of any ritual murder, and suggesting that Moritz be charged with perjury, proposing a punishment of a year in prison. The Jewish fear of the collapse of authority is shown to have been unfounded. While local hysteria may have enabled (or been caused by) the breakdown of authority through the corruption of the local landlord, the authority of Vienna remains inviolate.

Central to this reestablishment of order in the drama is a reenactment of the crime in the now wrecked and desolate synagogue, proving Moritz's account cannot be accurate given the placement of the table in the synagogue. It would have been impossible to see anything through the keyhole. Moritz finally admits that he saw nothing. The magistrate turns on him and accuses him of having lied to him, to which Moritz responds: "I have never lied. . . . I have always told the truth. . . . always the truth" (107). The tenuous relationship between truth and language is represented by the sense of the masculine being truthful or rooted in male symbols such as clothing or uniforms. What does the uniform represent in this context but a code of masculine behavior antithetical to that represented by the feminizing garb of the Eastern European Jewish male? The trial has undermined Moritz's sense of identity as a Jew, defined as the feminized masculine in this culture.

The final act of the play finds Moritz alone in the synagogue, where he is silently observed by the apostate Jakob (actually Johannes) Pfefferkorn and the prophet Elijah, who had been competing for his soul. Moritz's long monologue reveals his confusion, his inability to tell his lies from the truth. He asks, "Am I still a Jew? Perhaps I am still a Jew?" (112). He undresses, seeks out a shroud, places the point of a knife against his heart and commits suicide (113). The knife that he finds in the synagogue must have been the knife used in reenacting the ritual murder at the close of the previous scene. His suicide is thus an extension of the ritualization of death in the culture in which he lives. In his dying moment, he sees Elijah, who kisses him. Like the dying Faust at the close of the second part of the drama, Moritz is redeemed in his death, but here as a Jew. A suicide note written in the clearest and purest German is found next to his body: "No one murdered me, I murdered my self. I believed that I told the truth. The eternal one, blessed be he, will judge me" (121).

Suffering expressed in language are the hallmarks of the masculine in this world of words. The final scene in heaven brings the shadow of Moritz Scharf before Rabbi Akiva and the Baal Shem Tov to be judged. The Baal Shem Tov defends Moritz, noting, ". . . the suffering of the body was greater than a human being could bear. He was a boy, brother, who bore the suffering of a man" (122). Here the question of the suffering of the body and its relationship to masculinity defines the Jewish male. For Moritz is absolved of his betrayal because he was not a man, and yet his suffering made him into one. His role is that of Dreyfus, but a Dreyfus who broke and yet still was redeemed. God accepts the Baal Shem Tov's defense of Moritz, whereupon Moritz is truly saved as a man.

Zweig's fantasy introduces the idea of martyrdom and the temptation of the Diaspora into the very conclusion of the play. For the judgment of the soul of the dead child by the Baal Shem Tov and Rabbi Akiva is the judgment of two Jews, one of them the exemplary martyr. Akiva is one of the *asara harugei malkhut*, the ten victims of the Empire, tortured to death by Romans. His death comes to have an exemplary one in midrashic explanations of the relationship between non-Jewish power and the Jews of the Diaspora. Here the models of Jewish identity come to be Martin Buber's *fin-de-siècle* image of the anti-rational (and, therefore, anti-Enlightenment) Jew, the Baal Shem Tov, the founder of Hasidism and Akiva, the Jewish martyr for the Diaspora. Only they can judge the impact of the tempations of acculturation for the young Jewish suicide.

Here Kafka wept.

The reality of the actual trial is somewhat more banal. In the actual courtroom, the confrontation was indeed brutal. Móric was "invariably disrespectful, often curtly abusive. . . . He remained unremorseful and was visibly pleased by the prolonged cheering and applause that erupted at the conclusion of the proceedings of the day."[60] The cross-examination of the child eventually revealed his "systematic indoctrination under the watchful eyes of the county authorities" (132), and his mechanical answers made him an ineffective witness against his father and the other Jews. Indeed, the key moment in the actual trial was the tribunal's decision not to accept the child's testimony because he "displayed such blind, passionate hatred for his father, coreligionists, and faith," such "convincing evidence of his immaturity and lack of comprehension that he destroyed not only his own credibility but that of his testimony as well" (156). After the conclusion of the trial, Móric, along with the rest of his family, moved to Budapest. When asked by a reporter there what had actually happened in the synagogue on that Saturday, his reply was "Nothing happened there."[61]

Zweig's representation of the ritual murder trial incorporates another fantasy about the Jewish body. Only Jewish males were accused of ritual murder at the *fin de siècle*, which, to Kafka, represents the myth of Jewish male desire for the non-Jewish woman. But Zweig turns the charge of sexual excess against the nobility, in a rehearsal of the late nineteenth-century bourgeois preoccupation with the legendary *jus prima noctes*. To further sexualize the drama, Zweig makes the victim even older than she was in reality.

Miscegenation, or *Blutschande*, literally "violation of the blood," was a theme of the literature of the period, for example of Arthur Dinter's *Sin against the Blood* (1918). There, too, the *Mauscheln* of the Jew marked him as impossible to integrate. His immutability, like that of Moritz Scharf, means that he remains a Jew no matter what his physical transformation. It is Moritz Scharf who is the focus of Bernheim, Zweig, and presumably Kafka's concern. For the young Scharf embodies the fantasy of becoming the same as every one else in the society that persecutes him. His desire to become a soldier, which allows him to be seduced, is a promise to become like everyone else, to become fully male. Jewishness and citizenship, according to the young Zionist Arnold Zweig, are not incompatible, as long as the Jew maintains his difference. This reading is very different from Bernstein's, whose sense of Franco-Jewish identity may have been heightened by the Dreyfus Affair.

The feminized Jewish male, the barely pubescent thirteen-year-old who is only ritually a man, is revealed as powerless through the process of the trial. Like Dreyfus, he is accused arbitrarily, but unlike Dreyfus he capitulates to the accusation's potential to transform him. Dreyfus's body is transformed from the "French" soldier's body into the "Jewish" prisoner's, but his resolve never weakens; Moritz Scharf's physical transformation into a Hungarian peasant boy reflects his hopeless desire for a transformation. He remains the Jew, now the Jew as apostate. The boy retains his childish desires, even though at thirteen he is ritually a man. His suicide confirms his immaturity. Zweig's desire to "save" Moritz, to rescue him, is really his desire to save the language in which he writes and the culture it represents. Like Moritz, however, the language he uses remains the language of the oppressors. Even Zweig's imagery of ritual murder and ritual slaughter is part of this language. Even though authority finally dispenses justice in Zweig's play, the language of authority suborns the Jewish writer. Moritz's problem is thus the problem of the Jewish writer at the turn of the century. Does he write, does he tell the truth in a Jewish language, and is it then not read? Can he even assume that his Jewish readers will understand his use of the language of the oppressor, and will understand, somehow, that their truth is his truth? Or will he capitulate to the larger culture's false ideal of masculinity? Is not either a form of social emasculation?

Kafka's tears in reading Zweig mirror the tears he sheds in his "Letter to the Father" (written in 1919). There is a moment in that extraordinary documentary fiction where Kafka sees in his father the softness and kindness, the femininity, that he imagines in himself (L, 131). His father's tears when his mother is gravely ill, and his father's visit to him during Kafka's last illness when "you came tiptoeing to Ottla's room, to see me, stopping in the doorway, craning your neck to see me, and out of consideration only waved to me with your hand" (L, 131). Kafka's response then and now is to weep: "At such times one would lie back and weep for happiness, and one weeps again now, writing it down." The identification with the powerful and aggressive father's "feminine" qualities returns in the act of recording them. Tears are, as in the reading of Zweig's play about ritual murder, the result of the distancing of reality into the text. But they are tears that evoke the specter that Kafka will become his father. At this moment in Kafka's "Letter to the Father," he evokes the "good" father. In Kafka's reading of Zweig's play, it is the "bad" father that is presented, the father who had not given his son sufficient Jewish identity to remain true to his religious community. (This of course in the character's own reading of his son's actions.) Here Kafka's tears also evoke the father, who had, like the elder Scharf, "some traces of Judaism" from his own "ghetto-like village community" (L, 147). But what the son experiences in the small town in Hungary is the boredom and emptiness of a Jewish experience of "this transitional generation of Jews, which had migrated from the still comparatively devout countryside to the cities" (L, 148). Kafka's experience is in many ways that of Zweig himself and the young Scharf—Judaism is reduced to a "few flimsy gestures performed . . . with an indifference in keeping with their flimsiness" (L, 148). The attraction of the assimilationist model of masculinity in the drama—of the army—is thus clear, as it offers a meaningful, structured, and fully secular environment. Thus Kafka's tears reappear in 1919, after the onset of his tuberculosis, when he becomes aware of the limitations placed on his choices by the inevitability of becoming what he must become, a sick, male Jew, just like Hermann Kafka.

Both Zweig's fantasy about the Tisza-Eszlar ritual murder case of 1882 and Kafka's reading of his fantasy in 1917 are in light of the discourse about the more explicit association between ritual murder and ritual slaughter that was most clearly made in the Polna murder case of 1899. The accusation against the Jew Leopold Hilsner for the murder of a nineteen-year-old Christian woman haunted the streets of Prague for two years while Kafka was an upperclassman at the Altstädter Gymnasium. He was exposed to it in the pamphlets and posters that flooded the streets of Prague. In this discourse the link between ritual murder and ritual slaughter was explicitly made.

In his diaries, following his reading of Zweig, Kafka rehearses over and over again the scenario of the ritual murder in an effort to understand the position ascribed to the Jew as ritual murderer and/or ritual slaughterer. In his diary for September 16, 1915, he writes:

> Between throat and chin would seem to be the most rewarding place to stab. Lift the chin and stick the knife into the tensed muscles. But this stop is probably rewarding only in one's imagination. You expect to see a magnificent gush of blood and a network of sinews and little bones like you find in a turkey leg.[62] (D2, 130)

This passage evokes a very specific form of the ritual murder. The scene as Zweig describes it in his drama is the *locus classicus* for such murders—the victim is bound, the head held back, the throat slit, and the blood collected in vessels. It is the image drilled into young Moritz by the public prosecutor. Here Kafka is presenting the "real" problem of such a murder. And in doing it he (like Zweig) reflects the intense contemporary debate about the Jews and their killing of animals, a debate that is used to reflect on the nature of the Jew's soul and body as much as on Jewish ritual practices. It is the linkage of these two moments that reveals further aspects of the contemporary discourses about illness, ritual murder, and the Jews at the turn of the century.

SHEHITAH

The fantasy murder in Arnold Zweig's play is carried out by the butcher (*Schächter*), who, according the suborned witness, "cut her throat with the big calf knife and the others caught her blood in large, silver bowls" (76–77). This reference reflects the intense debate at the turn of the century about *Schächten* or *shehitah*, the Jewish ritual slaughter of animals for human consumption, closely associated with the charges of ritual murder and illness.[63] Two aspects of *shehitah* are particularly important: the act of slaughter itself, and the ritual examination of the carcass.

A contemporary, secular Jewish source describes *shehitah* in this fashion, stressing the painlessness of the act in spite of the physical torment the animals seemingly experience :

> Through bending the head backward the throat is exposed. Then a lightening fast cut across the throat using a long, razor sharp knife that cuts the softer parts of the throat through to the backbone. A huge amount of blood flows in thick streams from the severed veins and arteries, especially from the jugular. Because of the shock to the nerves as well as the sudden halting of blood to the brain there is immediate unconsciousness. The animal remains immobile until after about 3/4 a minute a purely mechanical autonomic reflex causes more or less powerful muscular reactions in the unconscious animal. Within 2 to 3 minutes these give way to the death cramps.[64] (Plate 29)

The *fin-de-siècle* Prague reading of *shehitah* is quite different from its contemporary Jewish defense. The most widely read *fin-de-siècle* work on public health in German was by Ferdinand Hueppe, who held the chair of hygiene in Prague beginning in 1889. His discussion of animal slaughter begins with a diatribe against ritual slaughter.[65] For him, slaughter must occur so as not to violate "our moral feelings." Animals should be anesthetized or at least stunned before slaughter. "From the ethical standpoint *shehitah* must be halted, because it is the crudest and most disgusting method. . . . [I]n *shehitah* the cramps as the animal bleeds to death are so horrible, so that any feeling human being, who has once seen it must turn from such primitive and disgusting techniques with abhorrence." Hueppe argues that the hygienic claim that meat that has been bled is healthier is false; indeed, "such meat is of lower quality." *Shehitah* is insupportable in "our climate and cultural conditions." Only the Jews, who belong in a foreign space and have a different culture, would advocate such a procedure. Thus the charges of cruelty, brutality, and indifference to suffering are lodged against the Jews in the light of their ritual practice of *shehitah*.

The societal response to the ritual slaughter of animals by Jews is itself brutal and direct.[66] The anticruelty forces in Europe and America teamed up closely with the anti-Semites, who saw everything associated with the Jews as an abomination, to label this form of slaughter cruel and barbaric. In Germany as early as the first Congress for the Protection of Animals (1860) there was a strong attack on ritual slaughter. This was in the light of contemporary views such as that of Arthur Schopenhauer, who saw in the Jews' refusal to use "humane" methods of slaughter such as "chloroform" a sign of their "unnatural separation" of human beings from the

PLATE 29. "Kosher Slaughter," from J. G. Lipman, "Shehitah," *The Jewish Encyclopedia,* 12 vols. (New York: Funk and Wagnalls, 1904), 11, 56. The use of an eighteenth-century, vaguely anti-Semitic image from a non-Jewish source in a *fin-de-siècle* Jewish reference work points toward the extreme ambiguity of ritual slaughter (National Library of Medicine, Bethesda).

animal world that he attributed to the spirit of Judaism.[67] Such attacks were virtually always accompanied by comments linking animal slaughter with other forms of Jewish "brutality." In 1885, the attack on ritual slaughter in Great Britain led the Lord Mayor of London to comment that the obsession with this Jewish practice recalled the ritual murder accusations from the time of Chaucer.[68] In the 1883 meeting of the Congress for the Protection of Animals in Vienna, the argument was made that the protection of ritual slaughter, or at least its lack of condemnation, was a sign that the Jews controlled the political process in Europe. By 1892, a law against ritual slaughter was passed in Saxony. And by 1897, there was a clear link between such attacks and the antivivisection movement, as the cruelest physicians were reputed to be Jews.[69] Even today ritual slaughter is banned in "liberal" Switzerland.

Indeed, Karl Liebknecht denounced on the floor of the Reichstag on April 24, 1899, the right-wing attacks on ritual slaughter as a further attempt to attack the Jews, and a colleague of his in the same debate simply labeled these attacks "anti-Semitic desires." Liberal newspapers such as the *Berlin Daily News,* in 1893, called those campaigning against ritual slaughter "pure anti-Semites." *The Nation,* in 1894, observed that "the cry against the so-called *Schächten* belongs to the best loved sport of the modern persecutor of the Jews."[70] It is no accident that the most repulsive anti-Semitic film of the Third Reich, Fritz Hippler's *The Eternal Jew* (1940), concludes with a scene of ritual slaughter, as conclusive evidence of the Jew's inhumanity.[71]

A typical text from this tradition is Ernst von Schwartz's 1905 monograph against the ritual slaughter of animals.[72] Schwartz begins by defending himself against the charge that he is simply an anti-Semite. He cites his Jewish landlord and his Jewish doctor as proof of his fairness. He defends the anticruelty forces as not being anti-Semitic. Nonetheless, like many intellectuals of his day, he isolates Jewish practices such as ritual slaughter as the barrier between Jews and their Christian neighbors: "Nothing is so disposed to increase the divide between Christians and Jews and to make Judaism be felt as a foreign element, than to demand the ability to do what is morally and legally forbidden to Christians" (21). But Jews, in their egoism, insist on their right to be different and still be part of the body politic.

Central to the ritual of *Schächten* is the purification of the animal's carcass by the elimination of its blood through the act of slaughter.[73] The religious argument is that the Jews (beginning with the biblical admonition in Genesis 9:4) were forbidden to eat blood. In the course of the late nineteenth century, this ritual argument was given hygienic content. But the refusal of the Jews to consume blood is a sign of the "hygienic" importance of ritual slaughter in the preservation of human life, especially its preservation from exposure to tuberculosis.[74]

In a basic statement made in 1889 by Henry Behrend, in the British periodical *The Nineteenth Century*, the hygiene argument is summarized.[75] Behrend, writing in the wake of the extraordinary popular acceptance of Robert Koch's discovery of the tubercular bacillus in 1882, argued that the present state of scientific knowledge demands that diseased meat be withheld from human consumption. This was very much in line with a general movement from treatment to prevention that developed in the 1880s.[76] We (in 1889) know the etiology of tuberculosis and other such infectious diseases (such as anthrax), and are now able to state without doubt how the disease can be passed on to human beings. Such meat "is not only deprived of most of its nutritive qualities, but is capable of communicating its specific malady to man, when taken as food" (410). The effects of the disease can be seen in the slaughtered animal, as the Sheriff-Principal of Glasgow comments: "The presence of the agent of the disease must precede the visible results of its action; indeed, the present case affords an illustration of the danger of inferring, from the absence of symptoms visible to the unaided eye, that the disease is localized" (411). In July of 1888, the International Congress of Tuberculosis in Paris stressed the dangers of eating infected meat. The assumption of the period was that there was an absolute association between the consumption of tainted meat and the acquiring of tuberculosis that would then be "transmitted to their unborn children" (412). Thus the eating of infected meat affected not only the present generation but all future generations.

Behrend rests his argument on two scientific premises: first, there is an absolute "identity of human and bovine tuberculosis," and second, tuberculosis is communicable to man "from the flesh of affected cattle" (413). This disease, Behrend claims, quoting a Dr. Klein from the Brown Institution, "is communicable by ingestion" (416). Thus the "comparative immunity from the tubercular diathesis" of the Jews can be explained by their dietary laws (418). Behrend's authorities support him in this matter. In 1885, Noël Guéneau de Mussy speaks before the Academy of Medicine in Paris of the "vitality of the Jewish race" depending on "the care exercised by them in the selection of their food supply" (418). This is especially evidenced in the relative low rate of infant mortality among the Jews, especially in Germany (419–420).

A belief in the continuity from Judaism to Christianity underpins much of this argumentation. For Behrend, Moses becomes the first bacteriologist, on the model of Koch and Pasteur:

> The idea of parasitic and infectious maladies, which has conquered so great a position in modern pathology, appears to have greatly occupied the mind of Moses, and to have dominated all his hygienic rules. He excludes from the Hebrew diet animals particularly liable to parasites; and as it is in the blood that the germs or spores of infectious disease circulate, he orders that they must be drained of their blood before serving for food. . . . What an extraordinary prescience! The contagion of tuberculosis has been proved only during the last few years; its transmissibility by food is not yet universally recognized, though the experiments of M. Chauveau render it almost certain; yet the law of Israel, thousands of years in advance of modern science, has inscribed in its precepts these ordinances, preventive of the malady. (417)

Both Jewish and Christian advocates of ritual slaughter take up this argument. At the Sanitary Congress at Brighton in 1881, a Dr. Carpenter commented, "obedience to the sanitary laws laid down by Moses is a necessary condition to perfect health, and to a state that shall give us power to stamp out zymotic diseases. If these laws were observed by all classes, the zymotic death-rate would not be an appreciable quantity in our mortality list."[77] The British Jewish anthropologist Lucien Wolf commented in 1884 that it was because of the "legalism" of the Jews, so disparaged by the anti-Semites of the day, that Moses "the lawgiver was not unmindful of the probable unwholesomeness" of animals declared to be not for consumption by Jews and especially that "the use of blood is emphatically and repeatedly forbidden."[78] The claim, made by physicians as well as the lay public, was that the Jews, through their religious practices, were following a basic model of hygiene, under the rubric that "we may go to Moses for instruction in some of the best methods in hygiene," according to William Osler in 1914.[79] But even the opponents of ritual slaughter, such as Ernst von Schwartz (1905), had to agree that "Moses was the great, wise reformer and hygienist."[80] But they disagreed that ritual slaughter was Mosaic and therefore divinely inspired; instead they considered it Rabbinic and corrupt.

The image of Moses as "a super-eminent, specially evolved and Divinely-led genius" is also the theme of Alexander Rattray's 1903 study of "divine hygiene."[81] His view is that the Bible is a "deep mine of most important medico-hygienic information" and seeks "to prove that this is directly or indirectly Divine." For all of Rattray's attention to the biblical admonitions concerning food, he neither mentions ritual slaughter (except to stress that removal of blood preserves meat), nor does he discuss tuberculosis and its dangers. Such an approach curtailed the discussion of ritual slaughter as divinely inspired, while stressing the potential benefits of ritually slaughtered flesh. Jews use the argument to argue for ritual slaughter; their opponents label it as an invention of the Jews, not of the divinely inspired Moses.

If the Jews have greater immunity to infectious illness through divinely inspired laws, this might account for their presumed longer life expectancy. (This is very much in line with the claim of the *Maskilim*, the followers of the Jewish Enlightenment, that Judaism is an essentially rational religion. Lucien Wolf, in 1881, states that in its ritual practices, "Judaism, as in everything, is strictly logical."[82]) Such information about disease and the blood is of importance for the society as a whole, and especially so for those insuring the lives of individuals, as one of Behrend's authorities, Professor Hosmer, states: ". . . at the present day in the life insurance offices the life of a Jew is said to be worth much more than that of men of other stock" (419). There is no discussion here of ritual slaughter and brutality, only of ritual slaughter and hygiene. Here the guidelines for the defense of *Schächten* are set—ritual slaughter is modern, hygienic, scientific, and important for actuarial tables; it prevents the pollution of future generations by controlling blood.

Blood, within the hygienic rationale of *Schächten*, is also considered to have a detrimental effect on the preservation of meat, and serves as one of the touchstones for the arguments both for and against the practice. For example: "To use blood as food approximates very closely to drinking urine, and is not merely loathsome but *pro tanto* unsafe."[83] The arguments against this rationale were striking in their bluntness. An anonymous tract from 1883 argues that ritual slaughter was not at all biblical in its origin but rather rabbinical and that, indeed, the Bible demands the least painful death for animals.[84] This view separated out the positive "religious" tradition that leads to Christianity from the negative "essentially" Jewish tradition of Rabbinic Judaism. The Bible, this view states, cannot condone evil things. Only Jews do. Again we can turn to Schwartz for an example. Blood, he states, is forbidden "because it is holy and not because it is unhealthy, for that which is holy cannot be sick, cannot be poisonous" (36). It is only the blood drawn from *ritually* slaughtered animals that is polluted, and can make one ill "because of the dirtying of it through the presence of vomit that will make it disgusting and poisonous" (37). It is thus logical that the Jews do not wish to consume such blood. But the Jews, because they are inherently hypocrites, Schwartz states, "will eat bloody meat: What Israelite has not already eaten bloody game?" (38). Then comes the final turning in Schwartz's argument. Jews say they don't eat blood because it is holy or because the way they handle it is polluting, but according to Schwartz they really do eat it any way—all contradictions to prove the Jew's lying nature even in regard to their own rituals.

One way of placing the practice of cleansing meat of blood into ill-repute is to vilify the Jews. For Jews do not only lie about eating bloody meat in practice, they are also the heirs of the most reprehensible culinary practice, the basis of ritual murder. Jews are cannibals—citing 2 Kings 6: 24–30, Schwartz argues that Jews have in the past eaten children. His statement is doubly ironic: "According to the dietary laws the enjoyment of human flesh was not directly outlawed, yet in the light of the dietary laws it must be accepted that it was forbidden. At least a passage in the tractate *Chullin* (Folio 92b) indicates that the flesh of the dead may not be weighed with a scale so that it cannot be *sold*" (33). Jewish ritual practices, such as *shehitah,* reveal the hidden, inner nature of the Jewish soul, which is cannibalistic as well as avaricious.

It is also marked in the form of the ill Jewish body. Jews have abnormal, ugly bodies because they eat meat that has been slaughtered in a ritual manner and has the blood drained from it. So at least opines Gustav Simons in 1907.[85] This body is marked by an arm "that is no longer able to work or eventually to strike out, but only able to collect the fruits of the work of others." It is marked by "flat feet and the characteristically less elastic pattern of walking." And all of this is the result of having eaten "mineral poor fruits of civilization and bled meat, which resulted in a poor skeleton." This combination of character and physique was the result of the practice of *shehitah.*

Shehitah was read as both a reflex of the Jewish soul, as well as part of a pattern of Jewish illness. In Thomas Mann's *The Magic Mountain* (1924), the figure of Leo Naphta, whom the protagonist Hans Castorp meets in the tuberculosis sanitarium at Davos, is immediately revealed to the reader as a Jew by his "corrosive ugliness": "Everything about him was sharp: the hooked nose dominating his face, the narrow, pursed mouth, the thick, beveled lenses of his glasses in their light frame, behind which were a pair of pale-gray eyes—even the silence he preserved, which suggested that when he broke it, his speech would be incisive and logical."[86]

Naphta's background reveals all the connections between the Jew, ritual murder and *shehitah*. Mann believed strongly in the inheritance of family characteristics and in degeneracy as the explanation of individual pathology.[87] For him, the Jew was the exemplary case and the ritual butcher the Jew's most intense representative. Leo, or as he was then called, Leib Naphta, came from the Eastern reaches of the Austrian Empire, from the Galician-Volhynian border, where his father Elie was a *schochet*, a ritual slaughterer. Mann's description of the act plays on the stereotype of the Jew as a "brooding and refining spirit":

> Standing near the victim, which was hobbled and bound indeed, but not stunned, he would lift the mighty slaughter-knife and bring it to rest in a deep gash close to the cervical vertebra; while the assistant held the quickly filling basins to receive the gushing, steaming blood, and the child looked on the sight with that childish gaze that often pierces through the sense into the essential, and may have been in an unusual degree the gift of the starry-eyed Elie's son. He knew that Christian butchers had to stun their cattle with a blow from a club before killing them, and that this regulation was made in order to avoid unnecessary cruelty. Yet his father, so fine and so intelligent by comparison with those louts, and starry-eyed as never one of them, did his task according to the Law, striking down the creature while its senses were undimmed, and letting its life-blood well out until it sank. The boy Leib felt that the stupid *goyim* were actuated by an easy and irreverent good nature, which paid less honor to the deity that did his father's solemn mercilessness; thus the conception of piety came to be bound up in his mind with that of cruelty, and the idea of the sacred and the spiritual with the sight and smell of spurting blood.[88]

This is a somewhat standard representation of ritual slaughter, but Mann, never one to leave well enough alone, provides us with the mythic continuum on which this spiritual type must be placed. For Elie Naphta is also a "familiar of God, a Baal-Shem or Zaddik, a miracle man" who can cure "a woman of a malignant sore, and another time a boy of spasms, simply by means of blood and invocations." The word "blood" seems to reflect the blood gathered by the *schochet* through the ritual slaughter; indirectly, it refers to the "race" of the Jews, to their blood. But Mann continues this line of associations, for in the very next sentences, he describes Elie Naphta's eventual fate: "But it was precisely this aura of an uncanny piety, in which the odor of his blood-bolstered calling played a part, that proved his destruction. There had been the unexplained death of two gentile boys, a popular uprising, a panic of rage—and Elie had died horribly, nailed crucifix-wise on the door of his burning home." Here the set of associations seems to be complete—ritual slaughter, the physiognomy and the psyche of the Jew, the Jew who cures through the blood, and the ritual murder accusation, which ends in the death of the Jew crucified as a Jew—here no trial supervenes, unlike the cases of Dreyfus and Josef Scharf.

Mann extends this chain of associations to include the ritual murder trials and the body of the Jew. For Leo Naphta is at Davos being treated for tuberculosis because his mother was tubercular. According to Mann, Leo has "the seeds of his lung disease" from his mother and from his father "beside his slenderness of build, an extraordinary intelligence." This follows the medical view of the turn of the century that tuberculosis was inherited through the mother rather than through the father![89] Mann evokes the Jew's characteristic slenderness along with his characteristic predisposition to tuberculosis. But here, like Naphta's Jewishness, the disease is labeled as an inheritance of the mother. Tuberculosis is not the inheritance of the ritual butcher, whose magic cures such illnesses. Tuberculosis, like Jewishness, is matrilineal. This explains why Naphta is the regressive pedagogical force (opposed to Settembrini and Peeperkorn) in the fictive world of Mann's "magic mountain." But the only truly modern figure in the novel remains the protagonist Hans Castorp, who learns from experience, under the motto *placet experiri,* rather than from books or tradition—and who is not actually tubercular! Nothing about him associates him with Thomas Mann's constructed image of the Jew in the novel.

The association between tuberculosis and ritual slaughter is not merely a "literary" one. It has a powerful link in the notion that *shehitah* was the central means by which the Jews avoided tuberculous infection. Among Jews (and their supporters) it was not "racial immunity" nor the "pathological constitution" of the Jews that rescued them from illness, but religious, that is hygienic practice. The ritual slaughter of cattle was followed by the *Bedikah*, the ritual inspection of the carcass for anomalies, especially in the pleura and viscera. The Talmudic practice (outlined in *Mishna Chullin* 3:1) delineates the various conditions of the pleura that would make the animal *treff* (unclean) under Halakhic law, and therefore inedible.

The two aspects of *shehitah*—the ritual slaughter and bleeding of the animal, and the examination of its pleura (*Bedikah ha Reah*)—are often linked as hygienic moments that prevent the transmission of disease (as understood in terms of the age of Pasteur and Koch). The leading Russian Jewish specialist on the topic, the St. Petersburg physician I. A. Dembo, stresses not the prevention of transmission of infection, but the increased health of those eating meat that can be kept fresh longer because of the bleeding process.[90] The association between hygiene and ritual slaughter is the basic proof of the need to bleed the animals. Such views were supported by two of the most important medical authorities of the day, Rudolf Virchow and Émile Du Bois-Reymond; Dembo dedicates his book to the latter.[91] And it is tuberculosis which is most greatly feared and is thus the disease best prevented by the entire ritual of slaughter. Indeed, in the *fin-de-siècle Jewish Encyclopedia*, the article on *Bedikah* stresses that the examination of pleura was to look for (among other things) *bu'ot*, defined in the article as "blisters or tubercles."[92]

Those who opposed the ritual killing of animals as inhumane because of the animal's conscious state also found themselves in opposition to the *Bedikah*. Thus Ernst von Schwartz could maintain that, while the Jews' claim that "the Jewish examination offers the best possible guarantee for healthy meat" (54), may have been true at one time, it is no longer the case. It may be that this inspection made sense in ancient times when the Jews were exposed to illnesses and lacked veterinary expertise, but today, he states, "this examination appears comical" (49). He quotes J. Goltz, the director of the public abattoir in Berlin, that "these rules speak more than any others against the hygienic importance of *Schächten*." The head of the Bremen abattoir, Koch, noted that "many animals are declared to be kosher that are then declared to be inedible by the official inspection" (51). Thus older Jewish religious practices, which are now labeled as "barbaric," were also understood as earlier forms of hygiene. They were both "bad" and "good"—but only for the Jews in their imagined proper time and place. And that time and place was not contemporary Europe. It is little wonder that the illnesses ascribed to the Jews did not include tuberculosis, for the magical power of *shehitah*, which paralleled the Catholic Mass, kept the illness apart from the Jews.

If Zweig's drama of ritual murder made Kafka weep, it is clear that the debate about *shehitah* gave Kafka a trope that linked "beauty/health" and "ugliness/illness" with the ritual practices of the Jew. Kafka's con-

PLATE 30. A 1893 cartoon in the Swiss periodical *Der Nebelspalter* of a *mauschelnd* David ritually slaughtering Goliath (National Library of Medicine, Bethesda).

text could have been the discussion of *shehitah* in Prague culture. But it is important to note that Kafka had actually read Jacob Gordin's Yiddish drama *Di Shekhite* (1899), in which the protagonist's act of murder using a knife is juxtaposed to the training of a *shochet.*[93] This seems to be one of the very few Yiddish works that Kafka actually read.[94] There too, if ever so ironically, ritual slaughter and murder are paired. Over and over Kafka rewrites *shehitah* in terms of an anti-Semitic culture that read *shehitah* as the model for the ritual murder as in an 1893 cartoon in the Swiss periodical *Der Nebelspalter* of a *mauschelnd* David ritually slaughtering Goliath (Plate 30). This image introduces the anti-Semitic fantasy of the weapon that Jews used for their ritual murder/*shehitah*. It is not a ritual slaughtering knife but a pointed and curved dagger.

Such pointed knives are a staple of representations of ritual murder from the early modern period, the fifteenth and sixteenth centuries, to the infamous illustration on the front of the "ritual murder" issue of Julius Streicher's notorious *Der Stürmer* of May 1, 1934.[95] Remember Kafka's own comment in his diaries, that the ritual of circumcision used "an ordinary knife, a sort of fish knife." (See Plate 5.) The ritual knife used for circumcision, like the knife used to butcher animals, is blunt rather than pointed. It would be useless for stabbing; its sharp edge is its significant feature (Plate 31). Nonetheless, in Kafka's description of ritual murder, the victim is "stabbed . . . between throat and chin."[96] (D2, 130). This is a fantasy; it is not *shehitah*. However, Kafka takes up the equation of ritual murder with ritual slaughter not out of ignorance, but in

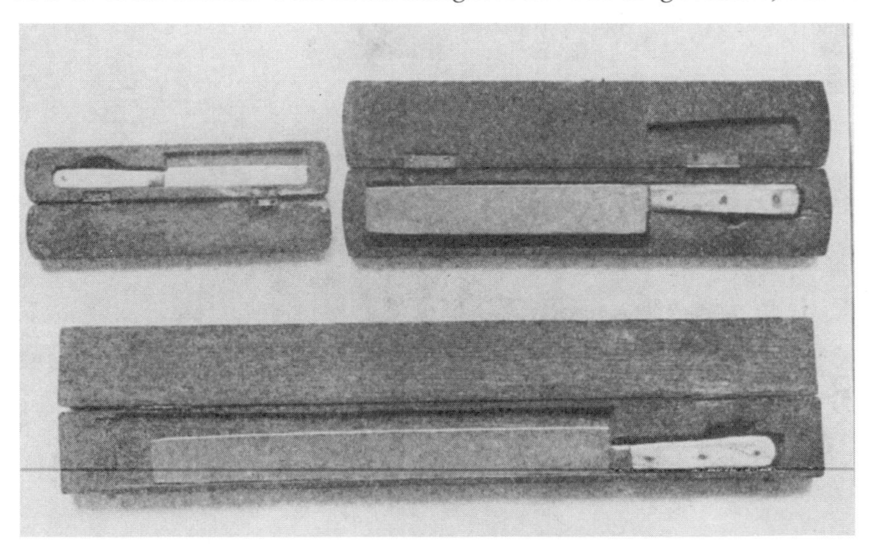

PLATE 31. The knives used in ritual slaughter, from J. G. Lipman, "Shehitah," *The Jewish Encyclopedia*, 12 vols. (New York: Funk and Wagnalls, 1904), 11, 56 (National Library of Medicine, Bethesda).

order to reflect on the discourse that produced it, the discourse on the Jew's immutability and unassimilability to Western culture.

The pointed knife is the link to the secular interpretation of *shehitah*, namely, ritual slaughter as a form of hygiene, part of the struggle against illnesses such as tuberculosis. For the image of the "battle" against tuberculosis is closely allied with the sharpened sword. In two posters from World War I this image is made overt. In a French image, the two enemies of civilization are the Germans and tuberculosis. The shedding of the blood of the German eagle represents the healing of the tubercular (Plate 32). In a contemporaneous Italian poster, the healing hand of the Red Cross nurse holds the dagger that impales the dragon of tuberculosis (Plate 33). In both of these images, it is the pointed knife or sword of hygiene that will destroy the danger to the body politic. The knives impale animals that represent danger, and these animals belong to the wider category of symbols that would include the "vermin" (*Ungeziefer*) that represent the Jews in the culture of the time. Thus the danger of disease becomes the danger of the Jews. There is a further set of visual associations within contemporary discourse to the struggle against tuberculosis represented by the practice of *shehitah*. It is, of course, a further echo of the bloody "battle" imagery, with its highly masculinized rhetoric (even in the case of the Red Cross nurse). For, as in the "struggle for Dreyfus," the struggle over disease and its meaning is a combat that defines the realm of the masculine for Kafka. But it is a battle that also evokes older, anti-Semitic myths about the dangers of Jewish practices such as circumcision, and images of Jews as carriers of disease.

Echoes of the ritual scene of the blood libel murder and its association with the (psychic) health of the Jew can be found in a number of Kafka's literary texts. As early as Kafka's "Description of a Struggle" (1906/1910), the image of the ritual shedding of blood serves as the focus for the closure of a text. There the "acquaintance," with no apparent motivation, " . . . pulled a knife out of his pocket, opened it thoughtfully, and then, as though he were playing, he plunged it into his left upper arm, and didn't withdraw it. Blood promptly began to flow. His round cheeks grew pale" (S, 50). It is clearly a pointed knife. The narrator's response is to pull "out the knife, cut up the sleeve of his overcoat and jacket" and tear his shirt sleeve open. "I sucked a little at the deep wound" (S, 50). Kafka conflates suicide, ritual bloodletting, and circumcision. The narrator assumes the role of the *mohel* as the acquaintance

PLATE 32. A French poster of the American Committee against Tuberculosis in France, representing the struggle against the Germans and tuberculosis from World War I (National Library of Medicine, Bethesda).

PLATE 33. An Italian poster by B. Casella representing the Red Cross's fight against tuberculosis (Wellcome Institute, London).

had assumed the role of the *schochet*. The image of the *mohel* sucking on the open wound is redolent with anxiety about the transmission of illnesses, including syphilis and tuberculosis, as well as with images of forbidden male/male contact. Self-mutilation reveals the depths of the acquaintance's despair. Kafka projects the interrelated discourses of ritual and madness applied to the Jew into this neutral world, in which no race "marks" his nameless characters.

The attack on *shehitah* as cruel and heartless compared to modern forms of animal slaughter is echoed in Kafka's later story "In the Penal Colony," when the Officer tries to second-guess his visitor's response to the machine: "Perhaps you object on principle to capital punishment in general and to such mechanical instruments of death in particular, besides you will see that the execution has no support from the public, a shabby ceremony—carried out with a machine already somewhat old and worn" (S, 155). This echoes the westernized Jew's view that ritual slaughter and circumcision, "have merely historical character, even as they are practiced today" (D1, 196). It has become a "shabby ceremony." However, the machine combines the modern forms of slaughter advocated by the opponents of *shehitah*, clearly condemning them, with the ritualism associated with *shehitah*.

Such complex play with images of knives and slaughter is not limited to "In the Penal Colony."[97] The masochistic, Jewish response to the Christian intolerance of Jewish ritual is ironically thematized in his tale, "Jackals and Arabs," first published in Martin Buber's periodical *The Jew*, in October 1917. This Jewish audience would have recognized the allusions to *shehitah* without any trouble. In Kafka's tale of "Jackals and Arabs," the jackals represent the Western fantasy of the Jews as always haunting the edges of "culture," unable to truly alter their instincts. This is a fantasy now shared by westernized Jews themselves. The jackals have all the Jewish markers of difference. They bear the *foetor judaïcus*, "a rank smell which at times I had to set my teeth to endure streamed from their open jaws" (S, 408). They *mauschel*, they have a "natural plaintiveness of . . . voice" (S, 409). But it is the eating habits of the jackal that most set them apart from their neighbors in the desert, the Arabs. The jackals detest the Arabs, who "kill animals for food, and carrion they despise" (S, 408). The jackals are appalled at their "exile among such creatures" (S, 408). All of the physical attributes of these animals reflect (and are reflected) in the representation of their character. Here it is the mode of feeding, of consumption, of becoming what one is fated to become through eating, that defines the jackal.

It is central to Kafka's representation of the jackals that they eat differently from the Arabs. According to their perspective, they eat "naturally," consuming carrion, while the Arabs "murder" their food. The jackals desire a world cleansed of such an enemy: "no more bleating of sheep knifed by an Arab; every beast to die a natural death; no interference till we have drained the carcass empty and picked its bones clean. Cleanliness, nothing but cleanliness is what we want" (S, 409–410). Hygiene, by which ritual slaughter is positively reinscribed in turn-of-the century rhetoric, is how the jackals rationalize their consumption of carrion. But the different eating habits of these two old foes signify their different character; they lie "in the blood, and perhaps will only end with it" (S, 408). What must be done, says one old jackal, is that "we shall draw blood from them, and the quarrel will be over." It is the drawing of blood that will cure. But they are too cowardly and weak to draw this blood themselves: "And so, sir," they say to the European visitor, "and so, dear sir, by means of your all-powerful hands slit their throats through with these scissors!" (S, 410). And what is provided for their execution is a "small pair of sewing scissors, covered with ancient rust." The weapon of choice has tiny, but distinctly pointed blades.

In "Jackals and Arabs," Kafka parodically rewrites the debate about *shehitah*. The "natural" manner of death, the eating of carrion, comes to represent the historicized ritual tradition of the marginalized Jews, whose means of slaughter provokes the disgust of their non-Jewish country people. The Jews argue that their means of slaughter is hygienic (clean), and that the killing of animals is barbaric and unclean. Like the Jews, the jackals drain the blood from the carcass. They are the ritual slaughters in reverse, who eat only *treff* meat from animals that have died a natural death, but who drain their blood. (Jews are forbidden to consume the flesh of animals that are not ritually butchered.). The jackals are also the ritual murderers in this ironic replay of the anti-Semitic stereotypes of the day. They want the throats of the next victims slit. Remember, it is the jackals who claim to eat only animals that have died "naturally." The Arabs, on the other hand, are not to be allowed to die naturally; they must be slaughtered as they have slaughtered the animals they consume. (The irony is that Jewish and Islamic ritual practices are certainly closer to each other than to European ideas of ritual slaughter.) But the weapon they provide is comical, a pair of rusty, sewing scissors, whose pointed blades evoke the pointed weapons supposedly used in ritual slaughter and ritual murder.[98]

The Arabs laugh at the jackals who offer these pathetic scissors to every European who passes through. And the Arabs treat these halakhically unclean animals as their "dogs." The Arabs throw a camel's carcass to them, and a jackal goes immediately "at the camel's throat, sinking his teeth straight into an artery" (S, 410). All of the jackals then pile onto the carcass. The "camel's blood was already lying in pools, reeking to heaven, the carcass was torn wide open in many places" (S, 411). What marks the "hatred" of the jackals for the Arabs is the jackal's nature, represented in this version by a parody of *shehitah*, with the (dead) animal's throat slashed and its body laid open for the European's inspection. It is this "nature" that fuels the enmity between the jackals and Arabs.

Here the narrator serves, as he does in "In the Penal Colony," as the outsider whose visit highlights the blindness of all involved to the senselessness of their world. Like the proverbial person from Mars, all of their pretensions are revealed to him, and potentially to us. For the readers of Buber's journal, Kafka's allusions to the debates about *shehitah* would have been clear, and would have called down the laughter both against those who attacked this practice as reflecting the essential Jewish character, and against those defenders who saw *kashruth* (ritual practice) as an essential part of the ritual definition of the Jew, but retrofitted it with a "modern," "hygienic" rationale. Kafka unsuccessfully tries to escape this double bind. He substitutes vegetarianism and Fletcherization, or the repetitive chewing of his food, for the laws of *kashruth*. His literary view mirrors this shift. Kafka links the punishment of the body with consumption of food. He certainly has models for this association. In Dreyfus's diary, it is the filthy, uncooked food given to him, in "In the Penal Colony," the foods prepared by the women for those about to be executed, and in the parody of "Jackals and Arabs," the ritual preparation of food. Food, with its evocation of ritual and hygiene, is linked to Kafka's sense that—whatever diet they consume—Jews remain Jews. And yet there is a meaningful variation in his discourse on food. Kafka writes of the antiquarian notions of ritualization of food, but acknowledges a world in which changing forms of ritualization shape each of his literary figures. Thus the rejection of older models of ritual (that are supposed to have a miraculous ability to ward off evils of all types), is replaced by new, "modern" rituals of eating, whose powers are also believed to be able to ward off the ultimate evil, the decay of the body. Food for the body becomes food for the soul.

In "The Investigations of a Dog" (1922), Kafka triples the roles of the Jew as dog (already present in the image of the jackals), the Jew as writer, and the Jew as pseudoscientist. This tale, which has been successfully read (by Kafka's friend Hugo Bergmann) as a representation of the "Zionist dream of Jewish life," centers this dream in the "science of nutrition"[99] (S, 302). In this tale you are literally what you eat. The conflict between pseudoscientistic discourse (whether racial Zionist, such as Buber, or reform religious) and religious revelation is at the core of this tale. The dog's fasting, for example, is not the mystic's fasting by choice, but fasting out of imposed necessity. The dog's interpretation of this act, however, turns necessity into the stuff of scientific examination cast in the positivistic discourse of the biological science of the day. However the contemporary Jewish references in this tale are read, this story's central trope of the scientific dog examining his own hunger concentrates on a major biological (and social) question of the late nineteenth century—what is the role of food in the shaping of the body and of society. This "scientific" search for knowledge is placed in a scientific discourse commanded by a talking dog. It is a search for knowledge that "crumbles away like a neglected ancestral inheritance and must laboriously be rehabilitated anew" (S, 287). The discourse of the scientific rationalization of Halakhic practices, as discussed in the case of ritual slaughter, by the Jews of the turn of the century attempts to "rehabilitate" their ritual laws by showing that they are really science. Here Kafka turns the trope of the Jew as dog into one of the Jew as scientist. The aggadic shape of the story itself places the Halakhic into question. Telling stories is better than providing laws, especially when those laws are "misread" as pseudoscience. Kafka's dog is both the scientist using Jewish law to explain how hygienic Jews really are, and also the object of scientific investigation. The epistemological problem of being simultaneously observer and observed is also that of the Jew as victim and as witness, as betrayed and as betrayer. Buried in this tale are reworkings of the dangers of being a Jew in a world in which laws, either scientific or legal, can suddenly come apart and make the observer the observed.

In his diaries, Kafka describes a "singular juridical procedure" in which a male victim is executed in his cell by a male executioner with a dagger (D2, 162–163). In Kafka's literary work, such a scenario reflects his reworking of the problem of the feminization of the victim. There the echoes from the problematic image of execution in Kafka's "In the Penal Colony" reverberate. For the cotton that wraps the prisoner reappears here as the "cotton sheath" holding the "new dagger" that is intended as the means of execution. The collection of blood and the risks that it implies are always present in these images of ritual murder.

No text is clearer in this regard than "A Fratricide" (1919) (S, 402–404). In this tale "Schmar, the murderer" whets "his weapon, half a bayonet and half a kitchen knife" on his boot while he waits for his victim, Wese. Schmar butchers Wese: "And right into the throat and left into the throat and a third time deep into the belly stabbed Schmar's knife." This ritual reenactment of *shehitah*—first the cutting of the conscious animal's throat, then *Bedikah*, the opening of the body—is heightened by Schmar's shriek: "The bliss of murder! The relief, the soaring ecstasy from the shedding of another's blood! Wese, old night bird, friend, alehouse crony, you are oozing away into the dark earth below the street. Why aren't you simply a bladder of blood so that I could stamp on you and make you vanish into nothingness?" (S, 403). His victim is not merely a "bladder of blood" but a living, breathing individual whose murder is ritualized with a pointed dagger, but in the end the murder is apprehended by the policeman. Order is restored, at least superficially. This text echoes the final scene in *The Trial* (1914), where K. is taken out and executed:

> The two of them laid K. down on the ground, propped him up against the boulder, and settled his head upon it. But in spite of the pains they took and all the willingness K. showed, his posture remained contorted and unnatural-looking. . . . Then one of them opened his frock coat and out of a sheath that hung from a belt girt round his waistcoat drew a long, thin, double-edged butcher's knife, held it up, and tested the cutting edges in the moonlight. . . . [K.] raised his hands and spread out all his fingers.
>
> But the hands of one of the partners were already at K.'s throat, while the other thrust the knife deep into his heart and turned it twice. With failing eyes K. could still see the two of them immediately before him, cheek leaning against cheek, watching the final act. "Like a dog!" he said; it was as if the shame of it must outlive him. (T, 227–229)

This scene alludes to contemporary associations of ritual murder with ritual practice. In the final scene in *The Trial*, K. is no longer completely convinced of his own innocence. Has he, like Moritz Scharf, become convinced of his guilt by the power of the accusation? Is he in the end the best witness against himself? Is he the apostate who has sold his birthright for a mess of pottage? Has he betrayed the Jew within, like the *Taufjude*, like the baptized Jew whom Kafka's contemporary Fritz Wittels describes as possessing the "heightened passion of the persecuted, who attempts to destroy the colossus of the state that will not give him his tiny bit of law, without which he would rather be a dog than a human being"?[100] Is he the tubercular, condemned by Kafka's father who complained "about a clerk with TB: 'The sooner that sick dog croaks the better'" (L, 136). This clerk is seen as a drain on the private and public coffers. Is the state therefore quite right in considering such betrayers of their own people as potential betrayers of the state?

The execution has more than a slight tinge of both ritual slaughter and ritual execution. The body is prepared in a parody of the *akedah*, the binding of Isaac, as it is in the ritual preparation of the victim in the discourse of the blood libel. (One should remember that the resolution of the *akedah* is God's directive to Abraham to circumcise the males in his family. Circumcision in this context substitutes for sacrifice, and the covenant against human sacrifice is thus inscribed on the Jew's body.) Kafka also draws on Zweig's depiction of the knife used in the suicide of Moritz Scharf. There, too, it is a butcher knife that the nameless executioner carries, and as one holds his throat (to prepare him for the blow) the other stabs him in the heart. Here the entire vocabulary of the ritual murder as suicide is reenacted. But a Jewish butcher's knife cannot stab; only a practitioner of the more "modern" and "humane" form of butchery, the pig butcher of Kafka's nightmares, can stab the victim in the heart. The knife that Moritz accuses the *schochet* of having used in his lying reconstitution of the ritual murder, the knife that he uses to kill himself, was itself "proof" of the falsity of the charge of ritual murder. Through the vehicle of Zweig's play, the two acts—the act that marks the accusation of the blood libel and labels the innocent Jew as a murderer, and the suicide of the self-hating Jew—can be linked. Here it is the opening of the body, the stab into the heart, that reveals the awful truth about what one has really been along. K.'s last thought is that he is being murdered like an unclean animal, a dog, rather than like a ritually pure one such as a steer. It is the dog from Kafka's "Jackals and Arabs" whose uncleanness is the reflection of the world's attitude toward the Jews. Here the weapon is not a pair of sewing scissors, but "a pork butcher's broad knife that quickly and with mechanical regularity chops into me from the side and cuts off very thin slices that fly off almost like shavings because of the speed of the action" (D1, 286–287). Kafka becomes the victim, robbed of his integrity and manliness, murdered ritually by the Christian world about him. The shame of his victimage will outlive him. This shame Kafka can represent in ironic and distanced abstraction in his texts, while weeping at its mimetic representation in Arnold Zweig's drama.

Masculinity and Homosexuality

If the anxiety at what he must become is central to Kafka's world and the subject of at least some of his literary representations, then the ambiguity of that ill, diseased, incomplete thing hidden within the father and the self makes the very notion of the "masculine" in Kafka suspect. Indeed, much of the critical literature argues that central to Kafka's sense of self is his repressed homosexuality.[101] These views depart from the antitheses "straight/gay" and "masculine/feminine" as articulated in the post-1960s era.[102] These antitheses simply do not hold up when one looks at the turn of the century. They must be modified in the light of the construction of "homosexuality" during this period.

Once "gay" was constructed as a psychopathology at the mid-nineteenth century, this psychopathology came to be given the medical label "homosexuality."[103] No longer a "sin," it became the concern of the physician. But at the turn of the century, the Jewish male came to be another version of the "third sex." The idea of a "third sex" had evolved with the work of the lawyer Karl Ulrichs in the 1860s, who argued that there were three "natural" sexes—males, females, and "uranians." By the 1890s, this view dominated the debates within the homosexual emancipation movement. Homosexual, Jewish scientists such as Magnus Hirschfeld transmuted Ulrichs's legal rhetoric into the language of medical science—and the idea of "sexual intermediary classes" was developed. This view dominated Otto Weininger's 1904 formulation of homosexual identity. Kafka's strong interest in Weininger, like that of many Jewish males of his day, reflected to no little degree Weininger's account of masculinity and Jewishness.[104]

The circumcised body of the Jew was neither heterosexual in a normative sense nor "homosexual," except by extension and metaphor. It was a "third" version of the male—heterosexuals, "homosexuals," and Jews. The Jewish body, like the other two, was born, not made. Circumcision came to be seen as the exterior sign of the inherently different nature of the Jewish male. Jews were more often understood as born circumcised.[105] The myth that understood male Jews as marked by congenital circumcision is part of the culture of the *fin de siècle.* The male Jewish body thus revealed itself as different. This difference was understood as pathological, as it mirrored the psychopathology of the Jew. This meant that, while different from the "heterosexual" body, the male Jew, no matter what his sexual orientation, was closely associated with the pathological category of the "homosexual." This sense of a special status can be judged by the simple fact that Jewish males were considered by Aryan science as particularly predisposed to homosexuality. It is, as usual, the body of the Jew that betrays him. Thus the (male) Jew is seen as having an arm span less than equivalent to his height, as does the woman.[106] This was the case with Kafka. It is of little surprise therefore that the Jew is seen as overwhelmingly at risk for being (or becoming) a homosexual. Moses Julius Gutmann observes, "all of the comments about the supposed stronger sexual drive among Jews has no basis in fact; most frequently they are sexual neurasthenics. Above all the number of Jewish homosexuals is extraordinarily high."[107] This view is echoed by Alexander Pilcz, Professor of Psychiatry at the University of Vienna, who noted, "there is a relatively high incidence of homosexuality among the Jews."[108] It is the biological (or "ontological") difference of the Jew that is the source of his feminized nature. Among Jews, according to a lecture in 1920, by the Professor of Anthropology at the University of Vienna, Robert Stigler,

> [T]he physical signs of the sexual characteristics are noticeably vague. Among them, the women are often found to have relatively narrow pelvis and relatively broad shoulders and the men to have broad hips and narrow shoulders. . . . It is important to note the attempt on the part of the Jews to eliminate the role that secondary sexual characteristics instinctively play among normal people through their advocacy of the social and professional equality of man and woman.[109]

But gay society of the *fin de siècle* also saw the Jew as different. Within gay culture in Germany, Jews were seen as essentially Jews even when they were also identified as gay. They were given Jewish nicknames (such as Sarah or Rebecca) even when their given names were in no ways identifiably Jewish.[110]

The concept of masculinity was thus extremely complex for Kafka, as he questions the ritual murder trials or the Dreyfus case. But Kafka's confrontations were always mediated by texts: the textual world is the one he wishes to control, control which the culture around him denies him. Through a look at Kafka's reading and his response, one specific moment in the intellectual relationship between notions of masculinity and anti-Semitism at the turn of the century can be revealed.

It is specifically in Kafka's reply to the works of Hans Blüher (1888–1955) that we can find a proof text for the development of his views and anxieties concerning the relationship between masculinity, illness, and race. In Blüher the question of the homoerotic plays a major role, and Kafka's own representation of this experience becomes a testing ground for the bounds of the masculine. Blüher is one of the most fascinating figures of the intellectual scene during the first half of the twentieth century. Involved in the formation of the German Youth Movement (*Wandervogelbewegung*) at the turn of the century, his two-volume study of the homoeroticism of the youth movement and his development of the concept of bisexuality were heavily indebted to Sigmund Freud's early work.[111] Blüher was an early follower of Freud, and was published by him in the *Imago*.[112] By 1926, he had broken with Freud as a Jewish thinker, and denounced psychoanalysis as anti- German.[113] Blüher's writing in many ways created the Youth Movement, by retrospectively giving it a coherence that it lacked in actuality. His history of the Youth Movement, *The Role of the Erotic in Male Society,* written under the impact of his early reading of Freud, captured Kafka's attention. In October, 1917, Kafka notes, "Am eager to read Blüher" (LF, 153).

What Kafka finally read impressed him. Blüher dismissed traditional education as training for the state, and saw in the structures of education an attempt to subvert the natural tendencies of young men to bond. Blüher captures the spirit of the *Wandervogelbewegung* as the antithesis of such education, as a space where bonding among male equals could take place. He thus *de facto* rejects the presence of women and Jews from his ideal society, while at the same time attacking the vague cult of "Germanness" that permeated the early movement. What struck Blüher was the persecution of homosexuals in the movement itself, which he saw as an unconscious suppression of the libidinal attachment to members of the same sex. It was a neurotic process caused by repression. To explain this "self-hatred," Blüher used a Freudian conception of the mechanisms of defense. Blüher offered Kafka a reading of an "ideal" male society where social repression might be suspended. Unfortunately, the very homoeroticism at the basis of this society was declared to be unhealthy.

Kafka expressed his first interest in Blüher during World War I, when his own sense of masculinity was affected by his own illness and by the highly visible definition of the masculine in a mobilized society. He evidently turned to the two volumes on the Youth Movement immediately. Max Brod writes to him on October 4, 1917:

> Incidentally I received two books yesterday, which can help me. Both by Hans Blüher. "The Role of the Erotic in Male Society" and "Volk and Führer in the Youth Movement."—It is a hymn to pederasty, from which all cultural progress is expected.—I read the books without being able to stop. Today I am already more sober and see in them the description of the *German* man as the essential man.[114]

Brod's sense of Blüher's agenda was better than most. It was one that Kafka surely sensed. A great number of Jews followed Blüher's claim about the relationship of homosexuality to cultural progress, and advocated the male society, the *Männerbund,* which was the *Wandervogelbewegung*. But its "Aryan" mentality made it impossible for Jews to truly become part of this masculine world, as Kafka quite correctly saw. Nevertheless Kafka begins to read his own experiences in terms of Blüher:

> If I go on to say that in a recent dream of mine I gave [Franz] Werfel a kiss, I stumble right into the midst of Blüher's book. . . . The book upset me; I had to lay it aside for two days. However, it shares the quality of other psychoanalytic works that in the first moment its thesis seems remarkably satisfying, but very soon after one feels the same old hunger. This is "of course" easily explained psychoanalytically: Instant Repression. The royal train gets fastest service.[115] (LF, 166)

Kafka's rebellion against psychoanalysis (he had indeed read his Freud) is an answer to the relatively schematic answers offered by contemporary psychoanalysis, especially the emphasis on the Oedipal and repression. But it is also a rebellion against a "Jewish" science, so understood at the time, that refused to acknowledge its Jewishness. Kafka condemns the universal hermeneutics of psychoanalysis, not its validity. Here the conflict between the Aryan world of Blüher and the Jewish world of Freud is played out—at this moment, Blüher embodies both, even though it is clear to Kafka that Blüher's idealized male society is in no way open to him as a Jew.

Kafka's anxiety about the homoerotic—the kiss he gives Franz Werfel, another Jewish writer, in his dreams—reflects his own ambiguity about his Jewish male body. For it is only the attraction between equals (here two Jewish writers from Prague) that is possible within Blüher's cult of masculinity. Yet the Jewish male body is also (if only in the rhetoric of the time) not a truly male body. It is the analog to the body of the homosexual. If Zweig's account of the ritual murder trial makes Kafka weep, then reading Blüher upsets him. Blüher's model of the homoerotic, male society rejects the very Jewishness with which Kafka is forced, by the anti-Semitic society in which he and Blüher lived, to identify. Is being a "real" male and being "Jewish" antithetical? According to Blüher it is. This is not an unusual problem for Jewish males of the turn of the century. The rise of the Jewish gymnastic societies throughout Central Europe, and the rise of Jewish fraternities (usually not dueling fraternities) at universities, speak of the desire to engage in analogous forms of male bonding. Kafka's intense preoccupation with sports is an extension of this anxiety, coupled with the notion of the need to re-form the Jewish body without and within.

Kafka's own homoerotic feelings and fantasies must be read in light of the elision of the homosexual and the Jew. His passionate relationship with Oskar Pollack, and the story written in December, 1902, in which Kafka writes of their relationship as "Shamefaced Lanky" to Pollack's "Impure in Heart," stressed the rhetoric of the body in a homoerotic setting (LF, 6–7). His statement, in 1912, that "I am supposed to pose in the nude for the artist [Ernst] Ascher, as a model for St. Sebastian," unofficial patron saint of the homosexual, again frames his body in this context (D2, 222).[116] The overt references to homosexual activity in Kafka's writing, such as the deleted passage describing the painter Titorelli and K. in *The Trial*, or the "embrace" between the narrator and the Inspector in the "Memoirs of the Kalda Railroad," all point toward a strong sense of the homoerotic as an aspect of Kafka's fantasy life (D2, 83). It is especially true that in Kafka's relationship with the itinerant Yiddish actor Yitshak Löwy he felt a powerful sense of attraction as well as danger. Kafka takes Löwy to the National Theater in October 1911, and Löwy on that occasion informs Kafka that he has gonorrhea. Kafka's response:

"[T]hen my hair touched his as I moved his head toward me, I became afraid of the possibility of lice."[117] The tension between attraction and infection is evident in the contact, no matter how trivial, between "equals." But in Kafka's reading of Blüher, the desired acknowledgment of the homoerotic as an acceptable sign of belonging to the world of the "modern" is denied. For the male Jew may look or even act as if he is a member of this world, but it is sham and illusion.

If we begin again with Alfred Dreyfus and the accusation of treason that robbed him of his role as a soldier and as a man, the primary witnesses against him at his first trial were revealed to have been homosexual. Their homosexuality plays an important role in the conventional understanding of the case, especially among the homoerotic culture of the French and German armies. The homosexual is ill or at least repressed in the medical discourse of the time, the homosexual is the Jew in that same discourse, and the homosexual is the false witness who betrays the Jew. These contradictions provide a slippery space in which all such categories are interdependent.

After World War I, the *Dolchstoßlegende*, the "legend of the stab in the back," became established in Germany and Austria. It was supposedly the Jews who failed in their roles as soldiers and betrayed Germany and the Habsburg Empire. This was the only thing that could account for the loss. This was analogous to the claim in French intellectual and popular circles that women and syphilis had caused the loss of the Franco-Prussian War. Blüher, having broken with Freud, accepted the legend, and argued openly for the exclusion of Jews as incapable of integration into German society. His 1922 pamphlet on this topic, *Secessio Judaica*, attracted Kafka's attention.

On March 15, 1922 Kafka notes: "Objections to be made against the book: he has popularized it, and with a will, moreover—and with magic. How he escapes the dangers (Blüher)" (D2 225). And then Kafka tries to write an answer to Blüher:

> **June 16, 1922.** Quite apart from the insuperable difficulties always presented by Blüher's philosophical and visionary power, one is in the difficult position of easily incurring the suspicion, almost with one's every remark, of wanting ironically to dismiss the ideas of this book. One is suspect even if, as in my case, there is nothing further from one's mind, in the face of this book, than irony. This difficulty in reviewing his book has its counterpart in a difficulty that Blüher, from his side,

> cannot surmount. He calls himself an anti-Semite without hatred, *sine ira et studio*, and he really is that; yet he easily awakens the suspicion, almost with his every remark, that he is an enemy of the Jews, whether out of happy hatred or out of unhappy love. These difficulties confront each other like stubborn facts of nature, and attention must be called to them lest in reflecting on this book one stumble over these errors and at the very outset be rendered incapable of going on. According to Blüher, one cannot refute Judaism inductively, by statistics, by appealing to experience; these methods of the older anti-Semitism cannot prevail against Judaism; all other peoples can be refuted in this way, but not the Jews, the chosen people; to each particular charge the anti-Semites make, the Jew will be able to give a particular answer in justification. Blüher makes a very superficial survey, to be sure, of the particular charges and the answers given them. This perception, insofar as it concerns the Jews and not the other peoples, is profound and true. Blüher draws two conclusions from it, a full and a partial one. (D2, 230–231)

Kafka's comments break off at this point. Unable to proceed, Kafka wrote to his friend Dr. Robert Klopstock on June 30, 1922:

> *Secessio Judaica*. Won't you write something about it? I cannot do it; when I try, my hand immediately goes dead, even though I, like everyone else, would have a great deal to say about it. Somewhere in my ancestry I too must have a Talmudist, I should hope, but he does not embolden me enough to go ahead, so I set you to it. It does not have to be a refutation, only an answer to the appeal. That ought to be very tempting. And there is indeed a temptation to let one's flock graze on this German and yet not entirely alien pasture, after the fashion of the Jews. (LF, 330)

Here Kafka mimics the rhetoric of the early Freudian Blüher, an Aryan arguing like a Jew, yet stresses his own Jewishness against Blüher's hypocritical "Germanness." This "Germanness" is one, however, shared by Kafka and Klopstock; it is "not entirely alien pasture." Blüher's case, according to Kafka, is one of a "happy hatred or . . . unhappy love" that Blüher feels for the Jews, embodied in his "very superficial survey, to be sure, of the particular charges and the answers given them." Kafka knows his psychoanalytic discourse well enough to point out to Klopstock, who certainly did also, the Freudian homoerotic in Blüher's text. This model, found in Freud's reading of the Schreber case, can be reduced to Kafka's formula: is Blüher in love with the Jews or does he hate the Jews because they make him love them? This is a far from unique reading of the anti-Semite as homosexual. Arnold Zweig evokes Schreber when, in 1933, he explains the anti-Semitic German as the psychotic homosexual.[118] If the homosexual is psychotic, shaped by the fixation of his own sexual identity at an earlier (anal) stage of development, then the real "primitive" is Blüher, who represents for Kafka the homoerotic. Kafka sees his own psyche as deformed by his Jewish ancestry ("Somewhere in my ancestry I too must have a Talmudist"). He claims to retain this intellectual proclivity, but is also self-aware of it. This mind-set is not that of the homosexual, for here Kafka sets himself apart from Blüher's paranoia. Blüher becomes "this German" (Schreber) who will be the object of study "after the fashion of the Jews" (Freud/Kafka).

What is unstated in Kafka's dismissal of the "very superficial survey, to be sure, of the particular charges and the answers given them," is that Blüher stresses the superficiality of the Jew's westernization.[119] For Blüher, the Jews remain the "Orientals," no matter how they seem to have physically changed. They regress to what they always have been, once they are removed from Western society. Blüher's text evokes in a powerful manner the idea of a Jewish racial type: "The Jews are the only people that practice mimicry. Mimicry of the blood, of the name, and of the body" (19). Here Blüher simply picks up the rhetoric of thinkers such as Werner Sombart, who argued, in *The Jews and Modern Capitalism*, that the Jewish body is inherently immutable. Sombart's notion of the immutable does not contradict his image of Jewish mimicry; for him, the Jew represents immutable mutability:

> The driving power in Jewish adaptability is of course the idea of a purpose, or a goal, as the end of all things. Once the Jew has made up his mind what line he will follow, the rest is comparatively easy, and his mobility only makes his success more sure. How mobile the Jew can be is positively astounding. He is able to give himself the personal appearance he most desires. . . . The best illustrations may be drawn from the United Sates, where the Jew of the second or third generation is with more difficulty distinguished from the non-Jew. You can tell the German after no matter how many generations; so with the Irish, the Swede, the Slav. But the Jew, in so far as his racial features allow it, has been successful in imitating the Yankee type, especially in regard to outward marks such as clothing, bearing, and the peculiar method of hairdressing.[120]

For Blüher, as for Sombart, the Jewish mind-set persists, though their bodies (and hairstyles) seem to be changing. Their corrupt, materialistic thought disrupts those among whom they dwell by generating ideas that seem universal, yet are inherently Jewish. And "the Jew Freud" and his notion of psychosomatic correlates represent only the most modern version of such corrosive Jewish thought (23). It is to be found already in Spinoza's *Ethics*, and it is the identity of body and spirit. For Spinoza, as for Freud, when something occurs in the body, it is because it occurs in the spirit (25). "Where ever spirit is there is also body. Every idea has a corporeal correlate" (25). The identity of mind and body, a central theme in Kafka's understanding of himself and his illness, is merely a Jewish "trick" to get Aryans to believe that their *Geist* (spirit) and their bodies are crassly, materialistically linked. What seems to be a "neutral" model of argumentation, the model of psychosomatic illness, is revealed to Kafka as "Jewish." Thus all the jokes about the "Jewish patient" recounted in Chapter Two turn out to have been rooted in the supposedly Jewish understanding of the body. Here they move from joke to "philosophy," and are therefore clothed in a more somber rhetoric. They claim to reveal the "truth" about the psychologizing of the body that Pierre Janet declared at the turn of the century: that psychoanalysis is a Jewish science, not a universal one, because it is the product of a Jewish mind.

Blüher argues that, with the social integration of the Jews into German culture, their physical being was modified by their internalization of their host's culture. But this is only superficial and temporary. Once the Jews are "reghettoized," once they are separated from the "body politic," their "mimicry" of the German body too will end:

> One will see the Jews in Germany as clearly as one sees them in Russia and Poland. No one there confused him with the autochtonic man. The senses will be sharpened, and one will be able to ascertain the Jewish essence with the same security as one today distinguishes an African sculpture from Praxiteles. One will have the sense of the movement of the Jew, his walk, his gestures, the way his fingers grow from his hand, the form of his hair on the nape of his neck, the eyes and the tongue, so that no further errors are possible, and then the latent ghetto in which the Jew lives today, become manifest. . . . [The ghetto] is foremost a psychic manifestation (55).

Thus there will be no more risk of intermarriage and the production of *Mischlinge*.

For Blüher, this separation is also necessary to save the Jews. If the Jews are not separated from Aryan society and reghettoized, there will be a "world pogrom" (57). But it will not be done by the Germans: "Germany will be the only land that will be frightened from the act of murder. . . . It is ignoble to torture an unarmed enemy. The German is no Frenchman" (57). The Jews are doomed, even if they attempt to separate themselves out into a new state, as Herzl wants. Blüher sees this as a result of the fact that the Jews have no "warrior caste" (58). The absence of the Jew as soldier indicates his effeminacy. All that can be done is to reghettoize the Jew, and thus keep the Jew both protected and controlled.

Kafka sensed the importance of Blüher's call for the exclusion of the Jews. And he is not alone. Benjamin Segal, the editor of the most important Jewish periodical dealing with the interaction of Eastern and Western Jews, *Ost und West*, closes the final issue of that journal with an editorial on Blüher's text. He is quite aware of the implications of Blüher's warning about "world pogrom." Yet Segal dismisses Blüher (and other such anti-Semites) as self-haters during the "Great War," and charges that they are now merely "mimicking" the enemies of the Fatherland. In other words, they are merely *Mischlinge* or baptised Jews in disguise.[121]

Kafka is not alone in seeing Blüher as a key to an understanding of fascist anti-Semitism. As a result of Blüher, one Jewish response comes to see fascism as homosexual and German/Greek in its exclusion of the Jews. The German Jewish psychoanalyst Wilhelm Reich noted that " . . . the sexual structure of the fascists, who affirm the most severe form of patriarchy and actually reactivate the sexual life of the Platonic era in their familial mode of living—i.e., 'purity' in ideology, disintegration and pathology in actual practice—must bear a resemblance to the sexual conditions of the Platonic era. [Alfred] Rosenberg and Blüher recognize the state solely as a male state organized on a homosexual basis."[122] This concept of a homosexual patriarchy is precisely the image of the Jews as the patriarchal religion that haunted turn-of-the-century Jews in Prague. Jews were "sick," and this sickness was related to the world of the fathers. For they saw in their fathers not a sign of powerful masculinity but rather weakened, marginal men.

Kafka links Blüher's condemnation of Jewish mimicry and his own anxiety about his self-definition as a writer. He writes concerning

Friedrich von der Leyen's *Deutsche Dichtung in neuer Zeit*,[123] a survey of contemporary "German" writing that "seems accompanying music to the *Secessio Judaica* and it is astonishing how within a minute a reader, to be sure a well-disposed one, can organize things with the help of the book, how the crown of half-familiar, surely honest creative writers who turn up in a chapter entitled 'Our Land' are classified by landscapes: German property must not be annexed by any Jews" (LF, 346–347). Von der Leyen places Jewish writing back into the ghetto. He stresses that they are a danger to German culture in that they control the press, publishing, and the theater, that they are "negative, judgmental, libelous, and destructive" (371). They are "the power which is destroying the new *Reich*" (346). These Jews are "rootless" and therefore "especially receptive for the new/innovative/modern" (347).

The "new German writing" is obscured by the Jew's presence. It is necessary to make "the German blood that runs through their veins visible again" (372). And thus von der Leyen can contrast Max Brod's Jewish, unhealthy image of the Thirty Years War with the healthy, German one of Hermann Löns. Brod's writing is clearly "colder and more artificial" than that of the real "German" author (304). And yet von der Leyen sees one important tenet of the literature of the *fin de siècle* as disproved by the new nationalism that followed the Great War: "Are then the insights of the present really so true, and are the dangers, which have been feared, really so fearful? The idea of inheritance, which underlies the tragedy of [Ibsen's] Dr. Rank [in *A Doll's House*] and [Ibsen's] *Ghosts*, is in our eyes a chimera. The passionate hopes, which the generations before us placed on an age of the woman—oh! how it is vanished in the light of reality!" (22). Inheritance, the bugaboo of the late nineteenth-century theories of degeneration, is a "chimera." Not the reform of breeding through eugenics, but the political striving of the pure and select for the new *Reich*, that is the centerpiece of the new culture, a culture minus the Jews. For the argument for a eugenic solution assumes the false, external mutability of the Jews; such an approach sees them and their cultural production as inherently and immutably marked by their difference from the Aryan "peoples and tribes."

In Kafka's tale, "A Little Woman," written in the last year of his life and included in the very last volume he wrote, *A Hunger Artist*, it is the Jewish woman who represents the difficult and complex group with whom the German *Gemeinschaft* must constantly deal.[124] The male narrator couches the qualities of the "little (*kleine*) woman," indeed the very embodiment of the "minor" (*kleine*) literature, completely within the Blüherian discourse about Jewish difference. Here the fantasy of the homoerotic and the Jewish merge completely, and the Jewish author becomes totally feminized. In *A Hunger Artist*, Kafka moves from the fantasy of the emaciated body of the Jew in the title story, unable to eat because of the nature of his body, to a fantasy of the feminized body of the Jew. The protagonist is "naturally quite slim," a natural quality of the feminized body, but what marks her body immediately is that "the impression her hand makes on me I can convey only by saying that I have never seen a hand with the separate fingers so sharply differentiated from each other as hers; and yet her hand has not anatomical peculiarities, it is an entirely normal hand"[125] (S, 317). This is, of course, one of Hans Blüher's markers of the male Jew, "the way *his* fingers grow from *his* hand" (see Plate 9). Kafka's former professor, Hans Gross, the Prague criminologist (and father of Kafka's friend, the psychoanalyst Otto Gross), understands this as the "little, feminine hand of the Jew."[126] This feminized hand of the Jew transmutes itself in *The Trial* into Leni's "right hand" with the "two middle fingers, between which the connecting web of skin reached almost to the top joint" (T, 110). This physical sign of the degenerate is echoed in *The Castle*, where K. observes Frieda's hands, which "were certainly small and delicate, but they could quite as well have been called weak and characterless" (C, 39). The hands of the woman and the Jew reveal their true character.

Echoes of such views, condensed for Kafka in his reading of Blüher, are found throughout this tale of the "little woman." They provide the core for the feminization of the male. She is a "frail sick woman" (S, 319). She is also "sharp-witted" (S, 320). Her dealings with the narrator cause her to be "almost unable to work" and are characterized as an "unclean affliction" (S, 318). But this illness, according to the narrator, could be a sham: "I say quite openly that even if I did believe that she were really ill, I should not feel the slightest sympathy for her" (S, 319). Kafka employs Blüher's notion that psychosomatic illness is a Jewish invention, for only Jews believe that their bodies are "merely" extensions of the psyche. Here the feminization of the Jew is complete: she is ill, the inherently ill woman within. Kafka constructs a narrative voice separate from this feminized, ill, Jewish Other, stressing the inexorable link between the "little woman" and the narrative voice, representing the ability of the male Jew to undertake the role denied him in Blüher's work, that of the creative artist.

Here the role that Kafka selected for himself, the role of the writer, is denied the male Jew. The Jew's culture, like that of his body, is superficial and "cold." It is intellectualized, and therefore not "German." The Jew, hidden within the chrysalis of his westernized male body, remains a Jew in all of his limitations and beliefs. His body reveals him and betrays him. He is fated, no, he is condemned to become that which he must become.

four

Tuberculosis as a Test Case

Tuberculosis: Its Meaning at the Turn of the Century

What was Franz Kafka's illness? To this point, we have considered Franz Kafka's illness, the tuberculosis, that finally killed him, in the context of numerous overlapping contemporary discourses: about race, about the nation, about masculinity, about disease. Clearly the Jewish patient played a role in all these discourses. But let us begin this chapter with a broader question: How was tuberculosis as such read by the general public at the turn of the century? Was there a specifically "Jewish" reading of this disease?

Like many infectious diseases, the public understanding of tuberculosis underwent a sea change during the closing decades of the nineteenth and opening decades of the twentieth centuries. In 1819, René- Théophile-Hyacinthe Laënnec, the inventor of the stethoscope, showed, in his classic study of auscultation, that the "reality" of pulmonary tuberculosis (*phthisis*) could be read in its specific "signs."[1] Suddenly there was a semiotics of tuberculosis: a reading could follow the entire pathophysiognomy of the illness. No longer did tuberculosis only manifest itself in exterior signs; now it could be read within the body through auscultation. This innovation enabled a new conception of a potential cure. In

1856, Hermann Brehmer declared pulmonary tuberculosis (*phthisis*) to be treatable, recommending treatment in "closed" institutions placed in a parklike landscape. His associate Peter Detweiler soon understood that it was not the "immune areas" constructed in the sanatoria that cured, but rather the psychological effect of such treatment on the patients. Detweiler's Falkenstein Clinic, which he took over in 1876, introduced the "fresh air" cure.[2]

By the latter half of the nineteenth century, then, symptomatic identification and modern courses of treatment defined the disease. But on March 24, 1882, Robert Koch, the major advocate of the bacterial theory of disease in Germany, spoke before the Physiological Society in Berlin on the simple topic of "Tuberculosis." There he revealed that he had isolated in humans the tubercular bacillus hidden in the tubercles, the abscesses that outwardly signified the disease. Koch had discovered the specific bacillus that caused tuberculosis. Wilhelm Conrad Röntgen's 1895 development of X rays provided another set of visual signs for pulmonary tuberculosis. By 1916, the stages of tuberculosis were well described, from the initial early infiltration to the secondary infections. But only in 1944 could Selman Waksman present the first generally effective therapy, streptomycin.

Here the story should truly end: once the signs, the etiology, and the treatment of a disease are all determined, mythmaking ought to be superfluous. This is not at all what happens in the complex discourses about tuberculosis at the turn of the century. One finds instead the coexistence of different views about the meaning of the signs, the significance of the treatment, and the interpretation of the etiology, both in the lay conception of the illness sketched by Susan Sontag, as well as in medical discourse.[3] Indeed, one can make a rather strong case that life-threatening diseases, and tuberculosis in particular, encourage the widest range of explanatory models even when "good" scientific evidence for a more limited view of the illness exists.

A popular history of tuberculosis, like all popular histories of medicine, would trace the history of this disease along an axis from ignorance to knowledge and finally cure.[4] I want to argue something different in my history of tuberculosis. There are very many errors and dead ends that are not covered by a triumphal history of tuberculosis, and these errors do not simply disappear but become part of the popular mythology of the disease. This mythology has different meanings to different groups and individuals as it becomes part of their mythopoesis of illness. So I want to look at Franz Kafka's discourse about his illness as a Jewish discourse, a discourse that is part of the complex history of tuberculosis.

Two concepts that should have vanished with Robert Koch's discovery of the tuberculosis bacillus nonetheless powerfully persist in the medical literature of the age. These are the assumption that there is a predisposition for the disease, whether inherited as an acquired characteristic or as a racial trait, and the assumption that the tubercular has a particular physical constitution, indicated by certain physical and psychological signs. Such assumptions would seem dispensable once the etiology of tuberculosis is established, but they stay in the discourse of tuberculosis after Koch, where they had been for centuries before him.[5] The retention of these older models of the tubercular accords with the suggestions made by Judith Walzer Leavitt, Nancy Tomes, and Naomi Rogers, that the imagined objectivity of science introduced by German laboratory science at the end of the nineteenth century was superficial at best.[6] I believe that one could add that, while the new bacteriology did restructure the image of disease and of the patient, older models of disease were also adapted within the new model, continuing pre-Kochian notions of group predisposition to tuberculosis.

Hermann von Hayek, in the standard early twentieth-century overview of the theoretical problems associated with the illness, points out how self-contradictory and often confusing these concepts are when applied to infectious diseases such as tuberculosis.[7] For Kafka, such contradictoriness does no damage to an already contradictory discourse on tuberculosis as a specifically Jewish disease to which there is also a specifically Jewish immunity. It is as if Koch and the discovery of the tuberculosis bacillus had no real impact on him. Kafka was interested foremost in the question of the particular character, or psychopathology, of the turn-of-the-century tubercular, and the relation of this character to written expression. The conventional *fin-de-siècle* interpretation of the relation of mind to body, on which conventions about the writer depend, is what Kafka is at pains to reverse. For the conventional models presuppose that a "special psychological character" is linked to the ill body. Kafka must reverse this model if he is to assert control over his body and his illness. And as we have seen, such a reversal was understood as revealing a Jewish mindset. This is a mask, however. For it is not the progress of his illness that is at the core of Kafka's anxiety about the body and its diseases, but the permanent predisposition of the body which will herald its inevitable collapse.

Books and tuberculosis were linked in unusual ways at the turn of the century. An anxiety about literally contracting tuberculosis from others by reading their books permeated Kafka's culture.[8] Reading was also metaphorically infectious: tuberculosis patients were seen as "novel-reading, pale-cheeked, enthusiastic teenagers" who would rather read novels than exercise and regenerate their bodies.[9] This literary model is the more important for Kafka, which is unsurprising, given his fixation on the meaning of writing. Over and over again in this book, we have found that it is not direct experience that Kafka evokes, but experience mediated through the written word. There is no more powerful example than in Kafka's revision of the discourse about tuberculosis, a disease from which he directly suffered, after all.

To examine the literary use of tuberculosis as a specifically Jewish illness in enlightened, late nineteenth-century, Christian Europe, we can turn to George Eliot's representation of the sick Jewish body and its recuperation. In *Daniel Deronda* (1876) there is an extraordinary reunion between Mordechai, the representative of an older Judaism, and the eponymous hero, representing Judaism's secular future.[10] The men met "with as intense a consciousness as if they had been two undeclared lovers" (552). Mordechai appears simultaneously as Jewish and ill, while Deronda is neither. Mordechai has the "pathetic stamp of consumption with its brilliancy of glance to which the sharply-defined structure of features, reminding one of a forsaken temple, give already a far-off look as of one getting unwilling out of reach." He has a "Jewish face naturally accentuated for the expression of an eager mind—the face of a man little above thirty, but with that age upon it which belongs to time lengthened by suffering, the hair and beard still black throwing out the yellow pallor of the skin, the difficult breathing giving more decided marking to the folded arms: then give to the yearning consumptive glance something of the slowly dying mother's look when her one loved son visits her bedside, and the flickering power of gladness leaps out as she says, 'My boy!'" (552–553). Deronda, on the other hand, is anything but Jewish: "a face not more distinctively oriental than many a type seen among what we call the Latin races: rich in youthful health, and with a forcible masculine gravity in its repose. . . ." (553). Mordechai is ill, feminized, and marked by his yellow skin and Jewish "nostrility"; Deronda is healthy, masculine, and passes for "Latin." Mordechai is the past; Daniel is the future. Here we have a juxtaposition like the one in Thomas Mann's *Magic Mountain*, except there Leo Naphta represents the unhealthy Jewish presence in the world, while Hans Castorp represents the potential for a healthy future development quite closed to the Jew.

Daniel Deronda is a seminal representation of the Jew, but tuberculosis is again the marker of difference. Jews are given both "feminine" (ill) and "masculine" (healthy) qualities. The old Jew is the feminine, and the new Jew is the masculine. The old Jew's essential infirmity can be read on his body, while the new Jew is robust, indistinguishable from the "normal" British citizen of the times. However, Eliot's representation is inconsistent with the conventional wisdom, accepted by virtually all of the physicians of the time, that Jews had a natural immunity against tuberculosis.

The relationship between Jews and tuberculosis was hotly debated during the close of the nineteenth century.[11] One exemplary exchange followed the Civil War in the United States, where racial questions were differently constructed. In an exchange of letters in 1874, in the prestigious Philadelphia *Medical and Surgical Reporter*, Madison Marsh, a physician from Port Hudson, Louisiana, argued that Jews had a much greater tolerance for disease than the general population, as evidence offering their supposed immunity from tuberculosis. The Jew, he wrote, "enjoy[s] a wonderful national immunity from, not only phthisis [tuberculosis] but all disease of the thoracic viscera," because "his constitution has become so hardened and fortified against disease by centuries of national calamities, by the dietetics, regimen and sanitas of his religion, continuing for consecutive years of so many ages."[12] Indeed, the one Jew who claimed to have phthisis "proved to be a mere hypochondriac" (343). This was the view of his time. Lucian Wolf, in a debate before the Anthropological Society of Great Britain and Ireland in 1885, stated categorically, "figures could also be given to prove the immunity of Jews from phthisis," and Dr. Asher, in that same debate, observed, "Jews had an extraordinary power of resistance to phthisis."[13] Jews, at least in the Diaspora, live longer, have lower child mortality, and are generally healthier than Christians. The Jew's "high average physique . . . is not less remarkable than the high average of his intelligence."[14] Jews are the "purest, finest, and most perfect type of the Caucasian race."[15]

American Jews strongly agreed. Rabbi Joseph Krauskopf informed his Reformed congregation in Philadelphia:

> Eminent physicians and statisticians have amply confirmed the truth: that the marvelous preservation of Israel, despite all the efforts to blot them out from the face of the earth, their comparative freedom from a number of diseases, which cause frightful ravages among the Non-Jewish people, was largely due to their close adherence to their excellent Sanitary Laws. Health was their coat of mail, it was their magic shield that caught, and warded off, every thrust aimed at their heart. Vitality was their birthright. . . . Their immunity, which the enemy charged to magic-Arts, to alliances with the spirits of evil, was traceable solely to their faithful compliance with the sanitary requirements of their religion.[16]

Marsh added one new twist: Jews are healthier, live longer, are more immune to disease, are more intelligent not only because of their healthful practices, such as diet, but also because they belong to the "white" race. At least this is how a rural Louisiana physician during Reconstruction saw the Jews.

A month after this report was published, it was answered in detail by Ephraim M. Epstein of Cincinnati, a Jewish physician who had earlier practiced in Vienna and in Russia. He rebutted Marsh's argument point by point. First, Jews have no immunity from tuberculosis, or any other disease, including those long associated with Jewish religious practices: "I am sure I have observed no Jewish immunity from any diseases, venereal disease not excepted."[17] Indeed Jews have *phthisis.* Epstein cites the "family of an aunt of mine, two grown-up children die of pulmonary consumption, it being an evident inheritance from their father's family" (44). Jews not only manifest the illness, they transmit it from generation to generation! Second, Jews do not have "superior longevity"; they have no advantage either because of their diet or because of their practice of circumcision. However, Jews possess a quality lacking in their Christian neighbors. What puts Jews at less risk is the network of support, their "close fraternity"; "one Jew never forsak[es] the material welfare of his brother Jew, and he knows it instinctively."[18] It is simply the "common mental construction" of the Jew that preserves his health. Finally, such health as the Jews possess is due to "the constitutional stamina that that nation inherited from its progenitor, Abraham of old, and because it kept that inheritance undeteriorated by not intermarrying with other races. . . ."[19]

Here the battle begins. The Southern, Christian physician had seen in the Jews' particular practices a way to racial and individual health, universalizable for Caucasians. Indeed, in standard textbooks of the period, such as one by the Viennese biologist Carl Claus, Jews are already "Caucasians."[20] However, this is not the issue that occupies Marsh. In the American South after the Civil War, the primary racial distinction for Marsh has to be the one between Negro and Caucasian. In other words, with good diet and collective fortitude, whites have the potential to bear oppression—Marsh's readers would understand this to mean Reconstruction—to be healthier, more intelligent, more immune from disease than—Marsh's reader's would understand—blacks. The Eastern European Jewish physician, in contrast, had seen any limited advantage accruing to the Jews as part of an inheritance to which non-Jews could have absolutely no access, indeed which by definition exclude them.[21]

Marsh's vituperative response to Epstein came in August 1874.[22] Initially, he called upon the statistical evidence from Prussian, French, and British sources to buttress his argument about Jewish longevity. He then dismissed Epstein's argument about Jewish risk for disease completely, and turned to the ritual that Epstein had described as "the moral cause that had prevented intermarriage of the Jews with other nations, and thus preserved intact their health and tenacity of life" (133). It was circumcision as a sign of Jewish particularity and exclusivity that Epstein had invoked as the proof for his case about Jewish difference. For Marsh, however, circumcision is a "sanitary measure and religious rite . . . in practice by the ancient Egyptians. . . . It never became a Hebrew institution until friendly relations had been established between Abraham and the Egyptians. Then it was initiated by the circumcision of Abraham and Isaac by the express command of God" (133). Circumcision was an Egyptian ritual, and Moses, "the great champion, leader and lawgiver of the Hebrew race, was himself an Egyptian priest, educated in all the deep research and arts of the Chaldean Mage and mystic philosophic development of Egyptian and Oriental science, and all that was then known of the science of medicine, in its general principles and in its application of details for the preservation of health and prevention of disease" (133). This ideology of hygiene has a "slight tinge of Egyptian and Indian, or Asiatic philosophy, and shadow of its teachings [that] pervade[s] all the books of Moses" (133). Jewish ritual practices are but an amalgam of received ancient knowledge. Their hygienic techniques are in no way their particular innovation. Thus Marsh returns them to Egypt, and the "damp and cobwebby mold of antiquity."

What could Epstein know about real medicine? Marsh dismisses Epstein as merely a Jew, who draws his authority solely from this fact:

"What evidence or authority does he bring to support his pretensions to superior knowledge? His being himself a Jew, per se. . . ." (134). He reiterates his view that the Jews possess a secret to greater health that they were unwilling to share with the rest of the world. The subtext to Marsh's argument is that the Jew has a special immunity, which however they do not deserve, since they stole it from others. Jewish doctors such as Epstein are charlatans who conceal their knowledge of the true secret of health. This is the typical hostility of anti-Semitism toward the Jewish body, and the Jews' sexual selectivity or *amixia*.[23] Marsh is as envious as he is angry, of course, as he wishes to share in the special health of the Jewish body.

Circumcision had become a major issue for medical practice in the United States. Indeed, the American physician Peter Charles Remondino, writing in the 1870s, could note, "circumcision is like a substantial and well-secured life annuity . . . it ensures them better health, greater capacity for labour, longer life, less nervousness, sickness, loss of time."[24] By the 1890s, Americans associated "uncircumcised" with "uncivilized."[25] So it is unsurprising that circumcision became part of a hygienic program, but circumcision by a physician, not in the Jewish ritual context which Epstein had outlined.

The debate between Epstein and Marsh strikingly summarizes the conflict between the world as it could be, where Jewish hygienic practices are effective buffers against dreaded illnesses such as tuberculosis, and the world where European Jews suffered as frequently and as intensely from tuberculosis as anyone else. The European medical literature of the period, which Marsh abundantly cites, clearly supports his contention about the fabled resistance of Jews to tuberculosis. The Italian Jewish forensic psychiatrist Cesare Lombroso's findings are perhaps the most widely cited in the late nineteenth-century medical literature. As a Jew, and one of the most distinguished medical scientists of the period, his authority was unassailable. In the late 1860s, he argued that while the Catholic population of Verona showed a seven percent incidence of tuberculosis, the Jews of Verona showed only a six percent incidence of the disease.[26] Jews suffered from a slightly lower rate of infection than the other group. Lombroso's explanation was environmental, not racial. Jews, he argued, were less exposed to the vicissitudes of weather than their Catholic fellow citizens because of their choice of occupation. (As early as the Italian Renaissance, physicians such as Girolamo Fracastoro had argued strongly that there were inherited predispositions to disease and immunity from disease in specific racial groups. In all of these discussions the Jews were treated as a single, unitary group rather than a set of complicated geographic, regional, and ideological subcategories associated by either the label of being "Jewish" or Jewish ritual practice. By the early twentieth century, some physicians began to point out the error of this unitary assumption.[27])

Lombroso's view commanded the attention of the epidemiological world of his time. The view that Jews had a lower rate of tubercular infection was maintained in spite of new data. The Viennese epidemiologist Eduard Glatter had examined the rate of illness in Pest during the early 1860s.[28] He determined that of every one thousand patients under treatment in Pest, seventeen Hungarians, twenty-nine Germans, fourteen Slovaks, thirty-nine Serbs and nineteen Jews suffered from tuberculosis. The normal population distribution of groups of the normal (that is, healthy) population is 534 Hungarians, 224 Germans, 182 Slovaks, 28 Serbs and 32 Jews per thousand. This would give the Jews a relatively higher rate of infection than would be expected from their representation in the population (.032 percent of tubercular Jews as against .019 percent of the population). Glatter reads his figures, however, to show a greater immunity among Jews against diseases of the lungs (46–47). Their immunity is not as great as that against convulsive seizures, even though they have a much higher than average incidence of skin diseases (*Judenkrätze*) and gastrointestinal illnesses than other groups. The type of argument brought by Lombroso and Glatter is echoed in numerous studies at mid-century. Whatever the evidence, Jews are seen to have a lower incidence of pulmonary illnesses, including tuberculosis.

Similar figures are brought again and again for the entire latter half of the nineteenth century. John S. Billings, the most important medical epidemiologist, in his survey of 60,630 Jews in the United States for the closing years of the 1880s, argued quite differently. He wanted to examine the "'Jewish race' and 'Jews' . . . as the descendants of those who returned to Palestine after the Babylonian captivity, but without reference to their religious beliefs or practices." That is, he wanted to examine the race with respect to its health or illness. Among American Jews, he found, "these Jews were much less affected with tubercular disease, and especially with tubercular consumption, than the average population. The total number of deaths reported from this cause was only 68, or 36.5 per 1,000 of all deaths in males, and 34 per 1,000 of all deaths in females. For the whole United States the number per 1,000 of deaths that were reported as due to consumption was in 1860 for males 108.8; females, 146.1. . . . In other words, the proportion of deaths among Jews was less than one-third for males, and less than one-fourth for females, of what it was among our average population."[29] In Australia, the President of the New South Wales Board of Health, in 1888, "adduced the remarkable fact, that among the Jewish population of New South Wales, numbering 4,000, a dwelling mostly in the towns, but one death from consumption had occurred in three years, whereas if the disease had been as prevalent among them as in the rest of the population, thirteenth or fourteen would have succumbed."[30] Similar sets of statistics can be found in the medical literature of the age for virtually every major city of Europe (for example London, Paris, Vienna, Berlin) as well as for New York City. Jews seem to suffer from a lower statistical rate of tuberculosis.[31]

Now there are two ways to read this "fact." The first, as we have seen, rests on specifically Jewish ritual or marriage practices which provide immunity. This is what Marsh and Lombroso argue. The second, espoused by Glatter and Billings, imputes a special quality to members of the race. This racial argument was supported by anthropologists such as Georg Buschan, in the major popular geographic journal of the day, who saw increased predisposition or increased resistance as defining signs of racial identity.[32] For Buschan, the "four to six times higher rate of mental illness" among the Jews must be the result of an inherited weakness of the central nervous system, since Jews do not evidence any of the sociopathic etiologies, such as alcoholism, which, according to him, cause mental illness. But if Jews can be predisposed to acquiring certain illnesses because of their racial identity, they can also be immune from certain diseases for the same reason. Thus he also sees the relative immunity of the Jews from cholera as a sign of their biological nature. Traditionally, claims about Jewish immunity to disease were part of accusations that a Jewish pact with the devil protected them, or that they had caused a plague by poisoning wells, from which they then avoided drinking. Jews thus had to be anxious about claims that they possessed special immunities. When scientists such as Buschan proposed an inherent racial predisposition to or against specific illnesses, they also implied that its signs could be read on the Jew's body. In the scientific discourse of the time, what is real is what is seen. And the nature of Jewish immunity had to be written on the body of the Jew.

Kafka's Discourse on His Illness

All of the central tropes in Franz Kafka's representation of his identity are interrelated. His anxiety about his inevitable fate as a male, as a Jew, and as a patient all overlap and intertwine. When we examine, then, the meaning of Kafka's body at the moment of the outbreak of his "real" illness, his tubercular hemorrhage in late August, 1917, we can see how he interprets it in the light of his anxiety of becoming what he always knew he would. His own texts representing his initial illness and its context reveal much of his attempt to give his tuberculosis a specific and directed meaning. But what is that meaning? He writes about the outbreak of his illness on September 9, 1917:

> I had a hemorrhage of the lung. Fairly severe; for 10 minutes or more it gushed out of my throat; I thought it would never stop. The next day I went to see a doctor, who on this and several subsequent occasions examined and X-rayed me; and them, at Max's insistence, I went to see a specialist. Without going into all the medical details, the outcome is that I have tuberculosis in both lungs. That I should suddenly develop some disease did not surprise me; nor did the sight of blood; for years my insomnia and headaches have invited a serious illness, and ultimately my maltreated blood had to burst forth; but that it should be of all things tuberculosis, that at the age of 34 I should be struck down overnight, with not a single predecessor anywhere in the family—this does surprise me. Well, I have to accept it; actually, my headaches seem to have been washed away with the flow of blood. (LF, 543)

In a world where the central trope about illness is centered on blood, it is no wonder to Kafka that "it is in the blood."[33] A contemporary psychoanalytic study, published in the psychiatrist Georg Groddeck's house journal, discussed the general consternation that early twentieth-century German patients reflected when they came to the physician. They immediately attempted to localize the source of their own disease. "I believe, it is in the blood," such patients tell their physicians. Much like the contemporary French preoccupation with their livers as the locus of disease, for the Germans at the beginning of the twentieth century, all pathology was in the blood. Blood, in this same culture, as we have seen, has many layers of meaning—from the blood associated with the blood libel trials to its role in purifying ritually slaughtered animals, from its function as the primary German marker of race to the parallel concern with blood as the proof of a eugenically "healthy" body politic.[34]

Yet in Kafka's first account of his illness, it is the blood that cleanses, that wipes out the old illness that dominated the body, and replaces it with a new sign of the state of his psyche. It is not only the blood suddenly gushing from the slit throat of the victim of the blood libel, or the animal ritually slaughtered through *shehitah* that reveals the truth about what Kafka was fated to become, but also the blood gushing from his own throat. But *both* moments are represented in Kafka's understanding of his hemorrhage as a cleansing. The tuberculosis of which the hemorrhage is the sign is repressed, and Kafka instead interprets his bleeding in the discourses of his time.

In all events, Kafka states that he clearly did not expect to become tubercular. His evident surprise at his hemorrhage leads us to assume that he expected his illness to take another, more familiar form, perhaps a cardiac condition like his father's. Here the notion of becoming what one is fated to become is violated. Kafka can only comprehend the enormity of becoming what he now is, a tubercular Jew, as an extended metaphor for his own illness of the soul, an illness he believes that he has inherited, as we have seen, from his mother. His implied immunity from tuberculosis was based on his view that there was no predisposition for the disease "anywhere in the family." This immunity through the lack of predisposition is, as we shall see, a central trope in the formation of a specifically Jewish response to tuberculosis at the beginning of the twentieth century. "Anywhere in the family" does indeed refer to his greater sense of his identity as a Jew in a racialist society, who has internalized the notion that he has inherited certain physical and psychological qualities that make him a Jew.

The inheritance of tuberculosis does not belong to that image of the Jew. Indeed, this "fact" comes to play a role even in Kafka's last medical record. On April 10, 1924, Kafka is admitted to the clinic of the Jewish laryngologist, Markus Hajek, brother-in-law of the dramatist Arthur Schnitzler, and the physician whose botched operation for oral cancer will almost kill Sigmund Freud a few years later. The patient's history is taken, and shows that all of the family members are "healthy," that is, that there is no tuberculosis in the family.[35] Hajek's history details the final stage of the tuberculosis as seen through the eyes of a laryngologist. He records that the patient feels "relatively good." Such a view of a dying, suffering patient can only be that of the physician-observer who is implicitly contrasting Kafka with other patients in the terminal stages of the disease.

In mid-September, 1917, Kafka's discourse about his illness begins to structure this notion of tuberculosis as a "family" illness, if in rather global terms. His initial surprise at his own vulnerability has given way to an infantilizing of his relationship to the illness. The illness has become like a mother, but also a disease he has acquired from his mother. As we have seen, what Kafka (and Hermann Kafka) believed that the son had acquired from his mother's family is his pathological mental state, his incipient madness. The madness inherited from his maternal line (whence his Jewish identity comes, according to ritual law) manifests itself as tuberculosis. This is very much in line with the medical view of the turn of the century, that tuberculosis was inherited through the (non-Jewish) mother rather than through the (non-Jewish) father![36] Kafka reads his illness retrospectively as psychogenic. It is caused by the madness that he has inherited from his mother's family. Thus Kafka can universalize the notion of his illness and place it within the model of illness that he has already developed for himself.

In November, 1917, Kafka wrote to Max Brod from his sister's farm in Zürau concerning his initial attempt at curing himself of tuberculosis. This self-cure was very much in the model of the rest cure advocated by the medical authority of the time, but importantly for Kafka, he was not to be confined within a "closed" hospital, but in the home of his sister: "Possibly I could find other places where I could lie outside more, where the air is more bracing, and so on, but—and this is very important for the state of my nerves, which is in turn important to my lungs—I would not feel so much at ease anywhere else" (LF, 163). Thus the trope of the psychosomatic nature of illness, specifically of his own tuberculosis, begins to evolve. Tuberculosis is an attenuated mental illness in physical guise. It is a psychosomatic (read: Jewish) illness, for Jews suffer from mental illnesses expressed in their bodies, as Blüher intimates.

Kafka had written to Grete Bauer as early as June 14, 1914, prior to developing any manifest signs of tuberculosis: "This state of health is also deceptive, it deceives even me; at any moment I am liable to be assailed by the most detailed and precise imaginings and invariably on the most inconvenient occasions. Undoubtedly an enormous hypochondria, which however has struck so many and such deep roots within me that I stand or fall with it" (LFe, 425). Well before he developed any signs of tuberculosis, well before he even knew that he was ill, he had evolved an explanatory model for his illness. Illness for Kafka was the baseline for his life, and defined his idea of health. The illness was fundamentally psychological, and not somatic; that is, his mental state predisposes him to a physical illness, and the precise form of that illness is arbitrary. In the age of psychoanalysis, the psychosomatic model offers a cure of the body by way of a cure of the psyche. Kafka's reading of Freud and his introduction to psychoanalysis through his friend Otto Gross meant that (even though he comes to doubt the efficacy of the method) he has an escape clause from the "merely" physical. On the other hand, he can also claim *not* to be suffering from mental illness.[37] "My mind is clear," he seems to say, "for all my symptoms are 'merely' physical." But health, according to Kafka, is illusion: all is illness. The ghost-in-the-machine here stems from Kafka's understanding that his illness is the result of Jewish, materialistic mind-set. The very form of this disease is not random, as we shall see, but lies within of the complex *fin-de-siècle* discourse on illness as the natural state of the Jewish body.

When Kafka writes about his tuberculosis to Max Brod he employs a maternal image:

> In any case my attitude toward the tuberculosis today resembles that of a child clinging to the pleats of its mother's skirts. If the disease came from my mother, the image fits even better, and my mother in her infinite solicitude, which far surpasses her understanding of the matter, has done me this service also. I am constantly seeking an explanation for this disease, for I did not seek it. Sometimes, it seems to me that my brain and lungs came to an agreement without my knowledge. "Things can't go on this way," said the brain, and after five years the lungs said they were ready to help. (LF, 138)

The trope of a psychosomatic illness satisfies his longing that his illness make sense. According to this explanation, his lungs are now directly affected by his psyche and express in physical symptoms (not mental illness) his disturbed emotional state. His disease clearly does not come from his mother, he states, but it should. Like Leo Naphta's tuberculosis in *The Magic Mountain*, it is the disease of the mother, the disease that, like the Jewishness carried by the mother, defines the contours of the son's body. Here the "regression to racial type," or racial atavism, of becoming what one inevitably must become, is tentatively broached.

His version of the first attack of the tuberculosis is psychologized and distanced in his letter to his sister Ottla on August 29, 1917. He writes:

> About three weeks ago, I had a hemorrhage from the lungs during the night. It was about four o'clock in the morning; I woke up, wondering at having such a strange amount of spittle in my mouth, spat it out, but then struck a light, strange, it's a blob of blood. And then it began. *Chrlení*, I don't know whether that's the way to spell it, but it is a good expression for this bubbling up in the throat. I thought it would never stop. How was I going to plug it since I hadn't started it? I got up, walked around the room, went over to the window, looked out, went back—still blood. Finally it stopped and I slept, better than I'd done in a long time. Next day (I was in the office) saw Dr. Mühlstein. Bronchial catarrh. He prescribed a medicine; I was to drink three bottles; return in a month; right away if blood came again. Next night, blood again, but less. Again to the doctor, whom I had not liked, by the way. I'll pass over the details; it would take too long. The result for me: three possibilities, first, acute cold; when the doctor said that, I contested it. Would I catch cold in August? And when I don't catch colds at all. Here at least the apartment might be at fault, this cold, stale, ill-smelling place. Secondly, consumption. Which the Dr. denies for the present. Anyhow, we'll see, all inhabitants of big cites are tubercular; a catarrh of the apex of the lung (that's the phrase, the way people say piglet when they mean swine) isn't anything so bad; you inject tuberculin and all's well. Thirdly: this last possibility I barely hinted to him; naturally he promptly warded it off. And yet it is the only right one and is also quite compatible with the second. Of late, I have again suffered dreadfully from the old delusion (LO, 19).

The "old delusion" becomes clearer when Kafka later refers to "the status of this mental disease, tuberculosis." For in this reading, the three possibilities are a cold, which Kafka dismisses as a sign of the incompetence of the physician, or tuberculosis, which is the same as a mental collapse. It is the fear of becoming the insane Jew hidden within himself that structures Kafka's initial response to his illness. Here Kafka may be drawing on a literary analogy that was certainly known to him. In a letter from Flaubert to Louise Colet (July 7–8, 1853), the tubercular author commented, "My nervous illness has been the froth of those little intellectual pranks. Each attack was like a hemorrhage of the nervous system."[38] It is with Flaubert, the son of a tubercular, that the tubercular Kafka will compare himself (as will be discussed below). Flaubert himself understood his illness as a mental illness, where "the soul was entirely folded in on itself, like a hedgehog wounding itself with its own quills." Or perhaps, like Kafka's tuberculosis as "a knife that stabs not only forward but one that wheels around and stabs back as well" (LFe, 544).

Kafka's view is that all urban dwellers are tubercular, yet his tuberculosis reflects his particular mental status. If the image of the Jew is as the quintessential urban dweller, with all of the diseases and ailments of the city, then Kafka's reading universalizes this anxiety to everyone in the city. And yet the signs point to that other illness of the urban Jew, the mental instability (using the psychosomatic model of illness that Kafka takes over without questioning) represented in the symptom of the bloody discharge. No simple cure, no injections of Robert Koch's miracle cure, tuberculin, will help, for the real problem resided in the psyche. Incidentally, tuberculin proved to be a chimera.[39]

In a letter to his soon-to-be-former fiancée Felice Bauer, he reads his illness as having its origin in his conflicted feelings for her. He writes to her on October 1, 1917, from his sister's farm at Zürau:

> Suddenly it appears that the loss of blood was too great. The blood shed by the good one (the one that now seems good to us) in order to win you, serves the evil one. Where the evil one on his own would probably or possibly not have found a decisive new weapon for his defense, the good one offers him just that. For secretly I don't believe this illness to be tuberculosis, at least not primarily tuberculosis, but rather a sign of my general bankruptcy. I had thought the war could last longer, but it can't. The blood issues not from the lung, but from a decisive stab delivered by one of the combatants.
>
> From my tuberculosis this one now derives the kind of immense support a child gets from clinging to its mothers' skirts. What more can the other one hope for? Has not the war been most splendidly concluded? It is tuberculosis, and that is the end. Weak and weary, almost invisible to you when in this state, what can the other one do but lean on your shoulder here in Zürau, and with you, the purest of the pure, stare in amazement, bewildered and hopeless, at the great man who—now that he feels sure of universal love, or if that of its female representative assigned to him—begins to display his atrocious baseness. It is a distortion of my striving, which in itself is already a distortion.
>
> Please don't ask why I put up a barrier. Don't humiliate me in this way. One word like this from you and I would be at your feet again. But my actual, or rather, long before that, my alleged tuberculosis would stab me in the face, and I would have to give up. It is a weapon compared to which the countless others used earlier, raging from "physical incapacity" up to my "work" and down to my "parsimony," look expedient and primitive.
>
> And now I am going to tell you a secret which at the moment I don't even believe myself (although the distant darkness that falls about me at

> each attempt to work, or think, might possibly convince me), but which is bound to be true: I will never be well again. Simply because it is not the kind of tuberculosis that can be laid in a deck chair and nursed back to health, but a weapon that continues to be of supreme necessity as long as I remain alive. And both cannot remain alive. (LFe, 545–546)

Here, in a self-consciously literary mode, Kafka begins to work out the notion of sacrifice that is central to the blood libel. It is not really tuberculosis, but rather blood from a "decisive stab" by one of the combatants in a struggle to the death. Here the notion of the male body as warrior is superimposed on the notion of illness. The struggle is between unequal foes, however, as in the act of ritual slaughter or blood libel—one must be defeated because the one (the body) is inferior to the other (the psyche). Here the notion of the competitive "stab" is put in its new context: "my alleged tuberculosis would stab me in the face, and I would have to give up." But this new context is his dependency on Felice and on this new substitute for her. For Kafka begins to define his illness as his "weapon" against the world about him. His tuberculosis is not a mere disease, "the kind of tuberculosis that can be laid in a deck chair and nursed back to health," but rather the new weapon in his psychic armament that has turned against his body. *It has become a new mother/lover as well as the new* schochet*/murderer for him.* Kafka begins to universalize and rationalize his very specific illness—it is not tuberculosis but rather his psychic state mirrored in the tuberculosis. Here we have a reflection of the central debate of the late nineteenth and early twentieth century about the predisposition of given individuals for this illness.

For Kafka, tuberculosis is an illness, but not *the* illness from which he suffered. It is merely a metaphor (and this is Kafka writing, not Susan Sontag), as he wrote in his diary during September, 1917: "You have the chance, as far as it is at all possible, to make a new beginning. Don't throw it away. If you insist on digging deep into yourself, you won't be able to avoid the muck that will well up. But don't wallow in it. If the infection in your lungs is only a symbol, as you say, a symbol of the infection whose inflammation is called F[elice], and whose depth is its deep justification; if this is so then the medical advice (light, air, sun, rest) is also a symbol. Lay hold of this symbol" (D2, 182). Of course, the tuberculosis was not simply a symbol: it was a reality, which Kafka needed to refashion into a symbol representing the ability to alter the emotional state that had "caused" the illness.

But the discourse about tuberculosis and mental states reflects Kafka's own concern about the meaning ascribed to the disease. On September 25, 1917, he writes in his diary: "Not entirely a crime for a tubercular to have children. Flaubert's father was tubercular. Choice: either the child's lungs will warble (very pretty expression for the music the doctor puts his ear to one's chest to hear), or it will be a Flaubert. The trembling of the father while off in the emptiness the matter is being discussed" (D2, 186–187). Well after Koch's discovery of the tuberculosis bacillus, physicians still ask the question: "Can a tubercular father pass the bacillus via the sperm to the egg?"[40] The image of "auscultation, and more particularly upon the absence or presence and distribution of the râles,"[41] the physician listening to the musical "warble" of the tubercular's lungs becomes a trope in the late works (such as the singing represented in "Josephine, the Singer"), and here it is brought into the context of the relationship between tuberculosis and creativity, a context that is understood in the discourse of the time as a sign of the psychopathology of the tubercular patient. But it is the father that Kafka sees as ill and providing through his susceptibility the wellspring of the son's creativity. The answer here to the anxiety of becoming what one is fated to become is that the fate may be transmuted from physical illness to the "disease" (or psychopathology) of creativity. For the creative, following Cesare Lombroso's model of "madness and genius," generally accepted in the late nineteenth century, was in many ways closely connected to the expression of illness, if it were not itself a form of madness. And here the doubling of the anxiety of the Jewish patient can be heard—for Jews, like tuberculars, were denied in popular thought the ability to be truly creative. Both seemed to be creative but were in fact merely "superior degenerates."

It is striking that, by the early twentieth century, the notion of the psyche and discourse of the tubercular patient have been canonized in the medical as well as the popular literature. People with tuberculosis are believed to think and express themselves in ways that are absolute reflections of the process of illness.[42] This tubercular psychopathology, as we shall see, may be understood as the predisposition to developing tuberculosis, as well as a symptom of the disease itself.[43] That a tubercular could imagine having children would certainly be understood as a sign of psychopathology: "The tubercular patient often loses an understanding that he out of various reasons cannot partake of the joys of love and should not place any more children into the world. He stomps on these general hygienic as well as eugenic, aesthetic and sociological premises."[44] In these words, the words of a medical specialist of the day, discourses that we would expect to remain discrete join in a univocal condemnation. Eugenic (purity of the race), hygienic (purity of the individual), and sociological (purity of the society) concerns should make a tubercular individual hesitate to have offspring—but this is finally an *aesthetic* argument, notwithstanding that it appears in the professional medical literature. The tubercular body is unaesthetic and will produce ugly (that is diseased) children. For Kafka, that possibility is linked to the notion that illness and creativity are linked, that tuberculars are also creative geniuses.

But they are also poor fathers. Max Salomon wrote in 1904 that people with tuberculosis should avoid marriage.[45] He presents four reasons for this. First, the effect of marriage on the tubercular: he argues that after marriage the illness worsens and assumes its "galloping" form, which quickly dispatches the patient. This is the result in the male of too easy access to coitus, and in the female the result of pregnancy and delivery (40). (Kafka's anxiety about coitus and its attendant uncleanness is reified here.) Second, he fears infecting his partner. Third, the resulting offspring would be predisposed to the illness as their parents had been, and would also be exposed to the bacillus. Salomon is quite pragmatic in his anxiety: children from such marriages must be isolated and separated from the infected parent(s), and the home must be free of dirt and alcohol (41–42). Finally, the life of a family left behind after the death of the breadwinner would be horrendous. These views are echoed in the standard handbooks for patients: "the marriage relation should be strictly taboo."[46]

Kafka's letter to Felice Bauer, and his comments on Flaubert, the "great tubercular," center on the related constructions of tuberculosis and sexuality. One aspect of the trope is well known from its literary representation in the novels of Thomas Mann and Klabund—people with tuberculosis have a more intense libido than do nontubercular individuals. Wilhelm Weygandt, the famed Professor of Psychiatry at the University of Hamburg, reported that the sexuality of patients was a special problem in German sanatoriums.[47] He claimed that anaphrodisiacs were added to the large quantities of milk given to patients in the sanatoria. According to Weygandt, there is a link between the inherent "optimism" of the tubercular patient and their increased libido. The American specialist on tuberculosis, Maurice Fishberg, stressed the hypersexuality of the tubercular patient.[48] For Fishberg this was a direct result of the infection that results in a tuberculous toxemia. It is not the result of any constitutional predisposition on the part of the patient, nor an artifact of the treatment: "there are other chronic diseases in which the patients are idle, eat well and may be despondent, yet they do not indulge in sexual excesses to the same extent as the tuberculous" (241). Here the notion is that the disease process or its mode of treatment increases the "abnormal" sexual drive of the patient.

The British physician D. G. Macleod Munro reverses the argument, seeing masturbation as a potential contributing factor for tuberculosis: "the advent of the sexual appetite in normal adolescence has a profound effect upon the organism, and in many cases when uncontrolled, leads to excess about the age when tuberculosis most frequently delivers its first open assault upon the body"[49] (33). The contemporary view that masturbation can cause a wide range of illnesses in the predisposed individual includes tuberculosis. Unsurprisingly, the tubercular evidences for Munro a "moral recklessness" (33). The proof is that the tubercular suffers from a higher rate of venereal disease (33). This only seems to be the result of the "idle life imposed upon the tuberculous patient" (34). Thus the patients are "morally reckless" and "obey this imperious craving," even if they hemorrhage immediately after. Thus "phthisical patients of the erethic type ought not to undertake marriage, or, if already married, indulge in marital intercourse" (35). But they do, in spite of all warnings! This is a clear sign of "mental instability and lack of self-control" (36). When they marry, they often negatively affect their partners: "Rarely have I been able to detect any physical signs in explanation of this. The consumptive person, in so intimate a relationship with a healthy consort, appears to me to have a vampire-like effect, sapping both the physical and mental vigor of the healthy partner" (39). In the language of the tubercular the vampire is more than a metaphor, for the healthy consort suffers from "some degree of anemia" (38). Kafka reverses this trope: Felice Bauer is the vampire draining his blood. She is the cause of his illness, the reason he is bleeding. Society warns that the ill partner will make the healthy partner ill as well—if the partner is predisposed to the illness. As Jews, however, neither Franz Kafka nor Felice Bauer should be immune because they are predisposed; or should both have Jewish immunity?

And yet these tubercular lovers are drawn to one another. Here too eugenic theory proposes an explanation. Why would tubercular individuals marry? The existence of tuberculosis in marriage partners may well depend more on the history of each member of the couple than on any infection, for individuals with the same inheritance tended to be attracted to one another: "the presence of tuberculosis in husband and wife . . . may depend on the extent to which assortative mating prevailed with regard to what we may term the tuberculosis diathesis."[50] That is, people who are predisposed to the same illness are attracted to one another. Kafka rejects Felice Bauer because she is also at risk, although he suspends this principle in his later relationship with Milena Jesenská, when he learns at the very beginning of their relationship of her tuberculosis.

This fantasy of the gain from illness parallels Kafka's concern about his father's understanding of his illness. In late July, 1922, he writes to Max Brod in terms reminiscent of his famed, unsent "Letter to the Father": "But in this case what is there for a father's eyes to light up? A son incapable of marriage, who could not pass on the family name . . . alienated from the Faith, so that a father cannot even expect him to say the prayers for the rest of his soul; consumptive, and as the father quite properly sees it, having gotten sick through his own fault, for he was no sooner released from the nursery for the first time when with his total incapacity for independence he sought out that unhealthy room at the Schönborn Palace. This is the son to rave about" (LF, 347–48). The son's brilliance is no recompense for his becoming like the father: not only ill, but emasculated by illness. He cannot even say a *Kaddish,* the prayer for the dead, since he expects to predecease his father. Here for the first time is the alternative to the "struggle between lung and head" as the explanation for the disease: his father's accusation, repeated in the "Letter to the Father," that Kafka is ill because he moved into a damp apartment after first leaving home. The father's materialist explanation denies that Kafka's illness is inherited. Kafka rejects his father's explanation: his ill health is not merely an accident of geography, of his poor choice of accommodations, of his abandonment of his family, but is part of his essence. He relies on the model of psychosomatic illness to counter his anxiety that he has inherited an immutably ill, distorted nature, revealed now in his body.

In order to do this he must also deny the specificity of his illness as tuberculosis. He writes to Max Brod in October, 1917: "I have come to think that tuberculosis, or the kind of tuberculosis I have, is no special disease, or not a disease that deserves a special name, but only the germ of death itself, intensified, though to what degree we cannot for the time being determine" (LF, 151). But it is specifically pulmonary tuberculosis from which Kafka suffers, not any random disease. His attempt to come to terms with this illness that took him by surprise, that was the wrong illness to develop, becomes his attempt to deal with who he was and how his body functioned.

The most elaborate account of the outbreak of his illness given by Kafka comes almost three years later, during April, 1920, at the point when his correspondent and lover Milena Jesenská discovers that she, too, has pulmonary tuberculosis:

> So it's the lung. I've been turning it over in my mind all day long, unable to think of anything else. Not that it alarms me; probably and hopefully—you seem to indicate as much—you have a mild case, and even full-fledged pulmonary disease (half of western Europe has more or less deficient lungs), as I have known in myself for 3 years, has brought me more good things than bad. In my case it began about 3 years ago with a violent hemorrhage in the middle of the night. I was excited as one always is by something new, naturally somewhat frightened as well; I got up (instead of staying in bed, which is the prescribed treatment, I later discovered), went to the window, leaned out, went to the washstand, walked around the room, sat down on the bed—no end to the blood. But I wasn't at all unhappy, since by and by I realized that for the first time in 3, 4 practically sleepless years there was a clear reason for me to sleep, provided the bleeding would stop. It did indeed stop (and had not returned since) and I slept through the rest of the night. To be sure, the next morning the maid showed up (at that time I had an apartment in the Schönborn-Palais), a good, totally devoted but extremely frank girl, she saw the blood and said: "*Pane doktore*, you're not going to last very long." But I was feeling better than usual, I went to the office and did not go see the doctor until later that afternoon. The rest of the story is immaterial. I only wanted to say: it's not your illness which scares me (especially since I keep interrupting myself to search my memory; and underneath all your fragility I perceive something like a farm girl's vigor and I conclude: no, you're not sick, this is a warning but no disease of the lung), anyway it's not that which scares me, but the thought of what must have preceded this disturbance. For the moment, I'm simply ignoring everything else in your letter, such as: not a heller—tea and apple—daily from 2 to 8—these are things I cannot understand which evidently

> require oral explanation. So I'll ignore all that (though only in this letter, as I cannot forget them) and just recall the explanation I applied to my own case back then and which fits many cases. You see, my brain was unable to bear the pain and anxiety with which it had been burdened. It said: "I'm giving up; but if anyone else here cares about keeping the whole intact, then he should share the load and things will run a little longer." Whereupon my lung volunteered, it probably didn't have much to lose anyway. These negotiations between brain and lung, which went on without my knowledge, may well have been quite terrifying.[51]

This version introduces new moments. Remember that like is supposed to attract like, that is, individuals with a "tuberculosis diathesis" should be attracted to one another.[52] Kafka has begun to change the grounds of interpretation. First, the disease is ubiquitous, affecting half the population of Europe, although not those with a "farm girl's vigor," such as Milena Jesenská. Here Kafka draws on the stereotypical distinction between healthy (Christian) Czech and the sickly Jew. Kafka had held this view well before he showed any symptoms of tuberculosis. In 1912 he commented on the incompetence of doctors, and the doctor's belief that there are "people whose physical condition is worthy of his [the doctor's] curative power and is produced by it, and he feels insulted, more than he is aware, by the strong nature of this country girl" who denies her illness and is simply well in spite of appearances (D2, 247). This distinction between the "beautiful" Milena Jesenská and the "ugly" Franz Kafka is part of the larger distinction between the truly healthy and the truly ill. For the assumption of the age, as we shall discuss, is that everyone is at risk for tuberculosis, but only some actually manifest the disease in its fatal form.

For the sufferer, relief sets in after the onset of the illness. It labels the person who is ill as inherently different and ugly. True cure (which would be the overcoming of illness as if it had not taken place) would be being powerful and beautiful. Kafka's illness proves to him that he has always been ugly, therefore true cure is impossible, since he cannot be what he has never been, namely beautiful. He cannot be cured. Tuberculosis means that he no longer can aspire to be other than what he is, he no longer suffers from that temptation: now he is *really* Jewish, free of any desire to be otherwise. Kafka thus imagines what it is like to be truly healthy, and it is not being Jewish. The image of the essentially healthy individual peasant haunts yet another recapitulation of Kafka's account of his illness, written to Oskar Baum in June of 1920: "Would you care for a lay diagnosis? The physical illness is only an overflow of the spiritual illness. Should one want to channel it once more, then the head naturally defends itself. For the head in times of need has spawned the lung disease and now they are trying to force it back into him, just when he feels the strongest urge to spawn still other illnesses. Moreover to begin with the head and cure him would require the strength of a furniture mover, which for the aforementioned reasons I will never be able to summon up" (LF, 239). The image of the "strength of a furniture mover" evokes the working-class Czech.

When Kafka, at a very late stage of his illness, actually agrees to enter a tuberculosis sanatorium, he comments on the serving women in a letter to Max Brod on March 11, 1921:

> I am firmly convinced, now that I have been living here among consumptives, that healthy people run no danger of infection. Here, however, the healthy are only the woodcutters in the forest and the girls in the kitchen (who will simply pick uneaten food from the plates of patients and eat it—patients whom I shrink from sitting opposite) but not a single person from our town circles. But how loathsome it is to sit opposite a larynx patient, for instance (blood brother of a consumptive but far sadder), who sits across from you so friendly and harmless, looking at you with the transfigured eyes of the consumptive and at the same time coughing into your face through his spread fingers drops of purulent phlegm from his tubercular ulcer. At home I would be sitting that way, though not quite in so a dire state, as "good uncle" among the children. (LF, 264)

Kafka separates the truly healthy and beautiful from the ill and ugly. The healthy come from "healthy stock, the kind that doesn't give up, even in extremity," like the "Warden of the Tomb" (1916/17) (219). This is not Franz Kafka. He is virtually the *blood* brother of one even more ill than himself. It is of course laryngeal tuberculosis from which Kafka will eventually die, robbed of speech and staring at those who come to visit him in hospital. The illness lies in the blood.

Kafka's surprise at the appearance of this illness was so great that he could forget the primary theme of his pathological predisposition, but this theme has finally returned. In all his accounts of the appearance of his tuberculosis, he stresses that he had expected to become ill, only not in this form. The unity of body and mind was the *fin de siècle*'s view on the origin and nature of disease, and "Kafka never doubted, nor ever ceased to believe, that what made him ill was the way he lived."[53] While Kafka might seem to have this image of the meaning of somatic illness in common with such thinkers of the time as Sigmund Freud and Georg Groddeck, it is evident that for him the "psychosomatic" model masks another model of pathological predisposition. Elias Canetti has commented: ". . . the myth about the two combatants within him . . . is an unworthy myth and a false one. The image of a struggle cannot encompass his inner processes; he distorts them by a kind of herniating of his hemorrhage, as if the struggle were indeed a bloody one."[54] The image of a combatant conceals someone else whom Canetti, himself a Sephardic Jew born in Bulgaria, could not bring himself to see: Blüher's concept of the Jew within.

Jews and the Illness Unto Death

The discourse on the history of psychosomatic illness at the turn of the century is double-edged, as we discussed in Chapter Two. Conceptions of psychosomatic illness at the turn of the century incorporate symptoms that cluster about the images of the hysteric and the neurasthenic. These include physical symptoms such as impairment of movement and gait, lethargy, difficulties in speaking and articulating, and so on.[55] This medical and philosophical discourse about "illnesses of the will," about which John Smith has so ably written in *Genders*,[56] assumes a specific meaning for Jewish males.

Kafka's understanding of his illness as psychosomatic reveals yet another discourse on race and masculinity. In contrast to the pessimism apparent from his writing about his illness, in his life Kafka struggled against the conception that illness was inscribed on his body. He, like many Jews of the turn of the century, hoped to circumvent his pathological predetermination. He indulged, indeed, often overindulged in sports and self-cure through various and sundry forms of dieting well before the onset of his tuberculosis. Thus on September 11, 1916, he recounts his visit to his family doctor, Dr. Mühlstein:

> As for my headaches, they have been variable recently, therefore on the whole quite bearable. The doctor whom I went to see, and who examined me as carefully as doctors generally examine one, was very pleasant. A quaint, rather funny man who nevertheless, by his age and

> physical bulk (how you could ever come to trust anything as long and thin as me is something I shall never understand)—as I was saying, by his bulk (thick lips, a broad rotating tongue), his neither excessive nor affected sympathy, his modesty in medical matters, as well as some other traits, inspired confidence. He declared he could find nothing but extreme nervousness. His suggestions were actually very funny: not too much smoking, not too much to drink (though a little now and then), eat more vegetables than meat, preferably no meat for supper, a visit to the swimming baths from time to time—and at night lie down quietly and go to sleep. (LF, 499)

Mühlstein's Jewish body is the very antithesis of the damaged Jewish body in the discourse of the time. The irony in Mühlstein's suggestions lay in the fact that Kafka had intensely pursued his formula for health for at least a decade prior to the onset of his illness, with, of course, no real effect.

It is evident that Kafka's intense preoccupation with his diet is part of a larger preoccupation, which incidentally was shared by other figures of the late nineteenth century such as Friedrich Nietzsche and Marcel Proust. As Mark Anderson notes, Kafka's compulsive chewing of food at the table, which followed the dictates of the system of Fletcherization; his vegetarianism; his intense fascination with systems of physical culture; all are part of a preoccupation with health and the body generally.[57] Such "modern" activities, often conceived as a return to the spirit of "Muscular Christianity," offer a socially acceptable quest for health to one who understands his body as innately ill. They also fill a cultural gap very evident to Kafka: they replace *kashruth*, the consumption of ritually slaughtered food, a "historical" practice that Kafka's parents had abandoned.

The meaning of kosher food for the turn of the century Jew is complex. It had lost any connection with traditional ritual well before Kafka's time. The *bal t'shuva*, the person returning to Judaism, whether in a religious or a political/cultural conception, and that Kafka certainly was, would have evoked kosher slaughter only in the context of the new, *fin-de-siècle* argument for "hygiene." It thus filled the same cultural space as did vegetarianism or Fletcherization or gymnastics. It was associated only with the concepts of health and hygiene, as we have seen.[58] Prophylaxis or self-cure, whether through the eating of kosher meat or Fletcherized food, became attractive alternatives to compulsory quarantine. One does not have to be cut off from society, one does not have to be labeled as ill, one has control over one's illness and life, if one eats properly. The replacement of a "Jewish" solution to illness (*kashruth*) with a neutral (read: Christian) solution, such as the gymnastic system of J. P. Müller with its Christian evangelical overtones, attempted to bridge the gap with the greater society while denying the specificity of the Jewish body and psyche. Indeed, Kafka's own haunting of spas during the period before the appearance of his tuberculosis, otherwise not unusual behavior among his contemporaries, was marked by his earlier visits to spas not usually open to Jews. Health and hygiene became "universal" (that is, not Jewish) analogs to popular therapies such as vegetarianism or Fletcherism. But for Jews such as Kafka, the power of the image of food and health was lodged in the ferocious debates about the meaning of kosher slaughter as a sign of the psyche of the Jews.

But all attempts at cure were in vain. Kafka feared that his future was unchangeable, for he had inherited an ill mind and an ill body, or at least a predisposition for illness, and this fear shimmers through all of his attempts to employ the psychosomatic model of illness. Most of these attempts focus on tuberculosis, for this illness reflects a confirmation of his inherently diseased state, as he wrote to Milena Jesenská on August 26, 1920: "I am dirty, Milena, infinitely dirty, this is why I scream so much about purity" (LM, 169). It is his sense that he is unhygienic that determines his sense of himself. In a rebuttal of psychoanalysis as an explanatory model for the relationship between his mind and body, his psyche and his disease, Kafka writes to Milena Jesenská in November, 1920, about the nature of disease:

> All these alleged diseases, sad as they may seem, are matters of faith, anchorages in some maternal ground for souls in distress. . . .those anchorages which are firmly fixed in real ground aren't merely isolated, interchangeable possessions—they are preformed in man's being, and they continue to form and re-form his being (as well as his body) along the same lines. And this the [psychoanalysis] hopes to heal?
>
> In my case one can image 3 circles: an innermost circle A, then B, then C. The center A explains to B why this man is bound to torment and mistrust himself, why he has to give up. . . . Nothing more is explained to C, the active human being; he simply takes orders from B. C acts under the greatest pressure, in a fearful sweat. . . . Thus C acts more out of fear than understanding; he trusts, he believes that A has explained everything to B and that B has understood everything and passed it on correctly. (LM, 216–217)

The matter of faith and belief is not only in the nature of disease but also in the question of cure and prevention. When one believes, as Kafka clearly did, that he was condemned to a life of illness and despair, explanation no long suffices. It is the coldness of inevitability, of becoming what one was fated to become, that haunts Kafka's sense of his own diseased body.

The "Jewish" science of psychoanalysis might have offered an alternative model, but Kafka's body is inherently ill. No model of struggling or repressed forces within the psyche will explain to Kafka why he cannot be healed. For his illness is ordained, it was inscribed on his body and is acted out materially, as he stresses with the insistence on "real ground." If not tuberculosis, then what? Certainly the cool, dispassionate account of the treatment of his tuberculosis that he gives to his parents during the final stages of his illness was an attempt both the assuage their anxiety about him as well as to fend off their intervention into his life in Berlin. But it was also an awareness of the inevitability of his own illness because of them, whom he sees as the inevitable originators of that illness.[59]

THE INHERITANCE OF TUBERCULOSIS: CONSTITUTION AND PREDISPOSITION

The notion of a racial predisposition to specific illnesses was ubiquitous. On March 7, 1913, Julius Tandler, the Jewish professor of anatomy and Viennese city councilor, addressed the German Society for Racial Hygiene (that is, Eugenics).[60] It is Tandler who, in 1924, intercedes for the terminally ill Franz Kafka at the behest of Kafka's friend Franz Werfel, and enables Kafka to get a bed at the Kierling Sanatorium, where he finally dies.[61] In this basic address, he attempts to align a series of concepts that were loosely used at the turn of the century, among them constitution, predisposition, and race. Tandler assumes that these aspects define the human being, and that they are present simultaneously. For him all of these categories are "predetermined at the moment of conception" (13). Anything that can be altered by environment is not constitutional. Constitution is the individual variation that is present in an individual once the qualities of type and race are subtracted. This would include any "inherent relative abilities" such as the specific "disposition" for an illness. Thus there are "tumor races" (20). (There is a slippage from constitution to race in Tandler's argument). According to Tandler, there are races who develop specific forms of tumors. Some racial groups, he argues, have a predisposition that grants them a specific form of immunity, such as the immunity of blacks to tetanus.

Tandler illustrates his distinction between constitution and race with a specific example. While some, he argues, see the shape of the nose as a constitutional sign, he sees it as racial. He observes that individuals with a "Jewish nose" (*Hakennase*) are born with a small, flat nose and the development of the Jewish nose takes place only in puberty (21). What is universal is the nose formed in the earliest stages of fetal development; what is specific to the race appears as the individual matures and becomes identified as a part of the race. Here Tandler seems to exclude the "exterior" presentation of the body, which might not reflect the internal habitus of the individual. That is, one may look different from what one truly is (see Plates 15–16). Tandler divides all individuals into three types based on musculature and muscle tone: the hypertonic, the normal-tonic, and the hypotonic. Note that this typology is not just physical but also psychological. Thus Botticelli is, for Tandler, the painter of the hypotonic, and Michelangelo the painter of the hypertonic (17–18). But this is because they themselves were hypo- or hypertonic: "Great artists as rigidly formed individuals cannot transcend their own muscle tone and they paint this. If they are hypotonic [they paint] only hypotonic individuals, if they are hypertonic, only hypertonic individuals" (17). The creative artist's manner of seeing the world is limited by habitus: epistemology is thus a reflex of biology.

All of Tandler's comments, as he himself notes with some pride, rest on his continued acceptance of the notion of the inheritance of acquired characteristics (23). The qualities found in the races and in the constitution of the individual reflect, therefore, historical processes and can be altered, over time and with difficulty, but they can be altered. Here the notion of racial hygiene (eugenics) comes into play, for through hygiene, we "can speak of a cleansing of the stream of life, as we speak of a self-cleaning of the rivers" (26). Thus racial constitutions can be improved from generation to generation through "the eugenically prescribed reproductive selection, that may seem in contradiction to self determination and individual freedom." Individual efforts will not bring about such selection; it must be made law (26).

Tandler's views on constitution have a strong analog in Prague. By 1893, Ferdinand Hueppe, the Prague hygienist discussed in Chapter Three, had classified three sets of conditions for the appearance of infectious illness: the media for illness (such as climate or social context), the stimuli for illness (infectious agents), and the predisposition for illness.[62] Hueppe stressed predisposition as the primary quality, thus articulating the view that there are racial types to which people will generally revert, especially in illness. In a speech in Nuremberg in 1893, he argued that the "so-called tuberculosis bacilli" affect different groups or species differently based on their "disposition."[63] It is no surprise that one of Hueppe's most aggressive supporters was the racial theorist Houston Stewart Chamberlain, who saw in Hueppe's work primarily the work of the racial hygienist (or eugenist). Chamberlain went so far as to advocate giving Hueppe a chair in Vienna, and thus recalling him to the German-speaking world from the "barbarism" of Prague.[64]

A further connection to Kafka is that Hueppe was a close friend and colleague of the contemporary Prague philosopher and cofounder of *Gestalt* psychology, Christian von Ehrenfels. Even in that writer's work, race claimed a central position. In a widely read book on human sexuality, Ehrenfels wrote of the competition between the "higher" and the "lower" races and about the "great problem of our time": how to respect racial imperatives in the face of the "liberal-humanistic fiction of the equality of all people."[65] For Ehrenfels, the purpose of "natural sexual morals" (which are for him a natural law) "is to conserve or improve the constitution of the tribe or people."[66] He saw the need for the "white, yellow, and black" races to remain "pure" and to avoid any sexual interbreeding. As with most of the racial scientists of his time, he justified colonial expansion with the rationale that the "sexual mission" of some races is best accomplished "if they place their generative powers in the service of others."[67] As the rhetoric of this statement seems to indicate throughout Ehrenfels's discussion of race, his prime example is the "Oriental." For Ehrenfels: "These same directives are applicable to the Jewish problem, in as much as these are the result of differences in their constitution and not—as is actually generally the case—the result of resolvable differences in their social milieu."[68] All of the discussions about race are actually encoded references to the Jewish question. For the Jews are understood as biologically different. Their strengths, like the strengths of each of the races, are preserved only when they remain within their own group. Intermixing leads to the corruption and the weakening of the race. Rather than intermixing with Aryans, the Jews, Ehrenfels implies, through their activity in Western culture, can place "their generative powers in the service of others." And yet the racial theorist who advocated the purity of the race and the distinction between the "higher" and "lower" races was himself Jewish by descent, even though raised as a Christian.

Ehrenfels publicly acknowledged his Jewish background, and was horrified at the rise of political anti-Semitism.[69] He saw in the work of Otto Weininger the "superficiality, impiety, frivolity, impudence, and desire for self-advertisement" that he ascribed to the Jews. Yet there was a sense of Weininger's project having touched on "true insights" that came from Weininger's Jewishness.[70] Ultimately, however, Ehrenfels subsumes all of this anxiety into a model of the "Orient." The real danger, he states in a talk given in 1911, is the "Yellow Peril," "hoards of Mongols" poised to confront the "Caucasian" race: "Among 100 whites there stand two Jews. The German peasant has been awakened and armed with the holy weapons of his ancestors—not to struggle against 80 million Mongols but to confront two Jews! Is this not the height of folly!"[71] By 1911 Ehrenfels comes to deny any substantial physiological difference between Aryans and Jews. Indeed, he now sees the Jews as suffering from all of the diseases and dangers of modern society: "They suffer more than we do from the present sexual and economic order."[72] For a number of thinkers of the period assumed that the Jews were the worst example of the impact of civilization because of their weak nervous system. Franz Kafka mentions a response that Ehrenfels made during a presentation by Felix Theilhaber on the "decline of Germany Jewry" to a public audience in Prague in January, 1912.[73] Theilhaber had recapitulated the thesis of his controversial book: that urbanization, the struggle for profit, as well as mixed marriages and baptism were causing German Jewry to vanish. (The latter argument was a social variant on the older biological argument that "mixed marriages between Jews and Aryans had a noticeably lower fecundity."[74]) Ehrenfels's response, as Kafka noted, was a "comic scene" where the philosopher (whose Jewish antecedents were well known) "smiling spoke in favor of mixed races." The "hybrid" who spoke now in favor of "racial mixing" violated the basic contention that body types could not be altered by race mixing, and that the immutability of the body was a sign of the predisposition of the individual. Ehrenfels's desire for a new race, comprised of the best qualities of the constitutive races, would have been read as a biological fantasy by Hueppe and those who stressed the pathology of inheritance.

The debates about physical constitution and body type in tuberculosis paralleled the general discussion about the meaning of fixed body types undertaken by physicians such as Ernst Kretschmer in the 1920s. This reaction to the Darwinian view of the mutability of form is best captured in the debates around the attempt, in the 1920s, to apply the body-type thesis of Ernst Kretschmer to racial biology.[75] Kretschmer's three body types (asthenic, athletic, pyknic) were associated with specific forms of mental illness. Given the general assessment that there was a close correlation between race and mental illness, it was not too long before this leap was made. Ludwig Stern-Piper, in a lecture at the 1922 Southwest German Psychiatric Conference, took the three body types outlined by Kretschmer, and claimed that they were basic racial types.[76] Kretschmer responded.[77] He saw the existence of all three body types in all races; indeed he saw a certain contradiction between the very concept of "racial" types and body types. Stern-Piper continued the argument, stressing the inherent racial makeup of each individual and the links between body type, illness, and race.[78] This debate was joined by clinicians such as the Munich physician Moses Julius Gutmann, who attempted to work out which mental illness dominates among Jews. Given the predominance among Jews, he notes, of the asthenic body type, of a long, lanky body, one would imagine that they would be particularly subject to schizophrenia, but in his own clinical work he sees a predominance of manic-depressive psychosis.[79] The way the Jew looks, like the way the criminal looks, is scientific evidence of the Jew's sociopathic condition.

The notion of body type plays a major role in the question of Jews and tuberculosis. But it is striking that it should. While the etiology of mental illness remains undiscovered, by the late nineteenth century science "knows" what causes tuberculosis. After Robert Koch's clarification of the etiology of tuberculosis, the central question came to be not what causes tuberculosis, but why it appears in only certain individuals. Everyone is exposed to the bacillus, as Julius Cohnheim's pre-Koch *bon mot* has it: "After all, everyone has a bit of tuberculosis."[80] The debate about the potential of inheriting tuberculosis gives way, in the course of the nineteenth century, to the myth about inheriting the tendency or predisposition to tuberculosis. Following on the work of Robert Koch, in 1883, Paul Clemens von Baumgarten declares that pulmonary tuberculosis (*phthisis*) is acquired *in utero*, but could be latent for a long time.[81] In

1898, Georges Kuss disproves the hypothesis of intrauterine inheritance.[82] But in 1899 Otto Naegeli undertakes a series of postmortem examinations that show the universal exposure to pulmonary tuberculosis (*phthisis*) but that only a small percentage actually become ill.[83] In 1894 Felix Wolff is already very careful about not speaking about the inheritance of the disease, which had been thoroughly disproved, but about inheriting the tendency or the predisposition to the illness. For him it is the intensity or severity as well as the frequency of the illness within a family that is the classic sign of the family's predisposition to the illness.[84] One had to accept Koch's evidence about the etiology of tuberculosis, so one had to find ways to retain the notion that body types offered clues to predisposition to infection. Unlike guinea pigs, human beings could not all simply fall victim to bacteriological exposure. Who is "excluded" from contagion? becomes the central question.[85] Many physicians sought to bring tuberculosis into a category with illnesses such as Basedow's Syndrome, for which there was already an established physiognomic or constitutional profile, in this case a "lympathic constitution."[86] Constitution could be inherited, even if a disease, as such, could not.

The insurance industry of the late nineteenth century was quite convinced of the potential of an individual to inherit at least a heightened predisposition for tuberculosis. Reginald E. Thompson, in the standard monograph on the topic, stated, "the evidence establishes the truth of the theory that phthisis is hereditary, and shows that the general laws of inheritance, which are known to hold good for other conditions and diseases, especially insanity, are observed in the transmission and development of the phthisical inheritance."[87] The pattern that Thompson recognizes is the inheritance of acquired characteristics: "Phthisis although acquired in one generation certainly may be transmitted by inheritance to the second generation" (188). Even Rudolf Virchow believed that heredity was a potent factor in the development of tuberculosis.

How to deal with the risk that such a predisposed individual poses for society? Karl Pearson, who coined the term "eugenics," writes in his first study of tuberculosis, published in 1907, "the discovery of the possibility of phthisical infection has led, I think, to underestimation of the hereditary factor. Probably few individuals who lead a moderately active life can escape an almost daily infection under urban conditions; but in the great bulk of cases, a predisposition, a phthisical diathesis, must exist, to render the risk a really great one. In this sense it is probably legitimate to speak of the inheritance of tuberculosis."[88] Charles Goring, a student of Pearson's, formulated it as a rule: "With an inherited diathesis, man is powerless: the bacillus is all powerful."[89]

The medical establishment considered such arguments conclusive. Indeed, the standard European handbook of medical eugenics, written by Baur, Fischer, and Lenz, maintains in the 1920s that tuberculosis is an infectious disease, but one to which certain individuals are predisposed through inheritance. For them, the asthenic constitution is the physical mark of this predisposition.[90] One can inherit the predisposition to tuberculosis even though one seems basically healthy[91] (1: 20–21). Like Pearson, the German tradition argues that the bacterial explanation misses the constitutional dimension (1: 213). For tuberculosis itself plays a eugenic role, as it "destroys weaker constitutions, specifically the asthenic or hypoplastic constitutions" (2: 22). Here again is the *habitus phthisicus*. Unsurprisingly, it turns out that entire races can possess the *habitus phthisicus*: those groups that have been exposed to the disease for centuries, that have been decimated by it because of their exposure to it, also develop a certain resistance to it, such as the Jews (2: 24).

In 1914, the Norwegian Professor Søren Laache publishes a groundbreaking summary essay on the constitutional aspects of pulmonary tuberculosis. [92] He attempts to correct the assumption that exposure to tuberculosis is the only cause of the illness. He argues that tuberculosis appears regularly in families, but in marriages, the uninfected partner not only outlives the infected partner, but rarely dies from tuberculosis, in contrast to syphilis. Racial predisposition, however, is what really interests Laache. He takes the example of the black, who has a substantially higher rate of tubercular infection in the United States than the general population. He believes that the "poorly filtered air through their 'platyrrhinie,' flattened noses" might lead to a higher rate of infection (133). Jews, on the other hand, have a higher rate of immunity (though they are in no way totally immune) to the disease. Here one can only attribute this to the "resistance that they develop over time" (134). One could argue (with Julius Tandler) that the Jewish nose is a racial indicator, and that unlike the flat nose of the black, it provides a better air filtration system, developed because of the long and constant exposure to tuberculosis in the Ghetto. On the other hand, Laache also believes strongly in the *habitus phthisicus*, of which the sunken chest is a sign (136). Thus Thomas Mann's view that the "Gaffky number," the designation of the degree to which the infection was present in the sputum, was totally unreliable: "Up on the Schatzalp," says Mann's protagonist Hans Castorp, "there is a man, a Greek peasant, an agent had him sent here from Arcadia, he has galloping consumption, there isn't the dimmest hope for him. He may die any day—and yet they've never found even the ghost of a bacillus in his sputum. On the other hand, that Belgian captain that was discharged cured the other day, he was simply alive with them, Gaffky ten—and only the very tiniest cavity."[93]

What can explain the low or absent bacillus count? It can only be the inheritance of a specific predisposition for tuberculosis that makes even the slightest infection dangerous. The model of the inheritance of acquired characteristics is already under attack by biologists, beginning with August Weismann, and will cease to be accepted within most serious academic biological circles by the 1920s. Nonetheless, it persists in popular opinion through the influence of the medical profession, most powerfully in the work of August Reibmayr, whose standard study of inheritance and marriage is cited over and over again in the medical literature of the period. Reibmayr gives the most detailed biological rationale for the anomalous relationship of the Jews to tuberculosis.

Reibmayr, in 1897, accepts the special (racial) status of the Jews. He stresses the source of the illnesses of the Jews in their sexual inbreeding (*Inzucht*). He provides a standard analogy between the inbreeding of the Jews and that of isolated Alpine communities. While Reibmayr considers the positive cultural effects of inbreeding, he concludes that inbreeding is obstructing progress. Regression to inbreeding can occur later in a group's history, as in his microhistory of the Jews: exogamy accompanied a higher level of development, and endogamy the beginning of the degeneracy of the group.[94] Reibmayr particularly stresses that this inbreeding develops (at least initially) a specific form of the Jewish body, one with "not physical strength, rather the finer development of the body, that under healthy conditions always stands in correlation to a finer development of the spirit" (181). In the Diaspora, Jews came to intermarry with other peoples, or so was the general view at the turn of the century (191). Persecution and the desire for economic gain had made the Jews into a wandering people, "unbound to the soil," who were then able to intermix with other groups (195). This could be seen especially among the Spanish and Portuguese Jews, whose long residency on the Spanish peninsula enabled them to intermix with the local Islamic population.

Thus they developed more positive attributes. For example, they speak the language of the nations where they now dwell "purely," while the "Jews of other lands speak the languages with a unique (Jewish [*jüdelnden*]) accent" (198). They are also cleaner than other Jews (199).

It is within the model of degeneration that Reibmayr places the problem of the marriage of the tubercular.[95] For Reibmayr the *habitus phthisicus*, the physical body of the person with tuberculosis, signals the decline of the "original racial type." The bad body thus drives out the good, racial body, as the race as a whole becomes more and more predisposed to tuberculosis. The changes in the body caused by the tubercular bacilli are inherited from generation to generation. Reibmayr's "proof" is the "change" in the German body from the sixteenth century, when the German physician Georg Agricola proclaimed, "Every German a born warrior!" to the 1800s, when of one thousand Germans called for military service, only half are declared able to serve (53). He also cites Austrian statistics according to which in 1858, 498 per one thousand were qualified for military service, while in 1892 only 206 per one thousand were qualified.

On the other hand, how is it that certain groups have an inherited resistance to tuberculosis? He comes to the conclusion that the presence of extremes moves the body into a resistant state (55–57). Thus the Jews, whom Reibmayr does not mention in this context, acquire their supposed immunity through long exposure to tuberculosis. Unfortunately, the benefits of such exposure are mitigated by inbreeding. For example, consanguineous marriages increase the chance that the offspring will acquire tuberculosis. Reibmayr attempts to balance the advantages and disadvantages of inbreeding for the Jews. The Jews do have a degree of "inherited resistance" to certain diseases, such as leprosy, the plague, and malaria (257). This comes from their early exposure to these illnesses in the "orient . . . their original home, and in Egypt" (257). But they have none for "modern" or "Western" illnesses such as cholera. (The Jewish immunity to cholera is a topos of the discussions of infectious diseases in the nineteenth century.[96] And yet it is clear that tuberculosis was a much greater and more constant danger than cholera, and was so perceived.[97] Cholera, which because of its epidemic nature served almost as a mask for tuberculosis, illustrated the Jews' immunity in an immediate and clear cut manner.[98]) Thus their resistance to tuberculosis is a reflex of their long exposure to this illness, an illness that is "certainly inherited," and the resistance to which is transmitted by inbreeding (260). What is significant is that Jews become ill from tuberculosis later in life and are able to reproduce, transmitting their acquired resistance. It is thus the "middle period" of the Jew's life (from thirty to forty) that is extended by his resistance to the illness. This period of resistance is also aided by social practices, such as the lower consumption of alcohol and "better material circumstances" (266). While Jews enjoy both lower and later mortality from tuberculosis, they do suffer from a host of other illnesses, such as "heart disease, cancer, diabetes, and especially illness of the central nervous system," to a degree greater than the general population (266–267).

The *habitus phthisicus* is "most firmly fixed" among the Jews (267). Jews are physically small, a sign of "Semitic blood." Jews have narrow chests and evidence early physical and mental development (267). Reibmayr's proof of the racial character of the form of the Jewish chest is the high rate of Jewish recruits dismissed from Russian military service. Here he counters Leroy-Beaulieu directly, who had argued that it was in the "least healthy race," among Polish Jews, that the narrowest chests were found, and who had the highest rate of rejection. Reibmayr argues that it is precisely among the orthodox Russian Jews, with their very low rate of intermarriage, that the greatest "physical and mental degeneration" is to be found (268). It is exactly among these Jews, with their "unhygienic life and the raw climate where they live" that "their natural resistance to tuberculosis is weakened" (268).

In sum, the Jews have, through inbreeding, "more quickly developed a resistance to acute infectious diseases" (269). On the other hand, inbreeding means that the "struggle of the organism with inherited diseases has attacked the nervous system" (169). "Every Jew today is already an evident neurasthenic, and the enormous increase of organic and psychic illnesses should be a warning sign. Nature is revenging itself, following its eternal law. And its eternal law is not only: Increase your numbers, but also interbreed!" (269–270).

Interbreeding is thus part of the classic double bind for the Jew: heal yourself by becoming other than what you are, or perpetuate the illness inherent within you! The double bind can be seen in Kafka's tale "The Vulture" (1920), one of the short animal stories that he wrote, but did not publish, during the final years of his illness.[99] With this tale we return to Kafka's deformed, Jewish feet, for the vulture is hacking at them in the opening sentence. "It had already torn my boots and stockings to shreds, now it was hacking at the feet themselves." The clothing that protected the dandy's body, or that he thought would disguise his body and make it look like everyone else's, is being destroyed by this eater of carrion, this icon of death. Vultures do not eat living things, unless they are so close to death that they appear dead. These literary vultures, like the jackals in "Jackals and Arabs," would find the eating of live animals or indeed their butchering anathema, at least according to German literary convention.[100] This body is thus dead in life. It is not the body of Prometheus, whose liver is pecked by an eagle for all eternity. This is the eternally diseased Jew.

A "gentleman" asks why the narrator is allowing his feet to be so butchered. The narrator's answer is that he would rather "sacrifice" his feet rather than his face. His face is his public aspect; but his feet, that reveal his diseased difference, have been hidden. The "torture" of the narrator is the inscription of his hidden difference on his visible body. The vulture thus substitutes for the machine in "In the Penal Colony."

A masculine gesture offers a false solution. The inquirer offers to shoot the vulture, and thus rescue the victim. He undertakes a soldier's role, the role of the armed hunter, as opposed to the stance of the victim. Once a possibility for rescue is promised, the vulture, like the intelligent jackals, "understood everything; it took wing, leaned far back to gain impetus, and then, like a javelin thrower, thrust its beak through my mouth, deep into me. Falling back, I was relieved to feel him drowning irretrievably in my blood, which was filling every depth, flooding every shore" (S, 443). The vulture "dies" killing his victim, dies in the blood hemorrhaging from his victim's throat. The victim's mock escape is to be found in his own blood, though whether it is the "blood" of race or the "blood" of illness is no longer distinguishable, as both discourses have merged. It is not the throat that Kafka evokes here but rather the narrator's mouth: the vulture attacks the narrator's language. The vulture is here the javelin thrower, the healthy sportsman with his hardened body, as opposed to the sickly body of the narrator-Jew. The narrator's language itself reveals his illness, his impaired masculinity, his Jewishness.

THE *HABITUS PHTHISICUS*

The *habitus phthisicus* was the clearest sign for the "inherited diathesis," the predisposition to tuberculosis, as early as the times of Hippocrates and Galen. Indeed, in the eighteenth century Friedrich Hoffmann believed that "tall people with long necks" were prone to tuberculosis.[101] The classic description for the nineteenth century was that of Christoph Wilhelm Hufeland (1762–1836), who stressed that "the constitutional consumption [the "habitus phthisicus," called by Hufeland the *phthisis constitutionalis*], innate in the organism by structure, hereditariness, and the corporeal disposition, endeavors through the whole period of life to develop itself; it can be delayed, but never entirely annihilated, and once developed, is incurable." The physical form of the *phthisis constitutionalis* was linked by Hufeland with the character of the predisposed individual. The *phthisis constitutionalis* was understood to:

> be marked by a flat thorax, narrow towards the side and back, shoulder blades protruding wing-like, long neck, slender body, and very white teeth, but above all, by a peculiar irritability of the vascular system and lungs; thence circumscribed red cheeks (called phthisical roses), appearing especially after eating, easily excited, over-heating and redness of the face on rising, hot hands after meals, cough easily excited; irritable, sanguine temper, but particularly by an indifference and a carelessness of their own health, especially concerning that of the lungs, so that they entirely overlook, in reporting their case, the difficulties in the lungs, or pass them over intentionally, and attribute their disease generally to some other part, especially to the abdomen.[102]

Thus body type and character are linked absolutely: the illness has a psychological dimension (denial) that is as much a sign as the "phthisical roses." The body type in Hufeland is closely associated with a humoral or character type, the sanguinary, represented by blood. The character type intensifies the meaning of the illness by placing it within the psyche as well as inscribing it upon the body.

Also prior to Koch, Carl Rokitansky, a leading exponent of the second Viennese school, described the *habitus phthisicus* in his classic textbook of 1842 to 1846:

> The compressed and shallow chest, flattened from before backwards, which the clavicles and projecting shoulders overhang like wings, and which expressed the phthisical constitution. There is no question, that a thorax of this form is often associated with a peculiarity of the whole organization; but it is the latter, and not the form of the thorax, which predisposes to tubercular disease of the lungs. What such a chest loses in breadth, and vaulted form, it gains in length; its capacity is by no means necessarily deficient, nor is that of the lungs within it; and that such a form of chest gives a predisposition to phthisis, is quite hypothetical.[103]

Rokitansky disputes whether it is the lung capacity (as in the discussions of chest capacity as a defining factor for military service) or the *thorax paralyticus* that defines the physical predisposition for tuberculosis. But that there is some type of external sign inscribed on the body is never in question.

By the close of the nineteenth century, the work of Hermann Brehmer, a founder of the sanatorium movement, and Berthold Stiller, the theoretician of constitutional types, establishes the *habitus phthisicus,* equivalent to the *habitus asthenicus,* as a given body type.[104] Brehmer believed that the body type of the tubercular was a sign of a weak heart, and sought treatment for this deficit as a means of preventing the onset of the disease. Exercise and hardening of the body could prevent or cure the *habitus phthisicus.* Stiller stressed that the inherited form of the body predisposed an individual to acquire tuberculosis. He saw an identity of the body type, the underlying constitution and the predisposition to illness. This tradition continues in the classic history of constitutional theory that opened the standard *fin-de-siècle* periodical on the topic.[105]

Hermann Strauss, whose work on tuberculosis and the Jews was important at the time, took up the classic description of the *habitus asthenicus* as the "graceful body type, usually pale appearance, weak development of the musculature and the fat layer . . . long face, with a small lower jaw and high gums, long neck, long torso, especially the abdomen—narrow and flat nature of the chest, that often shows a narrowness both at the upper as well as the lower apertures of the thorax."[106] On the physical "ground" of the *habitus asthenicus,* disease is more likely to flourish. Strauss ties the disposition to the form of the body. More importantly, he sees this as a "German" tradition, linked to Virchow's notion of pathological anatomy, and not to the less scientific, "French" conception of constitution. Of special interest to Strauss is the *habitus phthisicus* that predisposes an individual to tuberculosis. Following Brehmer, Strauss argues that one must treat such inherited body types to prevent them from actually contracting the disease. But Strauss, himself a Jew, and therefore potentially bearing the stigmata of the *habitus phthisicus,* has a solution. Strauss's suggestion is to discover such individuals as children, and force their body into the "correct" (that is, healthy) form with orthopedic corsets. The body is to be re-formed in order to make it healthy. Such views date well back into the nineteenth century. Daniel Gottlob Moritz Schreber, one of the most influential advocates of exercise as therapy, stressed that corrective exercises could prevent tuberculosis and asthma.[107] The idea of re-forming the body dominated the answer to degeneration theory at the turn of the century—regeneration. Karl Mann, in 1901, advocated "lung exercises, holding one's breath, hardening of the body through air and sun-baths, cleansing of the skin and in general rational training of the body" to "overcome the myriads of tubercular bacilli" that threaten everyone.[108] Appliances or exercise will alter the *habitus phithisicus.*

One of the most widely read popular books on tuberculosis at the turn of the century, Paul Niemeyer's *The Lungs*, also associates body type and difference.[109] Niemeyer devotes an entire chapter to a comparative study of two men—one with a healthy body type and one who represents the *habitus phthisicus.* The former has a breast circumference of 110 cm; the latter, one of 83 cm for more or less equivalent height and weight (Plates 34–35). The former represents for Niemeyer the "original Germanic type," and he quotes both the *Song of the Nibelungs* and Shakespeare to the effect that such a chest is a manly, healthy chest. He is a "thirty-year-old Teuton who has a primitive, powerful body . . . and represents what civilized society once again desires to have: the athletic body type" (109). His opposite number is described in much more detail. He is a thirty-three-year-old workman in charge of a railway bridge. (A favorite subject of the naturalist writers of the time, such as Gerhart Hauptmann, who sought degenerate types among the working class.) He is "thin, weakly muscled, only 'skin and bones'." And he is a prime candidate for tuberculosis. Through exercise, he overcomes his apparent degenerate state, and avoids infection. Fifteen years after his initial examination, he shows up, healthy, on his doctor's doorstep. Thus exercise can reduce the potential for tuberculosis even for body types predisposed by race or class to the illness.

But there is a group whose innate nature no exercise, no appliance can change—the Jews. They were the exception. Then Zionism and the German Jewish gymnastics movement came along to try to prove the common wisdom wrong, and reform the Jewish body. We can return to Dr. Wilhelm Pollack's description of Kafka's body for clues to Kafka's own reading of his body as the *habitus phthisicus*:

> His body is thin and delicate (*gracil*). He is relatively weak. His stride is secure, relaxed. The circumference of his neck is 37 cm. He shows no signs of goiter. His voice is pure and strong. He looks younger than

PLATES 34–35. The healthy "Germanic" physique of the middle classes and the *habitus phthisicus* of the working classes from Paul Niemeyer, *Die Lunge, ihre Pflege und Behandlung*

his age. The form and structure of his chest—his breast is raised, his clavicle is drumstick-shaped and indented at its ends. He has weak chest muscles. With a deep breath his chest circumference at level of his nipples is 82 cm and on expiration it is 78 cm. Both halves of his

im gesunden und kranken Zustande (Leipzig: J. J. Weber, *Illustrirte Zeitung*, 1913) (National Library of Medicine, Bethesda).

chest are equally developed but weak. He takes 16 breathes a minute when resting; and 19 per minute with exercise. The percussion of right upper lobe of his lung is dull as a result of an earlier rachitic deviation. No anomalies by auscultation; no anomalous sounds.

Pollack's description of Kafka's body, and his medical evaluation, would place Kafka within the *habitus phthisicus*. Kafka, in turn, thinks of the physical deformation as equivalent to his deformed psyche:

> It is certain that a major obstacle to my progress is my physical condition. Nothing can be accomplished with such a body. . . . My body is too long for its weakness, it hasn't the least bit of fat to engender a blessed warmth, to preserve an inner fire, no fat on which the spirit could occasionally nourish itself beyond its daily need without damage to the whole. How shall the weak heart that lately has troubled me so often be able to pound the blood through the length of these legs. It would be labor enough to the knees, and from there it can only spill with a senile strength into the cold lower parts of my legs. But now it is already needed up above again, it is being waited for, while it is wasting itself below. Everything is pulled apart throughout the length of my body. What could it accomplish then, when it perhaps wouldn't have enough strength for what I want to achieve even if it were shorter and more compact. (D1, 160)

When he turns this into a fiction in "Shamefaced Lanky and Impure in Heart," he, Lanky, has such long legs, "he'd stuck them out of the window for comfort; there they dangled pleasantly." He has "clumsy, skinny, spidery fingers. . . . He was ashamed of his height. . . . He has bony legs" (LF, 6–7). This body makes him vulnerable. In the tale it is a vulnerability tied to male-male bonding through the meaning attributed to Shamefaced Lanky's body. Impure in Heart states to him: "'Do you know what blood of blood is? one would answer with a leer, 'Yes, I have English cravats'." The "blood of blood" is the essential truth hidden within the spoken words, unuttered and unutterable, yet written in the blood. The answer is the answer of the dandy—I can cover my body (and my meaning) with fine clothes and be just like everyone else. This meaning in "blood" is the meaning ascribed to illness and masculinity. For, as we have seen, the *habitus phthisicus* is a sign of the lack of masculinity, as well as the prefiguration of illness, both aspects of the Jewish body. Kafka's role as St. Sebastian, his body pierced by arrows, his nude body exposed as an sign of his difference, is to be understood in much the same manner (D1, 222). The Jew as the first Christian martyr of the Jews—himself a Jew. The Jew as the visual representation of the homosexual body that is a Christian body. The irony is wonderfully circular! The image of the body represents the hidden disease within as the sign that one is fated to become what one must become, but, of course it does not resolve the ironic conflation of Jew with Christian.

The German physician and author Oskar Panizza similarly suggests, in a tale written in 1893, that the body of the Jew is not reformable. His tale depicts the careful reconstruction of the Jew Itzig Feitel Stern (one of the classic anti-Semitic literary characters of the mid-nineteenth century) into an "Aryan." The story begins with a detailed description of Stern's physiognomy—his Jewish "antelope's eye," his nose, his eyebrows, "his fleshly and overly creased" lips, his "violet fatty tongue," his "bow-legs," his "curly, thick black locks of hair."[110] But it is not just his body that marks him as a Jew. His language, whether French or High German, is "warped" by his "Palatinate-Yiddish."[111] He "meowed, rattled, bleated and also liked to produce sneezing sounds."[112] His speech was a "mixture of Palatinate Semitic babble, French nasal noises and some high German vocal sounds that he had fortuitously overheard and articulated with an open position of the mouth."[113] His body language was equally marked. His gait marked him as a Jew and it bore a striking resemblance to the way that "people with spinal diseases" walked.[114] His gesticulation was equally "Jewish." Stern's entire physiognomy indicates the perverted Jew.

Stern goes to Professor Klotz, the famous Heidelberg anatomist, to have his body reshaped. He is forced into orthopedic appliances, and has his movements retrained in order, in his own words, to "become such a fine gentilman just like a goymenera and to geeve up all fizonomie of Jewishness."[115] His "Palatinate-Yiddish" is rehabilitated and formed into a pure high German. But his Jewish soul remains. Stern desires a "chaste, undefined Germanic soul that shrouded the possessor like an aroma." To accomplish this, he medicalizes the old blood libel. Medicalizing the blood libel charge, he buys Christian blood and has it exchanged for his own. Thus transformed into an Aryan, Stern decides to marry a "blond Germanic lass."[116] Indeed, all of the physical changes that are necessary to make him into the ideal image of the Aryan have taken place—all but one. Feitel Stern remains circumcised. Panizza never mentions it, but there are procedures, many of them ancient, for the reversal of circumcision, procedures again in circulation at the close of the century.[117] The circumcision of the genitals is the outward sign of the immutability of the Jew within.

On his wedding night, Stern becomes intoxicated, and all of his newly acquired qualities of body, tongue and mind disintegrate. The *foetor judaïcus* that had been masked by the Christian blood that he had bought reappears and marks his final collapse as he lay "crumpled and quivering, a convoluted Asiatic image in wedding dress, a counterfeit of human flesh."[118] His efforts were futile. As Immanuel Kant had observed in his *Anthropology*: "Women, clergymen, and Jews ordinarily do not become drunk, at least they carefully avoid all appearance of it, because they are weak in civic life and must restrain themselves (for which sobriety is required)."[119] Jews become their true selves when the constraints of civilization are removed. And even more, you are truly what you eat, for, to paraphrase the old saw, in whiskey lies truth.

The restructuring of the Jewish body is, according to the anti-Semite, impossible because of its transhistorical immutability. In Panizza's text, unlike in most of the calls for the reform of the Jewish body at the turn of the century, the notion is that only the physician can cure. Self-help through exercise only is effective as part of a medical regime of body reshaping. And every aspect of the body points towards its relationship to illness. But here the problem arises again. How could the Jewish body type predispose one to illnesses such as tuberculosis, and yet the Jews have a substantially lower incidence of the disease?

By the end of the nineteenth century, every theory about predisposition to illness had been racialized. A race's physical characteristics as markers of this predisposition dominated discussion. The "national idiosyncrasy"[120] of the Jews and their "powerful struggle for life" *[Lebenszähigkeit]*[121] came to be the buzzwords for the rationale to their immunity. It was seen to be a "quality of their race or confession or specific qualities of life associated with these."[122] Such a description of Jews in Cracow, from 1914, elides the relation of racial predisposition and religious practice in a manner typical of this secularized age. The ethnographic explanation was that Jews produced their particular religion to satisfy biological purposes. Religious practices were considered a component of racial identity, and racial identity was biological.

This identity, finally, included all the stigmata of tuberculosis.[123] These were considered to be body weight, height, chest circumference, width, and depth. The formula was quite simple: $D = H - (P+C)$, where H is the body height/size, (P+C) the sum of weight and chest circumference. If the difference (D) is greater than 25, one should suspect a weakened constitution. The relationship of chest circumference to body size (height) will illustrate the pattern.

	.40–.45	.45–.50	.50–.55	44–.60	.60+
NHM	4.75	48.0	39.25	6.75	1.25
HM	8.1	53.3	31.5	6.6	0.5
NHW	15.4	58.2	24.3	2.1	—
HW	21.1	58.9	20.0	—	—

NHM = Nonhereditary Men; HM = Hereditary Men;
NHW = Nonhereditary Women; HW = Hereditary Women

The scale is the same for all of the other comparisons of the normal versus the *habitus phthisicus*. Not surprisingly, the "nonhereditary male" is *most* unlike the "hereditary woman," but the "hereditary male" forms an intermediate category between the most masculine (healthy) and the most feminine (ill).

Here we can return for the moment to the notion that the male Jew is feminized like the male tubercular. The tubercular's progressive feminization begins in the middle of the nineteenth century with the introduction of the term: *infemminire,* to feminize, which is supposedly a result of male castration.[124] By the 1870s, the term is used to describe the *feminisme* of the male through the effects of other disease, such as tuberculosis.[125] Henry Meige, at the Salpêtrière, saw this feminization as an atavism, in which the male returns to the level of the "sexless" child.[126] Feminization is therefore a loss, which can cause masturbation and thus illness in certain predisposed individuals. It is also the result of actual castration or its physiological equivalent, such as an intensely debilitating illness like tuberculosis, which reshapes the body.

What did the *habitus phthisicus* imply? First, it meant a lower cure rate for those who were constitutionally predisposed to the illness, as Paul Reichert argued in 1918. Such a constitution is not an artifact of the illness, but rather a sign of the initial predisposition, a "constitutional weakness and inferiority" (34). But this is, according to Reichert, no reason to despair: He recommends, against Strauss, avoiding professions where one must inhale dust, strengthening in one's youth through "hygienic" gymnastics, undertaking reasonably non-exhausting sports, and avoiding early marriage. The gymnastics in particular should undertake to strengthen the upper chest and help expand it.

Given the centrality of skin color as a marker for racial difference at the turn of the century, it is no wonder that it was also read as a stigma of the *habitus phthisicus.*[127] W. Schultz argued that groups with lighter skin color have a lower incidences of tuberculosis, while "divergent" (mixed) types, individuals with dark skin but light eye color, have a higher rate.[128] He thus accounted for the "relatively low number of cases of tuberculosis among the Jews" (65), as they were a "pure" race even though they had darker pigmentation. The *Judenkrätze* was also updated. Moro and Kolb found that "children with eczema who have dark hair and eyes" rarely have tuberculosis. They also deny the link between the *habitus phthisicus* and specific forms of head and face eczema in childhood. Childhood eczema seems to be preventative of tuberculosis.[129] The eugenist Fritz Lenz wanted to correlate skin pigment and hair color with the predisposition for tuberculosis.[130] John Beddoe argued that blond individuals had a lower rate of infection,[131] while Franz Koch argued quite the reverse.[132]

Franz Koch's 1909 presentation drew out all the connections between tuberculosis and other illnesses associated with degenerate behavior. For him, the weaker the race, the more potential for tuberculosis. Syphilis and alcoholism, in particular, are weakening the "northwestern cultures" (82), which for Koch leads to a distinction between a civilization full of bacteria, and the "tropical rain forest which is in bacteriological sense as good as sterile" (82). The most vulnerable are "those blond, long-skulled, blue-eyed Northerners" (83). They have an "ancient, inherited tendency" for tuberculosis that only became evident under the growth of modern civilization. Such a predisposition must have had a positive function "under natural conditions," he argues, but "under the influence of culture" it has become the *habitus phthisicus.* An "unhygienic manner of life and the unhygienic clothing" of civilization, specifically the wearing of suspenders, lead to tuberculosis (84). For the "greater gracefulness" of the skeletal structure of the "blond" race makes them more susceptible to such effects than the "coarse and short" skeletal structure of the dark races.

Since Koch obviously believes that acquired characteristics can be inherited, he proposes that "blond" children should be liberated from the compulsion to sit for hours at school, and that they should have compulsory sports until the circumference of their chest no longer marks them as of the *habitus phthisicus.* For "in the free competition of the races the educated, flat-chested eyeglass wearers will not triumph, but rather the races who harmonically develop their spiritual and physical advantages" (86). There is a clearly a racial divide between physicians such as Koch and Strauss, who demand to intervene, and those who wanted patients to help themselves. For Jewish physicians, such as Strauss, need to justify the profession that provides them with social status; a non-Jewish physician, such as Koch, whose status is unquestioned, can call for the self-reform of the Christian body, in spite of or because of the long association of gymnastics with germanophilia and anti-Semitism.

In 1938, Samuel Arthur Weisman, then an assistant professor of medicine at the University of Minnesota, offers a radical answer to the problem of the chest: "your chest should be flat."[133] For Weisman, the tuberculous chest is the "round, deep chest," a relict of the infantile body form, while the flat chest is a sign of the mature, nontubercular chest. After measuring 20,000 chests, "I had noticed that a number of tubercular clinic patients who appeared at first sight to have flat chests turned out to be deep-chested when told to sit or stand up straight and throw their shoulders back; while persons who enjoyed normal chest health were the ones who possessed flat, wide chests" (ix). His statistics undermine the legend of the *habitus phthisicus*. He throws the work of German racial scientists such as Ludwig Stern-Piper on the thoracic index of race into question. He finds that although "Jews showed some tendency toward a slightly deeper chest" (76), "one's ancestry—at least in the nationality groups we have been able to study—is not a very important factor in determining the type of chest development one is likely to have" (77). For Weisman to argue in 1938, after the Nazi seizure of power, that there is no racial measure of a predisposition for tuberculosis, is clearly a political act. Fifty years earlier, Jewish scientists had been much more divided on this issue.

FIN-DE-SIÈCLE JEWISH READINGS OF TUBERCULOSIS

Jewish physicians who had dealt with the special Jewish relationship to tuberculosis were divided on the primacy of nature or nurture.[134] In 1904, Maurice Fishberg, a recognized anthropologist and pathologist of the Jews, and as well as one of the foremost specialists on tuberculosis, offered a comprehensive overview of Jewish reflections on tuberculosis since the innovations of Koch.[135] Consumption infected Jews for three reasons: first, their urban living conditions in "crowded and insufficiently ventilated tenement-houses"; second, their "sedentary" occupations such as tailoring; and third, their "consanguineous marriages" (245).

Indeed, the very appearance of the "modern Jew leads one to suspect the presence of tuberculosis. He is more stunted in growth than almost any other European." In particular, "the exceptionally narrow girth of Jews gives them what is technically known as the lowest 'index of vitality.' All of these conditions, added to their poverty, constant grief, anxiety, and mental exertion, besides the ceaseless persecutions to which they are subjected, tend to make them ready victims to tuberculosis. . . ." (246). This is central to the discussions of the period. All Jews look tubercular and many Jews are tubercular!

Yet, in spite of the tradition that Jews *should* suffer a greater incidence of illness, that is, Epstein's tradition supported by Joseph Jacobs's summary of the medical literature on consumption in the 1880s, it is clear by the 1890s that Lombroso's view of Jewish immunity from tuberculosis dominates. Even though Jacobs correctly commented, "it is scarcely likely, however, that the Rabbins [*sic*] were in any sense anticipators of Koch and Pasteur, for they considered the function of the lungs to be to absorb the liquids of the body," nonetheless the notion of the greater resistance of the Jews remained dominant.[136] Fishberg cites study after study to show the lower rate of tuberculosis among poor Jews, but its gradual increase in New York City. But this he sees as an artifact of poverty and living conditions in New York (and, unstated, the fact that any one with signs of tuberculosis was excluded from admission to the United States). Indeed "the well-to-do Jews are even less liable to consumption than the unfortunate poor. . . ." (247). Fishberg presents a standard cultural rationale that seems to avoid any racial implications: "Jews abhor the dusting-brush. They wipe all dusty surfaces with damp cloths, in some instances several times daily. By this means less dust is raised, and the risk of inhaling air laden with tubercle bacilli is lessened" (247). But for Fishberg, the primary rationale is that given by most of those who accept the relative immunity of the Jews to tuberculosis. He sees it due to:

> the careful inspection of their meat, examination being made particularly as to disease of the lungs and pleura, and bovine tuberculosis being thereby intercepted. . . . It has been repeatedly shown that the flesh of tuberculous cattle sold for food is responsible for many cases of tuberculosis; and the rigid inspection of meat practiced by the Jews has, therefore, the effect of checking to a very great extent the ravages of the disease. . . . their comparative immunity from the disease is not due to any racial characteristic of a purely physiological nature, but to kasher [*sic*] meat and the non-abuse of alcohol. (248)

Fishberg leaves much unsaid, which we should fill in. As early as 1865 to 1868, Jean-Antoine Villemin's work could assume that bovine and human tuberculosis had the same origin. At the turn of the century, Koch, building on the work of Theobald Smith, proved that the bacilli in question are different, and at the Tuberculosis Conference in London, he denied that there was any risk to human beings from bovine tuberculosis.[137] On September 30, 1907, Koch, at a meeting of the International Tuberculosis Congress in Washington, erroneously argued that bovine tuberculosis could never or almost never be transmitted to humans.[138] This claim was not only wrong, it undermined the hygienic rationale for ritual slaughter as well as for the pasteurization of milk.

The debate on Koch's extraordinary paper was intense. Koch had argued that there was little or no evidence of pulmonary tuberculosis, the form of eleven of twelve tuberculosis cases, to be transmitted from animals. He argued that it was not proven, therefore, that bovine tuberculosis had contributed to any specific cases of human pulmonary tuberculosis. When confronted with the practical ramifications of his talk—should, for example, one ignore bovine tuberculosis and abandon pasteurizing milk to decrease the risks of transmission—Koch exploded. He refused to discuss "resolutions of a purely practical nature that were not on the agenda" (634). In a three-hour secret session, Koch acknowledged the possibility of transmission, but refused to change his views unless irrefutable evidence was presented. He was wrong, but his influence undermined the contemporary hygienic rationale for ritual slaughter. Following the London and Washington meetings, major research endeavors were undertaken to prove Koch's error, which was accomplished by World War I.[139] (Ironically, Koch's earlier attempt to develop "tuberculin" as a cure for human tuberculosis turned out to be ineffective. But Albert Calmette and Camille Guérin developed at this time a BCG vaccine based on a bovine strain of tuberculosis to immunize children from the disease.)

Koch indirectly undermined all the arguments that social practice and not inheritance gave the Jews immunity from tuberculosis. The elaborate hygienic justifications for ritual slaughter in the late nineteenth century seemed to collapse, reviving anti-Semitic arguments about Jewish brutality and cruelty. If ritual slaughter had no hygienic meaning, then it could have none at all. Once again, as Hans Blüher had argued in *Secessio Judaica*, the Jews could only fall back on Jewish arguments when their claims to universally applicable knowledge or practices were challenged. If "modern" medicine (and Jewish ritual that had reinterpreted itself as part of "modern" medicine) with its claims of science were of little use, perhaps alternative forms of self-cure would be effective.

Given the failed association of science and "Jewish" hygienic practices, it is little wonder that Kafka turned to dietary self-cures. If he ate food representing what he would like to be, perhaps he could avoid reverting to what he was supposed to be. In April, 1911, he visited Moriz Schnitzer, the health faddist, who gave his hygienic, vegetarian regime biblical underpinnings: "Moses led the Jews through the desert so that they might become vegetarians in these forty years."[140] Many tuberculosis patients considered such regimens. This letter to the physician/editor appeared in a German patient's magazine: "Can you cure TB by eating vegetarian food?" The answer: "No, we surely eat too much meat. . . . While the pleasure of eating vegetarian food can be a stimulant and thus have a positive effect on the organism of tuberculosis, it should not result in too great a loss of weight."[141] Kafka's move away from meat to vegetarianism thus avoids a number of problems: the relationship of meat to illness and infection, the condemnation of Jewish ritual slaughter. It further constitutes a refutation of the anti-Semitic charge of materialism against modern medicine and science, including psychoanalysis.

For Jewish medical scientists of his time, however, this way out was not possible. In 1911, in a standard study of *The Jews: A Study of Race and Environment*, Maurice Fishberg recapitulates all of his earlier argument. Now, however, he introduces his own view that the traditional hygienic virtues of Jewish law and family life enable Jews to have a lower incidence of tuberculosis only through the inheritance of acquired characteristics.[142] He argues that the generations in the ghetto have provided a type of immunity for the Jews:

> The Jew, living for centuries in the Ghetto, could under the circumstances have adapted his organism to an adverse milieu, to overcrowding, to dark and ill-ventilated dwellings, etc. Those Jews who could not adapt themselves to a confined atmosphere succumbed to various diseases that thrive in such a milieu, chief among which is tuberculosis, and they were eliminated from their midst, having had slight chances to perpetuate their kind. . . . Living under such conditions for eighteen hundred years has had the effect of weeding out a large proportion of those Jews who were excessively predisposed to tuberculous infection (293).
>
> The phthisical chest described by Hippocrates and Galen is today

> found in a large proportion of Jews. Indeed, that frail, undersized, emaciated body, with a long, narrow, flat chest, in which the ribs stand out prominently, the chest-bone is depressed, and the shoulder-blades project in the back like two wings, may be considered as characteristic of a large number of Jews. . . . Physically, the Jews can, under the circumstances, be considered predisposed to pulmonary diseases, especially consumption. (286)

This is a paradox. This *real* constitution that predisposes one to tuberculosis marks the Jews' bodies yet does *not* indicate their predisposition to tuberculosis. It is vital for Fishberg to argue that it is not race that predisposes the Jew to resist tuberculosis:

> [T]hat it is not a racial trait is seen from the fact that in the United States the number of Jewish consumptives is growing to an alarming extent. Racial immunities are not lost by a residence for a few years in a new country, or by a change of milieu for one generation. . . . Nor can we attribute it to the ritual inspection of meat practiced by the Jews, because in western countries, where they are not loth to consume meat not prepared according to the dietary laws, their tuberculosis mortality is lower than in the East, where they are very strict in this regard. They are better adapted to city life and overcrowding by a long sojourn in the Ghetto, and by a process of natural selection there were [*sic*] eliminated most of those who were predisposed to tuberculosis, thus giving them an advantage. (529)

Fishberg rejects any simple racialist definition of an immutable Jewish body. Rather he relies on the notion of the inheritance of acquired characteristics—Jews have over the years undertaken certain ritual practices that have left them unmarked by certain ailments such as tuberculosis:

> All these peculiarities in the comparative pathology of the Jews are not due to any ethnic, "biostatic," or racial characteristics of a purely anatomical or physiological nature in relation to non-Jews. They have their origin in the past history of the Jews, in their habits of life, and in the fact that syphilis and alcoholism have but rarely been seen among them. When the Jew is commingling with his Christian neighbors and adopts their customs and habits of life, he sooner or later loses his "racial characteristics," and his comparative pathology presents no special peculiarities.[143]

A. Legoyt, the chief of the division of general statistics in France, had followed much the same line of argument in the 1860s. According to

Legoyt, the reasons for the relative good health of the Jews were: (1) early marriages; (2) low child mortality; (3) low-risk occupations (they are neither farmers nor sailors nor miners but bankers or merchants or artists); (4) their adherence to rules of hygiene (central of which are the rules for ritual slaughter. His comparative comments on the kosher and general abattoirs of Paris are striking); (5) family cohesion; (6) sobriety; (7) charity; (8) serenity; and (9) morality.[144] Here the mix of "biological" rationales, such as "good" sexual practices; social rationales, such as ritual practices; and character traits provide an image of the idealized life, like that evoked by Marsh in the wilds of rural Louisiana. They provide a pattern with which any group can extend their lives.

Similarly, Jewish physicians in Germany during Kafka's lifetime try to explain the Jewish immunity from tuberculosis in terms of an ideal of Jewish family life. Schamschen Kreinermann, in one of the two great surveys in Germany of the question of the relationship of Jews to tuberculosis, also returns to this question.[145] He stresses over and over again, summarizing the literature from Lombroso to John Billings, while confusing "racial" with "environmental" arguments as all such summaries did, concludes that the Jews were less at risk for tuberculosis. He offers this as self-evident. He then summarizes the explanatory factors in detail. The Jews show the *habitus phthisicus,* defined by a "lack of the long-muscle in a weak, narrow chest, in the highly placed position of the ribs . . . in the extension of the clavicle, and the wing-like extension of the shoulder blades" (1554). Again, it is the weak, unmasculine chest, as proven in this instance with military statistics, that marks the Jew!

The second factor noted by Kreinermann is the ubiquity of what he calls the "exsudative diathesis," or, in simpler terms, our old friend the *parech* or *Judenkrätze*, that predisposes Jews "of the poorer classes" to tuberculosis. Here the nineteenth-century equation of scrofula with pulmonary tuberculosis links traditional images of Jewish skin disease with a category of Jews, namely the poor, who are supposed to be at greater risk for all forms of tuberculosis. Finally, the urban concentration of the Jews, their poverty-stricken domiciles and their concomitant urban occupations (tailor, shoemaker, hatmaker, glove maker, and so on) predispose them to the illness. Cigar makers, for example, are especially at risk for tuberculosis. To these "environmental" factors, one can add the squalor of their environments and the dirty, cramped schools (*Cheder*) where they study.

Then how can one understand the apparent immunity of the Jews for tuberculosis? Kreinermann dismisses the anthropological view that stresses illness as a marker of race. Like all Jewish physicians, he stresses the environmental explanation. After dismissing Lombroso's claim that the occupations of the Jews are the major predisposing factor, Kreinermann stresses the much lower incidence of alcoholism as a reason for the heightened immunity of the Jews. But he also argues that Jews have acquired an immunity through centuries of exposure. Jews present "a poorer source of sustenance" for the bacilli (1561). But Kreinermann finally returns to religious practice as the primary source of the diminished risk: visits to the sick, the suspension of laws concerning fasting for the ill, the cleaning of the home before the Sabbath, ritual bathing, but most of all ritual slaughter and the inspection of meat.

In 1925, the second major study on the relationship of the Jews to tuberculosis was presented in the major German medical periodical dealing with clinical treatment of tuberculosis. N. Haltrecht stressed the lower rate of infection and mortality among the Jews, acknowledging first the social-pathological reasons—the poor, dusty, squalid housing, the struggle for existence.[146] However, he noted that there seems to have been a much greater disparity between the relatively equal rate of morbidity and the much lower rate of mortality. Jews got sick with tuberculosis more or less at the same rate as Aryans or at a somewhat lower rate, but had a longer life span after onset. Jews seemed to evidence the same pattern of illness, but only "because of neurasthenic influence." That is, Jews complained much more about their symptoms: "Jews more often complain about chest pains. They are more often tortured by attacks of coughing, that are often accompanied by intense vomiting. Jews often suffer from insomnia and the loss of appetite. The expectoration of blood places them in a great panic, that leads to depression and neurosis" (452). Here Hufeland's hypothesis about the displacement of tubercular individuals' anxiety onto other organs or parts of the body is linked to the image of Jews as singularly nervous, such nervousness manifesting itself especially in those who are predisposed to tuberculosis.

The notion that hypochondriasis and hysteria precede tuberculosis goes back at least to Richard Morton, writing in 1689.[147] Felix Wolff still believes in 1894, as did many of his colleagues, that there is a tubercular character: "Character qualities form an important aspect of the etiology of tuberculosis. . . ."[148] This is not to ignore the infection itself. Wolff's question, however, is why certain individuals and not others develop the infection, as the bacillus appears to be ubiquitous. His signs of emotional predisposition are "sadness, worry, anger" as the significant affective signs of the predisposition. There are psychopathologies that particularly predispose the individual to the illness, most specifically, "severe, chronic depression" (57). By the early twentieth century, it had become one of the signs of the incipient stage of the disease. D. G. Macleod Munro, whose study of the psychopathology of the illness summarized the standard views of the period, views many patients "especially women, who have been treated for neurasthenia" as having "in fact been cases of incipient tuberculosis that has remained latent"[149] (7). The source of the psychopathology is in the "cerebral intoxication caused by the products of the tubercle bacillus" (8). These patients complain of an "unstable physical force and nerve-exhaustion" (9). They are "intelligent, highly strung, and emotional. There is nothing to call attention to the lungs, and the chest is often not examined. Like all neurasthenics, they have an accurate knowledge of their symptoms, and generally give a clear and concise description of them" (9). Among the clearest symptoms is the "indulgence in reverie and day-dreaming" (11). "Work that formerly was carried out with vigor is dreaded" (11). There is a "strange disinclination for physical and mental effort" (12). There is "in childhood . . . often an unusual development of mental alertness, the precocity of intellect and reasoning power being a source of great pride to the parents, and it is often unfortunately when it is too late that the facts of the case become patent" (17–18).

The cause of hysteria for the neurologist of the late nineteenth century was some form of psychical or physical trauma. Even though Freud advocated replacing the idea of trauma with the idea of a symbolic fantasy of trauma in the mid-1890s, the psychosomatic view of hysteria persisted well into the twentieth century. One unspoken and often overlooked view of the etiology of tuberculosis at the turn of the century is that trauma was a major predisposing cause. This is of interest as it was an arena where workman's compensation and public insurance institutions played a major role. It was a hotly-debated topic during the opening decade of the twentieth century. Thomas Mann ironically implies in his novella *Tristran* (1903) that the cause of Frau Klöterjahn's tuberculosis was the birth of her all-too-healthy child.[150] In medical circles, the work of J. Orth, in 1915 and 1916, is emblematic of this argument.[151] His evaluation of an extended series of cases argued that severe physical trauma exacerbated existing tuberculosis and could lead to death. Here the idea of the "cause" of tuberculosis in trauma is related to the idea that trauma is the cause of hysteria. For latent tuberculosis could be made manifest by trauma, just like latent hysteria in the model of J.-M. Charcot.

F. Köhler presents another model, in which the disease itself creates a specific psychopathological, or at least sociopathological, type. This type, like the type that predisposes an individual to tuberculosis, is characterized by "the disappearance of altruistic tendencies, the development of an egoistic emotional profile to an extreme degree and the extinguishing of a sensitivity that a normal person has for our societal organization. . . ."[152] Their egoism becomes a sign of their difference, manifested in extreme cases as mental illness, which is especially common among Jews. Their predisposition to "neurasthenic and hysterical symptoms, present before the on-set of the illness," finally appears when they become ill. Alfred Sokolowski, the noted Polish specialist in tuberculosis, observed that such illness appears especially with Jews, "who are well-known to have various forms of nervous illness."[153] F. Köhler describes a case of a "fifty-year-old man of Jewish faith whom I treated in the second year of an evident pulmonary tuberculosis, who suddenly developed signs of a hebrephenic psychopathology and had to be committed to a psychiatric hospital where he died after three years."[154] Jews are particularly at risk for the mental illnesses that appear when tuberculosis is present. Jews are essentially crazy. This craziness appears either as a result of, or is triggered by, tuberculosis.

In his long study of tuberculosis and the Jews, N. Haltrecht also examines the rituals concerning cleanliness and abstemiousness, as well as the ritual laws concerning slaughter and the inspection of the lungs of beef cattle (*Bedikah*). He dismisses them, eventually arguing that Jews acquire immunity through a lifetime of exposure to the bacillus. It is not the inheritance of immunity but the acquired immunity that is vital. He then traces a spectacular increase of tuberculosis among the Jews during the course of World War I.[155] Indeed, Jewish mortality doubled in Berlin between 1913 and 1917, an increase much greater than among the general population. But the Jews of Vilnius, Warsaw, Bialystok all saw spectacular increases up to 1917. Indeed, 1917 seems to have been the pinnacle for increases of all classes but especially the Jews. In Vilnius there was a ninety percent increase in deaths of Jews from tuberculosis from 1916 (208 deaths) to 1917 (496 deaths). In Bialystok, the rate among Jews went from 46.6 deaths from tuberculosis for every 10,000 Jews in 1916 to 72.8 in 1917. In Vienna, the mortality from tuberculosis among Jews in 1919 was 186 percent higher than in 1913 to 1914. The reasons are evident to Haltrecht—much poorer food was available in the cities, especially in the East, neutralizing the Jewish immunity. The disease also progressed more quickly because of the lower resistance caused by poor nutrition.[156] Gottstein showed in his comparative study of 1922 how starvation among the general population created a sudden and immediate outbreak of tuberculosis. Gottstein sees this as a sign of the constitutional aspect of predisposition to the illness. For the extremely cold and long winter of 1917, combined with the shortages of food and coal, led many more individuals to develop tuberculosis than in previous years, and raised the mortality rate radically.

Haltrecht's view was countered by Kreinermann's supervisor in Basel, Hermann Strauss, who by the 1920s had come to the Jewish Hospital in Berlin. In 1926, he answered Haltrecht, calling on his reading of Kreinermann's work and that of another his students, Isbert Werner.[157] Werner's work, published in 1925, surveyed the debate about Jews and pulmonary tuberculosis. What he found was that a substantial increase in cases of tuberculosis was found during the "hunger years" of World War I, and that at that point the rate of pulmonary tuberculosis among Jews increased to the level of the general population. He also found that there seemed to still be a marked differential between men and women—men having an almost ten percent higher rate of tuberculosis during this period of generally greater increase.

Strauss is more interested in the differential of age. He stresses that the majority of Jewish tuberculosis cases fall in the period after the age of thirty, in contrast with the general population. This implies, according to Strauss, a more positive prognosis. Thus he finds a much lower death rate among Jewish patients, as much as twenty-five percent lower. But for Strauss, as for Fishberg, the real question is about the predisposition of those Jews who actually become ill. He traces a twenty to thirty percent rate of "genetic predisposition" (*erbliche Belastung*) among Jews who become ill, i.e., they have family members who themselves have tuberculosis. Indeed, up to fourteen percent have siblings who are ill. He agrees with Fishburg's claim that it is the acquired resistance to the disease that enables the majority of Jews to be resistant to the illness (44). Yet Haltrecht's claim about the sudden increase of tuberculosis among the Jews in 1917 strikes a chord with Strauss. He agrees, based on his experience in Berlin, that the number of cases of tuberculosis among Jews from 1914 to 1924 increased greatly, the severity was greater, and the mortality rate higher. Yet he stresses that even given this radical change, "the resistance of Jews even during the war years to tuberculosis was relatively greater than among non-Jews" (43–44). And yet this acquired resistance was insufficient to overcome the worsened living conditions caused by the war (45).

Here Kafka's own complex sense of his illness must be stressed. We considered very early in this book the contradictory position that Jews were placed in regard to tuberculosis. Are they either immune by dint of ritual practice or inheritance, or are they predisposed because of the configuration of their bodies? Here was the great leveler—the "War to end all Wars," a war in which the enemy is equivalent to the tubercular (see Plate 32). In the great hunger and cold that result from the shortages in Germany and the Austro-Hungarian Empire, everyone was risk. Not parentage, race, nor age, but history seemed to place one potentially at risk. Kafka's sense of his own illness is bounded by his understanding of the war; his "toy pistol of a lung" marks his body as a casualty (LF, 156). But this war can never end—"each [war] will come to its end but none ever stops. Tuberculosis no more has its origin in the lungs than, for example, the World War had its cause in the ultimatum. There is only a single disease, no more, and medicine blindly chases down this one disease as though hunting a beast in endless forests" (LF, 275). Here the beast—whether vulture or mouse—is the disease hidden within, the destiny that seems historical but is primordial.

Jewish scientists such as Moses Julius Gutmann wrote against such blind pessimism. Gutmann, whose study of the pathology of the Jews remained a standard work for the 1920s, addressed the supposed immunity from tuberculosis and its implications in a long, 1926 essay on "Jewish Particularity and Modern Biology."[158] There he replicates the following arguments: Jews have lower rates of infection than the general population but higher rates of mortality from tuberculosis because of "selection" (acquired immunity) as well as "hygiene in the home, higher level of care, limited or no use of alcohol, nursing of infants, through which a certain level of protection is transferred to the child." But Gutmann is more practical and realistic than virtually any of the other commentators on this question of immunity. He notes: "With all illnesses which seem to occur less frequently among the Jews, it needs to be examined whether these illnesses are not often denied. There is a tendency among the Jewish population to deny inherited illnesses (among which the people [*Volk*] include tuberculosis)" (352).

In 1933, two of the most important eugenists of the Third *Reich*, Karl Diehl and Otmar Freiherr von Verschuer, undertook a major study of the inheritance of tuberculosis.[159] They applied the concept of the twin study, looking at development in identical (monozygotic) twins, to the patterns of tuberculosis in populations. They were confronted by an obvious contradiction. Jews, especially according to racist eugenic theory, have the "more susceptible and less resistant" body form, the *habitus asthenicus*, and yet they still have a lower rate of infection from tuberculosis. They see this as the result of a sexual selection, since the Jews, living in an urban environment, were more frequently ill with the disease, the healthy Jews self-selected and reproduced. Thus the Jews showed both the *habitus asthenicus* and a lower rate of infection, the former a sign of their predisposition, the latter a result of their patterns of sexual selection. Jewish sexual practices are at the source of their supposed immunity from tuberculosis.

In 1940, Emil Bogen presented a summary essay on the "strikingly lower death rate" among Jews for tuberculosis.[160] An American Jewish physician writing in the one short-lived American Jewish medical journal, he was constrained to argue against any "mysterious genetic or acquired constitutional cellular or humoral, immunological mechanism," and preferred to look at the lifestyle defined by Jewish ritual. He stresses the "Jewish diet . . . rich in protein and calories," which deters the "initial breakdown and progression" of tuberculosis. But much more important for Bogen is the belief that Jews get "early and adequate application of rest [which] depends on early diagnosis and recognition of the seriousness of the condition." This is the direct result of the "nervousness" of the Jew: "The very neurotic tendency that makes the Jew magnify minor symptoms, and go to bed on slight provocation, that the more stoical Indian or the more light-hearted Irishman would shake off in silence or bravado, may be actually one of the chief factors responsible for the low tuberculosis death rate among these people." Thus, "Jews enter sanatoria more readily and remain in them more persistently than other peoples. . . ." It is Jewish character that finally determines how the Jews respond to illness.

five

Conclusion

Kafka Goes to Camp

In July of 1923, the tubercular and feverish Franz Kafka found himself in the vacation town of Müritz, observing a group of "Eastern European Jews whom West European Jews are rescuing from the dangers of Berlin. Half the days and nights the house, the woods, and the beach are filled with singing. I am not happy when I'm among them, but on the threshold of happiness" (LF, 373). This summer camp had been created by Siegfried Lehmann, one of the leaders of Jewish education in Berlin, to bring inner city Eastern European Jewish children from the *Scheunenviertel*, the Jewish immigrant neighborhood in the middle of the city, out into the healthy countryside. Such "preventoria" were intended to decrease the number of cases of tuberculosis in the inner city. The children Kafka saw there were "healthy, cheerful, blue-eyed children," according to a letter to Max Brod (LF, 372), but they were also "Hebrew-speaking, healthy, and cheerful," according to a simultaneous letter to Robert Klopstock (LF, 372). Kafka reached the threshold of happiness observing this summer camp.

The countryside is the antithesis of the city. In the dark, cold cities, in Berlin and Vienna and Prague, Jews "to the European . . . have the same

Negro face" (LM, 136). In the country, all the Jewish children from the East are suddenly transformed into beautiful, healthy little "blue-eyed" Germans. These healthy children are the antithesis of the experience of the Western Jew in cities, the very Jews who are rescuing them! Berlin is for Kafka a place in which, "when I get out down there, at the Zoo, say, I have trouble with my breathing, start to cough, become more anxious than I ordinarily am, see all the dangers of this city uniting against me" (LF, 383). Berlin is the locus of illness and corruption, but in the country all of the Jews, at least all of the Eastern Jews, breathe well.

These Yiddish-speaking children, who were learning Hebrew at camp, provided Kafka with an indirect introduction to one of their counselors, the nineteen-year old Dora Dymant. From Galicia, she had been raised in the penumbra of the court of the *Gerer rebbe*. As a result, she spoke Yiddish, her mother tongue, but she also knew Hebrew well. As a young woman she came to Breslau, where she became involved with the secular world. In the summer of 1923, she was employed by Siegfried Lehmann's Jewish People's Home in Berlin as a counselor. By the beginning of August, the intensity of the relationship was such that Franz Kafka and Dora Dymant imagined a future life that would eventually move from an interim stop in Berlin to Palestine. Dymant was Kafka's last great love, but she, too, was part of the world of disease that formed Kafka's experience.

Kafka's Jewish experience is caught in the web of words that surrounded his life—words in Yiddish, in German, in Czech, and in Hebrew. These words were connected intimately to conceptions of nationhood, and were part of the national project to define the health or illness of its inhabitants. Kafka's world was one of people reduced to words, even his experience of the summer camp was one tied to the language(s) spoken by the "blue-eyed" healthy children. At that moment at the shore, Kafka looked and saw children playing, children brought to the West to help them recuperate or to help them build their bodies to resist the Jewish illnesses of the Pale and the city. And part of that recuperation was the Zionist dream of a Hebrew-speaking Jewry ready to recapture its nationalistic role in the Holy Land. Yet the positive isolation of the camp, its goal of strengthening the body, and its transformation (in Kafka's view) of Jews into "blue-eyed" Germans, all reflect a complex relationship to the idea of a special place where healing could take place. And part of that healing comes to be an understanding of his masculinity, the masculinity of the tubercular, in his relationship with Dora Dymant.

For Franz Kafka, the final moment in the meaning of tuberculosis comes in a double reading of therapeutic space as an answer to the anxiety about confinement and punishment that is intimately associated with the image of tuberculosis at the turn of the century. This anxiety takes on a very different meaning when read from a Jewish perspective as a commentary on the Jewish body. Here it is not Alfred Dreyfus's body—the Jewish body that denies its Jewishness—but rather the body of the person with disease, with tuberculosis, who cannot be Jewish because Jews, as we have seen, have a magical immunity from tuberculosis. Yet Dreyfus's exile is to a space where one had earlier isolated lepers ("*auf dem man früher die Aussätzigen interniert hatte*").[1] These are the original inhabitants of "Devil's Island," now replaced by *male* convicts. These contradictions in the space associated with specific illnesses enables Kafka's tale "In the Penal Colony" to be both about Jews and inherently not about Jews, drawing on discourses which are heavily coded as Jewish, but which self-consciously distance this labeling. Indeed, the focus on masculinity in that story (women are reduced to observers of male-male interaction) is one by-product of the image of Devil's Island as a space of illness. One might add that this tradition of associating Jews with infectious disease becomes part of the rationale for French anti-Semites in the 1940s. Under Pétain, the French "special police" in charge of rounding up Jews promised to obey a charter of twenty-one points, one of which was "For French purity and against Jewish leprosy."[2]

Walter Müller-Seidel has brilliantly illustrated how very important the notion of deportation was in the legal culture of the turn of the century. But banishment is also a set trope in the discourse of illness at the turn of the century—one was banished from society, whether one went into the hospital voluntarily or not.[3] Indeed, Peter Detweiler's idea of the "fresh air" cure for tuberculosis was tied to a controlling medical regime and the *de facto* isolation of the patient from the world. By the 1890s, at Davos, the site of Thomas Mann's *The Magic Mountain* (1924), the idea of Detweiler's sanatorium had reached a peak of efficiency in Karl Turban's closed and controlled environment, as much a "total institution," in Foucault's sense, as the prison-island. One could be indefinitely banished to this space of healing. As Thomas Mann observes, in *The Magic Mountain,* the degree of one's infection "infallibly reflected the chances of recovery with which the patient had to reckon; the number of months or years he must still remain could with ease be deduced from it, beginning with the six months that Hofrat Behrens calls a 'week-end,' and ending with the 'life sentence,' which taken literally, often enough meant very little indeed."[4] The use of a prison vocabulary to register the sense of isolation felt in sanatoria parallels the stigmatization of illnesses such as tuberculosis. For becoming ill was much like having committed a crime—both were evidence of degeneration, or a regression to the real degeneration which one had till then concealed.

According to the French physician Jules Héricourt, tuberculosis was a "social disease," like syphilis.[5] The stigma of disease was associated with the visible stigmata of disease written on the body. But these stigmata only revealed the innate nature of the body. Tuberculosis is the result of "the privations and the fatigue undergone by men of weakly constitution [that] end by reawakening attenuated or torpid cases of tuberculosis" (viii). The result of contracting this disease which one was predetermined to contract is the need to isolate patients in sanatoria and to have compulsory notification:

> It has been objected . . . that it would be cruel to inform patients that they are tuberculous, and would result in many tragedies of despair. It does not seem to us that this argument is valid: the consumptive, whose treatment is a matter of general hygiene rather than of medical therapeutics, has every reason for requiring to know what ails him if he wishes to recover, for he must in that case adopt a mode of life to which he would never constrain himself if he did not know himself to be seriously threatened. (47)

The patient must become his own jailer; he must acknowledge his own danger to the body politic through his own body.

Héricourt's British translator, Bernard Miall, provides the ultimate rationale for the compulsory reporting and hospitalization of the tuberculous patient—the need for a eugenics which would separate the healthy from the sick, the beautiful from the ugly:

> We need a religion of beauty, of perfection. It would be a simple matter to teach children to worship perfection rather than hate it because it reveals their own imperfection. For we cannot teach what beauty is without making plain the hideousness of egoism. Beauty is the outward and visible sign of health—perfection—virtue. Pleasure is the perception of beauty, or some of its elements. What makes for the fullness and perfection of life, for beauty and happiness, is good; what makes for death, disease, imperfection, suffering, is bad. These things are capa-

> ble of proof, and a child may understand them. Sin is ugly and painful. Perfection is beautiful and gives us joy. We have appealed to the Hebraic conscience for two thousand years in vain. Let us appeal to the love of life and beauty which is innate in all of us. A beauty-loving people could not desire to multiply a diseased or degenerate strain, or hate men and women because they were strong and comely and able. . . . The balance of the races is overset, and only the abandonment of voluntary sterility by the fit, and its adoption by the unfit—which is eugenics—can save us. (244–245)

The ugliness of the *habitus phthisicus* is a sign of its inward flaws, flaws of character in addition to the infection itself. The only thing to do with such degenerate types is to isolate them, to deport them to hospitals, where, in spite of their intense sexual drive, we can insure that they do not reproduce any further.

However, unsuspected by Müller-Seidel, deportation has a broader meaning during this period when it comes to disease. Hans Gross's views on deportation are closely connected to conjectures about degenerative illness and disease, and parallel the views of his hygienist colleague Hueppe.[6] Gross was one of Kafka's professors of law, whose views play a large role in Müller-Seidel's discussion of deportation because of the importance of his son, the radical psychoanalyst Otto Gross, in the Prague of Kafka's time.[7] One exiles the degenerate from society and places him or her into penal colonies. But degeneration is not manifested simply in crime, although the literature of the period insists that those predisposed to tuberculosis also manifest a higher rate of sociopathic acts.[8] Degeneration is more than the "morbid deviation from the type," to use the classic definition of the mid-nineteenth century. By the close of the nineteenth century, it also means the inheritance of negative acquired characteristics. In sheltering them, society spares these individuals the struggle for life, enabling them to develop and grow. Then they merely degenerate, and commit sociopathic acts. The degenerate criminal should be permanently exiled, recommends Gross, as he can no more be "cured" of his criminality than an amputee can be cured of a missing limb. For the period from 1890 to 1920 was the age of the great debate about the required reporting of tuberculosis and the resultant social status of those officially labeled as ill. This debate paralleled the growth of the sanatorium movement, especially the debates in Germany and Austria about the construction of state supported sanatoria.

The history of this question in Austria is not unimportant.[9] Up to 1882, the pattern for the control of infectious diseases in Austria is set: where multiple cases of a disease such as cholera appear, the local authorities had to turn to provincial (*Kreisamt*) doctors who declared an emergency. The ill were to be quarantined in their homes, and the authorities had to assure the "necessary isolation, hygiene and ventilation of the room." Only in exceptional cases could the health commission declare that an individual could be removed from the home by the police.

Tuberculosis was neither reportable nor quarantinable, as it rarely was seen as occurring in the appropriate number of cases (from four to ten) in one place at one time. With Robert Koch's discovery of the tuberculosis bacillus in 1882 came a greater interest in tuberculosis as a social and hygienic problem. But in 1888, when a requirement to report all infectious diseases was introduced in Austria, tuberculosis was excepted. By 1892 a form is prepared by the medical bureaucracy which lists all infectious diseases (such as measles), but not tuberculosis. The rationale is that there is no sense in requiring notification for a disease "unless the sanitary authorities were able to deal effectively with [it]."[10] Even the simple tabulation of death notifications from the disease was impossible to compile because of a lack of uniform reporting in Austria. But lurking behind this seeming inability is a high degree of awareness of the stigmatizing nature of tuberculosis. Indeed, reading the death statistics for the turn of the century in Austria is complicated by this stigmatization. In 1895, the standard death from lung disease came to be labeled "pneumonia" because of the unpleasant connotations of the label "tuberculosis" (315).

While hospitals dedicated to tuberculosis had existed in Austria as early as 1844, the first modern tuberculosis sanatorium was built in Austria only in 1898, and by 1911 there were only three large sanatoria and "three small sanatoria for Jews, all of which are charitable institutions erected by private initiative" (320). In 1903, the first organization to aid those suffering from tuberculosis (the *Hilfsverein*) was founded in Austria, followed in 1911 by the founding of the Austrian Central Committee to Counter Tuberculosis. Only in 1914, with the beginning of the war and the explosion of tuberculosis throughout the empire, were there the first requirements which dealt with tuberculosis as an infectious disease. In 1915 the first quarantine laws for tuberculosis were promulgated in Austria. This was followed in 1916 by the law depriving patients with tuberculosis of their civil rights and making them wards of the state. The debate still raged until 1917 whether the hospitals should be private or state-run, but that every person with tuberculosis should be hospitalized was no longer in doubt. In 1919, at the close of the war, Julius Tandler, now the Minister of Health of the new Republic of Austria, introduced the requirement of notification for pulmonary and laryngeal tuberculosis. And it was only in 1919 that The Masaryk League Against Tuberculosis was founded in Prague. After his death, Kafka's colleagues at the state-run insurance company where he worked contributed 330 crowns in his memory, in June 1924, toward the eradication of tuberculosis in Prague [see the Appendix].

All of these changes were preceded by intense public debate of which Kafka would have been well aware. Tuberculosis was thus understood as threatening isolation from society, either voluntary isolation (with the rise of the sanatorium movement) or compulsory isolation. Thomas Mann's *Magic Mountain* (in which Kafka appears as an exemplary tubercular) captured the anxiety about the former. Franz Kafka's work, especially *The Castle* (1914–15), captured the anxiety about the latter.[11]

The isolation of the castle and K.'s impossible struggle to attain access to it, are a simple reversal of the anxiety and attraction of the sanatorium. Kafka, who spent every possible vacation as an adult visiting health spas, knew of the attraction of being treated as a patient even when one's illnesses were psychosomatic. The placebo effect of living as a voluntary patient carried with it a frisson of being ill while not being ill. How different it was when one was truly ill, when the choice of coming and going was no longer one's own. It is important to understand that compulsory notification and compulsory treatment come to be a reality in Austria and Czechoslovakia only at the very moment when Kafka himself is ill. *The Castle* represents a world with heightened and focused sexuality. It is a world framed by a sense of the impossibility of entrance (escape) but the focused desire to access (escape) the confines of the castle. Indeed, the very physical presence of the castle looming on the hill overlooking the inn and the village suggests the isolation of the sanatorium. At the very time Kafka was writing the novel, there was an anxiety about being confined to a "criminal lunatic asylum (for hysterics or epileptics), or transportation for an indefinite period, with supervision from 5 to 10 years."[12] The crime so to be punished was "malicious injury or disfigurement; mutilation; rape or outrage with violence; restraint on personal liberty."

Being put into an asylum, if one were hysterical, or into a sanatorium, if one's hysteria came to be written on one's body as a somatic illness, became the same thing for Kafka.

It is during the war that the anxiety concerning the meaning of tuberculosis for Kafka becomes most acute. His understanding of his illness in 1917 falls very much in line with the increased number of cases of tuberculosis during the war, as Haltrecht discusses. No longer does the possibility exist of some type of acquired or racial immunity to tuberculosis or the illusion that "lifestyle choices," such as exercise, nude bathing, or Fletcherism will protect an individual from contagious illness. Indeed, Vera Pohland has argued quite convincingly that by 1917, when K. E. Ranke proposed a three-stage theory of tuberculosis on the model of syphilis, whatever "positive," aestheticizing features had been associated with tuberculosis in the nineteenth century had been completely abandoned.[13] By 1917, tuberculosis in central Europe is a completely and negatively stigmatizing illness. The seemingly attractive fantasy of the female tubercular in Dumas's *Lady of the Camellias* (set to music in Verdi's *Traviata*) or Murger's *Scenes de la vie de bohème* (set to music in Puccini's and Leoncavallo's *Bohème*) in the late nineteenth century was impossible. This alteration coincided, significantly, with the great tuberculosis epidemic associated with World War I, and with the final "proof" that Jews, wherever they lived, were just as likely to contract this illness as their non-Jewish neighbors.

All about him Kafka saw individuals whose immunity was supposedly greater than most, contracting this "social" illness that puts them on the wrong side of the debates about compulsory notification and hospitalization. When Kafka internalizes his sense of his own illness, when he comes to understand that self-cure is impossible and that he is becoming what he was fated to become, then the model of the unattainable castle (from which one is excluded) transforms itself into the sealed world of the late tale, "The Burrow" (1923–1924). The burrow of the nameless animal is the haven, fashioned with the animal's blood: "I was glad when the blood came, for that was proof that the walls were beginning to harden; and in that way, as everybody must admit, I richly paid for my Castle Keep" (S, 328). The inhabitant of this blood-soaked castle can sleep only "beneath the moss on the top of my bloodstained spoil" (S, 341). Even its own death would not be pointless in this protected warren, "even in my enemy's mortal stroke at the final hour, for my blood will ebb away here in my own soil and not be lost" (S, 340). Blood as a sign of purification, as in the ritual of *shehitah*, mixes with its perversion and misreading in the debates about ritual murder and ritual slaughter, and with the blood of Kafka's own experience of tuberculosis to provide a frame for this reversal of the "Castle" into the "Castle Keep."

"The Burrow" was one of the unpublished tales that was not included in *A Hunger Artist*. At the time of Kafka's death in 1924, he was reading the proofs of this small volume of four tales. "A Hunger Artist," the title story, reproduces much of the anxiety about confinement, exposure, the spectacle and emaciation of the body, and about becoming what one was fated to become by projecting it onto the social reality of the hunger artists who actually functioned as carnival geeks at the turn of the century. The anxiety becomes a positive quality that suffuses the entire narrative, and yet one can read in this reversal all of the anxiety that Kafka repressed. For Kafka's geek turns out in the end to have been a freak—he has no real control over his actions, he must become what he is fated to become, a hunger artist. "I have to fast, I can't help it . . . I couldn't find the food I liked. If I had found it, believe me, I should have made no fuss and stuffed myself like you and anyone else" (S, 277). Here Kafka evokes a ritual of starvation not through the agency of the artist but because of a programmed capacity of the artist's body over which he has no control. It is a specific form of anorexia nervosa from which this figure suffers, fashioned by the dictates of his body and his mind, as understood by the culture in which he lived.[14] His body manifests the predisposition of the Jewish or tubercular body to disease. It is also evident that this skeletal body, in the discourse of the time, was understood as a feminized body.[15] The claustrophobic sense of inevitability is heightened by its ending. The death of the protagonist and his replacement by a panther evokes more than Rilke's poem. We have in it a mindless, non-reflective but aesthetically pleasing, in other words healthy, body replacing the deformed and acutely self-reflexive hunger artist. This volume also includes "A Little Woman" and "Josephine, the Singer," each of which, as we have discussed, raises issues about illness, masculinity, and Jewish identity. These are never the sole focus of each tale, but are certainly indispensable components.

If we now turn to the final medical accounts of Kafka's body at the end of his life, we can see how the anxiety of becoming what one was fated to become has inscribed itself on Kafka's body as well as on his psyche. Kafka's physicians, beginning in 1918, see him as an extension of his lung. And they also begin to use euphemisms. Kafka comments to his sister Ottla that Dr. Mühlstein said it was "a catarrh of the apex of the lung (that's the phrase, the way people say piglet when they mean swine)" (LO, 19). (I am struck by the similarity of the doctor's comments in Thomas Mann's sanatorium novella *Tristan* [1903]: "It was, as we have heard, an affection of the trachea—a word that in Dr. Hinzpeter's mouth sounded so soothing, so consoling, so reassuring, that it raised their spirits to a surprising degree."[16]) In their medical records they are quite a bit more direct. Dr. J. Kodym documents the pulmonary tuberculosis on November 20, 1918, and Dr. Ernst Fröhlich attests to his illness on February 28, 1919[17] (see the Appendix). Each report reflects on the gradual disappearance of Franz Kafka in the eyes of his physicians and employer, and his replacement with Franz Kafka's lung. Thus the pulmonary specialist Dr. Leopold Strelinger documents Kafka's illness at the Slovakian sanatorium at Tatranské Matliary on March 2, 1921, concentrating only on the state of the various lobes of the lung. On May 5, 1921, he reports again to Kafka's employer about the state of his lungs, requesting a further five-month stay for Kafka. On April 10, 1924, in the final year of his life, Kafka is admitted to the clinic of the Jewish laryngologist Markus Hajek. Hajek's records focus on the profound destruction that the infection had caused within the body.[18] Here the importance of the relationship between the ill body and the ill mind, whether psychosomatic or inherited, whether predisposition to the *habitus phthisicus* or the immunity of the Jew, vanishes. What is left is the decaying lung and larynx as well as the heightened certainty of early death following chronic illness.

Franz Kafka reflects at the end of his life on his society's view of a sick, male Jew. His own explanations of his tuberculosis reflect its relationship to his self-diagnosed madness. Yet the working out of this "madness" with his letters and accounts of his illness has its own literary dimension. There is a constant inscription and reinscription, moving further from the notion of an illness predisposed because of his family's history to one inscribed in his lived experience. With all of the twisting and turning, there are still bits and pieces of the discourses about illness, masculinity and Judaism that remain accessible in Kafka's texts. In order to overcome his fundamental inability to control the cultural language of his time, Kafka provided a new literary discourse laced with irony in which these hanks of hair and bits of bone are contained. Thus the reader can return to the world of the literary text for a final rereading of Kafka's own sense of his body, that remains as tentative and bounded as his text.

ENVOI

At noon on Tuesday, June 24, 1924, Franz Kafka died of tuberculosis at the Kierling Sanatorium outside of Vienna. He had been brought to this refuge from the sanatorium run by Markus Hajek, whose cruel and heartless treatment of their friend appalled Kafka's friend, Robert Klopstock, and his last love, Dora Dymant. They accompanied him to the sanatorium. His death spared young Franz Kafka the fate of deportation and extermination experienced by most European Jews two decades later. Philip Roth imagines an expatriate Kafka, an émigré in New Jersey in the 1940s, teaching Hebrew to young American Jews like himself.[19] In reality, Kafka's world would have been quite different had he survived into the 1940s. Franz's beloved sisters, Ottla, Valli, and Elli, all died in the *Shoah,* murdered in Nazi death camps. Ottla, Kafka's favorite, was deported to Theresienstadt but voluntarily accompanied a transport of children to Auschwitz in October, 1943, where she was killed. At Auschwitz there is the faint chance that she could have met Madeleine Levy, the twenty-five year old granddaughter of Alfred Dreyfus, who was also murdered there. At the "selection," the infirm Franz Kafka would have been gassed immediately.

The importance for the Nazis of a fantasy about the Jewish body cannot be overstated. From Hitler's own obsession with Jews as carriers of disease, as the very emblems of the illness within the body politic, through to the ugly realities of the medical experiments in the concentration camps after 1941, the Jewish body stood at the very center of the Nazis' obsessions. One moment in this fanatical preoccupation shall close this study of Franz Kafka as a Jewish patient—a moment in which the preoccupation with tuberculosis and the Jewish body came together in another camp, at the concentration camp at Neuengamme in Hamburg.[20]

Here, in 1944, an experiment was undertaken upon twenty Jewish children between the ages of five to twelve who had been brought for this purpose from Auschwitz. These children (and a number of adult prisoners) were exposed to live tuberculosis bacilli through cutaneous scarring, injections, or the introduction of the tuberculosis bacillus directly into the lungs with a rubber tube. The "physician" who thought up this experiment was Kurt Heißmeyer. Heißmeyer's overt intent was to improve the treatment of tuberculosis by stimulating the immune system of the patient. He seemed to accept the idea that a secondary tubercular infection in the form of a supplementary skin tuberculosis would heighten resistance. This invalid theory had been put forward by the Austrian tuberculosis investigator Professor H. Kutschera-Aichbergen in the early 1930s, who, however, had warned specifically against the introduction of live bacilli into children. By 1944, Kutschera-Aichbergen's views were highly suspect. Heißmeyer's stated intent in his experiment, however, masked the real reason he was testing these children in these ways, indeed the real reason they were available to him for such experiments in the first place.

Heißmeyer's biological theory was deeply racialized. Trained at the medical school in Freiburg, and then at the sanatorium at Davos, Heißmeyer knew all of the post-World War I theories of racial predisposition to tuberculosis. By 1934 he was employed at the sanatorium at Hohenlychen, which was taken over in 1942 by the SS as their official sanatorium. Through this assignment, he met numerous leading figures in the Nazi medical hierarchy, including Fritz Fischer, one of the most notorious concentration camp "doctors." Heißmeyer joined the party in 1937 as a convinced Nazi.

Heißmeyer's own medical views concerning tuberculosis were very much in line with the racial arguments of the party ideologies, such as those of his uncle August Heißmeyer, the chief of the SS's central organization. In a "basic" position paper concerning the functioning of tuberculosis sanatoria, written in 1943 and published in the standard German medical periodical on tuberculosis, Kurt Heißmeyer recommended the concept of racial inferiority as a means of sorting those patients who warranted hospitalization. The "racial value" of the patient had to be used as a criterion of treatment, as much as "organic condition." "Useless life" had no place in sanatoria, which should be reserved for those who could contribute to the race. Central to Heißmeyer's argument is the idea that "racially less valuable individuals" were less able to withstand tubercular infection. Thus there was little purpose in treating them as individuals, since they would eventually succumb to the illness, but might be able, through prolonged treatment, to have children who would carry their stigmata of racial predisposition to tuberculosis. Heißmeyer's theory rested on the nineteenth-century view that everyone was, at one time or another, exposed to tuberculosis but that only those who were "exhausted," either because of racial inferiority or degenerate lifestyle, would actually develop the disease. Racially pure individuals were immune or could be easily cured once their lifestyles changed.

So Heißmeyer began to experiment with the induction of tuberculosis and the secondary exposure of those with tuberculosis to further infection. He was opposed to any experiments on animals, as such experiments would place the "constitution of the human being on the same plane as that of the animal."[21] Here is an echo of Koch's refusal to see the similarity of human and bovine tuberculosis. Central to the debate over this issue had been the possible relation of Jewish ritual practices to prophylaxis for tuberculosis. Clearly, Heißmeyer's position that the Jewish race is exhausted abandons the old position that they had a natural immunity to tuberculosis, which had been refuted in the medical literature following the great tuberculosis epidemic during World War I. Now Jews are considered among the most easily infected, and Jewish children, who would not have had time to develop an immunity, are even more at risk. Heißmeyer infects the children and the adults he has brought from the camps and follows up these acts by a series of surgical interventions to trace the development of the illness. By the spring of 1945 he is forced by the progress of the war to abandon his project. The infected children are taken out and murdered.

Kafka's hypochondria, his real and imagined illness, his Jewish, male body, his slow death at a sanatorium which would have thrown him out after 1941, all point to his internalization of the European conception of the Jewish body. Kafka internalized the understanding of the Jew's body that dominated his age. But it was a Jew's body that existed only in the collective imagination of the Jews and non-Jews in his time. This imaginary space became the space in which medical science came to construct the meanings associated with the Jew's body. By the 1940s, such fantasies became the basis for the senseless experimentation upon Jews. Jews were murdered in the *Shoah* because they were considered the sources of social and biological disease. In the malicious medical experiments undertaken in the camps, the fascination with the difference of the Jewish body continued to play a major role. The experiments at Neuengamme, the murder of the children on whom these experiments were undertaken, all point to the importance of the social construction of the Jewish body in the long turn of the century leading up to the *Shoah*.

The irony of the earlier view of the immunity of the Jews to tuberculosis occurs to at least one thinker in the *Shoah*. Deported to the Lodz ghetto from Prague in 1941, Oskar Rosenfeld, a Jewish writer of some reknown, editor of "New World," portrays the day-to-day horror of starvation and death in the ghetto.[22] A member of the archival collective designated to document daily life in the Lodz ghetto, he keeps a personal diary in which he records the anomalies of life. Upon first arriving in the ghetto, he sees the "blue-eyed, blond-haired girls and red-blond-haired boys" singing and playing in the streets. Their healthy appearance is truly deceptive, for the "majority suffers from rickets and tuberculosis." (69) Tuberculosis becomes a plague in the ghetto. At least sixty percent of the illnesses recorded in the ghetto are pulmonary tuberculosis (215). Rosenfeld's friends are dying one by one of hunger and tuberculosis (214). In March of 1942, he picks up a copy of a volume of *Meyer's Encyclopedia* of 1907 (vol. 10, p. 28) and copies the following into his diary verbatim:

> The greater the desire for life the less the predilection to disease! This is especially true of infectious diseases, such as tuberculosis, pneumonia, typhus. . . . All of these illnesses are to be found less frequently among the Jews and among them are of lesser intensity. This difference is especially to be noted in the case of tuberculosis even though the majority of the Jews live or lived in dirty and less hygienic circumstances. (Ghettos). . . . The source of this relative lesser receptivity for certain illness seem to be the strict ritual laws concerning food, the internal and pure family life and the lack of excess in eating and especially in drinking (alcohol). On the other side, however, the heightened disposition for other illnesses can be seen in the poverty, the dirt, and noise of the ghetto and the nerve-wracking struggle for existence. Even though all of these causes may add their weight as reasons for greater immunity or predisposition, they are not sufficient to this extraordinary occurrence; one can not avoid the explanation that a racial moment, i.e., a biological racial peculiarity plays a role. (201–202)

This passage is headed "Illness in the Ghetto." Surrounded by starvation and death, Rosenfeld quotes this passage from 1907 without comment. The irony of its racial message is brought home by the mundane reality in which he finds himself. His diary chronicled day by day starvation and disease altering the bodies of the Jews in this new ghetto. We observe through his eyes how the Jews condemned to a slow death in the Lodz ghetto see and feel their bodies alter, collapse, and become diseased.

Each Jew in the Lodz ghetto undergoes the transformation that Dreyfus had undergone on Devil's Island. Racial identity is no protection against disease in the new ghetto (any more than it had been in the old ghetto). In 1944 Rosenfeld observes that of the 78,000 Jews in the Lodz ghetto, 70,000 are ill and it is especially the children who are ill with pulmonary tuberculosis. In May of 1944, he reports that 13 people a day are dying of tuberculosis. (292–293) The "blue-eyed, blond-haired girls and red-blond-haired boys" from Germany die and are replaced by dark-haired Jewish children from the East—each group of children in turn die of tuberculosis. Those who survive hunger and disease are sent on to the ovens of the death camps.

Franz Kafka's early death spared him from the *Shoah*, but not from the system that labeled him as different, even in the meaning ascribed to the illness that finally killed him. In 1923, Kafka watches at Müritz the "healthy, cheerful, blue-eyed children" escaping the dangers of tuberculosis; in the city, in 1944, Kurt Heißmeyer at Hohenlychen inoculates these children (or others like them) with tuberculosis; in 1944 Oskar Rosenfeld sees the "blue-eyed, blond-haired girls and red-blond haired boys" dying of tuberculosis in the Lodz ghetto. Camps set up to protect Jewish children from infection are replaced by camps set up to infect them. Thus the fantasies about the Jewish body in the medicine of the *fin-de-siècle* become the horror of the *Shoah*.

appendix

Official Correspondence on Kafka's Illnesses

The originals of all materials are in the Památník Národnhího Písemnictví in Prague.

JUNE 17, 1909, PRAGUE [GERMAN]

Esteemed Administrative Board:
The respectful petitioner has for some time suffered from a pathologically nervous condition, expressed primarily in almost uninterrupted digestive problems and insomnia. The petitioner is therefore compelled to undergo a systematic cure in a sanatorium and requests the esteemed executive board to kindly grant him a week-long medical holiday in addition to his recreational holiday, which the petitioner would use for the said cure in a sanatorium.

The enclosed doctor's certificate confirms the above reasons for the request.

Dr. Franz Kafka, Clerk

AUGUST 18, 1909, PRAGUE [GERMAN]

DOCTOR'S CERTIFICATE
I hereby confirm on behalf of J. U. Dr. Franz Kafka, civil servant at the Workmen's Accident Insurance Institute in Prague, that as a result of work continued without interruption or holiday for almost two years, the above-named has recently begun to feel fatigued and nervous and to suffer from frequent headaches, as a result of which

it is necessary for him to take a holiday, even if only for a short time, in order to relax, after which he will certainly be able to return to work rested and strengthened.

M. U. Dr. Siegmund Kohn, practicing physician

AUGUST 19, 1909, PRAGUE [GERMAN]

Esteemed Administrative Board of the Workmen's Accident Insurance Institute for the Kingdom of Bohemia in Prague:

The respectful petitioner requests that he be kindly granted an 8-day holiday in consideration of the enclosed doctor's certificate.

J. U. Dr. Franz Kafka

PRAES. AUGUST 19, 1909, #60288 [GERMAN]

Esteemed Directors of the Workmen's Accident Insurance Institute for the Kingdom of Bohemia in Prague:

[in another handwriting:]
Employed by the company since July 30, 1908.
On April 1, 1909, not yet 1 year.

(Paragraph 26 of the employees' manual states that administrators, assistant administrators, and employees are entitled annually to a recreational holiday, provided that they have been with the company a full year).

[in Kafka's handwriting:] *J. U. Dr. Franz Kafka*
requests permission for an 8-day holiday.

1 Enclosure

NE.60.288 1909 [GERMAN]
AUGUST 20, 1909

J. U. Dr. Franz Kafka, civil servant, Loco.:
In reply to your petition dated August 19, 1909 for permission to take an 8-day holiday, you are hereby informed that the administrative board of the institute, during an open meeting held on the 19th of this month, has in consideration of [expert] medical opinion exceptionally granted you the requested holiday.
Post. exped. Videat "U"
to be noted and then returned
"P."

Dr. Odstrčil

AUGUST 19, 1909 [GERMAN]

MEETING
To grant J. U. Dr. Franz Kafka an 8-day holiday.
[another handwriting:] Granted under exceptional circumstances

[stamped and signed:] *Dr. Odstrčil*

JUNE 11, 1912., PRAGUE [GERMAN]

I confirm that it is urgently necessary for J. U. Dr. Franz Kafka, clerk for the Workmen's Accident Insurance Institute for Bohemia in Prague, to undergo at least a one-week systematic cure at a well-run institution because of digestive problems, weight loss, and a range of nervous complaints, and to this end he needs to be given at least a one-month holiday.

Dr. Siegmund Kohn, M.D., practicing physician

JUNE 19, 1912, # 52851 [GERMAN]

[in Kafka's handwriting:]
Esteemed Directors of the Workmen's Accident Insurance Institute for the Kingdom of Bohemia in Prague:

[in another handwriting:]
Began employment July 30, 1909
(3 years and 11 months)

[in Kafka's handwriting:]
Dr. Franz Kafka, clerk, requests a favorable recommendation for the enclosed application seeking permission for a week-long medical holiday.
1 Enclosure

[in another handwriting:]
Income:

Salary	*(in crowns)*	*2,350.00*
Housing	" "	*940.00*
Tax allowance	" "	*493.50*
		3,783.50 crowns

[in the other handwriting:]
In accordance with the administrative board's decision dated June 17, 1910, the length of the regular recreational holiday for a legal clerk of the institute is three weeks.

June 20, 1912 [German]

MEETING
To extend the 3-week holiday of Dr. Franz Kafka, legal clerk, by one week.

[in another handwriting:] *Extension by one week granted.*

NE 52851 [German]
June 21, 1912

Distinguished J. U. Dr. Franz Kafka, Legal Clerk of the Institute in Prague:
In reply to your application (dated the 17th of this month) for a one-week extension of your 3-week holiday, you are hereby informed that the administrative board of the company in its meeting of the 20th of this month has decided to grant you the requested extension of your 3-week recreational holiday by one week.

September 14, 1917, Prague [German]

The vice-secretary Dr. Franz Kafka has fallen ill with a medically confirmed apical lung catarrh and as of September 11 is on leave from work for one year.

[in another handwriting:] *Returned to work today, May 2, 1918.*

[signature]

Procházka

[No date: End of 1915] [German]

Dear esteemed Mr. [František] Khol,

I received your card only today. In the first place I do not live on Niklai St. anymore but at Old Town Ring 6 [Altstädter Ring 6], and in the second place the safer address for postal delivery is Pořic 7, which is my office; letters sent to my home address arrive first at the shop and are put into my hands only according to the moods of the apprentices.

There's nothing I like better than to give advice about sanatoriums. In the south I know of only one, Dr. Hartungen's in Riva. It has almost all the merits of a sanatorium at which one would not just then want to be cured of serious suffering. If one does want that, then one of course has to go to a sanatorium which is not run by doctors. But there are hardly any of these in the south. This leaves only the sanatoriums of Dr. Hartungen in Riva and of *Dr. Ernst in Pegli near Genoa*. I know the sanatorium in Riva, the sanatorium in Genoa is a dream of mine. Go there, one can reach it with the electric line; there is very little difference in price, [and] surely no difference in success, since success in less serious cases of course does not depend at all on the features of the cure, but rather on life at the sanatorium as a whole. Aside from that, in Genoa there is also Genoa, as well as the whole south. Definitely to Genoa. But you have to hurry and go there at once, without making a longer journey on the way. Travel afterwards, because the sanatorium in Genoa is closed during the summer months, I think from July to October. Naturally you should write to me before you go, and I will give you regards to pass on to an [female] acquaintance of mine. The selection of sanatoriums in the south is naturally bigger than these two; there is a Fellenberg Sanatorium on Lake Zurich where I spent a couple of days ["couple" crossed out], a sanat. in Lugano, which I have passed, and there is supposed to be a sanatorium near Florence, but I have only heard that briefly mentioned. Do not allow yourself to make a mistake: go to Genoa. One has to be able to get rid of one's suffering at least in beautiful surroundings.

My own visits to sanatoriums will have to stop for a while; to tell you the truth, I have become engaged, there not far from Mr. [in Czech] Josti. Thus does one tremble for years, then to fall, or thus does one lie quietly for years, then suddenly to stand up. Whichever you prefer!

Let me offer you heartfelt greetings and wish you a pleasant trip, an intelligent sanatorium choice and good luck.

Yours,

Franz Kafka

OCTOBER 14, 1918 [GERMAN]

Esteemed Head Inspector:
Be so kind as to excuse the absence of my brother. He is in bed with a high fever, and we have had to call a professor in to see him.

With which, esteemed Head Inspector, I send you my best wishes,

I remain,

Your

Ottla Kafka

OCTOBER 14, 1918 [GERMAN]

OFFICE MEMORANDUM
The Vice-Secretary Dr. Franz Kafka did not appear at work today.

The Head Inspector [signature]

[in another handwriting:] *Returned to work today, November 19, 1918.*

NOVEMBER 25, 1918 [GERMAN]

Esteemed Head Inspector:
Saturday afternoon and Sunday I lay in bed with a fever, though today I feel better. Either I have again caught a cold during the last week, which is readily possible, or the fever is directly related to my lungs, in which case the apical lung catarrh and lung inflammation have reappeared, brought on by this severe flu (42^{c} fever). The enclosed doctor's certificate from Dr. J. Kral will speak to the latter possibility, though it was written before the most recent attack of fever.

Up until five weeks ago, I had nothing to complain about in terms of my lungs; my present doctor, who knew nothing about my old catarrh, was unable to find anything on my lungs in the first two days of my bout with influenza; only on the third day did the old symptoms appear under the influence of this illness. So I have had a serious setback; I'm temporarily suffering from short, heavy breathing, weakness-inducing sweats at night, etc.

In spite of this, in consideration of my holiday last year, I would happily have tried to get over this without missing work if only the doctor had not *very seriously warned* me against it and if the present transitional period did not most easily excuse a work leave. If I feel a bit recovered, though, I will come to work, regardless of the doctor's orders.

I would ask, esteemed Head Inspector, that you pass this on to the Governmental Counsel. I would have liked to introduce myself to the Governmental Counsel in the last week, but I did not want to bother him with my private troubles when he is at present so overburdened. Should the Governmental Counsel make any demands of me with regard to my being away from work, then I beg, esteemed Head Inspector, that you would kindly let me know, so that I can immediately comply with them.

With kind regards,
Your ever respectful

Dr. F. Kafka
[Enclosure]

NOVEMBER 20, 1918, PRAGUE [GERMAN]

Doctor's Certificate,
Dr. Franz Kafka fell ill 4 weeks ago of influenza, which caused a lung inflammation. Because of this illness his apical lung catarrh, which had taken a favorable course during a cure last year ..., has again appeared. For this reason, Dr. F. Kafka must spend at least 4–5 weeks in the fresh air of the country, in order to prevent the impending deterioration of his condition.

J. Krol

JANUARY 3, 1919 [CZECH]

REPORT B.A.
This is to announce that Dr. Fr. Kafka, of the business division, did not appear at work today.

JANUARY 4, 1919

[in another handwriting:] *Returned again to work today.*

JANUARY 8, 1919 [CZECH]

[Kafka's handwriting:]
Dr. Josef Popper, M.D., is requested to provide a medical opinion regarding the state of health of Dr. Franz Kafka, vice-secretary of the institute.

JANUARY 8, 1919

[Popper's handwriting:]
In 1917 Dr. F. Kafka suffered an affliction of the lung apices which reappeared following a severe bout of influenza combined with pneumonia in October and November, 1918. This affliction requires lengthy treatment which must be combined with ample nourishment, particularly with milk and a sojourn in the fresh air. To this end a holiday of at least 3 months is recommended.

[signature]

J. Popper

PRAGUE, JANUARY 12, 1919 [CZECH]

Distinguished Administrative Board:
I have been suffering since 1917 from an inflammation of the lung apices. A long stay in the country markedly improved my condition, but as a result of a severe bout of influenza in the autumn of 1918 it has again become seriously worse. According to the enclosed statement from the institute's physician, a 3-month sojourn in the country is necessary for my health. I therefore request the esteemed board to kindly grant this holiday with the observation that I intend to reside not far from Prague in Libech, so that if called I could appear immediately at the institute, should any special work be required.

Dr. Kafka

[Overleaf] *Distinguished Directors:*
Dr. Franz Kafka, vice-secretary of the institute, requests a favorable recommendation for his petition to the administrative board.

JANUARY 14, 1919 [CZECH]

To Dr. Franz Kafka, Vice-Secretary of the Institute in Prague:
In reply to your request of the 14th of this month for a three-month recuperative holiday in the country due to a continuing serious illness, we hereby inform you that the head of the administrative commission of the institute, in consideration of the report from the institute's doctor, has granted you a three-week holiday on the understanding that, if work requires it, you would immediately step into your duties.

You must announce the start of your holiday to the directors of the institute.

[signature] Marschner
Post. rep. videat "bus. div."
To be noted, then returned. "P."

[NO DATE] [CZECH]

Esteemed Mr. Valenta,
I am lying in bed with a fever. Night fevers do not surprise me anymore, but I don't dare leave my bed with a morning fever. I do not, however, know how to explain it to the directors.

I hope that it will be possible for me to come to the office tomorrow in order to finish dictating something regarding the Škoda Works to the director, and then to leave Wednesday for the country.

With sincere greetings,
Yours

Dr. Kafka

JANUARY, 20, 1919 [CZECH]

REPORT P.O.
This is to announce that Dr. Franz Kafka, of the business division, did not appear for work today.

JANUARY 22, 1919 — Returned again to work today.

JANUARY 22, 1919 [CZECH]

Vice-secretary of the institute Dr. Franz Kafka announced that today he begins his three-week holiday.

PRAGUE, FEBRUARY 4, 1919 [CZECH]

Doctor's report on Dr. Kafka's request for an extension of his holiday.
The lung disease from which Dr. Kafka suffers cannot be expected to be cured in three weeks; I had suggested a holiday of three months, after which enough of an improvement could be expected to enable the above-named gentleman to be capable again of office work. I would therefore recommend a two-month extension of the holiday, during which time Dr. Kafka should place himself under medical supervision, preferably, if his financial means permit, at an institute equipped for the treatment of lung diseases.

[signature]
J. Popper

FEBRUARY 4, 1919 [CZECH]

The three-week holiday which the chief administrator kindly granted me is nearing a close. Overall my state of health has improved in the fresh air, though the main phenomena of my illness still continue. This result, however, conforms with the statement by the doctor from the institute, who remarked that this disease would require at least a three-month sojourn in the country.

I respectfully request an extension of my holiday.

Dr. F Kafka
Vice-secretary of the institute
c/o Pension Städl
Schelesen at Liběchov

FEBRUARY 4, 1919 [CZECH]
File Number 50.Praes.

[Kafka's handwriting:]
Distinguished Directors:

[another handwriting:]
Received from the board a three-week holiday on the understanding that he has to return to duty whenever called.

Began this holiday on January 22, 1919. Holiday will therefore end February 11, 1919.

[Kafka's handwriting:]
Dr. Franz Kafka, vice-secretary of the institute, begs the administrative board for an extension of his holiday.

FEBRUARY 6, 1919 [CZECH]

MEETING.
To extend the holiday of vice-secretary of the institute Franz Kafka from medical considerations.

[another handwriting:] *another 4 weeks.*

FEBRUARY 7, 1919 [CZECH]
File Number 50.Praes.

To J. U. Dr. Franz Kafka, Vice-Secretary of the Workmen's Accident Insurance Institute for the Kingdom of Bohemia in Prague,
temporarily at
Zĕlezy at Libĕchov.
Pension Städl

In reply to your request of the 4th of this month for an extension of your 3-week holiday on grounds of illness, we hereby notify you that the board of the institute at its meeting on the 6th of this month resolved, in light of the submitted doctor's certificate, to grant you another 4 weeks' holiday to March 11 of this year, inclusive, on the understanding that, if required at the institute, you will return to work immediately.

Post exped. videat
To be noted, then returned.

[signature] *Z. Valenta*

FEBRUARY 28, 1919, LIBOCH [CZECH]

Doctor's Certificate
J. U. Dr. Franz Kafka, Vice-Secretary of the Workmen's Accident Insurance Institute in Prague, who is at present a patient in my care, requires an extension of his illness leave until at least the end of March 1919 to assure a full recovery of his health.

Dr. Ernst Fröhlich, M.D., Liboch on the Elbe

March 1, 1919 [Czech]

Distinguished Administrative Board:
The holiday which the administrative board graciously granted me ends on the 11th of this month. According to the report of the doctor who cares for me here, however, my complete recovery would necessitate a holiday until the end of March. I am therefore compelled to respectfully request the distinguished administrative board for a further extension of my holiday.

I enclose the doctor's certificate.

Dr. Franz Kafka
Vice-secretary of the institute
Temporarily at the Pension Städl
Zělezy, post office Liběchov on the Elba

March 3, 1919 [Czech]
File Number 97.Praes.

Vice-secretary of the institute Dr. Franz Kafka, for an extension of his holiday to the end of March, 1919.

Single, born July 3, 1883, age 35 years. In the service of the institute from *July 30, 1908* (10 years, 7 months).

Received a 3-week holiday from the board on the understanding that he would return to duty whenever called.

Began this holiday *January 22, 1919* and ended it February 11, 1919. After repeated requests a 4-week extension of the holiday was permitted, until *March 11, 1919*.

March 6, 1919 [Czech]
File Number 97.Praes.

To J. U. Dr. Franz Kafka, vice-secretary of the Workmen's Accident Insurance Institute for the Kingdom of Bohemia, temporarily in Zělezy at Liběchov, Pension Städl.
In reply to your request to the board of March 3, 1919 for an extension of your holiday until the end of March of this year, we hereby notify you that the chairman of the administrative commission of the institute has granted the requested extension of your holiday, in light of the submitted doctor's certificate, on the understanding that you will return to duty immediately if work at the institute requires it.

[signature] ***Marschner***
Videat "Bus. div."
To be noted and returned, "P."

MEETING [Czech]
To extend the holiday of vice-secretary of the institute Dr. Franz Kafka due to illness until the end of March, 1919.

May 13, 1919 [Czech]

REPORT P.O.
This is to announce that Dr. Franz Kafka, vice-secretary, did not appear at work on May 12, 1919, due to illness.

Head of the department:

[signature] *Valenta*

May 17, 1919
Returned to work on May 15, 1919.

November 14, 1919 [Czech]

Esteemed Mr. Valenta,
I am meant to return to work on Monday, and indeed I think I will. But if the weather should remain as nice as today and yesterday, and if I am inclined to stay here another three days, then please, dear Mr. Valenta, be so kind and excuse my absence; I would then return on Thursday.

Sincere thanks and greetings,
Yours,
Dr. Kafka

[another handwriting:]
Vice-secretary Dr. Kafka did not appear at work today, November 17, 1919.

[signature] *Z. Valenta*

Returned to work today, November 20, 1919.

December 22, 1919 [Czech]

REPORT P.O.
This is to announce that J. U. Dr. Franz Kafka, vice-secretary of the business division, did not appear at work today.

Head of the division: [signature] *Z. Valenta*

Returned to work today. December 29, 1919

FEBRUARY 21, 1920, PRAGUE [CZECH]

OFFICE ANNOUNCEMENT
Secretary J. U. Dr. Franz Kafka requested his sister to excuse him, as he has fallen ill with influenza (fever).

[signature] *J.B. Procházka*

Returned to work today. February 24, 1919

FEBRUARY 25, 1920, IN PRAGUE [CZECH]

MEDICAL STATEMENT.
J. U. Dr. Franz Kafka manifests signs of a considerably advanced lung infiltration. He is markedly run-down and emaciated. A lengthy sojourn of up to 3 months in a sanatorium for lung diseases would be recommended for him. Medical treatment in a sanatorium would most likely bring about an improvement.

Dr. Kodym

FEBRUARY 26, 1920, PRAGUE [CZECH]

Distinguished Administrative Commission of the Workers' Accident Insurance Institute for Bohemia in Prague:
According to medical opinion I need a lengthy recuperative holiday, especially now in the early spring. I therefore respectfully request that a holiday be kindly granted to me for 6–8 weeks.

Dr. Franz Kafka

FEBRUARY 26, 1920 [CZECH]
File Number 73.praesidium

Distinguished Directors of the Workmen's Accident Insurance Institute for Bohemia in Prague:
J. U. Dr. Franz Kafka, secretary of the institute, requests the kind granting of a recuperative holiday.

FEBRUARY 26, 1920 [CZECH]

MEETING
To grant secretary of the institute *J. U. Dr. Franz Kafka* a holiday from medical considerations.

8-week sick leave permitted.

FEBRUARY 27, 1920 [CZECH]
File Number 73.praesidium/1920

To J. U. Dr. Franz Kafka, institute secretary in Prague:
In reply to your request of February 26 of this year for the granting of a holiday from medical considerations for a period of 6 to 8 weeks, we hereby inform you that the administrative board of the institute in its meeting of the 26th of this month, in light of the doctor's certificate, resolved to grant you an 8-week holiday.

You must announce the beginning date of the holiday to the directors of the institute in good time.

MAY 4, 1920 [CZECH]
Meran-Untermais
Pension Ottoburg

Distinguished Directors of the Workmen's Accident Insurance Institute:
By resolution of the administrative board I was granted an irregular 8-week holiday which ends on May 29. Apart from this I am owed the regular 5-week holiday. According to medical opinion it would significantly help my treatment if I could combine these two. I there respectfully request the distinguished directors to kindly allow me to do this; I would then return to work again on June 3.

Dr. F Kafka

MAY 14, 1920 [CZECH]
File Number 182. praesidium

Single, aged 37 years.
Secretary of the institute J. U. Dr. Franz Kafka, to extend his irregular holiday by his regular holiday time, through June 3, 1920, from medical considerations.

In service of the institute from July 30, 1908 (11 years, 9 months).

Remuneration: (1/IV)	
Salary	11,508.00 Crowns
Housing allowance	4,608.00 Crowns
	16,116.00 Crowns
2 Awards	2,686.00 Crowns
Bonuses	4,200.00 Crowns
Total	23,002.00 Crowns annually

Regular holiday: 5 weeks.
In the meeting of the administrative board of February 26 of this year he received an 8-week holiday from medical considerations, which began April 3 of this year and ends on May 28, 1920.

MAY 14, 1920 [CZECH]

MEETING
Institute secretary J. U. Dr. Franz Kafka, to extend his irregular 8-week medical holiday by another 5-week regular holiday.

[another handwriting:]
The irregular 8-week medical holiday extended by another 5-week regular holiday. May 14, 1920

MAY 15, 1920 [CZECH]
File Number 182.praesidium/1920

To J. U. Dr. Franz Kafka, secretary of the institute, temporarily in Merano:
With regard to your request of May 4 of this year, we hereby notify you that the administrative board in its meeting of the 14th of this month resolved to grant you an extension of the irregular 8-week medical holiday by another 5-week regular holiday for recuperation, to be taken until July 2 of this year, inclusive.
At the same time we wish you a full result with the treatment in the south.

[another handwriting:] *To be recorded in the list of holidays. May 20, 1920*

OCTOBER 14, 1920, IN PRAGUE [CZECH]

MEDICAL STATEMENT
J. U. Dr. Franz Kafka, secretary of the institute, is stricken with a double-sided infiltration of the lung apices. He declares that recently his body temperature has somewhat increased. It would be in his interest to attempt to improve or even cure his illness through treatment in a sanatorium. The time required for this would be at least three months.

Dr. Kodym

DECEMBER 13, 1920 [CZECH]
File Number 519.praesidium/1920

To Secretary J. U. Dr. Franz Kafka, head of the joint conceptual department for the agenda of premiums, in Prague:
With regard to the statement of the institute's doctor of October 14, 1920, the administrative board resolved in its meeting of October 21, 1920 to grant you a *3-month* recuperative holiday.
Since you intend to begin the holiday on *December 20, 1920,* it will end *March 20, 1921,* inclusive.

Director: Dr. Odstrčil

DECEMBER 16, 1920, IN PRAGUE [CZECH]
Workmen's Accident Insurance Institute.

RECEIPT
by which the undersigned confirms that he accordingly received a ruling from the Workmen's Accident Insurance Institute for Bohemia in Prague on December 13, 1920 (File Number 519.praesidium.1920) concerning his holiday.

Dr. Kafka

JANUARY 27, 1921 [CZECH]

Esteemed Director:
I have now been here for more than 5 weeks and thus having a certain overview on the possible effects of my sojourn here on my health, I am taking the liberty, esteemed director, of sending you a brief account of myself.

I am very well housed (Matliary in the Tatras, Villa Tatra); the prices here are considerably higher than in Merano, but with regard to prices in general in Slovakia, they are nonetheless quite moderate.

I am able generally to judge my illness and its improvement according to my body weight, fevers, cough and breathing stamina. My body weight and external appearance have significantly improved. I have already gained more than 4 kg. and I think that I may continue to gain weight. I have a fever less often, sometimes not at all for several days, and it is usually milder when it comes. However, I spend most of the day in bed and try to avoid any exertion. My coughing is about the same, but it's lighter, so that I can bear it more easily. And finally, my breathing stamina has barely changed. Of course it takes a long time; the local physician maintains that I should make a full recovery here, but one can't completely rely on such statements.

Taking my condition as a whole, I feel better here than in Merano and I hope also to come back from here with better results. It is also possible that I will not stay here the whole time, but may move to a sanatorium in Novy Smokovec or in Tatranska Poljanka.

I would like to take this occasion, esteemed director, to thank you repeatedly for the kindness you have shown in granting me this holiday and I send you sincere greetings.

Yours devotedly,

Dr. F. Kafka

MARCH 11, 1921
Matliary in the Tatras [German]

MEDICAL REPORT
Concerning Dr. Franz Kafka of Prague, who has been in my medical care here since December 20.

Lung diagnosis of December 20: Concerning the left upper lobes, relatively diminished resonance. On the back, the same to beneath the extension of the scapula. On the front, sharpened vesicobronchial breathing, covered to rib V. by crepitation. Left back upper lobe to below the spinal scapulae, sharpened vesicobronchial breathing, covered by profuse crepitation. From there to the middle of the lower lobes, semi-vesicular noises.

Right front to rib III., relatively diminished. On the back to the spinal scapulae, relative damping. On the front, sharpened vesicular breathing to the upper edge of rib III. Back the same and front to below the spinal scapulae.

Heart normal. No cardiac murmurs. Pulse at rest, 80, and during some movement, 96–100.

Lung diagnosis, March 11, 1921: The same perversion as on December 20 over the left upper lobe. Breathing at front: vesicobronchial midway on the clavicle, covered by profuse crepitation; from there to rib IV. scantier, middle-range noises. Left back, vesicobronch. breathing to beneath the spinal scapulae, covered by dry crepitation. From there, sharpened vesicular breathing accompanied by half-dry semi-vesicular coughing.

MARCH 16, 1921 [CZECH]

Distinguished Administrative Board:
The holiday which was granted me ends March 20.
According to the enclosed doctor's certificate, residence in Prague would still be dangerous to me at this point. I therefore respectfully request a further 2-month extension of my holiday.

Dr. F. Kafka
Matliary in the Tatras (Slovakia)
"Villa Tatra"

MARCH 20, 1921 [CZECH]
File Number 137.praesidium

[Kafka's handwriting:]
Distinguished Directors of the Workmen's Accident Insurance Institute for Bohemia:

[another handwriting:]
Single, aged 38 years (born July 3, 1883).
In the service of the institute since July 30, 1908.

Actual time in service:	*12 years, 7 months*
applicable to promotion (3 war yrs.):	15 years, 7 months
applicable to retirement (3 yrs.):	15 years, 7 months

Remuneration: (1/IV)

Salary	11,508.00 Cz. crowns
Housing allowance	4,608.00 Cz. crowns
	16,116.00 Cz. crowns

Temp. inflation weighting	4,200.00 Cz. crowns

One-time allowance	9,260.00 Cz. crowns
2 awards	*2,686.00* Cz. crowns
Total	32,262.00 Cz. crowns annually

On the basis of the resolution of the administrative board of October 21, 1920, Kafka was granted a medical holiday of *3 months* from December 20, 1920—March 20, 1921.

He previously had an 8-week medical holiday in conjunction with the 5-week regular holiday from May 20 to July 2, 1920.

[Kafka's handwriting:]
Dr. F. Kafka, secretary of the institute, requests an extension of his holiday.
One Enclosure

[another handwriting:]
The requested holiday is recommended on grounds of health.
March 13, 1921.

[another handwriting:]
Tel. number 4306— Dr. David!

MARCH 24, 1921 [CZECH]

MEETING
To extend the medical holiday of secretary J. U. Dr. Franz Kafka by another two months.
[another handwriting:] *Extension of his medical holiday by another two months granted.*

MARCH 25, 1921 [CZECH]
File Number 137.praesidium/1921

To J. U. Dr. Franz Kafka, Secretary of the Workmen's Accident Insurance Institute in Prague, temporarily at
Tatranskych Matliarech
Villa "Tatra"
Slovakia

This is to inform you that the administrative board of the institute, acting on your request of March 20, 1921, resolved at its meeting on the 24th of this month, with regard to the medical opinion of the doctor treating you and the recommendation of the institute's doctor, to grant you an extension of your present holiday by two months, until May 20, 1921, inclusive.

Director: Dr. Odstrčil

[NO DATE] [CZECH]
MEETING

J. U. Dr. F. Kafka, secretary of the institute, for an extension of his holiday until he substantially improves. *2 months*.

[this notice appears in the same handwriting twice, no date on either instance]

APRIL 3, 1921 [GERMAN]
Matliary

Esteemed Director:
I would have written before now, but I was ill in bed with a high fever; the illness is still not over and it still has not been established, at least in my opinion, what the illness actually is, whether a passing intestinal catarrh or something worse. It will in any case cost me much of my weight gain, though the lungs, according to the doctor's examination and statement today, remain undisturbed by this illness and have even recently further improved.

That I have again begged for an extension of my holiday comes out of my helplessness against this lung illness, whose real meaning I begin to recognize only here, now that I live among people so afflicted. The holiday request is made easier, even possible for me through the patience and goodness with which you, esteemed director, have received my sister and my petition—I dare not calculate how many I have made—and for that I am deeply grateful to you.
I remain, esteemed director, with devoted greetings.

Your

Dr. F. Kafka

MAY 5, 1921 [GERMAN WITH CZECH ADDENDUM]

MEDICAL JUDGMENT
concerning Dr. Franz Kafka of Prague, who is at present here in my medical care.

Dr. Kafka has a double-sided lung disease which is manifested in the following symptoms and findings:

Over the left lung, front, a relative vaporous sound reaching to the upper edge of the third rib. The same on the back to under the lysina leapulae.

Right front to under the clavicle a relative vaporous sound, the same on the back to the lysina leapulae.

Left back a sharpened coughing from half-dried, somewhat numerous to under the lysina leapulae. Left front breathing.

Right back moderately sharpened breathing, accompanied by *in*numerous semi-damped cracking to above the lysina leapulae.

On the grounds of these findings it is evident that Dr. Kafka is at present not yet capable of returning to work and that he needs another five-month period of recuperation in the Upper Tatras, calculated from the present moment, in order to attain a satisfactorily healthy condition.

Dr. L Strelinger
Medical Specialist in Lungs

[added to the same page:]
With regard to the state of the lungs as described, one judges further treatment to be necessary. If he [Kafka] were to return to work, it would probably not be for a long time and it is worth recommending that the treatment be extended until such time as a substantial improvement takes place.

May 12, 1921 *Dr. Kodym*

MAY 6, 1921 [CZECH]
Tatranska Matliary

Distinguished Administrative Board:
With regard to the enclosed medical report of May 5 of this year, I respectfully request that the holiday which was granted me until May 20 be kindly further extended.

Dr. F. Kafka

MAY 9, 1921 [CZECH]
File Number 234.praesidium

Distinguished Directors of the Workmen's Accident Insurance Institute in Prague.
Dr. Franz Kafka respectfully requests an extension of his holiday.

One enclosure.

MAY 12, 1921 [CZECH]

MEETING
Secretary J. U. Dr. Franz Kafka, to further extend his holiday from medical considerations.
[another handwriting:]
A further extension of his holiday from medical considerations by 3 months granted.

May 12, 1921

May 13, 1921 [Czech]
File Number 234.praesidium/1921

To J. U. Dr. Franz Kafka, Secretary of the Workmen's Accident Insurance Institute for Bohemia in Prague, temporarily at
Tatranských Matliarech
Villa "Tatra"
(Slovakia)

This is to inform you that the administrative board of the institute, regarding your request of May 6, 1921, resolved in its meeting on the 12th of this month, with regard to the medical opinion of the doctor treating you and the recommendation of the institute doctor, to grant you an extension of your present medical holiday by another *three months*, until *August 20, 1921, inclusive*.

Sent by registered post. May 13, 1921

May 18, 1921 [German]

Esteemed Director:
I wish to thank you sincerely, esteemed director, for granting me a renewed holiday and for the manner in which you granted it. How I shall ever pay back this debt of thanks to the institute, however, I must confess I don't know and that it troubles me.

My condition has improved much more in the last 2 months than in the preceding 3 months. My total weight gain amounts to about 8 kg. The coughing, expectoration, and fatigue have decreased, which I could not have thought possible 2 months ago; certainly, as with the improvement in my breathing stamina, the beautiful weather, the lighter air, and the lighter clothing all contribute to my improvement.

With my devoted greetings
I remain, esteemed director,

your Dr. F. Kafka

August 17, 1921 [Czech]

Esteemed Director:
I am writing this letter in bed. I wanted to return to Prague on the 19th of this month, but I am afraid that it won't be possible. For several months I have been almost free of fever, but on Sunday I woke up with a fever which climbed to over 38 degrees and still continues today. It's probably not the result of a cold, but one of those chance things common to lung disease which one cannot avoid. The doctor who examined me and found my lungs to be in good condition except for a stubborn remnant considers this acute fever to have little significance. Nonetheless, I still have to stay in bed while the fever persists. Hopefully, the fever will disappear by Friday, then I would get underway; otherwise I would have to stay several days longer, in which case I would bring with me a doctor's report.

This fever, from which I suffer a considerable loss of body weight anyway, is for me even sadder because it prevents me after such a long holiday from fulfilling even the minimal duty of appearing for work on time.

Respectfully devoted,
Dr. Kafka

[across the top in another handwriting:]
Returned to work at the institute August 29, 1921.

ENVELOPE POSTMARK: AUGUST 27, 1921 [CZECH]

Blessed Dr. Bedřich Odstřcil

Director of the Workmen's Accident Insurance Institute
Prague
Poric 7

Return Address: Dr. Kafka
Tatranska Matliary
Villa Tatra
Slovakia

AUGUST 25, 1921
Tatranska Matliary [German]

DOCTOR'S CERTIFICATE
By virtue of which I confirm that I have been treating Dr. Franz Kafka of Prague here from December 20, 1920 until the present day. Dr. Kafka, who suffered from a significant lung illness, improved markedly in connection with the treatment followed here. In the last few days, however, as a result of external temperature upheavals, the patient has suffered from a cold which brought forth a high fever, so that the patient was compelled to keep to his bed for several days.

The condition has improved greatly and the patient is leaving.

[signature], *Medical Specialist for Lungs*

SEPTEMBER 13, 1921, PRAGUE [CZECH]

DOCTOR'S REPORT
J. U. Dr. Fr. Kafka manifests signs of an infiltration of both upper lobes in the lungs. Compared to the findings before he began the sanatorium cure, an improvement has taken place and I have the impression that the disease is no longer advancing.

Prospective continuation of the sanatorium treatment would be recommendable from the medical point of view.

[signature] *Kodym*

SEPTEMBER 23, 1921, PRAGUE [CZECH]

Esteemed Director:
Since I have had an unusually strong cough during the last two nights, I am staying in bed today, though more from caution than necessity. I hope, however, that tomorrow I will certainly be able to come to work. I respectfully ask you to excuse my absence from the office and I send you my best regards,

with all respect,

Dr. Kafka

OCTOBER 17, 1921 [CZECH]

Esteemed Director:
Without my knowledge my parents arranged a medical examination for me with the physician Dr. O. Hermann (Prague 1, Mikulíš 17), to whose consulting room I am meant to come today at 8:30 a.m., because no other time was convenient for the doctor. According to the doctor, this examination will take 1 to 1 1/2 hours. Therefore I will not be able to come to the office until 10:30 a.m.

I respectfully ask you, esteemed director, to kindly excuse my absence from the office until then.

With all respect,

Dr. F. Kafka

[another handwriting:] *Appeared at work: 11:30 a.m., October 17, 1921.*

OCTOBER 19, 1921, PRAGUE [CZECH]

DOCTOR'S REPORT
Dr. Franz Kafka was thoroughly examined by me on October 17 of this year. At issue is a double-sided lung catarrh; on the left side it is just ending, on the right it is receding (Turban Gerhardt R II-III, L I-II.) Double-sided damping; on the left side up to the *crista scapulae*; on the right to the present *partii hili* (depressed area). On the left at the upper back a murky, on the right a bronchial breathing with rumbling. Egophony and increased *tremitus*. A veil, determined by X-ray, over both apices and *hili* (depressions) on glands on the right. In the sputum Much's granules. Moreover, there is with this illness an etiologically determined ossification of the sternoclavicular joint and consecutive neurasthenia.

Considering the state of this illness it is mandatory that the patient undergoes treatment for several months, remaining to begin with in Prague but away from work.

[signature] *Dr. Hermann*
Prague V
Mikulis 17a

October 22, 1921 [Czech]

DOCTOR'S REPORT
J. U. Dr. Franz Kafka is stricken with a chronic lung illness, which manifests an advance in the right apex.

The medically warranted treatment of the disease requires several months of complete physical rest; the requested holiday is therefore justified by this purpose.

What the outcome will be is not possible to predict, but a complete cure is improbable; one wonders whether retirement would not be more convenient for the ill employee as well as for the institute.

[signature] *Dr. Kodym*

October 25, 1921, Prague [Czech]

Distinguished Administrative Board:
With reference to the enclosed doctor's report, written by Dr. O. Hermann, M.D., allow the undersigned respectfully to request permission for a medical holiday, since according to the urgent advice of the doctors he must immediately undergo systematic treatment.

With all respect,

Dr. F Kafka

October 26, 1921 [Czech]
File Number 547.praesidium

[Kafka's handwriting:]
Distinguished Directors of the Workmen's Accident Insurance Institute:

[another handwriting:]
Single, aged 38 years (born July 3, 1883).
In the service of the institute since July 30, 1908.

Actual time in service:	13 years, 3 months
applicable to promotion (3 war yrs.):	16 years, 3 months
applicable to retirement (3 yrs.):	16 years, 3 months

Remuneration: 1/IV

Salary	11,508.00 Cz. crowns
Housing allowance	4,608.00 Cz. crowns
	16,116.00 Cz. crowns
Temp. inflation weighting	4,200.00 Cz. crowns
One-time allowance	9,260.00 Cz. crowns

2 awards	2,686.00 Cz. crowns
Total	32,262.00 Cz. crowns annually

Next regular promotion *March 1, 1924.*

Last began a holiday from medical considerations on *December 20, 1920* and did not return to work until *August 29, 1921* (8 months).

In 1920 he received an 8-week holiday from medical considerations and then began a regular 5-week holiday.(Absent therefore for 3 months, 1 week.)

[Kafka's handwriting:]
Dr. F. Kafka, secretary of the institute, requests permission for a medical holiday.

[another handwriting:]
In 1919 he received an irregular holiday on grounds of illness from January 22, 1919 to the end of March 1919 (2 months).

October 27, 1921 [Czech]

MEETING
To grant Secretary of the Institute J. U. Dr. Franz Kafka a holiday from medical considerations.

[another handwriting:] *Holiday from medical considerations granted for 3 months. October 27, 1921*

October 29, 1921 [Czech]
File Number 547.praesidium/1921

To J. U. Dr. Franz Kafka, Secretary and Head of the joint conceptual department in Prague.
The administrative board of the institute, acting in its meeting of the 27th of this month on your request of October 26, 1921 for the granting of a medical holiday, resolved, with regard to the certificate of the institute's physician, to grant you a *three(3)-month holiday*, until the *end of January, 1922.*

You must announce your intention to begin this holiday to the director *in good time.*

Director: Dr. Odstrčil [signature]

[No date] [Czech]

Distinguished Administrative Commission:
My holiday, which was previously granted by the administrative commission of the institute, ends on February 4 of this year.

I have used this holiday to undergo systematic treatment, which has achieved much better results than previous treatment(s) and which also offers much hope for permanent improvement of my condition in the near future. Dr. Kodym, M.D. compared the X-ray of my chest at present with that made three months ago and considered the difference favorable. The doctor treating me stated that after another three-month systematic treatment I would be able gradually to execute my duty again and then probably for good, that is, without danger of again being threatened by this illness.

[Kafka's handwriting, but no signature]

JANUARY 21, 1922 [CZECH]

I visited Dr. Herman[n], who is now treating the patient [Kafka]. By comparing roentgenological findings at the beginning of the treatment with those now, as well as taking the physical examination into account, it is possible to ascertain a substantial improvement in the state of the lungs. It would therefore be advisable, in the interests of an ideal, very good result from the treatment, to experiment with further treatment, which would require a period of 3–4 months.

[signature] *Dr. Kodym*

SUBMITTED JANUARY 24, 1922 [CZECH]
File Number 53.praesidium

[Kafka's handwriting:]
Distinguished Directors of the Workmen's Accident Insurance Institute in Prague:

Dr. F. Kafka, secretary of the institute, requests an extension of his holiday.

[another handwriting:]
Single, aged 39 years (born July 3, 1883).
In the service of the institute since July 30, 1908.

Actual time in service:	*13 5/12*
applicable to promotion (3 war yrs.)	16 5/12
applicable to retirement (3 yrs.)	6 5/12

Remuneration: 1/IV (from March 1, 1920)

Salary	11,508.00 Cz. crowns
Housing allowance	4,608.00 Cz. crowns
	16,116.00 Cz. crowns
Temp. inflation weighting	4,200.00 Cz. crowns
One-time allowance	9,260.00 Cz. crowns
2 awards	2,686.00 Cz. crowns
Total	32,262.00 Cz. crowns annually

Next regular promotion *March 1, 1924.*

[another handwriting:]
Holidays from medical considerations:
from November 1, 1921 - January 31, 1922 (3 months)
from December 20, 1920 - August 29, 1921 (8 months)

In 1920 he received an 8-week holiday and immediately thereafter began a regular 5-week holiday.(Absent for 3 months, 1 week.)
In 1919 from January 22, 1919 - March 31, 1919 (2 months)

JANUARY 26, 1922 [CZECH]

MEETING
To grant secretary of the institute Dr. Franz Kafka an extension of his irregular holiday from medical considerations.

[another handwriting:] An extension of the irregular holiday granted from medical considerations for another 3 months. January 26, 1922

JANUARY 27, 1922 [CZECH]
File Number 53.praesidium/1922

To J. U. Dr. Franz Kafka, Secretary of the Institute and Head of the joint conceptual department in Prague:
In response to your request of January 24, 1922 the administrative board of the institute resolved in its meeting of the 26th of this month, with regard to the opinion of the institute's physician, to grant you an extension of your present irregular holiday, from medical considerations, by yet *another 3 months*, that is, to the *end of April, 1922.*

Director: Dr. Odstrčil

APRIL 26, 1922, PRAGUE [CZECH]

DOCTOR'S REPORT
J. U. Dr. Franz Kafka is stricken with an advanced lung disease. After an improvement in his condition, the illness is now at a relative standstill, but it still does not allow the patient to resume his occupation.

It is not possible to expect that in the foreseeable future his health would improve to the point where Dr. Kafka could again begin his duty at the institute.

Dr. Kodym

JUNE 7, 1922, PRAGUE [CZECH]

DOCTOR'S REPORT
J. U. Dr. Franz Kafka is stricken with an advanced infiltration of the lungs which makes him incapable of service in the institute. In the foreseeable future a substantial improvement cannot be expected, though by continuing treatment perhaps after several years of appropriate therapy a certain improvement may appear.

Dr. Kodym

[NO DATE] [CZECH]

The regular holiday ends June 4, 1922.

JUNE 7, 1922 [CZECH]

Distinguished Administrative Board:
My present holiday ends on June 11 of this year. My medical condition has improved considerably in this time, during which it has been possible for me to devote myself to systematic treatment; nonetheless, according to medical opinion, I am not yet in a condition to allow me to begin regular work without the danger of my lung disease worsening, which would compel me shortly to request a new holiday. Since I do not wish to reach such a point and since the doctor assures me that with appropriate treatment and rest my health will within approximately 4 months be strengthened and made resilient, so that I could begin work without fear of a renewed breakdown, I wish now to petition respectfully for a transfer into temporary retirement, with the provision of pension benefits for the length of its duration.

With regard to the calculation of retirement benefits my service time shows only 17 years, so that my pension would be very small and would be completely inadequate with regard to necessary medical treatment. Allow me to submit a further request that my retirement benefits not be calculated from the first-grade salary of the 4th class, in which I am actually at present placed, but that they be calculated from the third-grade salary. I was namely placed in this latter grade by resolution of the administrative board, but effective only from the moment I return actively to work. Through no fault of my own, resuming active duty is still impossible for me because of the lung disease, and I therefore believe that the distinguished administrative board will not take it ill that I put forward the above request.

With deep respect,

Dr. F. Kafka

SUBMITTED JUNE 7, 1922 [CZECH]
File Number 446.praesidium

[Kafka's handwriting:]
Distinguished Directors of the Workmen's Accident Insurance Institute:
Dr. F. Kafka, secretary of the institute, requests a transfer to temporary retirement.

[another handwriting:]
Single, aged 39 years, born July 3, 1883.
In the service of the institute since July 30, 1908.
(ending June, 1922)

Actual time in service:	13 11/12
applicable to promotion (3 war yrs.):	16 11/12
applicable to retirement (3 war yrs.):	*16 11/12*

Remuneration: 1/IV (from March 1, 1920)
with regular promotion on *March 1, 1924*

Salary	11,508.00 Cz. crowns
Housing allowance	4,608.00 Cz. crowns
	16,116.00 Cz. crowns
Temp. inflation weighting	4,200.00 Cz. crowns
Temp. one-time allowance	9,260.00 Cz. crowns
2 awards (augmented)	3,808.00 Cz. crowns
[2 awards, original]	[2,686.00] Cz. crowns
Annual total.	33,384.00 Cz. crowns
	[32,262.00] Cz. crowns
Increased premium for holiday	2,465.00 Cz. crowns
Original " " "	*1,343*.00 Cz. crowns

By resolution of the administrative commission from February 3, 1922 he was appointed *head secretary* of the institute, and in the event of his taking up active duty in the institute he will receive remuneration at *8th[sic] salary grade, rank IV class*, effective from the *beginning of duty*, namely

with the salary	12,900.00 Cz. crowns
housing allowance	5,004.00 Cz. crowns
	17,904.00 Cz. crowns
temp. inflation weighting	4,200.00 Cz. crowns
" one-time allowance	9,260.00 Cz. crowns
and 2 awards (augmented)	4,106.00 Cz. crowns
Annual total	35,470.00 Cz. crowns

with retained position in promotion order, which promotion would place him on *March 1, 1924* into the *1st salary grade, rank V class.*

Holidays from medical considerations:
In 1922 = 5 months
" 1921 = 8 months
" 1920 = 3 months and 1 week
" 1919 = 2 months.

JUNE 12, 1921 [CZECH]

Proposal
for the temporary pensioning of head secretary of the institute
J. U. Dr. Franz Kafka

Synopsis

Pension according to *variant I* = *9,888.00* CzC annually, or
824.00 CzC monthly,
" according to *variant II* = *10,164.00* CzC annually, or
847.00 CzC monthly,
" according to *variant III*= *10,608.00* CzC annually, or
884.00 CzC monthly, and
" according to *variant IV* = *10,908.00* CzC annually, or
909.00 CzC monthly.

Pension with temporary inflation weighting
according to the law of March 3, 1921, No.995b.z.a.n.
concerning retirement benefits of government employees:

according to *variant I*:

pension (CzC)	9,888.00
inflation weighting (")	1,920.00
total (CzC)	11,808.00 annually,
or	984.00 CzC monthly

according to *variant II*:

pension (CzC)	10,164.00
inflation weighting "	1,920.00
total (CzC)	12,084.00 annually,
or	1,007.00 CzC monthly

according to *variant III*:

pension (CzC)	10,608.00
inflation weighting "	1,920.00
total (CzC)	12,528.00 annually,
or	1,044.00 CzC monthly

according to *variant IV*:

pension (CzC)	10,908.00
inflation weighting	1,920.00
total (CzC)	12,828.00 annually,
or	1,069.00 CzC monthly.

JUNE 12, 1922 [CZECH]

Transfer to temporary retirement: *July 1, 1922*!

PROPOSAL
for the temporary retirement of head secretary of the institute
J. U. Dr. Franz Kafka

Variant I
Remuneration at *1st salary grade, rank IV class*, to which he belonged at the time of transfer to retirement, with added remuneration for *earned time* extrapolated into the eventual *regular* promotion, that is, into *2nd salary grade, rank IV class*.

Length of service (paragraph 6):
from July 30, 1908 to June 30, 1922 = *13 11/12 years*

Length of service applicable to retirement:

actual years of service	= 13 11/12 yrs.
plus 3 credited war years	= *3 years*
total	= *16 11/12 yrs.*

Remuneration, from which is calculated 90% base pay
(paragraph 4): *1/IV, from March 1, 1920*

salary	11,508.00 CzC
housing allowance	4,608.00 CzC
holiday premium	1,343.00 CzC
	17,459.00 CzC

for earned time from March 1, 1920 to June 30, 1922

(2 years and 4 weeks)	*614.04* CzC
total	18,073.74 CzC

90% Base Pay (paragraph 4):
18,073.04 x 90% = *16,265.74 CzC*

Percentages (3) according to paragraph 3:

for 10 years	= 40
for 6 11/12 years	= *20.75*
total	= *60.75%*

Pension:

Basic 16,265.74 x 60.75% = 9,881.43 CzC,
rounded up to *9,888.00* annually, or *824.00* CzC monthly.

JUNE 12, 1922

Transfer to temporary retirement: *July 1, 1922*!

PROPOSAL

for the temporary retirement of head secretary of the institute
J. U. Dr. Franz Kafka

Variant II

Remuneration at *1st salary grade, rank IV class*, to which he belonged at the time of transfer to retirement, with added remuneration for *earned time* extrapolated into the eventual *regular* promotion, that is, into *3rd salary grade, rank IV class*.

Remuneration, from which is calculated 90% base pay
(paragraph 4):
1/IV, from March 1, 1920

salary	11,508.00 CzC
housing allowance	4,608.00 CzC
holiday premium	1,343.00 *CzC*
	17,459.00 CzC

for earned time from March 1, 1920 to June 30, 1922 (*2 years and 4 weeks*)	1,129.00 *CzC*
total	*18,588.80 CzC*

90% Base Pay (paragraph 4):

18,588.80 x 90% = *16,729.92 CzC*

Pension:

Basic 16,729.92 x 60.75% = 10,163.42 CzC,
rounded up to *10,164.00* annually, or *847.00* CzC monthly.

JUNE 12, 1922

Transfer to temporary retirement: *July 1, 1922*!

PROPOSAL

for the temporary retirement of head secretary of the institute
J. U. Dr. Franz Kafka

Variant III

Remuneration at *3rd salary grade, rank IV class*, to which he would be entitled after returning to active service following a lengthy holiday from medical considerations, but *without extrapolating earned time* into the eventual regular promotion, that is, calculated at *1st salary grade, rank V class.*

Remuneration, from which is calculated 90% base pay
(paragraph 4):
3/IV

salary	12,900.00 CzC
housing allowance	5,004.00 CzC
holiday premium	1,492.00 CzC
total	19,396.00 CzC

90% Base Pay (paragraph 4):
19,396.00 x 90% = *17,456.40 CzC*

Pension:
Basic 17,456.40 x 60.75% = 10,604.76 CzC,
rounded up to *10,608.00* annually, or *884.00* CzC monthly.

[lighter ink:]
Funeral allowance: Basic 17,456.40 : 4 = 4,364.10 CzC

JUNE 12, 1922

PROPOSAL
for the temporary retirement of head secretary of the institute
J. U. Dr. Franz Kafka

Variant IV
Remuneration at *3rd salary grade, rank IV class*, with added remuneration for earned time extrapolated into the eventual regular promotion, that is, into *1st salary grade, rank V class.*

Remuneration, from which is calculated 90% base pay
(paragraph 4):
3/IV

salary	12,900.00 CzC
housing allowance	5,004.00 CzC
holiday premium	1,492.00 CzC
	19,396.00 CzC

for earned time from March 1, 1920 to June 30, 1922

(2 years and 4 weeks)	534.80 CzC
total	19,930.80 CzC

90% Base Pay (paragraph 4):
19,930.80 x 90% = 17,937.72 CzC

Pension:

Basic 17,937.72 x 60.75% = 10,897.16 CzC,

rounded up to 10,908.00 annually, or 909.00 CzC monthly.

JUNE 21, 1922, PRAGUE [CZECH]

DOCTOR'S REPORT.
Dr. Franz Kafka still suffers from a lung infiltration. Much progress may be noted in the patient's recuperation, but he cannot be expected to resume his occupation sooner than 4 months from now.
Dr. Hermann
Expert for internal illnesses
Prague V, Mikuliska 17a

JUNE 28, 1922 [CZECH]

MEETING
To transfer Head Secretary of the Institute J. U. Dr. Franz Kafka to temporary retirement.

It is resolved to transfer Dr. K. to temporary retirement and to credit to his pension those two grades which his chronic illness effectively prevented him from attaining and to grant the inflation weighting which in similar cases is usual for government employees;
therefore, the pension amounts to

	CzC. 10,608.00	annually
inflation weighting	" 1,920.00	"
total	CzC.12,528.00	

JUNE 30, 1922 [CZECH]
File Number 446.praesidium.1922

To J. U. Dr. Franz Kafka, Head Secretary of the Workmen's Accident Insurance Institute for Bohemia in Prague:
Old Town Square No. 6/V

The administrative commission of the Workmen's Accident Insurance Institute for Bohemia in Prague resolved in its meeting of June 29, 1922, with regard to your request of June 7, 1922, to accept the proposal of the administrative board, following paragraphs 1-7 and paragraph 32 of the pension standard, effective since July 1, 1921, based on your exceptionally accorded remuneration level at 3rd salary grade, rank IV class for definitive officers of the institute, to transfer you, beginning *July 1, 1922*, into temporary retirement with the following benefits:

1) *pension* (paragraphs 2-7) in the amount of 60.75% of base pay 17,456.40 CzC (*without extrapolation of served time into your eventual normal promotion to 1st salary grade, rank V class*), that is, *10,608.00* CzC, or *ten-thousand, six-hundred and eight Czech crowns* yearly, rounded up, which means *884.00 CzC*, or *eight-hundred and eighty-four Czech crowns* monthly,

and

2) *temporary inflation weighting*, assessed according to the law of March 3, 1921, Number 995b.z.a.n.(rate I/A) concerning retirement benefits of government employees, in the amount of *1,920 CzC*, or *one-thousand, nine-hundred and twenty Czech crowns* annually, which means *160 CzC*, or *one-hundred and sixty Czech crowns* monthly.

As a result of the resolution of the administrative commission of the institute, therefore, your total retirement benefits are *12,528.00 CzC*, or *twelve-thousand, five-hundred and twenty-eight Czech crowns* annually, which means *1,044 CzC* or *one-thousand, forty-four Czech crowns* monthly.

The pension, with temporary inflation weighting, will be paid to you starting *July 1, 1922* through the bursary in monthly allotments, payable at the beginning of each month.

At the same time we herewith stop the payment of your present remuneration through the bursary of the institute as of *June 30, 1922*.
For receipt of payment of the temporary retirement pension you must show *proof of life*.

Director: Dr. Odstrčil
[stamp:] Remitted by postal check on July 7, 1922, Check 6, series 394, number 118.

[separate page:]

June 30, 1922
Videat Dr. P. and Bursary
Memorandum to end payments of all present remuneration due to head secretary of the institute

J. U. Dr. Franz Kafka
on *June 30, 1922*
and

to pay him through the bursary *the above-mentioned temporary retirement pension with temporary inflation weighting* as of *July 1, 1922*.

The pension should be billed to the account of the *pension fund*, but the temporary inflation weighting to the account of the *overhead fund*.

II.

Videat Dr.
To be noted and used for further office actions, then returned.

Director: Dr. Odstrčil

December 23, 1923 [Czech]

Esteemed Director:
I would like to announce my desire to reside for some time in Steglitz near Berlin; please allow me to explain the circumstance briefly as follows:

The condition of my lung illness in the autumn and winter of last year was not good and was further worsened by painful stomach and intestinal cramps of uncertain origin, which several times struck with full force. The lung fever and these cramps caused me to keep to my bed for several months.

In the spring these problems improved, but they were replaced by complete insomnia, an illness which has already for years accompanied my lung disease, though only intermittently rather than fully and always from clear causes; this time, however, the insomnia was without cause and permanent, and sleeping pills were almost useless. My condition, nearly bordering on the intolerable, lasted several months and on top of that caused a deterioration in my lungs.

In the summer I traveled with the help of my sister—alone I was incapable of any decision or undertaking—to Müritz on the Baltic Sea; my illness did not actually improve there, but an opportunity presented itself for me to go to Steglitz in the autumn, where some friends wanted to care for me somewhat, though of course under Berlin conditions, already then difficult, which made their help a prerequisite for my journey, since given my medical condition I would not be able to live alone in a foreign city at all.

A temporary stay in Steglitz seemed to me beneficial for, among other things, the following reasons:

1) because of a complete change of surroundings and all its attendant consequences; I promised myself that this would have a positive influence particularly on my nervous disorder. I thought of the lung disease only secondarily, because most crucial to my condition was to do something immediately for the welfare of my nerves.

2) It came out, however, that by chance my choice of location—as also predicted by my Prague physician who knows Steglitz—was not unprofitable to my lung disease either. Steglitz is a semi-rural suburb of Berlin, resembling a garden town. I live in a small villa with a garden; a half-hour walk through gardens takes me to the woods; a large botanical garden is ten minutes away; other parks are also close and from my residence every path leads through a garden.

3) Also quite important for my decision finally was the hope that in Germany my pension would go further than in Prague. This expectation, however, has not been fulfilled. Two years ago it certainly would have been, but just now in the autumn the cost of living first reached and then for the most part considerably surpassed world prices, so that I can barely get by, and that only because my friends advise me and because I have not sought medical treatment.

In general I can report that the stay in Steglitz so far is having a positive effect on my health. I would therefore very much like to stay here for some time still, assuming of course that the high cost of living does not force me into a premature return.

I respectfully request, esteemed director, the consent of the institute to my residence here and I would like to make a further request that my pension benefits be sent to the address of my parents.

To explain my second request, I would like to point out that any other form of remittance would harm me financially and, given my scant means, I would feel even the smallest financial loss very strongly. I would suffer damage by any other form of remittance, regardless whether in marks (—I would then bear the burden of the exchange rate and expenses—) or in Czech crowns (—then I would bear even larger expenses—), whereas my parents will always find some opportunity to send me the money free of charge and possibly for two months at a time through the medium of some friend traveling to Germany. In remitting the money to my parents, of course, proof of life will eventually be demanded, so please inform me about the forms and time tables, so that I may send it directly from here to the institute.

Begging again, esteemed director, that you favorably judge my present request, which is not unimportant for me, I send you sincere greetings and express myself.

With deep respect,
Dr. F. Kafka
Berlin-Steglitz
Grunewaldstrasse 13
c/o Mr. Seifert

[another handwriting:] *Received December 28, 1922*
File Number 1,132. praesidium

DECEMBER 31, 1923, PRAGUE [CZECH]

To J. U. Dr. Franz Kafka, retired Head Secretary of the Workmen's Accident Insurance Institute for Bohemia in Prague, temp. at
Berlin–Steglitz:

In reply to your letter of the 20th of this month, we inform you that we gladly grant your request for remittance of your retirement benefits directly to your parents, provided that you send us a simple statement (without duty stamp) assigning power of attorney to your parents to accept the payment.

Aside from that, please send us every month or even once every several months —as you wish—a proof of life as verified by the local police, which must be dated on the first or some following day of the month in which the benefits are to be remitted.

If you should, however, wish to settle *permanently* in Germany or any other place abroad, you would be required to inform us and request a further remittance of your uncurtailed retirement benefits.

At the same time, I wish you the greatest improvement in the coming new year and hope that your sojourn at the present residence will bring you true and continuing benefit.

Director: Dr. Odstrčil

JANUARY 18, 1924 [CZECH]

OFFICE MEMORANDUM

J. U. Dr. Franz Kafka, retired head secretary of the institute, now dwelling temporarily in

Berlin-Steglitz:

The director of the institute has granted his request of December 20, 1993 for the remittance of his retirement and maintenance benefits to his parents,

Mr. *Hermann Kafka* and
Mrs. *Julia Kafka* in *Prague I,*
Old Town Square no. 6/4th floor,

provided he furnishes a simple statement granting power of attorney to his parents to accept the payment and, in addition, that every month or once every several months — as he likes — he furnishes a proof of life, verified by the local police, which must be dated by the first or some following day of the month in which the pension benefits are to be remitted.

Since Dr. Kafka has already furnished the required statement, only the proof of life is still awaited; thereafter his pension benefits will be remitted *directly* to his parents beginning *February 1, 1924* and continuing for the months, inclusive, in which the proof of life is verified by the pertinent police.

[signature:] *Procházka*

MARCH 19, 1924, PRAGUE [CZECH]

Esteemed Director:
Because my health has deteriorated considerably since the beginning of winter, I am now going to Davos, supported by my uncle/doctor. It is not possible for me to come to the office, honored director, since fever prevents me from leaving my bed. After my arrival in Davos, I will again send a report.

With respectful greetings,
Yours devotedly,

Dr. F. Kafka

JUNE 11, 1924, PRAGUE [CZECH]
611.praesidium

The Masaryk League Against Tuberculosis in Prague-II:
Please be respectfully informed that we have today remitted to you a postal check to honor the memory of the deceased head secretary of our institute, J. U. Dr. Franz Kafka, in the sum of 330.00 CzC (three-hundred and thirty Czech crowns),

contributions to which were made by Director and Lecturer Bedřich Odstrčil, Counsels to the Director J. U. Dr. Frantisek Trnka and J.U.C. Antonín Hlavatý, head secretary J.U.C. Josef Kraetzig, secretary J.U.C. Michal Treml and legal clerks J. U. Dr. Václav Mazanek and J. U. Dr. Bohumil Sochr.

Director: Dr. Odstrčil

[NO DATE] [CZECH]

Contributions to The Masaryk League for the Eradication of Tuberculosis in Prague to honor the memory of the deceased Dr. Franz Kafka.

Director J. U. Dr. B. Odstrčil	100 CzC
Hlavatý	50 CzC
Dr. Trnka	50 CzC
J. Kraetzig	50 CzC
M. Tremml	40 CzC
Dr. Mázanek	20 CzC
Dr. Sochr	20 CzC
Dr. Kohlík	on holiday

JUNE 23, 1924, PRAGUE [CZECH]

Number 5803/D/1
[from] The Masaryk League Against Tuberculosis
Prague II, Spaleni St. 28

To the Workmen's Accident Insurance Institute for Bohemia in Prague:
We received on June 14 of this year, based on your honorable letter of June 11, 1924, a postal check to honor the memory of the deceased head secretary of your institute J. U. Dr. Franz Kafka, in the sum of *330.00 CzC* (three-hundred and thirty Czech crowns), and we ask that the Directors voice to the magnanimous donors our thanks and a request for further favor.

With deep regard
for:

[signature]
secretary

[signature]
vice chairman

[signature]
treasurer

[signature]
general secretary

Notes

CHAPTER ONE: ON DIFFERENCE LANGUAGE AND MICE

1 Of help in locating Kafka in this context is the autobiographical essay by Hans Tramer, "Prague—City of Three People," *Leo Baeck Yearbook* 9 (1964), 305–342; the excellent anthology by Wilma Abeles Iggers, ed., *The Jews of Bohemia and Moravia: A Historical Reader* (Detroit: Wayne State University Press, 1993); the basic study by Gary B. Cohen, *The Politics of Ethnic Survival: Germans in Prague, 1861–1914* (Princeton, NJ: Princeton University Press, 1981); and the recent thesis by Scott Spector, "Prague Territories: Nationality, Culture, and the German-speaking Jewish Writers of Prague from Fin-de-Siècle to World War I," (Diss., The Johns Hopkins University, 1993).

2 Karl A. Menninger, "The Genius of the Jew in Psychiatry," *Medical Leaves* (1937): 127–32, here 127.

3 Jean Baudrillard, "The Obese," in *Fatal Strategies*, trans. Philip Beitchman and W.G.J. Niesluchowski (New York: Semiotext(e)/Pluto, 1990), 23–27 and Jean Baudrillard, "The Anorectic Ruins," in Jean Baudrillard et al., *Looking Back at the End of the World*, eds. Dietmar Kamper and Christoph Wolf, trans. David Antal (New York: Semiotext(e) Foreign Agents Series, 1989), 27–39.

4 See my *Inscribing the Other* (Lincoln: University of Nebraska Press, 1991); *The Jew's Body* (New York: Routledge, 1991); *Rasse, Sexualität, Seuche: Stereotype aus der Innenwelt der westlichen Kultur* (Reinbek: Rowohlt, 1992);*The Case of Sigmund Freud: Medicine and Identity at the Fin de Siècle* (Baltimore: The Johns Hopkins University Press, 1993); *The Visbility of the Jew in the Diaspora: Body Imagery and Its Cultural Context*. The B.G. Rudolph Lecture for 1992 (Program in Jewish Studies:

Syracuse University, 1992); *Freud, Race, and Gender* (Princeton: Princeton University Press, 1993).

5 Elaine Scarry, *The Body in Pain: The Making and Unmaking of the World* (1985; New York: Oxford University Press, 1987), 14.

6 Hannah Arendt, "Franz Kafka" (1946) in Kenneth Hughes, ed. and trans., *Franz Kafka: An Anthology of Marxist Criticism* (Hanover: University Press of New England, 1981), 17.

7 Eric Santner, "History Beyond the Pleasure Principle: Some Thoughts on the Representation of Trauma," in Saul Friedlander, ed., *Probing the Limits of Representation: Nazism and the "Final Solution"* (Cambridge: Harvard University Press, 1992), 143–154, here 152–153.

8 Elias Canetti, *Kafka's Other Trial: The Letters to Felice*, trans. Christopher Middleton (New York: Schocken, 1974), 116.

9 Ernst Pawel, *The Nightmare of Reason: A Life of Franz Kafka* (1984; London: Collins Harvill, 1988), 82.

10 Stanley Corngold, *Franz Kafka: The Necessity of Form* (Ithaca, NY: Cornell University Press, 1988), 105–138.

11 The literature on Kafka is accessible through a number of overlapping bibliographies and handbooks. See Peter Beicken, *Franz Kafka: Eine kritische Einführung in die Forschung* (Frankfurt a.M.: Fischer, 1974); Hartmut Binder, ed., *Kafka-Handbuch in zwei Bänden.*, 2 vols. (Stuttgart: Kröner, 1979); Hartmut Binder, *Kafka-Kommentar zu den Romanen, Rezensionen, Aphorismen und zum Brief an den Vater* (München: Winkler, 1976), and his *Kafka-Kommentar zu sämtlichen Erzählungen* (München: Winkler, 1982); Maria Luise Caputo-Mayr, *Franz Kafka: eine kommentierte Bibliographie der Sekundärliteratur (1955–1980, mit einem Nachtrag 1985)* (Bern: Francke, 1987), and her *Franz Kafkas Werke: eine Bibliographie der Primärliteratur (1908–1980)* (Bern: A. Francke, 1982); N. Y. Hoffman, "Franz Kafka—His Father's Son: A Study in Literary Sexuality," *Journal of the American Medical Association* 229 (1974), 1623–1626; Stanley Corngold, *The Commentators' Despair: The Interpretation of Kafka's "Metamorphosis"* (Port Washington, NY: Kennikat Press, 1973); Ludwig Dietz, *Franz Kafka*, 2nd ed., Sammlung Metzler, vol. 138 (Stuttgart: Metzler, 1990); Ludwig Dietz, *Franz Kafka: die Veröffentlichungen zu seinen Lebzeiten (1908–1924): eine textkritische und kommentierte Bibliographie* (Heidelberg: Stiehm, 1982); Angel Flores, ed., *The Kafka Problem* (New York: New Directions, [1946]; reprint, New York: Gordian Press, 1975); Angel Flores, ed., *The Kafka Problem. With A New, Up-To-Date Bibliography & A Complete List of Kafka's Works in English* (New York: Octagon Books, 1963); Angel Flores, *A Kafka Bibliography, 1908–1976* (New York: Gordian Press, 1976); Françoise Tabéry, *Kafka en France: essai de bibliographie annotée* (Paris: Minard, Lettres modernes, 1991); Ritchie Robertson, "In Search of the Historical Kafka: A Selective Review of Research, 1980–92," *The Modern Language Review* 89 (1994), 107–137. Kafka's library is catalogued in Jürgen Born, ed., *Kafkas Bibliothek: ein beschreibendes Verzeichnis mit einem Index aller in Kafkas Schriften erwähnten Bücher, Zeitschriften und Zeitschriftenbeiträge* (Frankfurt a. M.: Fischer, 1991).

The major biographical sources for my present study are: Christoph Bezzel, *Kafka-Chronik*: [Daten zu Leben u. Werk] (München/Wien: Hanser, 1975); Hartmut Binder, *Franz Kafka: Leben und Personlichkeit* (Stuttgart: A. Kröner, 1983); Hartmut

Binder, *Kafka, ein Leben in Prag* (München: Mahnert-Lueg, 1982); Max Brod, *Franz Kafka, A Biography*. 2nd ed., trans. G. Humphreys Roberts and Richard Winston (New York, Schocken Books, 1960); Gerhard Kurz, ed., *Der junge Kafka* (Frankfurt a. M.: Suhrkamp, 1984); Rotraut Hackermuller, *Das Leben, das mich stört: eine Dokumentation zu Kafkas letzten Jahren 1917–1924* (Wien: Medusa, 1984; reprint, München: P. Kirchheim, 1990); Ronald Hayman, *Kafka: A Biography* (New York: Oxford University Press, 1982); Gustav Janouch, *Gespräche mit Kafka: Aufzeichnungen und Erinnerungen* (Frankfurt a. M.: Fischer, 1981); Gustav Janouch, *Conversations with Kafka*, trans. Goronwy Rees. 2nd ed., rev. and enl. (New York: New Directions 1971); Frederick Robert Karl, *Franz Kafka, Representative Man* (New York: Ticknor & Fields, 1991); Peter Alden Mailloux, *A Hesitation before Birth: The Life of Franz Kafka.* (Newark: University of Delaware Press, 1989); Anthony Northey, *Kafkas Mischpoche* (Berlin: K. Wagenbach, 1988); Anthony Northey, *Kafka's Relatives: Their Lives and His Writing* (New Haven: Yale University Press, 1991); Ernst Pawel, *The Nightmare of Reason: A Life of Franz Kafka* (1984; London: Collins Harvill, 1988); Marthe Robert, *As Lonely as Franz Kafka*, trans. Ralph Manheim (New York: Schocken Books, 1986); Christoph Stölzl, *Kafkas böses Bohmen: zur Sozialgeschichte eines Prager Juden* (Frankfurt a. M.: Ullstein, 1989); Joachim Unseld, *Franz Kafka, ein Schriftstellerleben: die Geschichte seiner Veröffentlichungen mit einer Bibliographie sämtlicher Drucke und Ausgaben der Dichtungen Franz Kafkas, 1908–1924* (München: C. Hanser, 1982); Klaus Wagenbach, *Franz Kafka in Selbstzeugnissen und Bilddokumenten* (Reinbek bei Hamburg: Rowohlt, 1964); Klaus Wagenbach, *Franz Kafka: Eine Biographie seiner Jugend* (Bern: Francke, 1958).

In addition to specific works cited in the text, I have used the following studies of Kafka: Lovis M. Wambach, *Ahaser und Kafka: Zur Bedeutung der Judenfeindschaft in dessen Leben und Werk* (Heidelberg: Carl Winter, 1993), Lippman Bodoff, "Letters to Felice—Kafka's Quest for Jewish Identity," *Judaism* 40 (1991), 263–280; Mark Anderson, ed., *Reading Kafka: Prague, Politics, and the Fin de Siècle* (New York: Schocken Books, 1989); Giuliano Baioni, *Kafka: letteratura ed ebraismo* (Torino: Giulio Einaudi, 1984); Dagmar Fischer, *Der Rätselcharakter der Dichtung Kafkas* (Frankfurt a. M.: Peter Lang, 1985); Harold Bloom, *The Strong Light of the Canonical: Kafka, Freud and Scholem as Revisionists of Jewish Culture and Thought* (New York: City College of New York, 1987); Iris Bruce, "A Life of Metamorphosis: Franz Kafka and the Jewish Tradition," (Diss., Toronto, 1991); Max Brod, "Kafkas Krankheit," *Therapeutische Berichte* 39 (1967), 264–272; Ida Cermak, *Ich klage nicht. Begegnungen mit Krankheit in Selbstzeugnissen schöpferischer Menschen* (Wien: Amalthea, 1972), 153–184; Laurent Cohen, *Variations autour de K. Pour une lecture juive de Franz Kafka* (Paris: Intertextes éditeur, 1991); Christian Eschweiler, *Der verborgene Hintergrund in Kafkas "Der Prozess"* (Bonn: Bouvier, 1990), and his *Kafkas Erzählungen und ihr verborgener Hintergrund* (Bonn: Bouvier, 1991); M. M. Fichter, "Franz Kafkas Magersucht," *Fortschritt der Neurologie und Psychiatrie* 56 (1988), 231–238; Marina Cavarocchi, *La certezza che toglia la speranza: Contributi per l'approfondimento dell'aspetto ebraico in Kafka* (Florence: La Giuntina, 1988); Valerie D. Greenberg, *Transgressive Readings: The Texts of Franz Kafka and Max Planck* (Ann Arbor: University of Michigan Press, 1990); Karl Erich Grözinger, Stéphane Mosès, Hans Dieter Zimmermann, eds., *Kafka und das Judentum* (Frankfurt a. M.: Jüdischer Verlag/Athenäum, 1987); Karl Erich Grözinger, *Kafka und die Kabbala: Das Jüdische in Werk und Denken von Franz Kafka* (Frankfurt a. M.: Eichborn, 1992); Georg Guntermann, *Vom Fremdwerden der Dinge beim Schreiben: Kafkas Tagebücher als literarische Physiognomie des Autors* (Tübingen: Niemeyer,

1991); Jürg Beat Honegger, "Kafkas Verständnis seiner Krankheit," *Das Phänomen der Angst bei Franz Kafka* (Berlin: Erich Schmidt Verlag, 1975), 114–120; Uwe Jahnke, *Die Erfahrung von Entfremdung: Sozialgeschichtliche Studien zum Werk Franz Kafkas* (Stuttgart: Hans-Dieter Heinz, 1988); Gerhard Irle, "Krankheitsphänomene in Kafkas Werk," in his *Der psychiatrische Roman* (Stuttgart: Hippocrates, 1965), 83–100; Jean Jofen, *The Jewish Mystic in Kafka* (New York: Peter Lang, 1987); Detlef Kremer, *Kafka: die Erotik des Schreibens: Schreiben als Lebensentzug* (Frankfurt a. M.: Athenäum, 1989); Ghyslain Levy and Serge Sabinus, *Kafka: Le corps dans la tête* (Paris: Scarbee, 1983); Brigitte Luhl-Wiese, *Ein Käfig ging einen Vogel suchen: Kafka, Feminität und Wissenschaft* (Berlin: Merve–Verlag, 1980); Britta Mache, "The Noise in the Burrow: Kafka's Final Dilemma," *The German Quarterly* 55 (1989), 526–540; Günter Mecke, *Franz Kafkas offenbares Geheimnis: Eine Psychopathographie* (München: Wilhelm Fink, 1982); Walter Müller-Seidel, *Die Deportation des Menschen: Kafkas Erzählung "In der Strafkolonie" im europäischen Kontext* (Stuttgart: Metzler, 1986); Peter Neesen, *Vom Louvrezirkel zum Prozess: Franz Kafka und die Psychologie Franz Brentanos* (Göppingen: Alfred Kümmerle, 1972); Ernst Pawel, "The Judaism of Franz Kafka," *Journal of the Kafka Society of America* 10 (1986), 80–82; Heinz Politzer, *Franz Kafka: Parable and Paradox*, rev. ed. (Ithaca, NY: Cornell University Press, 1966); Marjorie Edna Rhine, "Inscriptions and Incisions: Writing and the Body in the Works of Franz Kafka and Yukio Mishima (Diss., University of Wisconsin, 1992); Jill Robbins, *Prodigal Son/Elder Brother: Interpretation and Alterity in Augustine, Petrarch, Kafka, Levinas* (Chicago: University of Chicago Press, 1991); Ritchie Robertson, *Kafka: Judaism, Politics, and Literature* (Oxford: Clarendon Press; New York: Oxford University Press, 1985); Helmut Schink, *Jugend als Krankheit?* (Linz: OLV Buchverlag, 1980), 68–99; Ernestine Schlant, "Franz Kafka's Historical Consciousness," *Newsletter of the Kafka Society of America* 4 (1980), 15–20; Bernhard Siegert, "Kartographien der Zerstreuung: *Jargon* und die Schrift der jüdischen Tradierungsbewegung bei Kafka," in Wolf Kittler und Gerhard Neumann, eds., *Franz Kafka, Schriftverkehr* (Freiburg: Rombach, 1990), 222–247; Mitchell Silver, "The Roots of Anti-Semitism: A Kafka Tale and a Sartrean Commentary," *Judaism* 30 (1981), 263–268; Enzo Traverso, "Rationalité et barbarie: Rélire Weber, Benjamin et Kafka après Auschwitz," *Les Temps Modernes* 568 (November 1993), 7–29; Leopoldo Cortejoso Villanueva, "La construcción de Kafka y el sentimento de tuberculofobia," *Medicamenta* (Madrid) 40 (1963), 164–5; Joseph Vogl, "Schöne Körper," in his *Ort der Gewalt: Kafkas literarische Ethik* (München: Wilhelm Fink, 1990), 32–53; John S. White, "Psyche and Tuberculosis: The Libido Organization of Franz Kafka," *The Psychoanalytic Study of Society* 4 (1967), 185–251; Melvin Wilk, *Jewish Presence in T.S. Eliot and Franz Kafka* (Atlanta, GA: Scholars Press, 1986).

12 See the discussion of Kafka in my *Jewish Self-Hatred*, 282–285.

13 Mark Anderson, *Kafka's Clothes: Ornament and Aestheticism in the Habsburg Fin de Siècle* (Oxford: Clarendon Press; Oxford, New York: Oxford University Press, 1992).

14 Nancy Stepan and Sander L. Gilman, "Appropriating the Idioms of Science: Some Strategies of Resistance to Biological Determinism," in Dominick LaCapra, ed., *The Bounds of Race* (Ithaca, NY: Cornell University Press, 1991), 72–103.

15 See my "A View of Kafka's Treatment of Actuality in *Die Verwandlung*," *Germanic Notes* 2 (1971), 26–30.

16 All references are to Anatole Leroy-Beaulieu, *Israel among the Nations: A Study of the Jews and Antisemitism*, trans. Frances Hellman (New York: G. P. Putnam's Sons, 1895), here 258. This was first published as Anatole Leroy-Beaulieu, i.e., Henry Jean Baptiste Anatole, *(Les) juifs et l'antisémitisme: Israël chez les nations*. (Paris: Lévy, 1893). This went through at least seven printings in 1893 alone. Of his other works, see *La Révolution et le libéralisme; essais de critique et d'histoire* (Paris: Hachette, 1890), and his pamphlet *Les immigrants juifs et le judäisme aux États-Unis* (Paris: Librairie nouvelle, 1905). On his work, Martha Helms Cooley, "Nineteenth-century French Historical Research on Russia: Louis Leger, Alfred Rambaud, Anatole Leroy-Beaulieu" (Diss., Indiana University, 1971).

17 *Mischling* is a particularly offensive term from the pseudo-biological rhetoric of the late nineteenth century through the Nazi period. It evokes all of the questions of race, race-crossing, and racial purity that was inherent to the ideologies of the period. More recent terms, as shall be discussed below, have attempted to recuperate this term. I have chosen to keep the original German term, *Mischling*, rather than try to translate it either into contemporary English terminology or into the English scientific discourse of the *fin de siècle*. I have tried to show how this term comes to be incorporated with all of its complicated negative associations within Kafka's world of images.

18 Werner Sombart, *Die Zukunft der Juden* (Leipzig: Duncker & Humblot, 1912), 44.

19 W. W. Kopp, "Beobachtung an Halbjuden in Berliner Schulen," *Volk und Rasse* 10 (1935), 392.

20 All references are to William Thackeray, *Vanity Fair* (London: J. M. Dent, 1912).

21 Josefa Berens-Totenohl, *Der Femhof* (Jena: Eugen Diederichs, 1934), 29.

22 Max Warwar, "Der Flucht vor dem Typus," *Selbstwehr* 3 (April 30, 1909), 1–2.

23 On Kafka and the model of the "Orient" see the first-rate essay by Rolf J. Goebel, "Constructing Chinese History: Kafka's and Dittmar's Orientalist Discourse," *PMLA* 108 (1993), 59–71.

24 M. Lerche, "Beobachtung deutsch-jüdischer Rassenkreuzung an Berliner Schulen," *Die medizinische Welt* 1 (September, 17 1927): 1222. In long letters to the editor, the Jewish sexologist Max Marcuse strongly dismissed the "anti-Jewish" presuppositions of Lerche's views, while at the same time Professor O. Reche of the University of Leipzig saw in her piece a positive contribution to racial science (*Die medizinische Welt* 1 [October, 15 1927], 1417–19). Lerche responded to Marcuse's call for a better science of race to approach the question of the *Mischling* with her own claim that her work was at best the tentative approach of a pedagogue. She also disavowed any "anti-Jewish bias" on the part of her study (*Die medizinische Welt* 1 [November 12, 1927], 1542).

25 Leroy-Beaulieu, 261.

26 Leroy-Beaulieu, 178.

27 Leroy-Beaulieu, 194.

28 Leroy-Beaulieu, 217–218.

29 Gloria Anzaldúa, *Borderlands/La Frontera: The New Mestiza* (San Francisco: Spinsters/Aunt Lute, 1987), 79–81.

30 Christine Welsh, "Women in the Shadows: Reclaiming a Métis Heritage," *Descant* 24 (1993), 89–103.

31 Ernst Lissauer, "Deutschtum und Judentum," *Kunstwart* 25 (1912), 6–12, here 8.

32 Helen Milfull, "'Weder Katze noch Lamm? Franz Kafka Kritik des 'Westjüdischen,'" in Günter Grimm, Hans-Peter Bayerdorfer, and Konrad Kwiet, eds., *Im Zeichen Hiobs: Jüdische Schriftsteller und deutsche Literatur in 20. Jahrhundert* (Königstein/Ts.: Athenäum, 1985), 178–192.

33 Hartmut Binder, *Kafka in neuer Sicht: Mimik, Gestik und Personengefüge als Darstellungsformen des Autobiographischen* (Stuttgart: J. B. Metzler, 1976), 588, n. 77.

34 Leroy-Beaulieu, 229.

35 *Theodor Gomperz: ein Gelehrtenleben im Bürgertum der Franz-Josefs-Zeit: Auswahl seiner Briefe und Aufzeichnungen, 1869–1912*, ed. Robert A. Kann (Vienna: Verlag der Österreichische Akademie der Wissenschaften, 1974), 226.

36 See the discussion in Gilles Deleuze and Félix Guattari, *Kafka: Toward a Minor Literature*, trans. Dana Polan (Minneapolis: University of Minnesota Press, 1986), 66–67.

37 See Walter Sokel's critique of their position in his "Two Views of 'Minority' Literature: Deleuze, Kafka, and the German-Jewish Enclave of Prague," *Quarterly World Report* 6 (1983), 5–8.

38 Gilles Deleuze, "Coldness and Cruelty," in *Masochism*, trans. Jean MacNeil (New York: Zone, 1991), 9–142, here 60–61.

39 Cited in the translation from Mark Anderson, ed., *Reading Kafka*, 260.

40 Oskar Negt and Alexander Kluge, *Geschichte und Eigensinn: Geschichtliche Organization der Arbeitsvermögen. Deutschland als Produktionsöffentlichkeit, Gewalt des Zusammenhangs* (Frankfurt a.M.: Zweitausendeins, 1981), 105.

41 "Das Mauscheln kann man ererben, aber nicht erlernen. (Deutschland)" quoted with the greatest hesitancy from the classic Nazi compilation of negative proverbs about the Jews, Ernst Hiemer, *Der Jude im Sprichwort der Völker* (Nürnberg: Der Stürmer Buchverlag, 1942), 15.

42 Heinz Politzer, ed., *Das Kafka-Buch* (Frankfurt: Fischer, 1980), 16.

43 Heymann Steinthal, "Reindeutsche Sprache," in his *Über Juden und Judentum*, ed., Gustav Karpeles (Berlin: M. Poppelauer, 1910), 79–80.

44 Max Brod, *Rassentheorie und Judentum* (Prague: J. A. Verb. Barissa, 1934), 12–14.

45 Gabriele von Natzmer Cooper, *Kafka and Language in the Stream of Thoughts and Life* (Riverside, CA: Ariadne, 1991), 47.

46 See, for example, Kafka's suggestions of Löwy's readings from Bialek, Shalom Aleichem, Peretz as well as Morris Rosenfeld. (The latter was a guest of the Central Zionist Organization in Prague in 1908. His poems were translated into German by Friedrich Thieberger, Kafka's Hebrew teacher.) Franz Kafka, *Tagebücher*, eds. Hans-Gerd Koch, Michael Müller, Malcolm Pasley (Frankfurt a. M.: S. Fischer, 1990), 88–89.

47 Franz Kafka, *Hochzeitsvorbereitungen auf dem Lande*, ed. Max Brod (Frankfurt a. M.: Fischer, 1989), 306–309.

48 Franz Rosenzweig, "Vom Geist der hebräischen Sprache," in *Gesammelte Schriften* III: *Zweistromland*, ed. Reinhold and Annemarie Mayer (Dordrecht: Martinus Nijhoff, 1984), 719–721.

49 Ludwig Wittgenstein, *Culture and Value*, ed. G. H. von Wright and Heikki Nyman (Oxford: Blackwell, 1980), 18–19.

50 Margot Norris, *Beasts of the Modern Imagination: Darwin, Nietzsche, Kafka, Ernst, and Lawrence* (Baltimore: Johns Hopkins University Press, 1985).

51 Herbert Böhme, *Tuberkulöse Dichter der S–1 Struktur* (Diss., Marburg 1932; München: Knorr & Hirth, 1939).

52 Anthony Storr, *Churchill's Black Dog, Kafka's Mice and Other Phenomena of the Human Mind* (New York: Ballantine, 1965), 76–77.

53 Pawel, *The Nightmare of Reason*, 9.

54 *"Die Juden thun ebenso viel Nutz in der Welt schaffen wie die Mäuß im Weitzen* (Deutschland); *Die Juden seyn einem Land so nutz wie die Mäuß auf dem Getraideboden und die Motten im Kleid,"* Hiemer, 36.

55 Wilhelm Marr, *Goldene Ratten und rothe Mäuse* (Chemnitz: Antisemitische Heft 2, 1881). I am grateful to Jay Geller for providing me with a copy of this text.

56 Solomon A. Birnbaum, "Der Mogel," *Zeitschrift für deutsche Philologie* 74 (1955), 249.

57 See Mark Johnson, *The Body in the Mind. The Bodily Basis of Meaning, Imagination and Reason* (Chicago: University of Chicago Press, 1987), 126–36; as well as Edward Shorter, *From Paralysis to Fatigue: A History of Psychosomatic Illness in the Modern Era* (New York: Free Press, 1992).

58 I. M. Arluck and I. J. Winocouroff, "Zur Frage über die Ansteckung an Tuberkulose jüdischer Kinder während der Beschneidung," *Beiträge zur Klinik der Tuberkulose* 22 (1912), Supplement 3, 341–349, with a summary of the older literature.

59 Max Scheimpflug, "Über den heutigen Stand der Frage nach der Erblichkeit der Tuberculose," L. von Schrötter, ed., *Die Tuberculose* (Vienna: Wilhelm Braumüller, 1898), 1–44, here 29 with the detailed literature.

60 Clarence A. Lucas, *Tuberculosis and Disease Caused by Immoral or Intemperate Habits* (Indianapolis: Bookwalter-Ball, 1920). Such arguments are very much in line with the notion, introduced in the first decade of the twentieth century by K. E. Ranke, that tuberculosis was an illness that developed along the same tripartite model as did syphilis. This view matched a substantial increase in the reporting of the older category of "lung-syphilis" after 1916. See Richard Bochalli, *Die Entwicklung der Tuberkuloseforschung in der Zeit von 1878–1958* (Stuttgart: Georg Thieme, 1958).

61 Jules Héricourt, *The Social Diseases: Tuberculosis, Syphilis, Alcoholism, Sterility*, trans. with a final chapter by Bernard Miall (London: George Routledge and Sons, 1920).

62 Jonathan Boyarin, *Storm from Paradise: The Politics of Jewish Memory* (Minneapolis: University of Minnesota, 1992), 97.

63 See the defense of "Jewish genius" in Leroy-Beaulieu, 225–262.

CHAPTER TWO: KAFKA'S BODY IN THE MIRROR OF HIS CULTURE

1 Frederick Robert Karl, *Franz Kafka, Representative Man* (New York: Ticknor & Fields, 1991), 185.

2 I am grateful to the Assicurazioni Generali in Trieste for making the forms of Pollack's examination available to me.

3 "Docteur Celticus," *Les 19 Tares corporelles visibles pour reconnaître un Juif* (Paris: Librairie antisémite, 1903).

4 *"Die Religion ist einerlei / In der Rasse liegt der Schweinerei,"* cited from Ernst Hiemer, *Der Jude im Sprichwort der Völker* (Nürnberg: Der Stürmer Buchverlag, 1942), 10.

5 *"Er hat e Gang wie ä Judd* (Westmark)," Hiemer, 12; *"Er hat jüdische Platten* (Plattfüße) *(Franken),"* 14; *"Gott schütze uns vor Trichinosen und Judennosen* (Süddeutschland)," 13; *"Es gibt keinen Juden ohne Räude* (Bulgarien)," 38; "*Er wird sich jetzt seiner Arbeit rühmen wie der Jude seiner Krätze* (Ostland)," 38; "*Er übernimmt das wie der Jude die Räude* (Ostland)," 39; "*Er ist grindig wie ein Jude* (Ungarn)."

6 All references are to Anatole Leroy-Beaulieu, *Israel Among the Nations: A Study of the Jews and Antisemitism*, trans. Frances Hellman (New York: G. P. Putnam's Sons, 1895).

7 William Osler, *Men and Books*, ed. Earl F. Nation (Pasadena, CA: Castle Press, 1959), 56.

8 Diana Trilling, "Intellectuals in Love," *The New York Times Book Review* (October 3, 1993), 15.

9 William Z. Ripley, *The Races of Europe* (New York: D. Appelton, 1899), 384.

10 See my "Salome, Syphilis, Sarah Bernhardt and the 'Modern Jewess'" *German Quarterly* 66 (1993), 195–211.

11 M. J. Gutmann, *Über den heutigen Stand der Rasse- und Krankheitsfrage der Juden* (Berlin: Rudolph Müller & Steinecke, 1920), 14.

12 Gutmann, 18.

13 Martin Engländer, *Die auffallend häufigen Krankheitserscheinungen der jüdischen Rasse* (Vienna: J. L. Pollak, 1902), 11–12.

14 Heinrich Singer, *Allgemeine und spezielle Krankheitslehre der Juden* (Leipzig: Benno Konegen, 1904), 9, 13.

15 The originals of the materials are in the Památnik Národnhího Písemnictví in Prague, see the Appendix.

16 Rotraut Hackermuller, *Das Leben, das mich stört: eine Dokumentation zu Kafkas letzten Jahren 1917–1924* (Wien: Medusa, 1984), 12.

17 Edward Shorter, *From the Mind into the Body: The Cultural Origins of Psychosomatic Symptoms* (New York: Free Press, 1994), 90–117. This is an extension of Edward Shorter, *From Paralysis to Fatigue: A History of Psychosomatic Illness in the Modern Era* (New York: Free Press, 1992). Shorter, however, accepts the idea that there was an actual increase in illnesses among Jews that exacerbated the idea of a Jewish disease and a Jewish hypochondria. This is much too reductionist, and overlooks the possibility that Jews, too, could manipulate these illnesses as part of a strategy of resistance.

18 Gustav Hochstetter and Georg Zehden, *Mit Hörrohr und Spritze: Ein lustiges Buch für Aerzte und Patienten* (Berlin: Verlag der Lustigen Blätter, 1910), 98 (on bathing and numbers), 100 (Schminkeles). On doctors and their patients, see Edward Shorter, *Doctors and Their Patients: A Social History* (New Brunswick, NJ: Transaction Books, 1991).

19 M. Nuél, *Das Buch der jüdischen Witze* (Berlin: Gustav Rieckes, 1904), 43–44.

20 "Der jüdische Patient," *Selbstwehr* 8 (March 6, 1914), 3–4.

21 Cited (with photographs) in Joseph Jacobs, *Studies in Jewish Statistics* (London: D. Nutt, 1891), xl. These plates were reproduced from scholarly journals. (In *The Photographic News* 29 [April 17, 1885 and 24 April 1885], as unnumbered insets and as the frontispiece to vol. 16 (1886) of *The Journal of the Anthropological Institute,* which included the first publication of Joseph Jacobs, "On the Racial Characteristics of Modern Jews," 23–63, as well as A. Neubauer, "Notes on the Race Types of the Jews," 17–22.) See Nathan Roth, "Freud and Galton," *Comprehensive Psychiatry* 3 (1962), 77–83. On the tradition of photographic evidence in the history of anthropology see Alan Sekula, "The Body and the Archive," *October* 39 (1986), 40–55, and Joanna Cohan Scherer, ed., *Picturing Cultures: Historical Photographs in Anthropological Inquiry, Visual Anthropology* (Special Issue) 3 (2–3) 1990. It is also in the work of Lombroso that the image of race plays a major role. See F. Bazzi and R. Bèttica-Giovannini, "L'atlante fisiognomonico e frenologico del sig. Ysabeau tra quelli di Lavater e di Fall e quello di Lombroso," *Annali dell' Ospedale Maria Vittoria di Torino* 23 (1980), 343–416, and A. T. Caffaratto, "La raccolta di fotografie segnaletiche del Museo di Antropologia Criminale di Torino: la fotografia come documento e testimonianza dell'opera di Cesare Lombroso," *Annali dell' Ospedale Maria Vittoria di Torino* 23 (1980), 295–332. The tradition of fixing the racial gaze continues into the world of the scientific motion picture in the 1890s, such as the chronophotograph. See Elizabeth Cartwright, "Physiological Modernism: Cinematography as a Medical Research Technology," (Diss., Yale, 1991), 38.

22 Francis Galton, "Photographic Composites," *The Photographic News* 29 (17 April 1885), 243–246; here, 243.

23 Carl Heinrich Stratz, *Was sind Juden? Eine ethnographisch-anthropologische Studie* (Vienna: F. Tempsky, 1903), 7. Stratz is citing Joseph Deniker, *Races of Man* (London: W. Scott, 1900), 423.

24 Robert Burton, *The Anatomy of Melancholy*, ed. Holbrook Jackson (New York: Vintage, 1977), 211–212.

25 Hans F. K. Günther, *Rassenkunde des jüdischen Volkes,* 70 (on the physiology of the Jewish eye); 210–211 (Galton's photographs); 217 (on the Jewish gaze).

26 Joseph Roth, *Briefe 1911–1939,* ed. Hermann Kesten (Köln: Kiepenheuer & Witsch, 1970), 251.

27 Redcliffe N. Salaman, M. D., "Heredity and the Jew," *Eugenics Review* 3 (1912), 190.

28 Léon Poliakov, *The Aryan Myth: A History of Racist and Nationalist Ideas in Europe*, trans. Richard Howard (New York: Basic Books, 1974), 155–182.

29 Arthur de Gobineau, *The Inequality of Human Races*, trans. Adrian Collins (New York: Howard Fertig, 1967), 122.

30 Hannah Arendt, *The Origins of Totalitarianism*, Part I: *Antisemitism* (New York: Harcourt, Brace & World, 1968), 93.

31 On the background and reception of the Dreyfus Affair see Ernst-Otto Czempiel, *Das deutsche Dreyfus-Geheimnis* (München: Scherz, 1966); Jesus Jareño Lopez, *El Affaire Dreyfus en España, 1894–1906* (Murcia: Godoy, 1981); Danielle Delmaire, *Antisémitisme et catholiques dans le nord pendant l'affaire Dreyfus* (Lille: Presses universitaires de Lille, 1991); Nelly Wilson, *Bernard-Lazare: Antisemitism and the Problem*

of Jewish Identity in Late Nineteenth-Century France (Cambridge: Cambridge University Press, 1978); Nicholas Halasz, *Captain Dreyfus: The Story of a Mass Hysteria* (New York: Simon and Schuster, 1955); Egal Feldman, *The Dreyfus Affair and the American Conscience, 1895–1906* (Detroit: Wayne State University Press, 1981); Stephen Wilson, *Ideology and Experience: Antisemitism in France at the Time of the Dreyfus Affair* (Rutherford, [NJ]: Fairleigh Dickinson University Press; London: Associated University Presses, 1982); David L. Lewis, *Prisoners of Honour: The Dreyfus Affair* (London: Cassell, 1975); A. Maria. Cittadini Ciprî, *Proust e la Francia dell'affaire Dreyfus* (Palermo: Palumbo, 1977); Richard David Sonn, *Anarchism and Cultural Politics in Fin de Siècle France* (Lincoln, NE: University of Nebraska Press, 1989); Richard Griffiths, *The Use of Abuse: The Polemics of the Dreyfus Affair and Its Aftermath* (New York: Berg; St. Martin's Press, 1991); Elisabeth-Christine Mülsch, *Zwischen Assimilation und jüdischem Selbstverständnis: David Léon Cahun (1841–1900) ein Journalist und Jugendbuchautor im Umfeld der Dreyfus-Affäre* (Bonn: Romanistischer Verlag, 1987); Albert S. Lindemann, *The Jew Accused: Three Anti-Semitic Affairs (Dreyfus, Beilis, Frank) 1894–1915* (Cambridge/New York: Cambridge University Press, 1991); Michael Burns, *Dreyfus: A Family Affair, 1789–1945* (New York: HarperCollins, 1991).

32 All references are to Alfred Dreyfus, *Five Years of My Life, 1894–1899* (New York: McClure, Phillips & Co., 1901) here, 3. The German edition was Alfred Dreyfus, *Fünf Jahre meines Lebens* (Berlin: John Edelheim, 1901).

33 Karl, *Franz Kafka*, 501.

34 Cited by Maurice Paléologue, *An Intimate Journal of the Dreyfus Case*, trans. Eric Mosbacher (New York: Criterion, 1957), 21.

35 Léon Daudet, "Le châtiment," *Le Figaro* (January 6, 1895). On the image of Dreyfus see John Grand-Carteret, *L' affaire Dreyfus et l' image* (Paris Flammarion, 1898) esp. 48 for German images, and *Le Sifflet* 1–2 (Paris) February 17, 1898–June 16, 1899. See also the most recent catalogue: Laurent Gervereau and Christophe Prochasson, eds., *L'affaire Dreyfus et le tournant du siècle (1894–1910)* (Paris: BDIC, 1994).

36 Maurice Barrès, "La parade de Judas," *Scènes et doctrines du nationalisme* (Paris: Félix Guven, 1902), 132–143, here, 135.

37 Jean-Denis Bredin, *The Affair: The Case of Alfred Dreyfus*, trans. Jeffrey Mehlman (New York: Georg Braziller, 1986), 23. I am obviously indebted to Bredin's account.

38 Cited by Paléologue, 53.

39 *La Croix* (November 14, 1894).

40 Cited by Paléologue, 51.

41 Report of the investigating magistrate, quoted in Bredin, 85.

42 Cited by Paléologue, 49.

43 Alfred Dreyfus, *Cinq années de ma vie, 1894–1899* (Paris, E. Fasquelle, 1901). See note 32 for the English and German translations that appeared the same year. In addition, translations into Spanish, *Cinco anos de mi vida (1894–1899)*, trans. Ramon Orts-Ramos (Barcelona: Maucci, 1901), Italian, *Cinque anni della mia vita* (Milano: Sonzogno, 1901), and Ladino *Sinko anios de mi vida*, trans. Yitshak Gabai (Konstantinopla: Emprimeria Arditi, 1901) appeared that year. An earlier set of texts, the letters to his wife, was excerpted in this volume. See Alfred Dreyfus, *Lettres d'un innocent* (Paris: Stock, 1898).

44 Alfred and Pierre Dreyfus, *The Dreyfus Case*, trans. Donald MacKay (New Haven: Yale University Press, 1937), 74.

45 Cited by Paléologue, 247–248.

46 The image of Dreyfus on board the cruiser *Sfax* in 1899 shows him in this state. See Alfred and Pierre Dreyfus, opposite 106.

47 Bredin, 404.

48 Maurice Barrès, *Scènes et doctrines du nationalisme* (Paris: Félix Guven, 1902), 138.

49 Cited by Paléologue, 227.

50 Alfred and Pierre Dreyfus, *The Dreyfus Case*, 270–272.

51 Arendt, 82.

52 Karl, 423.

53 Hiemer, 34–40.

54 Jonathan Hutchinson, *Syphilis* (London: Cassell & Co., 1887), 458–460. The German translation is Jonathan Hutchinson, *Syphilis*, trans. Artur Kollmann (Leipzig: Arnold, 1888).

55 Hutchinson, 115–118.

56 Benedict Spinoza, *The Political Works*, trans. A. G. Wernham (Oxford: Oxford University Press, 1958), 63. I am grateful to Jay Geller for this source.

57 Hartmut Binder, *Kafka in neuer Sicht: Mimik, Gestik und Personengefüge als Darstellungsformen des Autobiographischen* (Stuttgart: J. B. Metzler, 1976), 588, n. 77.

58 On the family, see Anthony Northey, *Kafka's Relatives: Their Lives and His Writing* (New Haven: Yale University Press, 1991); Ernst Pawel, *The Nightmare of Reason: A Life of Franz Kafka* (1984; London: Collins Harvill, 1988), 9–12.

59 Pawel, 182.

60 Cesare Lombroso, *L'antisemitismo e la scienze moderne* (Turin: L. Roux, 1894), 102–103. On the history of the idea of the heart and its illness, see H. P. Kafka, "Silent Defects," *Journal of the American College of Cardiology* 13 (1989), 1451–1452 and on the historical context of heart illness see Saul Jarcho , ed., *The Concept of Heart Failure from Avicenna to Albertini* (Cambridge: Harvard University Press, 1980).

61 Engländer, 12–13.

62 Otto Binswanger, *Die Pathologie und Therapie der Neurasthenie* (Jena: G. Fischer, 1896), 46.

63 Alfred Lee Loomis and William Gilman Thompson, eds., *A System of Practical Medicine*. 4 vols. (New York/Philadelphia: Lea Brothers, 1897–1898), 4, 553.

64 Pawel, 260.

65 Pawel, 104, 134, 195.

66 Max Brod, *Über Franz Kafka* (Frankfurt: Fischer, 1977), 14.

67 Franz Kafka, *Tagebücher*, eds. Hans-Gerd Koch, Michael Müller, Malcolm Pasley (Frankfurt a. M.: S. Fischer, 1990), 778.

68 Pawel, 343.

69 Cited by Peter J. Swales, "Freud, His Teacher, and the Birth of Psychoanalysis," in

Freud: Appraisals and Reappraisals, ed. Paul E. Stepansky, 2 vols. (Hillsdale, N J: Analytic Press, 1986), 28.

70 Benjamin Franklin, *Leben und Ausgewählte Schriften* (Leipzig: Georg Wigand, 1838).

71 Rudolf Virchow, "Gesamtbericht über die Farbe der Haut, der Haare und der Augen der Schulkinder in Deutschland," *Archiv für Anthropologie* 16 (1886), 275–475.

72 George L. Mosse, *Toward the Final Solution: A History of European Racism* (New York: Howard Fertig, 1975), 90–91.

73 This report was submitted to Congress on December 3, 1910, and issued on March 17, 1911. A full text was published by Columbia University Press in 1912. Boas summarized his findings (and chronicles the objections to this report) in his *Race, Language and Culture* (New York: Macmillan, 1940), 60–75. On Boas, see Leonard B. Glick, "Types Distinct from Our Own: Franz Boas on Jewish Identity and Assimilation," *American Anthropologist* 84 (1982), 545–565.

74 Boas, 83.

75 Dr. Alfred Damm in his periodical *Wiedergebürt der Völker* (January, 1892), 31. I am grateful to Chris Kenway for this citation.

76 Alfred Damm, *Die Entartung der Menschen und die Beseitung der Entartung* (Berlin: W. Bruer & Co., 1895), 59.

CHAPTER THREE: MALES ON TRIAL

1 This aspect of my work has been greatly influenced by the work of George L. Mosse, especially his ground-breaking study *Nationalism and Sexuality: Middle-Class Morality and Sexual Norms in Modern Europe* (New York: Howard Fertig, 1985), and especially his chapter "Race and Sexuality: The Outsider," 133–152. I quote here from his introduction, 17. An excellent collection of essays has followed up Mosse's suggestions: Andrew Parker, Mary Russo, Doris Sommer, and Patricia Yaeger, eds., *Nationalisms and Sexualities* (New York: Routledge, 1992).

2 Richard Lichtheim, *Das Programm des Zionismus* (Berlin: Zionistische Vereinung für Deutschland, 1913), 14. (In Kafka's library, with a dedication by Max Brod.)

3 So, for example, Gershom Gerhard Scholem, *Sabbatai Sevi: The Mystical Messiah, 1626–1676*, trans. R. J. Zwi Werblowsky (Princeton: Princeton University Press, 1973).

4 Tom Pitt-Aikens and Alice Thomas Ellis, *Loss of the Good Authority: The Cause of Delinquency* (London: Penguin, 1989).

5 Hannah Arendt, *The Origins of Totalitarianism*, Part I: *Antisemitism* (New York: Harcourt, Brace & World, 1968), 91.

6 Sholom Aleichem, *Selected Stories* (New York: Modern Library, 1956), 269–273.

7 Arthur Schnitzler, *Plays and Stories*, ed. Egon Schwarz (New York: Continuum, 1982), 256. On the impact of this model see Thomas Freeman, "Leutnant Gustl: A Case of Male Hysteria?" *Modern Austrian Literature* 25 (1992): 41–51.

8 Ernst Pawel, *The Nightmare of Reason: A Life of Franz Kafka* (1984; London: Collins Harvill, 1988), 176.

9 Max Nordau, *Zionistische Schriften* (Köln: Jüdischer Verlag, 1909), 379–381. This

call, articulated at the second Zionist Congress, followed his address on the state of the Jews which keynoted the first congress. There he spoke on the "physical, spiritual and economic status of the Jews." In July, 1902 Nordau recapitulated his views in an essay in the *Jüdische Turnzeitung*, entitled "Was bedeutet das Turnen für uns Juden" (*Zionistische Schriften*, 382–384). On Nordau see M. Baldwin, "Liberalism, Nationalism, and Degeneration: The Case of Max Nordau," *Central European History* 13 (1980), 99–120.

10 Pawel, 205.

11 Sander L. Gilman, *The Jew's Body* (New York: Routledge, 1991), 38–59.

12 Franz Kafka, *Tagebücher*, ed., Hans-Gerd Koch, Michael Müller, Malcolm Pasley (Frankfurt a. M.: S. Fischer, 1990), 768.

13 Oskar Panizza, *The Council of Love*, trans. O. F. Pucciani (New York: Viking, 1979), 79. See, in this context, the discussion of Panizza in Claude Quétel, *History of Syphilis*, trans. Judith Braddock and Brian Pike (London: Polity Press, 1990), 45–49.

14 Johann Jakob Schudt, *Jüdische Merkwürdigkeiten* (Frankfurt am Main: S. T. Hocker, 1714–1718), 2, 369. On the later ideological life of this debate, see Wolfgang Fritz Haug, *Die Faschisierung des bürgerlichen Subjekts: Die Ideologie der gesunden Normalität und die Ausrottungspolitiken im deutschen Faschismus* (Berlin-West: Argument Verlag, 1986).

15 All quotations are from the English translation, Otto Weininger, *Sex & Character* (London: William Heinemann, 1906), 303. On Weininger, see my *Jewish Self-Hatred: Anti-Semitism and the Hidden Language of the Jews* (Baltimore: The Johns Hopkins University Press, 1986), 244–251; Jacques Le Rider, *Der Fall Otto Weininger: Wurzeln des Antifeminismus und Antisemitismus*, trans. Dieter Hornig (Vienna: Löcker Verlag, 1985); Jacques Le Rider and Norbert Leser, eds., *Otto Weininger: Werk und Wirkung* (Vienna: Österreichischer Bundesverlag, 1984); Peter Heller, "A Quarrel over Bisexuality," Gerald Chapple and Hans H. Schulte, ed., *The Turn of the Century: German Literature and Art, 1890–1915* (Bonn: Bouvier, 1978), 87–116; Franco Nicolino, *Indagini su Freud e sulla Psicoanalisi* (Naples: Liguori editore, n.d.), 103–110.

16 Joseph Roth, "Das Spinnennetz," Joseph Roth, *Werke*, ed. Hermann Kesten. 4 vols. (Cologne: Kiepenheuer & Witsch, 1975), vol. 1, 57.

17 Milena Jesenská, *Alles ist Leben*, ed. Dorothea Rein (Frankfurt a. M.: Neue Kritik, 1984), 132–135.

18 See the discussion in *The Jew's Body*, 38–59.

19 See the first–rate study by Anna Foa, "Il nuovo e il vecchio: L'insorgere della sifilide (1494–1530), *Quaderni Storici* 55 (1984); 11–34, trans. Carole C. Gallucci, in Edward Muir and Guido Ruggiero, *Sex and Gender in Historical Perspective* (Baltimore: the Johns Hopkins University Press, 1990), 24–45. On Jews and syphilis, see also Klaus Theweleit, *Male Fantasies*, trans. Erica Carter and Chris Turner, 2 vols. (Minneapolis: University of Minnesota Press, 1987–1989), 2, 16.

20 Emil von Behring and Shibasaburo Kitasato, "Über das Zustandekommen der Diptherie-Immunität und der Tetanus-Immunität bei Thieren," *Deutsche medizinische Wochenschrift* 16 (1890), 1113–1114.

21 Bertha Pappenheim with Sara Rabinowitsch, *Zur Lage der jüdischen Bevölkerung in Galizien: Reise-Eindrücke und Vorschläge zur Besserung der Verhältnisse* (Frankfurt a. M.: Neuer Frankfurter Verlag, 1904), 46–51.

22 Adolf Hitler, *Mein Kampf*, trans. Ralph Manheim (Boston: Houghton Mifflin Company, 1943), 247.

23 Compare Edward J. Bristow, *Prostitution and Prejudice: The Jewish Fight against White Slavery, 1870–1939* (Oxford: Clarendon, 1982), and J. L. Joseph, "The Mafkeh and the Lady: Jews, Prostitutes, and Progressives in New York City, 1900–1930" (Diss., State University of New York, Stony Brook, NY, 1986).

24 On the meaning of this disease in the medical literature of the period, see the following dissertations on the topic: Michael Scheiba, *Dissertatio inauguralis medica, sistens quaedam plicae pathologica: Germ. Juden-Zopff, Polon. Koltun : quam ... in Academia Albertina pro gradu doctoris ... subjiciet defensurus Michael Scheiba ...* (Regiomonti: Litteris Reusnerianis, [1739]), and Hieronymus Ludolf, *Dissertatio inauguralis medica de plica, vom Juden-Zopff ...* (Erfordiae: Typis Groschianis [1724]).

25 Joseph Rohrer, *Versuch über die jüdischen Bewohner der österreichischen Monarchie* (Vienna: n.p., 1804), 26. The debate about the special tendency of the Jews for skin disease, especially *plica polonica*, goes on well into the twentieth century. See Richard Weinberg, "Zur Pathologie der Juden," *Zeitschrift für Demographie und Statistik der Juden* 1 (1905), 10–11.

26 Wolfgang Häusler, *Das galizische Judentum in der Habsburgermonarchie im Lichte der zeitgenössischen Publizistik und Reiseliteratur von 1772–1848* (Vienna: Verlag für Geschichte und Politik, 1979). On the status of the debates about the pathology of the Jews in the East after 1919, see *Voprosy biologii i patologii evreev* (Leningrad: State Publishing House, 1926).

27 Arthur Schopenhauer, *Parerga and Paralipomena*, trans. E.F.J. Payne. 2 vols. (Oxford: Clarendon Press, 1973), 2, 357.

28 D. Chwolson, *Die Blutanklage und sonstige mittelalterliche Beschuldigungen der Juden: eine historische Untersuchung nach den Quellen* (Frankfurt a. M.: J. Kauffmann, 1901).

29 Paul Lawrence Rose, *Revolutionary Antisemitism in Germany from Kant to Wagner* (Princeton: Princeton University Press, 1990), 44–50, 252–262.

30 Voltaire, *Philosophical Dictionary*, ed. Theodor Besterman (Harmondsworth: Penguin, 1971), 256–257.

31 See *The Jew's Body*, 104–127.

32 Friedrich Nietzsche, *Ecce Homo*, trans. R. J. Hollindale (Harmondsworth: Penguin, 1983). On Kafka and Nietzsche, see Patrick Bridgwater, *Kafka and Nietzsche* (Bonn: Bouvier, 1974).

33 Erika Weinzierl, "Katholizismus in Österreich," in Karl Heinrich Rengstorf and Siegfried von Kortzfleisch, eds., *Kirche und Synagoge: Handbuch zur Geschichte von Christen und Juden*, 2 vols. (Stuttgart: Ernst Klett, 1970), 483–531, here, 507–513.

34 The debate and texts of the *fin de siècle* as well as the background material are documented by Hugo Hayn, *Übersicht der (meist in Deutschland erschienenen) Litteratur über die angeblich von Juden verübeten Ritualmorde und Hostienfrevel* (Jena: H. W. Schmidt, 1906). See Alan Dundes, "The Ritual Murder or Blood Libel Legend: A Study of Anti-Semitic Victimization through Projective Inversion," *Temenos* 25 (1989), 7–32 as well as his anthology of readings on the topic, Alan Dundes, ed., *The Blood Libel Legend: A Casebook in Anti-Semitic Folklore* (Madison, WI: University of

Wisconsin Press, 1991). On the general historical background see also R. Po-chia Hsia, *Trent 1475: Stories of a Ritual Murder Trial* (New Haven: published in cooperation with Yeshiva University Library, Yale University Press, 1992) as well as his classic work, *The Myth of Ritual Murder: Jews and Magic in Reformation Germany* (New Haven: Yale University Press, 1988). On questions of ritual murder and ritual slaughter in Germany at the turn of the century, see Mordechai Breuer, *Jüdische Orthodoxie im deutschen Reich, 1871–1918: Sozialgeschichte einer religiösen Minderheit* (Frankfurt a. M.: Jüdischer Verlag bei Athenaeum, 1986). On the situation in turn-of-the-century Prague, see *Thomas G. Masaryk and the Jews: A Collection of Essays*, trans., Benjamin R. Epstein (New York: B. Pollak, 1945). See also Stefan Lehr, *Antisemitismus, religiöse Motive im sozialen Vorurteil: aus der Frühgeschichte des Antisemitismus in Deutschland 1870–1914* (München: Kaiser, 1974); Ezekiel Leikin, ed. and trans., *The Beilis Transcripts : The Anti-Semitic Trial That Shook the World* (Northvale, NJ: Jason Aronson, 1993); Gavin I. Langmuir, *Toward a Definition of Antisemitism* (Berkeley: University of California Press, 1990), Stefan Rohrbacher, "Ritualmord-Beschuldigungen am Niederrhein: Christlicher Aberglaube und antijüdische Agitation im 19. Jahrhundert," *Menora* 1 (1990), 299–326; Wolfgang Treue, "Schlechte und gute Christen: Zur Rolle von Christen in antijüdischen Ritualmord- und Hostienschändigungslegenden," *Aschkenas* 2 (1992), 95–116.

35 Bracha Rivlin, "1891: Blood-Libel in Corfu," *The Jewish Museum of Greece Newsletter 27* (1989), 1–7. Lectures on the Corfu riots were held in Germany and Austria in 1891. See Ludwig Gorel, *Das Blutmärchen: Seine Entstehung und Folgen bis zu den jüngsten Vorgängen auf Korfu* (Berlin: J. Gnadenfeld, 1891).

36 Hermann L. Strack, *The Jew and Human Sacrifice*, trans. Henry Blanchamp (London: Cope and Fenwick, 1909), 212–235.

37 *Die Fackel* (October, 1899), 23–26.

38 Arnold J. Band, "Kafka and the Beilis Affair," *Comparative Literature,* 31–32 (1982), 168–183; and Ritchie Robertson, *Kafka: Judaism, Politics, and Literature* (Oxford: Clarendon Press; New York: Oxford University Press, 1985), 11–12.

39 Hans Gross, *Handbuch für Untersuchungsrichter als System der Kriminalistik* 2 vols. (München: Schweitzer, 1908), 2: 766.

40 T. G. Masaryk, *Die Notwendigkeit der Revision des Polnaer Mordes* (Prague: n.p., 1899). See Františěk Cěrvinka, "The Hilsner Affair," in Alan Dundes, ed., *The Blood Libel Legend: A Casebook in Anti-Semitic Folklore* (Madison: University of Wisconsin Press, 1991), 135–161.

41 Larry Wolff, *Postcards from the End of the World: An Investigation into the Mind of fin-de-siècle Vienna* (London: Collins, 1989), 102–110.

42 Rudolf Kleinpaul, *Menschenopfer und Ritualmorde* (Leipzig: Schmidt & Günther, 1892), 1–2.

43 Robertson, 11.

44 Frederick Robert Karl, *Franz Kafka, Representative Man* (New York: Ticknor & Fields, 1991), discusses Polna on 75ff.

45 Hippolyte Bernheim, *Die Suggestion und ihre Heilwirkung*, trans. Sigmund Freud (Leipzig/Vienna: Franz Deuticke, 1888), 152–154.

46 Felix Goldmann, *Taufjudentum und Antisemitismus* (Frankfurt a. M.: J. Kaufmann, 1914).

47 Abraham Grünberg, *Ein jüdisch-polnisch-russisches Jubiläum (Das große Pogrom von Siedlice in Jahre 1906)* (Prague: Selbstverlag, Ende Oktober, 1916) with the dedication of the author to Kafka.

48 Friedrich Nietzsche, *Thus Spoke Zarathustra*, trans. Walter Kaufmann (Harmondsworth: Penguin, 1983).

49 Houston Stewart Chamberlain, *Foundations of the Nineteenth Century*, trans. John Lees. 2 vols. (London: John Lane/The Bodley Head, 1913), 1, 324.

50 Arnold Zweig, *Ritualmord in Urgarn: Jüdische Tragödie in fünf Aufzüger* (Berlin: Hyperionverlag, 1914). Kafka's awareness of this play may be dated somewhat earlier. In *Selbstwehr*, the Zionist newspaper to which Kafka contributed, the account of Kafka being awarded the Fontane Prize is linked with Zweig, as the author of this play, having been awarded the Kleist Prize (December 10, 1915). Excerpts from the play appeared in the *Selbstwehr* on October 11, 1916. A discussion of the actual ritual murder trial had appeared on April 24, 1916.

51 Arnold Zweig, *Die Sendung Semaels: jüdische Tragödie in fünf Aufzügen* (München : K. Wolf, 1920).

52 I rely here on the detailed account by Andrew Handler, *Blood Libel at Tizsaeszlar* (New York: Columbia University Press, 1980). On the medical testimony during the trial, see Edith Stern, "Gerichtsmedizinische Bezüge zu dem Ritualmordprozess von Tiszaeszlar, Ungarn, 1882–1883," *Monatsschrift für Kriminologie und Strafrechtsreform* 67 (1984), 38–47.

53 Felix A. Theilhaber, *Der Untergang der deutschen Juden: Eine volkswirtschaftliche Studie*, 2nd Edition (Berlin: Jüdischer Verlag, 1921). On the general background of such arguments, see D. E. C. Eversely, *Social Theories of Fertility and the Malthusian Debate* (Oxford: Clarendon Press, 1959), and E. Hutchinson, *The Population Debate: The Development of Conflicting Theories up to 1900* (Boston: Houghton Mifflin, 1967). On Theilhaber, see H. Lehfeldt, "Felix A. Theilhaber—Pioneer Sexologist," *Archives of Sexual Behavior* 15 (1986), 1–12.

54 Theilhaber, 93.

55 Arthur Ruppin, *Die Juden der Gegenwart* (Berlin: Jüdischer Verlag, 1904).

56 Arthur Ruppin, *The Jews of the Modern World* (London: Macmillan & Co., 1934), 76.

57 Franz Kafka, *Tagebücher*, ed., Hans-Gerd Koch, Michael Müller, and Malcolm Pasley (Frankfurt: S. Fischer, 1990), 370–371.

58 Heinrich Singer, *Allgemeine und spezielle Krankheitslehre der Juden* (Leipzig: Benno Konegen, 1904), 25.

59 "Ritualmordhetze in Prag und die Staatsanwaltschaft," *Selbstwehr* (April 26, 1912), 5.

60 Handler, 128.

61 Handler, 131.

62 Kafka, *Tagebücher*, 754.

63 See Meyer Kayserling, *Die rituale Schlachtfrage oder ist Schächten Thierquälerei?* (Aarau: n.p., 1867); Wilhelm Landsberg, *Das rituelle Schächten der Israeliten im Lichte der Wahrheit* (Kaiserlautern: E. Crusius, 1882); C. Bauwerker, *Das rituelle*

Schachten der Israeliten im Lichte der Wissenschaft (Kaiserslautern: n.p., 1882); *Auszüge aus den Gutachten der hervorragendsten Physiologen und Veterinärärzte uber das "Schächten"* (Frankfurt a. M.: Louis Golde, 1887); Komite zur Abwehr antisemitischer Angriffe, ed., *Gutachten über das judisch-rituelle Schlachtverfahren ("Schächten")* (Berlin: E. Apolant, 1894); Friedrich Weichmann, *Das Schächten : (das rituelle Schlachten bei den Juden)* (Leipzig: I. C. Heinrichs, 1899); U. Liebling, "Das rituelle Fleischbeschau," *Österreiche Monatsschrift für Tierheilkunde* 12 (1900), 2241–2250; Aaron Zebi Friedman, *Tub Taam, or a Vindication of the Jewish Mode of Slaughtering Animals for Food Called Shechitah* (New York: n.p., 1904); Hirsch Hildesheimer, *Das Schächten* (Berlin: n.p., 1905); Hirsch Hildesheimer, ed., *Neue Gutachten uber das jüdische-rituelle Schlächt-verfahren (Schächten)* (Berlin: n.p., 1908); *Aus den Verhandlungen des Deutschen Reichstags uber das Schächten: 18. Mai 1887, 25. April 1899 und 9. Mai 1899* (Berlin: n.p., 1909); Eduard Biberfeld, *Halsschnitt nicht Hirntertrümmerung* (Berlin: L. Lamm, 1911); Thomas Barlow Wood, *The Jewish Method of Slaughtering Animals for Food* (London: n.p., 1925); Board of Deputies of British Jews, *Opinions of Foreign Experts on the Jewish Method of Slaughtering Animals* (London: n.p., 1926); Bela Galandauer, *Zur Physiologie des Schlachtschnittes: ist das Schächten eine Tierquälerei?* (Berlin: Reichszentrale für Schlachtangelegenheiten, 1933). On slaughter and its ritual meaning see Keith Thomas, *Man and the Natural World: Changing Attitudes in England, 1500–1800* (New York: Viking Penguin, 1984). This is still a topos for anti-Semitic writing; see Arnold Leese, *The Legalised Cruelty of Shechita: The Jewish Method of Cattle-Slaughter* (Hollywood, CA: Sons of Liberty, n.d.)

64 "Schächten," *Jüdisches Lexikon*, ed. Georg Herlitz and Bruno Kirschner, 4 vols. in 5 (Berlin: Jüdischer Verlag, 1927–1930), 4/2, 134–137, here 134–135.

65 Ferdinand Hueppe, *Handbuch der Hygiene* (Berlin: August Hirschwald, 1899), 275–277.

66 On the question of anti-Semitism and ritual slaughter, see Michael F. Metcalf, "Regulating Slaughter: Animal Protection and Antisemitism in Scandinavia, 1880–1941," *Patterns of Prejudice* 23 (1989), 32–48; Brian Klug, "Overkill: The Polemic against Ritual Slaughter," *The Jewish Quarterly* 34 (1989), 38–42; Antony Kushner, "Stunning Intolerance: A Century of Opposition to Religious Slaughter," *The Jewish Quarterly* 36 (1989), 16–20; Brian Klug, "Ritual Murmur: The Undercurrent of Protest against Religious Slaughter of Animals in Britain in the 1980s," *Patterns of Prejudice* 23 (1989), 16–28; Temple Grandin, "Humanitarian Aspects of Shehitah in the United States," *Judaism* 39 (1990), 436–46 and Mordechai Breuer, *Modernity within Tradition: The Social History of Orthodox Jewry in Imperial Germany*, trans. Elizabeth Petuchowski (New York: Columbia University Press,1992). On the general anxiety concerning health, blood, and slaughter see Noélie Vialles, *Le sang et la chair: Les abattoirs des pays de l'Adour* (Paris: Éditions de la Maison des sciences de l'homme, 1987).

67 Schopenhauer, *Parerga and Paralipomena*, 2, 375.

68 On anti-Semitism and *shehitah* see Friedrich Külling, *Bei uns wie überall? Antisemitismus* (Zurich: Schweizer Israelitischer Gemeindebund, 1977), 249–385, from which these examples were taken.

69 On the general background of this question in England see the debate outlined in Harriet Ritvo, *The Animal Estate: The English and Other Creatures in the Victorian Age* (Cambridge, Mass.: Harvard University Press, 1987). Two questions that are reflect-

ed in the anti-Semitic rhetoric against ritual slaughter and also turned into aspects of the debate about vivisection are the madness of the antivivisectionist and the notion of "sacrifice." See Craig Buettinger, "Antivivisection and the Charge of Zoophil-Psychosis in the Early Twentieth Century," *The Historian* 55 (1993), 277–288, and Michael E. Lynch, "Sacrifice and the Transformation of the Animal Body into a Scientific Object: Laboratory Culture and Ritual Practice in the Neurosciences," *Social Studies of Science* 18 (1988), 265–289.

70 Cited by Ernst von Schwartz, *Das Betäubungslose Schächten der Israeliten* (Konstanz: Ackermann, 1905), 21.

71 See David Welch, *Propaganda and the German Cinema 1933–45* (Oxford: Clarendon Press, 1983) and Yizhak Ahren, Stig Hornshoj-Moller, Christoph B. Melchers, *"Der ewige Jude" - wie Goebbels hetzte: Untersuchungen zum nationalsozialistischen Propagandafilm* (Aachen: Alano, 1990).

72 Schwartz, *Das Betäubungslose Schächten der Israeliten, op. cit.*

73 On the history of the medicalization of diet among the Jews, see Luis Garçia-Ballester, "Dietetic and Pharmacological Therapy: A Dilemma among 14th-Century Jewish Practitioners in the Montpellier Area," *Clio Medica* 22 (1991), 23–37; and M. Sackmann, "Fleischhygienische Verordnungen im Alten Testament," *Deutsche Tierartzliche Wochenschrift* 95 (1988), 451–453.

74 On the relationship between tuberculosis and slaughter, see E. H. Lochmann, "Folgenschwere Irrtümer bei der Beurteilung tuberkulöser Schlachtrinder," *Archiv für Lebensmittelhygiene* 20 (1969), 155–158; T. Schliesser, "Die Bekämpfung der Rindertuberkulose—'Tierversuch' der Vergangenheit," *Praxis der Pneumologie* 28 (1974) Supplement: 870–874; E. H. Lochmann, "Zur lebensmittelrechtlichen Beurteilung tuberkulöser Schlachtrinder im ausgehenden 18. Jahrhundert—Zugleich eine Studie zur Stellung des Tierarztes im öffentlichen Dienst jener Zeit," *Deutsche Tierarztliche Wochenschrift* 99 (1992), 345–346.

75 Henry Behrend, "Diseases Caught from Butcher's Meat," *The Nineteenth Century* 26 (1889), 409–422. The importance of this essay can not be underestimated. It is cited as the epigraph to the pro-*Schächten* pamphlet *Herrn Otto Hartmann in Cöln und sein Kampf gegen die Schlachtweise der Israeliten ... von einem Collegen* (Frankfurt a. M.: M. Slobotzky, 1889).

76 Roger-Hénri Guerrand, "Guerre à la tuberculose!" *Histoire* 74 (1984), 78–81.

77 Quoted in Lucien Wolf, "What Is Judaism? A Question of Today,"*Fortnightly Review* NS 36 (1884), 237–256, here 250.

78 Lucien Wolf, 246–247.

79 William Osler, "Israel and Medicine" (1914) William Osler, *Men and Books*, ed. Earl F. Nation (Pasadena, CA: Castle Press, 1959), 56.

80 Schwartz, 37.

81 Alexander Rattray, *Divine Hygiene: Sanitary Science and Sanitariness of the Sacred Scriptures and Mosaic Code*, 2 vols. (London: James Nisbet, 1903), 1, 200–253 on "Food," specifically, 227, on the selection of uninfected meat.

82 Lucien Wolf, 251.

83 Lucien Wolf, 247.

84 J. St., *Das Schächten. Streitschrift gegen den jüdischen Schlachtritus* (Leipzig: Kössling/Gustav Wolf, 1883).

85 Gustav Simons, "Rasse und Ernährung," *Kraft und Schönheit*. Rasse Sondernheft (1907): 21–24, here 23.

86 Thomas Mann, *The Magic Mountain*, trans. H. T. Lowe-Porter (New York: Knopf, 1982), 372. On the medical accuracy of the novel see Humphreys, "*The Magic Mountain*—A Time Capsule of Tuberculosis Treatment in the Early Twentieth Century," *Bulletin of the Canadian History of Medicine* 6 (1989), 147–163; L. E. Montiel Llorente, "La ciencia medica en *La montana magica* de Thomas Mann," *Asclepio* 32 (1980), 271–285; H. Saueressig, "Literatur und Medizin. Zu Thomas Manns Roman *Der Zauberberg*," *Deutsche Medizinische Wochenschrift* 99 (1974), 1780–1786. On Mann and his attitudes toward the Jews see Alfred Hoelzel, "Thomas Mann's Attitudes to Jews and Judaism: An Investigation of Biography and Oeuvre," *Studies in Contemporary Jewry* 6 (1990), 229–253.

87 A most incisive psychoanalytic reading of this fascination is given by Fredrick A. Lubich, "Thomas Manns *Der Zauberberg*: Spukschloß der Großen Mutter oder Die Männerdämmerung des Abendlandes," *Deutsche Vierteljahrsschrift für Literaturwissenschaft und Geistesgeschichte* 67 (1993), 729–763.

88 Thomas Mann, *The Magic Mountain*, 440–41.

89 Max Scheimpflug, "Über den heutigen Stand der Frage nach der Erblichkeit der Tuberculose," L. von Schrötter, ed., *Die Tuberculose* (Vienna: Wilhelm Braumüller, 1898), 1–44, here, 41 with the detailed literature.

90 (Isaak Aleksandrovich) J. A. Dembo, *Das Schächten im Vergleich mit anderen Schlachtmethoden. Vom Standpunkte der Humanität und Hygiene* (Leipzig, H. Roskoschny, 1894); trans. *The Jewish Method of Slaughter compared with other Methods from the Humanitarian, Hygienic, and Economic Points of View* (London: Kegan Paul, Trench, Trubner, 1894).

91 Their statements are included in H. Ehrmann, ed., *Thier-Schutz und Menschen-Trutz: Sämmtliche für und gegen das Schächten geltend gemachten Momente kritische beleuchtete* (Frankfurt a. M.: J. Kaufmann, 1885), 64–65 (Du Bois-Reymond), and 122 (Virchow).

92 Bernard Drachman, "Bedikah," *The Jewish Encyclopedia* 12 vols. (New York: Funk and Wagnalls, 1904), 2: 627–628.

93 Kafka, *Tagebücher*, 265. See the discussion in Evelyn Torton Beck, *Kafka and the Yiddish Theater: Its Impact on His Work* (Madison: University of Wisconsin Press, 1971), 177–178.

94 Robertson, 18.

95 For the earlier images see Dundes, 294–295.

96 Kafka, *Tagebücher*, 754.

97 See Margot Norris, "Sadism and Masochism in 'In the Penal Colony' and 'A Hunger Artist'," in Mark Anderson, ed., *Reading Kafka: Prague, Politics, and the Fin de Siècle* (New York: Schocken Books, 1989), 161–176 as well as Marc Kipniss, "The Threat of the (Marginal) Feminine: Decolonizing Kafka's *Strafkolonie*," *Journal of the Kafka Society of America* 16 (1992), 46–51.

98 A parallel reading would be to see them as a parody of the ritual knife used in cir-

cumcision. See William C. Rubinstein, "Kafka's 'Jackals and Arabs'," *Monatshefte* 59 (1967): 13–18.

99 See the detailed discussion and survey of the literature in Jens Tismar, "Kafka's *Schakale und Araber* im zionistischen Kontext betrachet," *Jahrbuch der deutschen Schillergesellschaft* 19 (1975), 306–323 and Iris Bruce, "'Aggadah raises its Paw against Halakha': Kafka's Zionist Critique in 'Forschungen eines Hundes'," *Journal of the Kafka Society of America* 16 (June, 1992), 4–12.

100 Fritz Wittels, *Der Taufjude* (Wien: M. Breitenstein, 1904), 32.

101 On Kafka and homosexuality, see Evelyn Torton Beck, "Kafka's Triple Bind: Women, Jews and Sexuality," in Alan Udoff, ed., *Kafka's Contextuality* (Baltimore : Gordian Press/Baltimore Hebrew College, 1986), 343–388; Elmer Drost, "War Kafka schwul? Ein Versuch, seine Texte neu zu lesen," *TAZ* (August 22, 1983); Günter Mecke, *Franz Kafkas offenbares Geheimnis: Eine Psychopathographie* (München: Wilhelm Fink, 1982); Ruth Tiefenbrun, *Moment of Torment* (Carbondale, IL: Southern Illinois University Press, 1973).

102 Compare Wolf Kittler, "Die Klauen der Sirenen," *MLN* 108 (1993), 500–516.

103 David F. Greenberg, *The Construction of Homosexuality* (Chicago: The University of Chicago Press, 1988), 408–409.

104 Hartmut Binder, *Kafka in neuer Sicht: Mimik, Gestik und Personengefüge als Darstellungsformen des Autobiographischen* (Stuttgart: J. B. Metzler, 1976), 380. The fascination with Weininger continued for Jews even in the *Shoah*. See Oskar Rosenfeld, *Wozu noch Welt: Auszeichnungen aus dem Getto Lodz*, ed., Hanno Loewy (Frankfurt am Main: Neue Kritik, 1994), p. 215 and 282.

105 See my essay "The Indelibility of Circumcision," *Koroth* (Jerusalem) 9 (1991), 806–817.

106 M. J. Gutmann, *Über den heutigen Stand der Rasse- und Krankheitsfrage der Juden* (Berlin: Rudolph Müller & Steinecke, 1920), 18.

107 Gutmann, 25–26.

108 Cited by Hans F. K. Günther, *Rassenkunde des jüdischen Volkes* (Munich: J. F. Lehmann, 1931), 273 (first published in 1922).

109 Robert Stigler, "Die rassenphysiologische Bedeutung der sekundären Geschlechtscharaktere," *Sitzungsberichte der anthopologischen Gesellschaft in Wien* (1919/1920), 6–9, here, 7. Published as a special number of the *Mitteilungen der anthropologischen Gesellschaft in Wien* 50 (1920).

110 Albert Moll, *Die konträre Sexualempfindung* (Berlin: Fischer, 1893), 116.

111 Hans Blüher, *Die Rolle der Erotik in der männlichen Gesellschaft*, 2 vols. (Jena: E. Diederichs,1917). The second volume is: *Führer und Volk in der Jugendbewegung*. On Blüher and Kafka see especially Binder, *Kafka in neuer Sicht, op. cit,* 346–395.

112 Hans Blüher, "'Niels Lyhne' von J. Jakobsen und das Problem der Bisexualität" *Imago* 1 (1912), 386–400, and "Über Gattenwahl und Ehe" *Imago* 3 (1914), 477–498. Of importance in his discussion of homosexuality and his debt to Freud is his "Die drei Grundformen der sexuellen Inversion" *Jahrbuch für sexuelle Zwischenstufen* 13 (1913), 1–79.

113 *Traktate über die Heilkunde, insbesondere die Neurosenlehre* (Jena: E. Dietrichs, 1926).

114 Malcolm Pasley, ed., *Max Brod-Franz Kafka: Eine Freundschaft*, 2 vols. (Frankfurt a. M.: S. Fischer, 1989), 2: 176 (my translation).

115 Brod-Kafka, 196.

116 On this theme in art see: James Saslow, "The Tenderest Lover: St. Sebastian in Renaissance Painting: A Proposed Iconology for North Italian Art, 1450–1550," *Gai saber* 1 (1) (Spring 1977), 58–66; François Le Targat, *St-Sébastien dans l'histoire de l'art depuis le 15e siècle* (Paris: Paul Vermont, 1977); *St-Sébastien: Adonis et Martyr* (Paris: Editions persona, 1983); Georges Eekhoud, "St-Sébastien dans la peinture" *Akademos* 1 (Feb 15, 1909): 171–175. On the role of this image in gay iconography see my "Touch, Sexuality and Disease," in William Bynum and Roy Porter, eds., *Medicine and the Five Senses* (Cambridge: Cambridge University Press, 1993), 198–224.

117 Kafka, *Tagebücher*, 93.

118 Arnold Zweig, *Bilanz der deutschen Judenheit 1933* (Amsterdam: Querido, 1934), 63–66.

119 All references are to Hans Blüher, *Secessio Judaica: Philosophische Grundlegung der historischen Situation des Judenthums und der antisemitischen Bewegung* (Berlin: Der weisse Ritter, 1922). On Blüher's extraordinary impact on Jewish thinkers of the time, see Alex Bein's autobiographical footnote on Blüher in Alex Bein, "The Jewish Parasite," *Leo Baeck Yearbook* 9 (1964), 3–40, here, 14, n. 39.

120 Werner Sombart, *The Jews and Modern Capitalism*, trans. M. Epstein (Glencoe, IL: The Free Press, 1951), 272. See also Jeffrey Herf, *Reactionary Modernism: Technology, Culture, and Politics in Weimar and the Third Reich* (New York: Cambridge University Press, 1984), 130–55.

121 "Philosophie des Pogroms," *Ost und West* (March/April 1923), 59–82, here 80.

122 Wilhelm Reich, *The Mass Psychology of Fascism*, trans. Vincent Carfagno (1943; New York: Noonday, 1993), 93.

123 Friedrich von der Leyen, *Deutsche Dichtung in neuer Zeit* (Jena: Diedrichs, 1922).

124 See the discussion in Jost Schillemeit's summary of the literature on the late writing in Hartmut Binder, ed., *Kafka-Handbuch in zwei Bänden*. 2 vols. (Stuttgart: Kröner, 1979), 2, 378–401.

125 On hands and their meaning in Kafka—excluding the racial implications—see Hartmut Binder, *Kafka in neuer Sicht*, 240–265.

126 Hans Gross, *Kriminal-Psychologie* (Leipzig: F.C.W. Vogel, 1905), 121.

CHAPTER FOUR: TUBERCULOSIS AS A TEST CASE

1 René-Théophile-Hyacinthe Laënnec, *De l'auscultation médiate, ou traité du diagnostic des maladies des poumons et du coeur* (Paris: Brosson & Chaudé, 1819).

2 Hermann Brehmer, *Die Therapie der chronischen Lungenschwindsucht* (Wiesbaden: Bergmann, 1887).

3 Susan Sontag, *Illness as Metaphor* (New York: Farrar, Straus and Giroux, 1978). See also E. Augstein, *Medizin und Dichtung. Die pathologischen Erscheinungen in der Dichtkunst* (Stuttgart: Enke, 1917); C.A.M. Noble, *Krankheit, Verbrechen und künstlerisches Schaffen bei Thomas Mann* (Bern, Herbert Lang, 1970); Tullo Hostillio Montenegro, *Tuberculose e literature: notas de pesquisa* (Rio de Janeiro: Casa do

Livro, 1971); Michele Anzalone, *Negli orti della regina: malati tra invenzione e realta* (Bologna: M. Boni, 1977); Vera Pohland, *Das Sanatorium als literarischer Ort. Medizinische Institution und Krankheit als Medien der Gesellschaftskritik und Existenzanalyse* (Frankfurt a. M.: Peter Lang, 1984); Jeffrey Meyers, *Disease and the Novel, 1880–1960* (New York: St. Martin's Press, 1985); Brigitta Schader, *Schwindsucht—Zur Darstellung einer tödlichen Krankheit in der deutschen Literatur vom poetischen Realismus zur Moderne* (Frankfurt a. M.: Peter Lang, 1987); Thomas Anz, *Gesund oder krank?: Medizin, Moral und Ästhetik in der deutschen Gegenwartsliteratur* (Stuttgart: J.B. Metzler, 1989).

4 Such as Frank Ryan, *Tuberculosis: The Greatest Story Never Told* (Bromesgrove, England: Swift Press, 1992). Except for his account of the recent reappearance of the disease, Ryan's popular history is not far from the tone of earlier histories, such as that of Lawrence F. Flick, *Development of Our Knowledge of Tuberculosis* (Philadelphia: 738 Pine Street, 1925); Richard Bochalli, *Die Entwicklung der Tuberkuloseforschung in der Zeit von 1878–1958* (Stuttgart: Georg Thieme, 1958) or F. B. Smith, *The Retreat of Tuberculosis, 1850–1950* (New York: Croom Helm, 1988). Much better are the specific social histories of the disease: Roy Porter, "The Case of Consumption," in Janine Bourriau, ed., *Understanding Catastrophe* (Cambridge: Cambridge University Press, 1992),179–203; Isabelle Grellet and Caroline Kruse, *Histoires de la tuberculose: Les fièvres de l'âme 1800–1940* (Paris: Ramsay, 1983); Barbara Bates, *Bargaining for a Life: A Social History of Tuberculosis, 1876–1938* (Philadelphia: University of Pennsylvania Press, 1992) (on the USA); F. B. Smith, *The Retreat of Tuberculosis 1850–1950* (London: Croom Helm, 1988) (on the UK); R. Y. Keers, *Pulmonary Tuberculosis: A Journey down the Centuries* (London: Baillière Tindall, 1978); Marc Bloch, *The Royal Touch: Sacred Monarchy and Scrofula in England and France*, trans. J. E. Anderson (London: Routledge and Kegan Paul, 1973); Wolfgang Seelinger, *Die "Volksheilstätten–Bewegung" in Deutschland um 1900: Zur Ideengeschichte der Sanatoriumstherapie für Tuberkulose* (München: Profil, 1988); Linda Bryder, *Below the Magic Mountain: A Social History of Tuberculosis in Twentieth-Century Britain* (New York: Oxford University Press, 1988); Peter Reinicke, *Tuberkulosefürsorge: Der Kampf gegen eine Geißel der Menschheit dargestellt am Beispiel Berlins 1895–1945* (Weinheim: Oterstudien Verlag, 1988); Richard Bochalli, *Die Entwicklung der Tuberkuloseforschung in der Zeit von 1878–1958* (Stuttgart: Georg Thieme, 1958); M. Piéry and J. Roshem, *Histoire de la tuberculose* (Paris: G. Dom et Cie, 1931).

5 See, in this context, Elizabeth Lomax, "Heredity or Acquired Disease? Early 19th-Century Debates on the Cause of Infantile Scrofula and Tuberculosis," *Journal of the History of Medicine and Allied Sciences* 32 (1977), 356–374; and Marion M. Torchia, "The Tuberculosis Movement and the Race Question, 1890–1950," *Bulletin of the History of Medicine* 49 (1975), 152–168.

6 Judith Walzer Leavitt, "'Typhoid Mary' Strikes Back: Bacteriological Theory and Practice in Early Twentieth-Century Public Health," *Isis* 83 (1992), 608–629; Nancy Tomes, "The Private Side of Public Health: Sanitary Science, Domestic Hygiene, and the Germ Theory, 1870–1900," *Bulletin of the History of Medicine* 64 (1990), 509–539; Naomi Rogers, *Dirt and Disease: Polio before FDR* (New Brunswick: Rutgers University Press, 1992).

7 Hermann von Hayek, *Das Tuberkulose-Problem* (Berlin: Julius Springer, 1921), 21–27.

8 Gerald S. Greenberg, "Books as Disease Carriers, 1880–1920," *Libraries and Culture* 23 (1988), 281–294.

9 Karl Mann, "Athletischer Körperbau," *Kraft und Schönheit*, Sandow Sonderheft (1901), 14–15.

10 All references are to George Eliot, *Daniel Deronda*, ed. Barbara Hardy (Harmonsworth: Penguin, 1967). On Eliot's novel, see Ingrid Kuczynski, "Der Blick auf das Andere. Das Konstrukt des Judentums in George Eliots Roman Daniel Deronda," Inge Stephan, Sabine Schilling, Sigrid Weigel, eds., *Jüdische Kultur und Weiblichkeit in der Moderne* (Cologne: Böhlau, 1994), 73–84.

11 One can note that this was not limited to the nineteenth century. A limited survey of this literature can be found in Max B. Lurie, *Resistance to Tuberculosis: Experimental Studies in Native and Acquired Defensive Mechanisms* (Cambridge, MA: Harvard University Press, 1964), 115–180; on the Jews, see 117–118. Lurie accepts the notion of a "native resistance of the Jews acquired through years of urbanization."

12 Madison Marsh, "Jews and Christians," *The Medical and Surgical Reporter* 30 (1874) (Philadelphia), 343–344, here, 343.

13 See the debate following the presentation of Joseph Jacobs, "On the Racial Characteristics of Modern Jews," *The Journal of the Anthropological Institute* 16 (1886), 23–63, here 56 and 61.

14 Marsh, 344.

15 Marsh, 344.

16 Joseph Krauskopf, *Sanitary Science: A Sunday Lecture* (Philadelphia: S. W. Goodman, 1889), 7.

17 Ephraim M. Epstein, "Have the Jews any Immunity from Certain Diseases?" *The Medical and Surgical Reporter* (Philadelphia) 30 (1874), 440–442; here 440.

18 Epstein, 441.

19 Epstein, 441.

20 Carl Claus, *Grundzüge der Zoologie zum Gebrauche an Universitäten und höheren Lehranstalten sowie zum Selbststudium*, 2 vols. (Marburg: N. G. Elwerts Universitäts-Buchhandlung, 1872), 2: 123.

21 On the German version of this argument concerning tuberculosis, see Alexander Riffel, *Die Erblichkeit der Schwindsucht und tuberkulosen Prozesse, nachgewiesen durch zahlreiches statistisiches Materiel und die praktische Erfahrung* (Karlsruhe: Gutsch, 1891), and his *Mittheilungen über die Erblichkeit und Infekiosität der Schwindsucht* (Braunschweig: Bruhn, 1892).

22 Madison Marsh, "Have the Jews Any Immunity from Certain Diseases?" *The Medical and Surgical Reporter* (Philadelphia) 31 (1874), 132–134.

23 On the history of this concept, see Sander L. Gilman and Steven T. Katz, eds., *Anti-Semitism in Times of Crisis* (New York: The New York University Press, 1991), 29.

24 Peter Charles Remondino, *History of Circumcision from the Earliest Times to the Present. Moral and Physical Reasons for Its Performance, with a History of Eunuchism, Hermaphroditism, etc., and of the Different Operations Practiced upon the Prepuce* (Philadelphia: F. A. Davis, 1891), 186. Remondino's book was published in 1892, but he notes in his introduction that it had been written decades earlier.

25 Stuart Creighton Miller, *"Benevolent Assimilation": The American Conquest of the*

Philippines, 1899–1903 (New Haven: Yale University Press, 1982), 75.

26 Cesare Lombroso, "Sulla mortalità degli Ebrei di Verona nel Decennio 1855–1864," *Rivista Clinica di Bologna* 6 (1867), 3–37.

27 Fracastoro is cited in this context in Fritz Schiff, "Person und Infekt," in Th. Brugsch and F. H. Lewy, eds., *Die Biologie der Person: Ein Handbuch der allgemeinen und speziellen Konstitutionslehre.* 4 vols. (Berlin: Urban & Schwarzenberg, 1926), 1, 595–732, here 662. When a more differentiate definition of the "Jew," was made, such as looking specifically at the Jews in the Holy Land, quite sophisticated comments about the risk for infection, given the social and economic status of the "Jew," were made. See Hans Much, *Eine Tuberkuloseforschungsreise nach Jerusalem* (Wurzburg: C. Kabitzch, 1913).

28 Eduard Glatter, "Das Racenmoment in seinem Einfluss auf Erkrankung," *Vierteljahrsschrift für gerichtliche und öffentliche Medicin* 25 (1864), 38–49.

29 John S. Billings, "Vital Statistics of the Jews," *North American Review* 76 (January 1891), 70–84, here, 78–79.

30 Cited by Henry Behrend, "Diseases Caught from Butcher's Meat," *The Nineteenth Century* 26 (1889), 409–422, here 413.

31 See the general discussion in Georg Cornet, *Die Tuberkulose*, 2 vols. (Wien: Alfred Hölder, 1907), 1, 490.

32 Georg Buschan, "Einfluß der Rasse auf die Form und Häufigkeit pathologischer Veränderungen," *Globus* 67 (1895), 21–24, 43–47, 60–63, 76–80, here 45–46, 60–61.

33 Hermann Runge, "*Ich glaube, es liegt im Blut*," *Die Arche* 13 (October 28, 1925), 1–7.

34 Christina von Braun, "Die 'Blutschande'—Wandlung eines Begriffs: Vom Inzesttabu zu den Rassengestetzen," *Die schamlose Schönheit des Vergangenen: Zum Verhältnis von Geschlecht und Geschichte* (Frankfurt a. M.: Verlag Neue Kritik, 1989), 81–112; and Jay Geller, "Blood Sin: Syphilis and the Construction of Jewish Identity," *Faultline* 1 (1992), 21–48.

35 Rotraut Hackermuller, *Das Leben, das mich stört: eine Dokumentation zu Kafkas letzten Jahren 1917–1924* (Wien: Medusa, 1984), 108–109.

36 Max Scheimpflug, "Über den heutigen Stand der Frage nach der Erblichkeit der Tuberculose," L. von Schrötter, ed., *Die Tuberculose* (Vienna: Wilhelm Braumüller, 1898), 1–44, here, 41 with the detailed literature.

37 Jennifer E. Michaels, *Anarchy and Eros: Otto Gross' Impact on German Expressionist Writers—Leonard Frank, Franz Jung, Johannes R. Becher, Karl Otten, Curt Corrinth, Walter Hasenclever, Oskar Maria Graf, Franz Kafka, Franz Werfel, Max Brod, Raoul Hausmann, and Berlin Dada* (New York : P. Lang, 1983).

38 Quoted in D. J. Enright, ed., *Ill at Ease: Writers on Ailments Real and Imagined* (London: Faber and Faber, 1989), 290.

39 On tuberculin as a "magic bullet" for tuberculosis see D. Leibowitz, "Scientific Failure in an age of Optimism: Public Reaction to Robert Koch's Tuberculin Cure," *New York State Journal of Medicine* 93 (1993), 41–48; J. M. Schmidt, "Geschichte der Tuberkulin–Therapie—Ihre Begründung durch Robert Koch, ihre Vorläufer und ihre weitere Entwicklung," *Pneumologie* 45 (1991), 776–784; B. Elkeles, "Der 'Tuberkulin-

rausch' von 1890," *Deutsche Medizinische Wochenschrift* 115 (1990), 1729–1732; E. Shapiro, "Robert Koch and his Tuberculin Fallacy," *Pharos* 46 (1983), 19–22.

40 Paul Jacob and Gotthold Pannwitz, *Entstehung und Bekämpfung der Lungentuberkulose*, 2 vols. (Leipzig: George Thieme, 1901), 1, 193.

41 Lawrason Brown, "The Visit in 1900," *The Story of Clinical Pulmonary Tuberculosis* (Baltimore: Williams and Wilkins, 1941), 73–109, here, 103.

42 Erich Hugo Ebstein, *Tuberkulose als Schicksal: Eine Sammlung pathographischer Skizzen von Calvin bis Klabund 1509–1928* (Stuttgart: Enke, 1932).

43 This theme is repeated constantly in the popular as well as medical literature of the late nineteenth and early twentieth centuries. See Lewis Moorman, *Tuberculosis and Genius* (Chicago: University of Chicago Press, 1940), on the "great tuberculars."

44 F. Köhler, "Die psychische Einwirkung," *Beiträge zur Klinik der Tuberkulose* 22 (1912), Supplement 3, 2–8, here, 4.

45 Max Salomon, *Die Tuberkulose als Volkskrankheit und ihre Bekämpfung durch Verhütungsmassnahmen: Ein Mahnruf an das deutsche Volk* (Berlin: S. Karger, 1904).

46 Fred G. Holmes, *Tuberculosis: A Book for the Patient* (New York: D. Appleton-Century, 1935), 186.

47 Wilhelm Weygandt, "Der Seelenzustand der Tuberkulösen," *Medizinische Klinik* 8 (1912), 91–95 and 137–140, here, 93. On the question of the stereotypes of race and disease in German culture of the *fin de siècle,* see the essay written for one of my summer seminars for college teachers, Dan Latimer, "Erotic Susceptibility and Tuberculosis: Literary Images of a Pathology," *MLN* 105 (1990), 1016–1031.

48 Maurice Fishberg, *Pulmonary Tuberculosis* (Philadelphia: Lea and Febiger, 1916), 241. It is important that Fishberg also denied the existence of an inherited habitus. He claims that what appears as the *habitus phthiscus* in children is merely the result of early infection (404).

49 D. G. Macleod Munro, *The Psycho-Pathology of Tuberculosis* (London: Oxford University Press, 1926).

50 Ernest G. Pope, *A Second Study of Pulmonary Tuberculosis: Marital Infection. Draper's Company Research Memoirs—Studies in National Deterioration*, 3 (London: Dulau and Co., 1908), 1.

51 (LM 5–6) The serving girl is his servant whose name is Ruzěka, LM, 162.

52 Ernest G. Pope, *A Second Study of Pulmonary Tuberculosis*, 1.

53 Ernst Pawel, *The Nightmare of Reason: A Life of Franz Kafka* (1984; London: Collins Harvill, 1988), 207.

54 Elias Canetti, *Kafka's Other Trial: The Letters to Felice*, trans. Christopher Middleton (New York: Schocken, 1974), 116.

55 See the discussion in Edward Shorter, *From the Mind into the Body: The Cultural Origins of Psychosomatic Symptoms* (New York: Free Press, 1994), 90–117.

56 John Smith, "Abulia: Sexuality and Disease of the Will in the Late Nineteenth Century," *Genders* 6 (1989), 102–24.

57 See Mark Anderson, *Kafka's Clothes: Ornament and Aestheticism in the Habsburg Fin de Siècle* (Oxford: Clarendon Press; Oxford; New York: Oxford University Press, 1992), 74–97.

58 On the politicization of illness and health, see Ute Frevert, *Krankheit als politisches Problem 1770–1880: Soziale Untersuchungen in Preußen zwischen medizinischer Polizei und staatlicher Sozialversicherung* (Göttingen: Vandenhoek und Ruprecht, 1984).

59 Josef Cermák and Martin Svatos, eds., Franz Kafka, *Briefe an die Eltern aus den Jahren 1922–24* (Frankfurt a. M.: S. Fischer, 1990).

60 Julius Tandler, "Konstitution und Rassenhygiene," *Zeitschrift für angewandte Anatomie und Konstitutionslehre* 1 (1914), 11–26.

61 Rotraut Hackermuller, *Das Leben, das mich stört: eine Dokumentation zu Kafkas letzten Jahren 1917–1924* (Wien: Medusa, 1984), 120.

62 The best overview of Hueppe's views is an article in English: Ferdinand Hueppe, "The Causes of Infectious Diseases," *The Monist* 8 (1898), 384–414.

63 Ferdinand Hueppe, "Über die Ursachen der Gährungen und Infectionskrankheiten und deren Beziehungen zur Causalproblem und zur Energetik," *Verhandlungen der Gesellschaft deutscher Naturforscher und Ärzte*. 65. Versammlung zu Nürnberg. 11.–15. September 1893, (Leipzig: F.C.W. Vorgel, 1893), 134–158, here 151.

64 Houston Stewart Chamberlain, "Der voraussetzungslose Mommsen," *Die Fackel* 87 (1901), 1–13, here 11.

65 On his debt to Freud, see Christian von Ehrenfels, *Sexualethik* (Wiesbaden: J. F. Bergmann, 1907). This is reprinted in Christian von Ehrenfels, *Philosophische Schriften*. ed., Reinhard Fabian, 4 vols. (Munich: Philosophia Verlag, 1982–1990), 3, 265–356. All references are to this edition, 296, n. 1; on the problem of our time, 362; on the question of the "higher" and "lower" races, see his essay "Über den Einfluss des Darwinismus auf die moderne Soziologie," *Volkswirtschaftliche Wochenschrift* (Vienna), 42 (1904), 256–259, and *Die Wage* (Vienna), 7 (1904), 363–364, 382–385; *Philosophische Schriften*, 3: 251–264.

66 *Sexualethik*, 275.

67 *Sexualethik*, 276.

68 *Sexualethik*, 356.

69 On Ehrenfels's sense of his own Jewish ancestry, see Max Brod, *Streitbares Leben* (Munich: Herbig, 1969), 211.

70 Cited from Ehrenfels's review of Otto Weininger's monograph, "Geschlecht und Charakter," *Politisch-anthropologische Revue* 3 (1904), 481–484, here, 483.

71 Christian von Ehrenfels, "Rassenproblem und Judenfrage," *Prager Tageblatt* 36 (December 1, 1911), 1–2. Reprinted in *Philosophische Schriften*, 4, 334–342, here, 337.

72 *Philosophische Schriften*, 4, 341.

73 Franz Kafka, *Tagebücher*, ed. Hans-Gerd Koch, Michael Müller, and Malcolm Pasley (Frankfurt: S. Fischer, 1990), 370–371.

74 Heinrich Singer, *Allgemeine und spezielle Krankheitslehre der Juden* (Leipzig: Benno Konegen, 1904), 25.

75 Ernst Kretschmer, *Körperbau und Charakter: Untersuchungen zum Konstitutionsproblem und zur Lehre von den Temperamenten* (Berlin: Springer, 1922).

76 Ludwig Stern–Piper, "Zur Frage der Bedeutung der psycho-physischen Typen," *Zeitschrift für die gesamte Neurologie und Psychiatrie* 84 (1923), 408–414.

77 Ernst Kretschmer, "Konstitution und Rasse," *Zeitschrift für die gesamte Neurologie und Psychiatrie* 82 (1923), 139–147. One can note that Kretschmer was refused a chair in psychiatry at Tübingen in January, 1945 because of his "political world view," i.e., because of his refusal to accept the arguments of racial science. See the letter of Stickl, the Rector of the University of Tübingen in Kretschmer's "Personalnotizen" (1945), from "Der Bevollmächtigte für das Sanitäts- und Gesundheitswesen" at the Berlin Documentation Center.

78 Ludwig Stern-Piper, "Konstitution und Rasse," *Zeitschrift für die gesamte Neurologie und Psychiatrie* 86 (1923), 265–273.

79 M. J. Gutmann, "Geisteskrankheiten bei Juden," *Zeitschrift für Demographie und Statistik der Juden* N.S. 3 (1926), 103–117, here 109.

80 Julius Friedrich Cohnheim, *Die Tuberkulose vom Standpunkte der Infectionslehre* (Leipzig : A. Edelmann, 1880), 34.

81 Paul Clemens von Baumgarten, *Über Tuberkel und Tuberkulose* (Berlin: Hirschwald, 1885) and his *Lehrbuch der pathologischen Mykologie*, 2 vols. (Braunschweig: Bruhn, 1886–1890).

82 Georges Kuss, *De l'hérédité parasitaire de la tuberculose humaine* (Paris: Asselin et Houzeau, 1898).

83 Otto Naegeli, *Allgemeine Konstitutionslehre* (Berlin: Springer, 1927).

84 Felix Wolff, *Die moderne Behandlung der Lugenschwindsucht* (Wiesbaden: J. F. Bergmann, 1894), 36–37.

85 J. Bartel, "Das Konstitutionsproblem in der Tuberkulosefrage," *Zeitschrift für Tuberkulose* 27 (1917), 40–50.

86 Arnold Paltauf, "Über die Beziehung der Thymus zum plötzlichen Tod," *Wiener klinische Wochenschrift* 2 (1889) (46), 876–881 and 3 (1890) (9), 172–175.

87 Reginald E. Thompson, *Different Aspects of Family Phthisis in Relation Especially to Heredity and Life Assurance* (London: Smith, Elder and Co., 1884), 175.

88 Karl Pearson, *A First Study of the Statistics of Pulmonary Tuberculosis. Draper's Company Research Memoirs—Studies in National Deterioration* 2 (London: Dulau and Co., 1907), 1.

89 Charles Goring, *On the Inheritance of the Diatheses of Phthisis and Insanity. A Statistical Study Based upon the Family History of 1500 Criminals. Draper's Company Research Memoirs—Studies in National Deterioration*, 4 (London: Dulau and Co., 1909), 19.

90 Erwin Baur, Eugen Fischer und Fritz Lenz, *Menschliche Erblichkeitslehre und Rassenhygiene*. 3 vols. (München : J. F. Lehmann, 1921), 1: 213.

91 See John M. Efron, *Defenders of the Race: Jewish Doctors and Race Science in fin–de-siècle Europe* (New Haven: Yale University Press, 1994), 26–28.

92 Søren Laache, "Über die konstitutionellen Anteil am Entstehen der Lungenschwindsucht," *Zeitschrift für angewandte Anatomie und Konstitutionslehre* 1 (1914), 130–138.

93 Thomas Mann, *The Magic Mountain*, trans. H. T. Lowe-Porter (New York: Knopf, 1982), 345.

94 Albert Reibmayr, *Inzucht und Vermischung beim Menschen* (Leipzig: Franz Deuticke, 1897), 128–129 (on the negative effects of inbreeding on culture); 175–211 (on inbreeding and interbreeding among the ancient Jews); 238–244 (on inbreeding in the mountains).

95 Albert Reibmayr, *Die Ehe Tuberculoser und Ihre Folgen* (Leipzig/Wien: Franz Deuticke, 1894).

96 A. Legoyt, "De certaines immunités biostatiques de la race juive en Europe," *Journal de la société de statistique de Paris* 10 (1869), 81–98, 109–124, here, 118–119.

97 Richard J. Evans, *Death in Hamburg: Society and Politics in the Cholera Years 1830–1900* (Oxford: Clarendon, 1987), 296, 475, states that tuberculosis was a greater killer than cholera.

98 See the discussion in Maurice Fishberg, "The Comparative Pathology of the Jews," *New York Medical Journal* 73 (1901), 537–543, 576–582, on cholera, 540–541.

99 See James K. Mish'alani, "Kafka: Text's Body, Body's Text," *Philosophy and Literature* 10 (1986), 56–64.

100 A. E. Brehms, *Illustrirtes Thierleben*, 6 vols. (Hildburghausen: Bibliographiches Institut, 1866), 3, 570–573.

101 Cited by Richard Burke, *A Historical Chronology of Tuberculosis* (Springfield, IL: Charles C. Thomas, 1938), 17.

102 Christoph Wilhelm Hufeland, *Enchiridion medicum: or The Practice of Medicine*, trans. Caspar Bruchhausen (New York: William Radde, 1844), 288 (phthisis constitutionalis); 285 (description). (The original was *Enchiridion medicum der Anleitung zur medizinischen Praxis. Vermächtniss einer funfzigjährigen Erfahrung* [Berlin: Jonas Verlagsbuchhandlung, 1836]).

103 Carl Rokitansky, *A Manual of Pathological Anatomy*, 4 vols. (London: The Sydenham Society, 1850), 3, 251–252.

104 See Brehmer, *op. cit.*, and Berthold Stiller, *Die asthenische Konstitutionskrankheit* (Asthenia universalis congenita. Morbus asthenicus), (Stuttgart: Ferdinand Enke, 1907), and his "Der Thorax phthisicus und die tuberkulose Disposition," *Berliner klinische Wochenschrift* 49 (1912), 97–101. This is countered by the work of Carl Hart and Paul Harrass, *Der Thorax phthisicus: Eine anatomisch-physiologische Studie* (Stuttgart: Enke, 1908), who stress the notion that the *habitus phthisicus* is one of many predisposing factors.

105 Max Neuburger, "Zur Geschichte der Konstitutionslehre," *Zeitschrift für angewandte Anatomie und Konstitutionslehre* 1 (1914), 4–10.

106 Hermann Strauss, "Über den Habitus phthisicus und seine klinische Bedeutung," *Berliner klinische Wochenschrift* 31 (January 1910), 207–210, here, 208.

107 Daniel Gottlob Moritz Schreber, *Das Pangymnastikon* (Leipzig: Friedrich Fleischer, 1862), 237, 241, 249, 260.

108 Karl Mann, "Athletischer Körperbau," *Kraft und Schönheit*, Sandow Sonderheft (1901), 14–15.

109 Paul Niemeyer, *Die Lunge, ihre Pflege und Behandlung im gesunden und kranken Zustande* (Leipzig: J. J. Weber, Illustrirte Zeitung, 1913). This is the tenth edition edited by Franz Carl Gerster; the first edition appeared in 1872. An English edition also appeared: *The Lungs in Health and Disease* (London: Scott, 1908).

110 The translation is by Jack Zipes, Oskar Panizza, "The Operated Jew," *New German Critique* 21 (1980), 63–79. See also Jack Zipes, "Oscar Panizza: The Operated German as Operated Jew," *New German Critique* 21 (1980), 47–61.

111 Panizza, 68.

112 Panizza, 64.

113 Panizza, 65.

114 Panizza, 64.

115 Panizza, 68.

116 Panizza, 77.

117 On posthioplasty see Thomas J. S. Patterson, ed., trans. and revised, *The Zeiss Index and History of Plastic Surgery 900 B.C.–1863 A.D.* (Baltimore: Williams and Wilkins, 1977), 250–254 and *The Patterson Index 1864 A.D. to 1920 A.D.* (Baltimore: Williams and Wilkins, 1978), 437–428. On the general history, see Jody Rubin, "Celsus' Decircumcision Operation: Medical and Historical Implications," *Urology* 16 (1980), 121–124.

118 Panizza, 79.

119 Immanuel Kant, *Anthropology from a Pragmatic Point of View*, trans. Victor Lyle Dowdell (Southern Illinois University Press, 1978), 60. See Nathan Rotenstreich, *Jews and German Philosophy: The Polemics of Emancipation* (New York: Schocken Books, 1984).

120 A. Legoyt, "De certaines immunités biostatiques de la race juive en Europe," *Journal de la societé de statistique des Paris* 10 (1869), 81–98, 109–124, here, 122.

121 Eduard Glatter, *Über die Lebens-Chancen der Israeliten gegenüber der christlichen Confessionen. Biostatische Studie gelesen in der Sitzung der mathematisch-naturwissenschaftlichen Classe der ungarischen Akademie den 5. Mai 1856* (Wetzlar: Gedruckt bei Rathgeber u. Cobet, 1856), 44.

122 Ludwig Teleky, *Vorlesungen über soziale Medizin* (Jena: G. Fischer, 1914), 123.

123 Paul Reichert, "Über Thorax- und Körpermasse bei Lungentuberkulösen und ihre Beziehungen zur Lehre von der Disposition," *Beiträge zur Klinik der Tuberkulose* 39 (1918), 24–36. Chart from p. 29.

124 Cesare Taruffi, *Hermaphrodismus und Zeugungsunfähigkeit: Eine systematische Darstellung des Missbildungen der menschlichen Geschlechtsorgane*, trans. R. Teuscher (Berlin: H. Barsdorf, 1903), 97.

125 Ferdinand-Valère Faneau de la Cour, *Du féminisme et de l'infantilisme chez les tuberculeux* (Paris: A. Parent, 1871).

126 Henri Meige, "L'infantilisme, féminisme et les hérmaphrodites antiques," *L'Anthropologie* 15 (1895), 257–264.

127 Karl Eisenstaedt, "Gibt es äußere Kennzeichen einer phthisischen Konstitution?" *Zeitschrift für Tuberkulose* 55 (1929), 27–40. Eisenstaedt is arguing against such signs but provides a detailed overview of the arguments for them prior to 1926.

128 W. Schultz, "Pigmentation und Lungentuberkulose," *Beiträge zur Klinik der Tuberkulose* 1924 (59), 65–73.

129 E. Moro and L. Kolb, "Über das Schicksal von Ekzemkindern," *Monatschrift für Kinderheilkunde* 9 (1910), 428–446, here 441–442.

130 Erwin Baur, Eugen Fischer und Fritz Lenz, *Menschliche Erblichkeitslehre und Rassenhygiene* 3 vols. (München : J. F. Lehmann, 1921), 1, 32.

131 John Beddoe, *The Races of Britain: A Contribution to the Anthropology of Western Europe* (Bristol: J. W. Arrowsmith, 1885).

132 Franz Koch, "Tuberkulose und Rasse," *Zeitschrift für Tuberkulose* 15 (1909), 82–86.

133 S. A. Weisman, *Your Chest Should be Flat: The Deep Chest Makes Better Soil for Tuberculosis* (Philadelphia: J. B. Lippincott, 1938).

134 I am using the term "Jewish physician" to refer to those physicians who either self-label themselves as Jews or are so labeled in the standard reference works of the time. See, for example, the listing in Solomon R. Kagan, *Jewish Medicine* (Boston: Medico-Historical Press, 1952).

135 Maurice Fishberg, "Consumption," *The Jewish Encyclopedia,* 12 vols. (New York: Funk and Wagnalls, 1904), 4, 245–248; see also Maurice Fishberg and Joseph Jacobs, "Anthropological Types," *The Jewish Encyclopedia,* 12: 291–295. See also the discussion in Maurice Fishberg, "The Comparative Pathology of the Jews," *New York Medical Journal* 73 (1901), 537–543, 576–582, here, 541–542, as well as his *Health Problems of the Jewish Poor: A Paper Read before the Jewish Chautauqua Assembly on Monday, July 27, 1903, at Atlantic City, N.J.* (New York: Cowen, 1903). With the shift in political discourse during the 1930s, Fishberg came to have a very different view. See Franz Boas, *Aryan and Semite, with Particular Reference to Nazi Racial Dogmas. Addresses delivered before the Judaeans and the Jewish Academy of Arts and Sciences, March 4th, 1934, in New York City, by Prof. Franz Boas, Dr. Maurice Fishberg, Prof. Ellsworth Huntington, Max J. Kohler, presiding* (Cincinnati: B'nai B'rith, 1934). On the general context of Fishberg's work (from a social historical point of view), see Deborah Dwork, "Health Conditions of Immigrant Jews on the Lower East Side of New York: 1880–1914," *Medical History* 25 (1981), 1–40, and Jacob Jay Lindenthal, "Abi Gezunt: Health and the Eastern European Jewish Immigrant," *American Jewish History* 70 (1981), 42–41. On the general question of Jewish health, see Stephen Jay Gould, "Science and Jewish Immigration," *Natural History* 89 (1980), 14–19.

136 Joseph Jacobs, *Studies in Jewish Statistics* (London: D. Nutt, 1891), iv–vi.

137 On Koch and bovine tuberculosis see R. A. Packer, "Veterinarians Challenge Dr. Robert Koch Regarding Bovine Tuberculosis and Public Health," *Journal of the American Veterinary Medical Association* 196 (1990), 574–575; Barbara Rosenkrantz, "The Trouble with Bovine Tuberculosis," *Bulletin of the History of Medicine* 59 (1985), 155–175; D. Karasszon, "Robert Kochs Forschungen zur Rinder-Tuberkulose," *Wissenschaftliche Beiträge der Martin Luther Universität Halle Wittenberg* 80 (1983), 111–116; H. Reimer, "Robert Koch und die Rindertuberkulose," *Zeitschrift für die Gesamte Hygenie* 28 (1982), 156–160.

138 Robert Koch, "Das Verhältnis zwischen Menschen- und Rindertuberkulose," Robert Koch, *Gesammelte Werke*, ed. J. Schwalbe 3 vols. (Leipzig: Georg Thieme, 1912), 1: 624–635.

139 See the discussion by Nathan Raw, *The Control of Bovine Tuberculosis in Man* (London: Baillière Tindall & Cox, 1937), and René and Jean Dubos, *The White Plague: Tuberculosis, Man, and Society* (1952; New Brunswick: Rutgers University Press, 1987), 109.

140 Cited by Frederick Robert Karl, *Franz Kafka, Representative Man* (New York: Ticknor & Fields, 1991), 270. See also Pawel, 224–225.

141 *Auf dem Liegestuhl: Die Zeitschrift des Lungenkranken* 1 (1927), 20. See also Barry Smith, "Gullible's Travails: Tuberculosis and Quackery, 1890–1930," *Journal of Contemporary History* 20 (1985), 733–756.

142 Maurice Fishberg, *The Jews: A Study of Race and Environment* (New York: Walter Scott, 1911) (published in German translation in 1913).

143 Maurice Fishberg, "The Comparative Pathology of the Jews," *New York Medical Journal* 73 (1901), 537–543, 576–582, here 581.

144 A. Legoyt, "De certaines immunités biostatiques de la race juive en Europe," *Journal de la société de statistique de Paris* 10 (1869), 81–98, 109–124, here, 123–124.

145 Schamschen Kreinermann, "Über das Verhalten der Lungentuberkulose bei den Juden," *Correspondenz-Blatt für Schweizer Ärtze* 45 (1915), 1546–1564.

146 N. Haltrecht, "Das Tuberkuloseproblem bei den Juden: Eine rassen- und sozialpathologische Studie," *Beiträge zur Klinik der Tuberkulose* 62 (1925), 442–480.

147 Richard Morton, *Phthisiologia; seu, Exercitationes de phthisi tribus libris comprehensae* (Londini: Imprensis Samuelis Smith, 1689).

148 Felix Wolff, *Die moderne Behandlung der Lungenschwindsucht* (Wiesbaden: J. F. Bergmann, 1894), 43.

149 D. G. Macleod Munro, *The Psycho-Pathology of Tuberculosis* (London: Oxford University Press, 1926).

150 Thomas Mann, *Death in Venice and Other Stories*, trans. H. T. Lowe-Porter (New York: Vintage, 1936), 324.

151 J. Orth, "Trauma und Lungentuberkulose," *Zeitschrift für Tuberkulose* 25 (1915), 21–35, 328–48; 26 (1916): 264–277.

152 F. Köhler, "Tuberkulose und Psyche," *Medizinische Klinik* 7 (1911), 1808–1813, here, 1881.

153 Alfred Sokolowski, *Klinik der Brustkrankheiten,* 2 vols. (Berlin: A. Hirschwald, 1906), 2, 345.

154 F. Köhler, "Psychopathologie der Tuberkulose und ihre kriminelle Bedeutung," *Zeitschrift für Tuberkulose* 15 (1909), 31–55, here, 37.

155 See the figures from 1910 to 1950 in appendix C to Dubos, *White Plague*, and compare the British discussion summarized in Linda Bryder, "The First World War: Healthy or Hungry?" *History Workshop Journal* 24 (1987), 141–157.

156 A. Gottstein, "Tuberkulose und Hungersnot," *Klinische Wochenschrift* 1 (1922), 572–575.

157 Isbert Werner, "Über das Verhalten der Lungentuberkulose bei den Juden)," *Zeitschrift für Tuberkulose* 43 (1925), 130–135.

158 M. J. Gutmann, "Jüdische Eigenart und moderne Biologie (Probleme der Biologie und Pathologie der Juden)," in Max Eschelbacher and Adolf Sindler, eds., *Zur Hygiene der Juden* (Düsseldorf: Synagogengemeinde Düsseldorf, 1926), 350–362.

159 Karl Diehl and Otmar Freiherr von Verschuer, *Zwillingstuberkulose: Zwillingsforschung und erbliche Tuberkulosedisposition* (Jena: Gustav Fischer, 1933), 54–55.

160 Emil Bogen, "Tuberculosis among the Jews," *Medical Leaves* 3 (1940), 123–124.

CHAPTER FIVE: CONCLUSION

1 Alfred Dreyfus, *Fünf Jahre meines Lebens* (Berlin: John Edelheim, 1901) 104.

2 Ted Morgan, "The Hidden Henchman," *New York Times Magazine* (May 22, 1994), 31–78, here 39.

3 See the discussion in Nan Marie McMurry, "'And I? I Am in a Consumption': The Tuberculosis Patient, 1780–1930," (Diss.: Duke University, 1985), Pierre Guillaume, *Du désespoir au salut: les tuberculeux aux 19e and 20e siècles* (Paris: Aubier 1986), 132–169; and Sheila M. Rothman, *Shadow of Death: Tuberculosis and the Social Experience of Illness in American History* (New York: Basic Books, 1994), especially chapter 15, 226–466. I am grateful to Sheila Rothman for sharing the manuscript of her study with me prior to publication.

4 Thomas Mann, *The Magic Mountain*, trans. H. T. Lowe-Porter (New York: Knopf, 1982), 345.

5 Jules Héricourt, *The Social Diseases: Tuberculosis, Syphilis, Alcoholism, Sterility*, trans. with a final chapter by Bernard Miall (London: George Routledge and Sons, 1920). Originally published as *Les maladies des sociétés: tuberculose, syphilis, alcoolisme et sterilité* (Paris: Flammarion, 1918).

6 Hans Gross, "Degeneration und Deportation," *Politisch-Anthropologische Revue* 4 (1905–1906), 281–286.

7 See M. Slavetínský´, "History of Campaigns against Tuberculosis in Moravia," (in Czech) *Vnitrňé lék*, 26 (1980), 515–516.

8 F. Köhler, "Psychopathologie der Tuberkulose und ihre kriminelle Bedeutung," *Zeitschrift für Tuberkulose* 15 (1909), 31–55.

9 I rely here on Julius Uffelmann, *Darstellung des auf dem Gebiete der öffentliche Gesundheitspflege in ausser-deutschen Ländern bis jetzt Geleisteten* (Berlin: G. Reimar, 1878), 83–102 and 448–467, as well as Paul Slezak, *Geschichte der österreichischen Sanitätsverwaltung* (Wien: Urban und Schwarzenberg, 1956), 42–47.

10 See F. Schürer von Waldheim and J. Kafka, *Aerzte-Codex: Eine Sammlung von den Arzt betreffenden österreichischen Gesetzen* (Wien: A. Hartleben, 1897), as well as W. Fornet, "The Movement in Germany, Austria, and Hungary," in Halliday G. Sutherland, ed., *The Control and Eradication of Tuberculosis* (Edinburgh: William Green, 1911), 231–330, here 314.

11 See Karoline Auguste Krauss, "Kafka's K. versus the Castle: The Self and the Other," (Diss.: University of Utah, 1993).

12 Enrico Ferri, *Criminal Sociology* (New York: D. Appelton, 1899), 204.

13 Vera Pohland, "From Positive-Stigma to Negative-Stigma. A Shift of the Literary and Medical Representation of Consumption in German Culture," in Rudolf Käser and Vera Pohland, eds., *Disease and Medicine in Modern German Cultures* (Ithaca, NY: Western Societies Program, 1990), 144–168.

14 Maud Elmann, *The Hunger Artists: Starving, Writing, and Imprisonment* (Cambridge, MA: Harvard University Press, 1993) as well as Leslie Lynne Heywood, "'Dedication to Hunger': Anorexia and the Gender of Literary Modernism" (Diss. , University of California at Irvine, 1993) and on the medical background see Joan Jacobs Brumberg, *Fasting Girls: The Emergence of Anorexia Nervosa as a Modern*

Disease (Cambridge, MA: Harvard University Press, 1988). See also George Yudice, "Feeding the Transcendent Body," *Postmodern Culture* 1 (September 1990).

15 Susan Bordo, "Reading the Slender Body," in *Women, Science, and the Body Politic: Discourses and Representations*, eds. Mary Jacobus, Evelyn Fox Keller, and Sally Shuttleworth (New York: Methuen, 1989), 83–112.

16 Thomas Mann, *Death in Venice and Other Stories*, trans. H. T. Lowe-Porter (New York: Vintage, 1936), 325.

17 The originals of all the materials are in the Památnik Národnhího Písemnictví in Prague [see the Appendix].

18 These records are reproduced in Rotraut Hackermuller, *Das Leben, das mich stört: eine Dokumentation zu Kafkas letzten Jahren 1917–1924* (Wien: Medusa, 1984).

19 Philip Roth, "'I always wanted you to admire my fasting' or, Looking at Kafka" (1973), reprinted in J. P. Stern, ed., *The World of Franz Kafka* (New York: Holt, Rinehardt and Winston, 1980), 202–217.

20 The information on the tuberculosis experiments at Neuengamme is taken from Otto Prokop and Ehrenfried Stelzer, "Die Menschenexperiment des Dr. med. Heißmeyer (Medizinische und kriminalistische Erhebung)," *Kriminalistik und forensische Wissenschaft* 3 (1970), 67–104, and Günther Schwarberg, *Der SS-Arzt und die Kinder vom Bullenhuser Damm* (Göttingen: Steidl, 1988). On Neuengamme, see Bogdan Suchowiak, *Die Tragödie der Häftlinge von Neuengamme* (Reinbeck: Rowohlt, 1985).

21 Cited by Prokop and Stelzer, 75.

22. All references are to Oskar Rosenfeld. *Wozu noch Welt: Auszeichnungen aus dem Getto Lodz,* ed., Hanno Loewy (Frankfurt am Main: Neue Kritik: 1994) I want to thank Jakov Hessing (Jerusalem) for drawing my attention to this text.

Index

Page numbers in boldface type refer to illustrations.